A History of American Life

PAUL LAUNE

A HISTORY OF AMERICAN LIFE

IN

TWELVE VOLUMES

ARTHUR M. SCHLESINGER
DIXON RYAN FOX
Editors

ASHLEY H. THORNDIKE   CARL BECKER
Consulting Editors

THE MACMILLAN COMPANY
NEW YORK · BOSTON · CHICAGO · DALLAS
ATLANTA · SAN FRANCISCO

MACMILLAN & CO., Limited
LONDON · BOMBAY · CALCUTTA
MELBOURNE

THE MACMILLAN CO. OF CANADA, Ltd.
TORONTO

1. Red Stockings
2. Steel Converters
3. At the Seaside
4. The Negro Vote

5. Transcontinental Railroad
6. The Farmer in Politics
7. The Great Strike

The Emergence of Modern America

A HISTORY OF AMERICAN LIFE
Volume VIII

THE EMERGENCE
OF MODERN AMERICA
1865-1878

BY
ALLAN NEVINS
PROFESSOR OF AMERICAN HISTORY, CORNELL UNIVERSITY
Sometime Editorial Associate on the New York World

New York
THE MACMILLAN COMPANY
1927

Nay, tell me not today the publish'd shame,
Read not today the journal's crowded page,
The merciless reports still branding forehead after
*   forehead,*
The guilty column following guilty column. . . .

Through all your quiet ways, or North or South,
*   you equal States, you honest farms,*
Your million untold manly healthy lives, or East
*   or West, city or country,*
Your noiseless mothers, sisters, wives, unconscious
*   of their good,*
Your mass of homes nor poor nor rich, in visions
*   rise—(even your excellent poverties)*
Your self-distilling, never-ceasing virtues, self-denials,
*   graces,*
Your endless base of deep integrities within, timid
*   but certain,*
Your blessings steadily bestowed, sure as the light,
*   and still. . . .*
These, these today I brood upon. . . .

WALT WHITMAN, "Old Age Echoes" (winter of 1873).

CONTENTS

27539

973.8 N41

CHAPTER   PAGE

I. THE DARKEST DAYS IN THE SOUTH (1865-
1873) 1

II. THE INDUSTRIAL BOOM IN THE NORTH
(1865-1873) 31

III. URBAN LIVING AND ROUTES OF TRAVEL . 75

IV. THE TAMING OF THE WEST (1865-1873) . 101

V. THE WEST AT WORK (1865-1873) . . . 124

VI. THE REVOLT OF THE FARMER (1868-1874) 154

VII. THE MORAL COLLAPSE IN GOVERNMENT
AND BUSINESS (1865-1873) 178

VIII. THE EVERYDAY LIFE OF AMERICANS . . 203

IX. THE BROADENING OF AMERICAN CULTURE 228

X. THE DEEPENING OF AMERICAN CULTURE . 264

XI. TWO MEMORABLE YEARS: 1873 AND 1876 . 290

XII. HUMANITARIAN STRIVING 318

XIII. RECOVERY IN SOUTH AND WEST (1873-
1878) 349

XIV. EMBATTLED INDUSTRY (1873-1878) . . 380

XV. CRITICAL ESSAY ON AUTHORITIES . . . 408

INDEX 433

ILLUSTRATIONS

(By the Editors)

PLATE

I. THE EMERGENCE OF MODERN AMERICA . . *Frontispiece*

(a) Top, left: The Cincinnati "Red Stockings", the first professional baseball team in America (see page 220). From *Harper's Weekly*, XIII, 421 (July 3, 1869). A good picture of a game may be seen in the same publication, XIV, 424-425 (July 2, 1870).

(b) Top, right: Bessemer steel converter (see page 33). From *Harper's Weekly*, XX, 252 (March 25, 1876).

(c) Top, center: The seaside. Note the costumes; even life guards wore long sleeves and long trousers, generally of heavy woolen material. From *Harper's Weekly*, XVI, 724 (Sept. 14, 1872).

(d) Middle row, left: The Negro vote (see chap. i). Detail from cut no. 5 in the double-sheet illustration printed in *Frank Leslie's Illustrated Newspaper*, XXVI, 169-170 (Nov. 30, 1867).

(e) Middle row, center: Meeting of the Union Pacific Railroad and the Central Pacific Railroad, thus completing the transcontinental railway (see page 56). Detail from illustration in *Harper's Weekly*, XIII, 356 (June 5, 1869).

(f) Middle row, right: The farmer in politics (see chap. vi). Detail from drawing by J. B. Beale in *Frank Leslie's Illustrated Newspaper*, XXXV, 397 (Aug. 30, 1873). A banner shown beyond the speaker reads: "We are the Laborers—Free Trade and Farmers' Rights—We Feed the World." In the full picture are other signs reading: "President's Salary $50,000 a year. Congressman $7000. Farmer 75 cts. a week;" "No more Credit Mobilier nor Congressional Grab;" "Brothers, Let us Organize for Knowledge and Power," the last-named being attached to the band wagon.

(g) Bottom: The great railroad strike—Burning the roundhouse at Pittsburgh (see page 388). Detail from illustration in *Harper's Weekly*, XXI, 628 (Aug. 11, 1877).

Note: In the arrangement of these seven pictures the Editors have attempted to follow the taste of the period, the very sense of congestion being familiar to all who have studied contemporary illustration. The rounded corners represent another favorite feature; for example, every illustration in the *New York Ledger* (weekly) for 1870 has rounded corners at the top. Many of the other illustrations

PLATE   PAGE

in the present volume are details from large pictures so designed. All pictures in this volume from *Frank Leslie's
Illustrated Newspaper* are used by permission of the Judge
Publishing Company; those from *Harper's Weekly* by permission of *Harper's Magazine.* Borders by Paul Laune.

II.   THE POSTWAR SOUTH . . . . *facing*   26
      (a) The ruins of Columbia, S. C., after Sherman's army
had passèd. From a drawing by Theodore R. Davis in
Harper's Weekly, X, 449 (July 21, 1866). "The sketch
is taken near the ruins of the Court-house in which locality
there is a large number of squatters." Our reproduction
clipped chiefly at left and right margins.
      (b) A Georgia plantation, 1860.
      (c) The same, 1880. Note the spread of the Negroes'
cabins as they passed from the status of slaves to that of
tenants. Both maps from *Scribner's Monthly*, XXI, 882-
883 (April, 1881). All pictures in this volume from
Scribner's Monthly are used by permission of the Century
Company, New York City, the old *Scribner's Monthly*
having become the *Century Magazine* in November, 1881.
      (d) Negro camp meeting. Portion of full-page draw-
ing by Sol Eytinge, jr., in *Harper's Weekly*, XVI, 620
(Aug. 10, 1872). In these "shouts" were heard the dirge-
like airs now known as spirituals.
      (e) A tournament. The surviving romanticism in the
South is well illustrated in a full-page drawing by W. S. L.
Jewett in *Harper's Weekly*, XIII, 780 (Dec. 4, 1869),
from which this section is taken. "It is a good representa-
tion of the tournament as it now exists in some of our
Southern (especially the border) States." For other pictures see *Frank Leslie's Illustrated Newspaper*, XXXI, 429,
and F. H. Norton, ed., *Frank Leslie's Historical Register of
the U. S. Centennial Exposition* (N. Y., 1877), 204.
Our reproduction, clipped on all sides, shows about half
the drawing.

III. GLIMPSES OF THE CITIES . . . . . . *facing*   82
      (a) The ballet at Niblo's Garden, New York. Scene
from the spectacle, "The White Fawn." Section of illustration in *Frank Leslie's Illustrated Newspaper*, XXV, 329
(Feb. 8, 1868). In the article on the following page it is
said: "The 'Black Crook' is dead! Long live the 'White
Fawn'!"
      (b) "Two Sides of the Way"—a study in contrasts
along upper Fifth Avenue, New York, by Thomas Worth.
From *Hearth and Home*, II, 172 (March 5, 1870). Worth
is best remembered for his "Darktown" comic lithographs.
      (c) A carnival at Louisville. Detail from drawing in

PLATE   PAGE

Frank Leslie's Illustrated Newspaper, XXXV, 29 (March 22, 1873). The French carnival spirit spread from New Orleans up the Mississippi Valley. For pictures of carnivals in New Orleans and Memphis see Edward King, *The Great South* (Hartford, 1875), 38, 40, 41, 43, 45, 268.

(d) "A Broadway Swell." From *Gleason's Monthly Companion*, I, 541 (Nov. 1872). For illustrated advertisements of tonics that were guaranteed to grow such whiskers, see, for example, *Scribner's Monthly*, XI, in advertising section, and *Harper's Weekly*, XX, 75. Cf. long-whiskers advertisement at the beginning of the period, *Frank Leslie's Illustrated Newspaper*, XXII, 319 (Aug. 4, 1866).

(e) Philadelphia Quakers. From *Harper's Weekly*, XX, 292 (April 8, 1876). The peculiar Quaker costume was still worn in this period.

(f) "Silver Palace Sleeping Car, Pennsylvania Central, Pittsburgh, Fort Wayne and Chicago Railroads." From a woodcut in *Frank Leslie's Illustrated Newspaper*, XXVI, 332 (Aug. 8, 1868). "We open the door leading into the main salon and a scene of unparalleled magnificence bursts upon the view—everything seems to be a blaze of silver." Each car cost $15,000, and was heated by a safe-like furnace underneath the floor.

(g) After the Chicago fire. The drawing in *Harper's Weekly*, XV, 1053 (Nov. 11, 1871), from which this section is taken, suggests the courageous spirit of rebuilding so strikingly shown by the citizens of Chicago.

(h) First elevated railroad, Greenwich St., New York. From a sketch by Stanley Fox in *Harper's Weekly*, XII, 476 (July 25, 1868). It had been tried out over its route from the Battery to Cortlandt St. on July 3, and attained a speed of fifteen miles an hour. So far it had cost $100,000.

IV.   THE INVASION OF THE WEST   .   .   .   .   *facing*   114

(a) Indians attacking an overland coach. From *Hearth and Home*, I, 173 (March 6, 1869). In the full-size illustration the words "Overland U. S. Mail" and "Wells, Fargo & Co." are easily discernible on the coach.

(b) Shooting buffalo from the train—the last word in useless slaughter. From *Frank Leslie's Illustrated Newspaper*, XXXI, 193 (June 3, 1871).

V.   WORK IN THE FAR WEST   .   .   .   .   .   *facing*   134

(a) "Kansas—Transport of Texas Beef on the Kansas-Pacific Railway—Scene at a Cattle-Shoot in Abilene, Kansas." From a full-page woodcut in *Frank Leslie's Illustrated Newspaper*, XXXII, 385 (Aug. 19, 1871). Abilene,

PLATE | PAGE

the county seat of Dickinson County, was an important concentration point for eastward shipment of Texas and Mexican longhorns.

(b) A Colorado mountain honeycombed with gold and silver mines. From a drawing by Frenzeny and Tavernier in *Harper's Weekly*, XVIII, 597 (July 18, 1874). The veins now and then came close to the surface.

VI. THE WESTERN FARMER—TWO STAGES . . *facing* 170

(a) A Kansas dugout. From Edward Ingersoll, *Knocking 'Round the Rockies* (N. Y. 1883), 95. The front of the dugout was covered with rawhide. The floor was of earth, on which oftentimes the inmates slept, though the more luxurious households had a cot bed as well as a table and benches.

(b) A Subordinate Grange meeting in an Illinois schoolhouse. From a sketch by Joseph B. Beale in *Frank Leslie's Illustrated Newspaper*, XXXVII, 341 (January 31, 1874).

VII. "WHOLESALE AND RETAIL" . . . . . *facing* 184

A cartoon by Thomas Nast published in *Harper's Weekly*, XV, 865 (Sept. 16, 1871). The persons represented in the "Wholesale" picture are A. J. Garvey, A. O. Hall (mayor), R. B. Connolly, W. M. Tweed and P. B. Sweeney. It represents an attitude and spirit then found, of course, in state and national governments as well.

VIII. THE AMERICAN HOME, 1865-1878 . . . . *facing* 204

(a) A bedroom set. From advertisement of Gould & Co. in *Harper's Weekly*, XX, 14 (Jan. 1, 1876), with legend.

(b) Bayard Taylor's house, "Cedarcroft," Kennett Square, Pa., an example of the "Italian" style. From *The Art Journal*, new ser. (Am. edn.), III, 264.

(c) A Rogers group—"Checkers up at the Farm." Such parlor groups sold at from $10 to $25. Rogers' lawn statuary brought from $25 to $100.

(d) A courthouse. From Amos J. Bricknell, *Village Builder* (Troy, N. Y., 1870).

(e) Parlor of the Roosevelt Museum, birthplace of Theodore Roosevelt, 28 East 20th St., New York. From photograph furnished by R. W. G. Vail, librarian. This represents the best taste of the period. The price of such mantel mirrors may be judged from a description of one similar in *Demorest's Illustrated Monthly Magazine*, VIII, 23 (Jan., 1871), 72 in. x 55 in., which cost $300. Before 1878 lambrequins over windows were being supplanted by hangings on rings sliding on a pole, and the decorated nail for supporting pictures by the molding hook; see illustrations in *Scribner's Monthly*, XI, 491, 494

PLATE   PAGE

(Feb., 1876). The picture hanging over the piano is the famous steel engraving by A. H. Ritchie (1822-1895), after the painting of "Lady Washington's Reception" by Daniel Huntington (1816-1906), the original being in the Brooklyn Museum. Note whatnot, glass-covered wax flowers, etc.

IX. SPORT AND FASHION . . . . *facing* 220

(a) Children's fashions. From *Peterson's Magazine*, LVI, plates for Sept., 1869. The velocipede shown here had been introduced from France in the middle sixties, but had been improved in America. See pictures in articles in the *Scientific American*, XIX, 120, 389 (Aug. 19 and Dec. 16, 1868).

(b) Croquet dress of black alpaca, trimmed with bands of green silk cut out in points. Detail from a steel engraving, *Godey's Lady's Book*, LXXII, 299 (April, 1866); described on page 382, same work.

(c) "Indiana divorce." From a decoration accompanying a satirical valentine, *Demorest's Illustrated Monthly Magazine*, VIII, 37 (Feb., 1871). The verse beside it reads, "If we can't pull together, we can easily get a divorce."

(d) The silhouette of 1877. From *Godey's Lady's Book*, XCV, 369 (Nov., 1877); described on page 443, same work. Carriage dress of dark gray silk and velvet brocade, trimmed with fringe. The bustle was now supplanting the hoops.

(e) The carriages of Leonard W. Jerome and August Belmont on the road to the race course at Jerome Park, Fordham, near New York. Section of an illustration in *Harper's Weekly*, X, 649 (Oct. 13, 1866). Our reproduction clipped on all sides. The race course, with its 230 acres, had been opened Sept. 25, in the presence of such notables as General Grant and Mme. Ristori.

(f) General Grant and family at Long Branch, N. J. Section from an illustration in *Frank Leslie's Illustrated Newspaper*, XXVIII, 321 (Aug. 7, 1869). President Grant spent so much time at Long Branch that he was criticized for neglecting his duties; the Republicans retorted by showing how much more time Thomas Jefferson had spent away from Washington. Pictures of Grant's two cottages may be found in *Harper's Weekly*, XIV, 525.

(g) Costume for tennis. From an advertisement for sporting goods in *Scribner's Monthly*, XVI, 1878 (bound in at back, Columbia University copy).

X. THE LYCEUM . . . . *facing* 238

"The Lyceum Committeeman's Dream—Some Popular Lecturers in Character." By Charles Stanley Reinhart

PLATE   PAGE

(1844-1896), in *Harper's Weekly*, XVII, 1013 (Nov. 15, 1873). Unfortunately no key or other descriptive matter was published with the illustration. We identify the figures as follows, reading the rows from left to right: William H. H. Murray, Charles Bradlaugh, James Parton, Bayard Taylor, —————, —————, David R. Locke ("Petroleum V. Nasby"), Louis Agassiz, John B. Gough, Henry Ward Beecher, Theodore Tilton, Elizabeth Cady Stanton, William Lloyd Garrison, Susan B. Anthony, —————, Thomas Nast, Samuel L. Clemens ("Mark Twain"), Wilkie Collins, Henry W. Shaw ("Josh Billings"). F. Weitenkampf, *American Graphic Art* (N. Y., 1924), 191, speaks of Reinhart's "forceful directness."

XI. SCIENCE AND SCHOLARSHIP . . . . . *facing* 276

(a) Major Powell's expedition down the Colorado. [Smithsonian Institution], *Exploration of the Colorado River of the West* (Washington, 1875), 82. For comment on this engraving see W. J. Linton, *History of Wood-Engraving in America* (Boston, 1882), 41. Our reproduction, for decorative value, has been rounded at the top and patched at the bottom.

(b) President Andrew D. White, aged about forty-one. From *Harper's Weekly*, XVII, 528 (June 21, 1873).

(c) President Charles W. Eliot, aged about thirty-nine. From *Scribner's Monthly*, XII, 351 (July, 1876).

(d) Laboratory of Massachusetts Institute of Technology. From *Frank Leslie's Illustrated Newspaper*, XXIX, 228 (Dec. 18, 1869). Clipped on all sides.

XII. 1873 AND 1876 . . . . *facing* 314

(a) Closing the Stock Exchange, New York, 1873. From *Frank Leslie's Illustrated Newspaper*, XXXVII, 66 (Oct. 4, 1873).

(b) The Republican elephant beside the Tammany tiger's grave. Cartoon by Thomas Nast in *Harper's Weekly*, XXI (March 24, 1877). After the close campaign of 1876 and the succeeding electoral dispute, the elephant says, "Another such victory and I am undone." Nast had originated the Republican elephant in the early autumn of 1874 to indicate the anticipated majority for that party in the coming congressional elections, an expectation unrealized. He had invented the Tammany tiger three years before. The Democratic donkey was about forty years older. See Albert B. Paine, *Th. Nast* (N. Y., 1904), 299-300. Paine's implication that Nast invented the paper cap of labor is disproved by Reinhart's picture; see above, plate x.

(c) The Centennial. Section from double-page illustration in F. H. Norton, ed., *Frank Leslie's Historical*

PLATE

PAGE

Register of the United States Centennial Exposition, 88-89.
President Grant's party is being introduced to the foreign
commissions.

XIII. MAKING LIFE MORE BEARABLE . . . . *facing* 334

(a) Clearing out a rookery. Section from illustration
in *Frank Leslie's Illustrated Family Almanac for 1872*
(N. Y. 1871), 60. The tenants of a five-story tenement
in Cherry Street, New York, had been warned to move so
that alterations might be made in the interest of health.
Police coercion proved necessary. The tenement, twenty
years old, was 50 x 240 feet in size, the only outside light
being from West Gotham Court, ten feet wide. Floors "accommodating" four families were refitted for two, refuse
vaults were taken out of the cellar, the open sewer was
closed, etc.

(b) Preventing cruelty to animals. Henry Bergh stopping a crowded car. From a drawing by Sol Eytinge, jr.,
in *Harper's Weekly,* XVI, 741 (Sept. 21, 1872). He
might have intervened as well, it would seem, on behalf
of the passengers. *Harper's Weekly,* XI, 189 (March 23,
1867), in connection with these pictures illustrating the discomfort in packed street cars, prints a set of verses from
which the following is extracted:

He's jerked abroad by sleeve and shoulder,
Shoved inside to sweat and moulder.
Toes are trod on, hats are smashed,
Dresses soiled—hoop-skirts crashed. . . .

XIV. WHITE SUPREMACY IN THE SEVENTIES . . . *facing* 376

(a) Anti-Chinese sentiment in California. From *Scribner's Monthly,* X, 279 (July, 1875).

(b) The attack on John Campbell by the Ku Klux Klan
in Moore County, N. C. From *Frank Leslie's Illustrated
Newspaper,* XXXIII, 60 (Oct. 7, 1871). "The pro-
gramme was interrupted by United States Detective Hester,
who saved the victims and captured the villains, with the
paraphernalia of the Order. These masks and dominoes
were carefully preserved, and after being submitted to the
jury, were arranged on a party of gentlemen who *posed* in
the postures occupied by the prisoners at the time of the
attempted murder, while the photographer, Mr. John O.
Johnson, took several negatives, from one of which our
engraving is composed." Probably very few graphic evidences remain of the operation of the Klan which are nearer
to the fact than this.

XV. STRIKES . . . . *facing* 388

(a) During a coal-mining strike in Pennsylvania, 1871.
From a drawing by Joseph Becker in *Frank Leslie's Illustrated Newspaper,* XXXII, 17 (March 25, 1871).

PLATE   PAGE

" 'Blacklegs,' or Working Operatives at Mahanoy City, Hooted by the Society Men and their Wives." Clipped at the sides.

(b) In the days of the great railroad strike of 1877. From a photograph in *Harper's Weekly*, XXI, 617 (Aug. 11, 1877). The Sixth Maryland Regiment of militia on its way to suppress riots in the western part of the state was attacked by a mob in the streets of Baltimore; nine citizens were killed. *Cf.* plate i.

EDITORS' FOREWORD

THE cross section of American civilization which Professor Nevins uncovers in this volume is one of the most varied and complex in the whole history of American life. In the South the whites were struggling against bitter odds to readjust their economic and social life to the conditions imposed by their defeat in the Civil War, while the Negroes, dazed by their new-found freedom, were groping their way toward a secure place in the new social organism. Beyond the Missouri a flood of population was rushing toward the last frontier, revealing to the older settled regions a new and colorful America, one built on heroic dimensions and characterized by kaleidoscopic change. In the Northeast machine-industry was rapidly asserting its supremacy, revolutionizing the older methods of carrying on business, and strongly affecting the life of all classes of society. Middle America continued to maintain its identity as a rural region, and yet, more than any other section, felt the unsettling impact of Eastern industrialism. Everywhere American life showed traces of the great struggle from which the country had so recently emerged, and public life in city, state and nation was stricken with the moral sickness which followed the war. It was a period of striking contrasts, of contending aspirations, of new life crowding out the old.

It has been Professor Nevins's task to describe the varicolored strands, social, economic and cultural, that entered into the pattern of postwar life, to trace the subtle interaction of these elements, and to appraise their significance. This, we believe, he has achieved with notable success, enriching his account with illustrative material gathered from a wide range of sources—newspapers, magazines, official reports, personal narratives. The same period has been traversed by other historians, notably James Ford Rhodes, W. A. Dunning and John W. Burgess, but their principal concern was with political and constitutional problems. Even Ellis Paxson Oberholtzer, writing with greater attention to economic and social development, takes little account, in his three volumes on this period, of many of the threads which are here seen to be woven tightly into the fabric of American civilization.

Professor Nevins makes it clear that each great section of the country had its own contribution to make to the national culture—to economic growth, intellectual life, social idealism. In his swiftly moving narrative the "Coal-Oil Johnnies," the swaggering gamblers in Wall Street, the railway and mining kings, picturesque but evanescent figures, are offset by the bold standard bearers of new university ideals, the venturesome creators of a new American literature and the pioneers of the test tube and microscope. The older ideas of Reconstruction are certain to be revised in the light of the author's demonstration that Southern progress did not halt even in the darkest days, since only a small part of the producing area was affected by the Reconstruction maladies. Incidentally it may be noted that it is possible for the social historian to treat the whole episode of Reconstruction without a single reference to either Charles Sumner or Thaddeus Stevens. As the author sets forth, the financial and economic crisis of 1873 divides these years into two distinct parts, with consequences of vital import not only to business development but also to the whole social program of this and succeeding generations. The reconstructive forces at work in common-school education, less significant in the life of this generation than of the next, have been left for treatment in a later volume of the series. As he comes to the end of this volume, the reader may well feel that the United States of Lincoln and Lee has dissolved before his eyes and that he sees before him at last the main outlines of "modern America."

A. M. S.
D: R. F.

THE EMERGENCE
OF MODERN AMERICA
1865-1878

THE EMERGENCE
OF MODERN AMERICA

CHAPTER I

THE DARKEST DAYS IN THE SOUTH
(1865-1873)

THE eleven states over which defeat spread its black wings in the spring of 1865 contained slightly fewer than five million white inhabitants and three and a half million Negroes. Of this number, about one million were men who had served in the field, many of whom were left crippled or debilitated by the war. A full quarter of a million had died in the armies, either in battle or from wounds or disease. The number who were actually left with the colors when the war guttered out was smaller than might have been supposed. At Appomattox Lee surrendered 26,765 men, the discouraged remnant of about 50,000 with whom he had begun the final hopeless campaign. These troops dispersed immediately to their homes. Within the next few weeks the remaining Confederate armies, Joseph E. Johnston's, Richard Taylor's, and E. Kirby Smith's singularly destitute force west of the Mississippi, surrendered also. The whole number of troops who turned their faces toward their families and the tasks of peace was 174,233, a body which was quickly absorbed by the remaining eight and a quarter million Southerners.[1]

[1] J. F. Rhodes, *History of the United States from the Compromise of 1850* (N. Y., 1893-1919), V, 187; E. P. Oberholtzer, *History of the United States since the Civil War* (N. Y., 1917-1926, in progress), I, 51; T. L. Livermore, *Numbers and Losses in the Civil War* (Boston, 1900), 1-65.

1

A determination on the part of Northern generals to cripple the resources of the South in every way had added greatly to the destruction which always attends a clash of armies. Virginia had suffered in almost every section. From Harper's Ferry to Newmarket the Shenandoah Valley had been turned into a desert by Sheridan and Hunter.[1] The barns, mills and haystacks were all burned with many of the houses; the bridges had been demolished; the livestock had been destroyed and fences had disappeared. Eastward, the whole region between Alexandria and Richmond had been overrun again and again, and villages, farmhouses, churches and timber swept away. Much of the country was a mere commons with all landmarks obliterated save here and there a blackened chimney keeping watch like a grim sentinel over the desolation.[2] Through the Carolinas and Georgia Sherman's army had cut a broad swath of destruction—destruction so complete that one federal officer had boasted that agriculture and trade could not be effectively revived in a generation.[3] Wide areas in northern Alabama had been ravaged by contending armies and guerrilla bands, and the Valley of the Tennessee in particular showed scenes of appalling ruin. Other states had suffered hardly less. In Arkansas Governor Murphy reported that the desolations of the conflict were beyond description; guerrilla bands and scouting parties had pillaged the country so savagely that two thirds of the counties were full of destitution.

The South from Virginia to Texas was dotted with towns which had been partly or completely ruined. The

[1] "Report of the Joint Committee on Reconstruction," *House Rep.*, 39 Cong., 1 sess., no. 30, pt. ii, 68 ff.

[2] M. P. Andrews, *Women of the South in War Times* (Balt., 1920); Susan D. Smedes, *Memorials of a Southern Planter* (Balt., 1887), 225; Myrta L. Avary, *Dixie after the War* (N. Y., 1906), 158 ff.

[3] G. W. Nichols, *The Story of the Great March* (N. Y., 1865), chaps. xxviii-xxix.

business section of Richmond had been laid waste by
the fire which accompanied the Confederate evacuation,
and other parts of the city plundered.   In Columbia,
South Carolina, eighty blocks, with 1386 buildings,
had been turned into a chaos of crumbling walls.
Charleston had suffered from two disastrous conflagrations and from repeated bombardments; and to Northern
visitors the summer after the war, seeing it half in ruins,
with vacant houses, rotting wharves, grass-grown streets
and pavements torn up to make fortifications, its old-
time beauty and pride seemed as dead as those of Athens.[1]
Atlanta, a thriving little mushroom city when the war
began, was now half in ashes, with thousands of tons
of débris strewing the ways and thirty-five thousand
people in the immediate vicinity dependent upon charity
for sustenance.   In Mobile a terrible explosion had converted nine blocks into a smoldering waste; the wharves
were partly torn up for firewood; the harbor had been
obstructed by the federal forces; and an atmosphere of
decay enveloped the narrow, dirty streets, in which men
loafed dispiritedly.[2]   So the story went.   Even in New
Orleans, which had suffered little physical damage, the
energy and confidence of the people were gone.   Many
of them were exiled, half the stores were locked and
empty, and flashy gamblers furnished the chief sign of
animation.[3]

Transportation, of course, had utterly broken down
throughout a great part of the South.   The direct line
from Richmond to Lynchburg was disrupted, and other
Virginia railways were virtually out of commission.

---

[1] Sidney Andrews, *The South since the War* (Boston, 1886), chaps.
i-ii; Whitelaw Reid, *After the War: a Southern Tour* (Cincinnati,
1866), 57 ff.

[2] *American Annual Cyclopedia* (N. Y., 1861-1903), V (1865),
391 ff.; W. L. Fleming, *Civil War and Reconstruction in Alabama* (N. Y.,
1905), chap. v, sec. 1.

[3] *Nation* (N. Y.), II (1866), 270.

Sherman had torn up the Georgia lines for three hundred miles from Atlanta to Savannah, and turning northward, had destroyed every rail in South Carolina that was within his reach and of value to the Confederacy. Mississippi had boasted the best equipped railway in the South, the two-hundred-mile line of the New Orleans, Jackson and Great Northern, today a part of the Illinois Central, which had cost seven million dollars. Now the stations were burned, the rolling stock had disappeared, and most of the roadbed and the bridges had been destroyed.[1] In Alabama nearly all of the eight hundred miles of railway were useless. From Mobile communication with the interior by rail was at first quite cut off, and passengers could reach Montgomery only by a week of risky steamboating on the tortuous Alabama River; at Selma, 'on the same stream, they found the depots, shops and foundry in total ruin. River traffic also was frequently interrupted, for the channels had been neglected, the levees allowed to collapse, and the boats had broken down.[2]

Everyone, with the exception of a small class of speculators and war profiteers, was impoverished.[3] Not only had the whole property in slaves, estimated at almost two billion dollars, been swept away, but land values had become incredibly low. The banks of the South had been submerged beneath a sea of worthless Confederate paper, and their capital, another billion dollars, was gone. The Southern insurance companies were bankrupt and dead. Mills, factories and mines were closed, and had little prospect of reopening in the near

[1] J. W. Garner, *Reconstruction in Mississippi* (N. Y., 1901), 137 ff.

[2] Fleming, *Reconstruction in Alabama*, chap. v, sec. 1. For much matter on the destruction of railways, see *House Rep.*, 39 Cong., 2 sess., no. 34.

[3] For speculation, profiteers and the newly enriched Southerners, see C. Mildred Thompson, *Reconstruction in Georgia* (Columbia Univ., *Studies*, LXIV), chap. v.

future. Many plantations were heavily mortgaged, and their owners knew that unless they got upon their feet at once they would lose their homes. This gave rise to an atmosphere of nervous anxiety, which infected those not engaged in agriculture. Worst of all was the irretrievable human ruin, physical and moral. Mississippi alone had fully ten thousand orphans; a family there which had not lost a member seemed a rarity, and observers said that half of the adult male population appeared to be gone. The destruction of character and courage—the effect of ruin, camp dissipation and guerrilla warfare—was more saddening than poverty or death.[1]

It was no wonder that, as Carl Schurz reported, many men who were stripped of all their available means, with nothing but perhaps some infertile land left, seemed sunk in despondency. But there were many more whose courage created their own opportunities, men like General W. N. Pendleton of Virginia, who, settling down on a farm near Lexington, began tilling it in such ragged clothes that passers-by took him for a farm hand; or men like Washington Duke, a hill farmer of North Carolina, who drove a covered wagon laden with hand-manufactured tobacco to the Capehart herring fishery on Albemarle Sound—a week's trip over rough and muddy roads—bartered his tobacco for salt herring, and traded the herring in turn for fresh pork, which the Raleigh merchants bought at a good price. Out of his profit he bought a dollar's worth of brown sugar and took it home to his hungry boys, one of them James B. Duke who was to become the founder of the American tobacco trust.[2]

[1] Reid, *After the War*, 360.
[2] W. K. Boyd, *Story of Durham* (Durham, 1925), 80-93. For another instance, see M. G. Fulton, *Southern Life in Southern Literature* (Boston, 1917), 373. Robert E. Lee turned heroically to education.

In many Southern communities the reign of violence and terrorism continued after the war. Thus in southeastern Alabama guerrillas and deserters from both armies continued for a year to plunder helpless countrysides; the Saunders gang was especially active till in 1866 Saunders was killed after fleeing to Georgia. The rivers were infested with cotton thieves, who landed at flourishing cotton fields, stole the cotton and carried it down to market. A band of outlaws even took passage upon an Alabama river steamboat and overcame the crew and the passengers. In upper South Carolina gangs of Negro robbers, one captained by a white man, were reported. Throughout the South horse and cattle thieves were active. Beyond the Mississippi, in the wilder parts of Arkansas and Texas, desperadoes scoured the country, driving off livestock, robbing men, and cutting throats.[1] Most alarming of all, the relations between whites and blacks were tinged by a steadily increasing turbulence, which showed itself not only in isolated affrays and murders but also in such bloody and frenzied race riots as that which disgraced New Orleans in July, 1866.[2]

Conquered and policed by Northern armies, how rapidly could the eight million Southerners struggle back to prosperity? The section had one great fundamental factor in its favor—it was preëminently an agricultural region. It suffered from two cardinal disabilities—its governing population of able-bodied white men had been reduced by one third or one fourth, while liberation had rendered much of its Negro labor indisposed to regular employment. Recovery for a farming re-

---

[1] See Charles Seymour, ed., *The Intimate Papers of Colonel House* (Boston, 1926), I, chap. ii, for Texas disorders; H. H. Bancroft, *Pacific States of North America* (San Fran., 1882-1890), XI, 480 ff.

[2] Fleming, *Reconstruction in Alabama*, chaps v-vi; *House Rep.*, 39 Cong., 2 sess., no. 16, 12 ff.

gion is usually only a question of one or two good crops accompanied by favorable markets. The South had no great industrial population to house and employ, and no large cities dependent upon a precarious supply of provisions and fuel.[1] When the war began New Orleans alone, with its 168,000 people, had reached the dignity of a metropolis. No other center boasted more than a quarter as many. The one problem was, in the face of a total lack of ready money and usable implements, a paralyzing scarcity and uncertainty of labor, and formidable difficulties in transporting and marketing crops, that of bringing a half-million farms and plantations back to solvency or prosperity.

The first twelve months after the war saw a hectic and deceptive flush of activity spread through most of the towns of the South. The need for the commonest articles of life was exigent and there was a modest amount of cotton for sale at the famine price of $125 a bale. A summer which began in stagnation thus ended with a brisk trade. By September, 1865, cotton was pouring into New York and Boston in unexpected quantities, while a stream of necessities—clothing, groceries, farm machinery, household wares, schoolbooks—flowed south. A. T. Stewart, Claflin & Company, and other New York firms reported that the section was taking about one fourth as much as in 1860 in bulk, or, because of the inflated prices, an equal amount measured in dollars.[2]

In Richmond the late autumn found scores of business houses in process of construction, and the mechanics fully employed. When Grant's troops entered the city there had not been ten thousand dollars in fed-

[1] Sir S. M. Peto, *Resources and Prospects of America* (London, 1866), sec. vii.
[2] *Commercial and Financial Chronicle* (N. Y.), Sept. 16, 23; Oct. 14, 1865; *N. Y. Eve. Post*, Sept. 29, 1865.

eral currency within it; now there were millions.[1]
Visitors to Mobile the same month rubbed their eyes
at the sight of bustling streets, overflowing hotels and
warehouses rising on the ruins of former structures.
New Orleans was slower in catching the stride, but by
the new year trade had approached its old volume, and
the ballrooms, theaters and opera were crowded. The
ruined New Orleans, Jackson and Great Northern Railroad, placed under the presidency of General P. T.
Beauregard, had been rebuilt with astonishing celerity;
in less than a year seventy-eight bridges were constructed
and long freight trains set in motion.[2] But it was
Atlanta which offered the most encouraging spectacle.
The four railways centering here were burdened to their
utmost; the trade of the city, measured in currency, was
already one third greater than before the war.[3]

But at bottom the prosperity of the Southern towns
was dependent upon that of the rural regions, and the
farmers and planters had to climb a steep and flinty
path to recovery. The materials with which to create
capital—livestock, machinery and seeds—were largely
gone. For example, Georgia in 1860 had two hundred
and thirty-two thousand horses and mules, and six years
later only one hundred and thirty-two thousand, a loss
of three draft animals in seven. It had possessed more
than a million cattle, and was left with little more than
half that number. Louisiana likewise had lost more
than half her draft animals.[4] For the first time many
Southern farmers used oxen for plowing, and there were
instances in which the plowshare was drawn by men

[1] *Richmond Inquirer*, Nov. 13, 1865.
[2] Garner, *Reconstruction in Mississippi*, 143 ff.
[3] Andrews, *South Since the War*, chap. xxxviii. The *N. Y. Herald*,
Dec. 27, 1865, reported that Texas was full of traders and that goods
were being rapidly shipped in.
[4] *Am. Ann. Cyclop.*, VI (1866), 8 ff.

and women. What seed existed was poor, the harness was a patchwork of strings and wires and the craziest homemade implements had to be used.

Above all, the problem of labor tormented the agriculturist with anxieties he had never anticipated. Neither the whites nor the Negroes had any practical acquaintance with the wage system, and circumstances impeded their efforts to learn; for few white employers had any money to pay their hands till the crop was marketed, while the Negroes generally confounded freedom with the right to be idle. On each side was an attitude of distrust, the whites frequently believing it impossible to make the Negroes work without compulsion, and the Negroes sullenly suspecting that the whites would browbeat or overreach them. In many areas the result was a temporary demoralization of farming.

Two symbols of his new estate appealed to every freedman—to change his name and to wander away from his plantation.[1] "I's free as a bird," he said, and proved it by setting out along the road. This aimless migration of Negroes was one of the picturesque social results of the war. More than twenty thousand Negroes found their way to Washington alone by the summer of 1865, and the labor market of all the border cities was overstocked. While thousands of long-scattered families, whose members had been sold apart, were joyously reunited, other families were disrupted.[2] Of course great numbers of freedmen did not move at all, and a majority of the others quickly returned to their old homes, but a general spirit of unrest was in the air.

[1] B. T. Washington, *Up from Slavery* (N. Y., 1901), chap. ii. Washington states that a little later the ambitious freedmen were dominated by "the craze for Greek and Latin learning" and "a desire to hold office."

[2] B. C. Truman, "Report," *Senate Exec. Doc.*, 39 Cong., 1 sess., no. 43.

The difficulties of Southern agriculture were accentuated by the onerous direct taxes laid by the federal government, and by the plundering and cheating practised by federal officers.[1] Under the circumstances the first three years after the war were inevitably, among whites and Negroes alike, years of the direst destitution which has ever been witnessed under the American flag. The very hand of nature seemed against the South. The crops of 1865, owing to the shortage of labor and implements and a terrible drought, were calamitously poor. The yield was less than half as much as in the crop year just before the war.[2] The same story was repeated in 1867, when not only did the crops come to grief through bad weather, insects and the idleness of Negro hands, but prices fell to less than half the expected level, completing the ruin of many planters.[3]

The result of these bad seasons was profound discouragement and the sharpest want. By the close of the crop year 1867, innumerable Negroes and many whites had no money, no decent clothing and not a week's supply of any food except cornmeal. In the four years after Appomattox, the Freedmen's Bureau alone had to issue nearly twenty-one million rations, of which more than fifteen million went to the freedmen.[4]

[1] For outrages against the Negroes by the "poor whites" of the Appalachian belt, and for the friction between former Unionists and former Confederates in these districts, see J. T. Trowbridge, The South (Hartford, 1866), 240; "Report of the Joint Committee on Reconstruction," House Rep. 39 Cong., 1 sess., pt. 1, 109 ff. On the labor question, see O. O. Howard, Autobiography (N. Y., 1907), II, 245-265; Carl Schurz, "Report," Senate Exec. Doc. 39 Cong., 2 sess., no. 6, 144, 156 ff. The sufferings of the South from seizures of Confederate cotton and the subsequent cotton tax are described in W. L. Fleming, ed., Documentary History of Reconstruction (Cleveland, 1906-1907), I, 25.

[2] Fleming, Reconstruction in Alabama, 200 ff.; Am. Ann. Cyclop., V (1865), 6, 788 ff.

[3] Am. Ann. Cyclop., VII (1867), 518 ff.; Com. and Fin. Chron., Oct. 12, 1867; Sept. 19, 1868.

[4] Secretary of War, Annual Reports, 1866-1868, passim; Howard,

Although the destitution was visible throughout the South, it was worst in Georgia, South Carolina and Alabama. In Alabama the ravages by the armies and by guerrillas contributed to such a paralysis of agriculture that the first crop was hardly one tenth of that raised before the war, and not before 1880 did the improved acreage equal that of 1860. During the first winter of peace many white families near Talladega lived in the woods, with no shelter save pine boughs, and when spring came three fourths of the eighty thousand widows of the state were said to be in want of the bare necessities of life. Many instances of outright starvation were reported in the northern part of the state of Alabama. Federal, state and private agencies had to distribute food unstintedly, the Freedmen's Bureau reporting in the fall of 1867 that ten thousand whites and fifty thousand Negroes were without means of subsistence.[1] In South Carolina many once wealthy families, especially in Charleston, parted with their plate and other heirlooms to buy bread; here, too, some actually starved to death. The fiery poet, Henry Timrod, whose lyrics had animated Southern hearts during the war, suffered constantly from hunger during the latter part of 1865 and died two years later in utter poverty. William Gilmore Simms sold a few copies of Timrod's volume of poems to obtain money for the family, but Simms himself, with his country home burned down and his library destroyed by Sherman's troops, was ruined.[2] In Georgia during 1865 pitiful scenes were described by the press correspondents. "In

Autobiography, II, 163-445 P. S. Peirce, The Freedmen's Bureau (Univ. of Iowa, Studies, III, no. 1), 1-191.

[1] N. Y. Eve. Post. Nov. 14, 1865; Am. Ann. Cyclop., VI (1866), 12 ff; Fleming, Reconstruction in Alabama, 200 ff.

[2] J. S. Pike, The Prostrate State, South Carolina under Negro Government (N. Y., 1874), 117 ff.; W. P. Trent, William Gilmore Simms (Boston, 1892), 294-300.

many whole counties," wrote one observer, "the merest
necessaries of life are all any family have or can afford,
while among the poorer classes there is great lack of even
these." Early in 1866 the legislature appropriated
$200,000 to buy food. In Mississippi the year after
the war Governor Humphrey recommended that one
fifth of the state revenues be applied immediately to the
succor of widows, orphans and other needy persons.[1]

Mentally and spiritually the white South suffered the
most in these dark three years; physically the black
South endured the most. While slaves, the Negroes had
been cared for, in health and sickness, by their masters;
now they were left to their own ignorance and carelessness. In the "contraband camps" and the mushroom
Negro colonies in the cities, the sanitary conditions were
horrifying. Inevitably epidemics, of which smallpox
was the deadliest, swept away great numbers, while the
ravages of tuberculosis were heavy. The Negro children, without proper care or diet, died like flies and for
several years almost none were to be seen in some districts. It was remarked that some new Herod would
seem to have slaughtered the innocents.[2] The Freedmen's Bureau, which gave at least a million ailing people
medical assistance, established hospitals and dispensaries,
but they could not check the epidemics. "A negro
woman will come in with her sick child at the morning
hour," reported a British observer, "but does not return
in the afternoon or next day as she ought, but makes
her appearance a few days after to announce that she
administered some charm of her own, and that the
little patient is dead."[3] Just how great was the loss

[1] *Am. Ann. Cyclop.*, V (1865), 29, 392; VI (1866), 521.
[2] George Petrie, "William F. Samford," Alabama Hist. Soc., *Trans.*,
IV, 465-485; *Nation*, XV, Aug. 15, 1872.
[3] Robert Somers, *The Southern States since the War, 1870-1871*
(N. Y., 1871), 52 ff.

of life it is difficult to determine, but some clue is afforded by the statistics of Charleston. Here, where the two races were not far from equal in numbers, there were years between 1866 and 1871 when the Negro mortality was twice that of the white citizens. The relative mortality of Negro children under five was even more shocking. Thus in 1868 there were one hundred and thirty-six deaths of white children and nearly three times as many—three hundred and seventy-two—of black; in 1869 the figures were one hundred and eighty-one and four hundred and sixty-one.[1] In some crowded, unhealthy communities of the South one fourth or one third of the Negroes died during the first years of readjustment.[2]

This harvest of death was but one of the many aspects of the Negro's forced and rapid adjustment to a totally new condition—a social revolution the most sweeping and sudden that has ever affected a large part of the American population and an almost unique event in history. Benefits and evils seemed for a time hopelessly confused. For the first time the Negroes could contract marriages in the ordinary legal fashion and regard their family life as possessing permanence; thousands of Negro couples in 1865 hastened to ratify their informal unions of old plantation times. On the other hand, some Negro circles considered it unprogressive for a man to remain tied to an ugly old wife, taken in slavery days, and a brood of troublesome children. Desertions were innumerable in 1865, and caused much suffering. Later a shocking laxity was shown by the very Negroes who, by virtue of property or office, should have been examples to their race. For the first time, also, Negroes had an opportunity to worship without interference by the

[1] *Nation*, XV, Aug. 15, 1872.
[2] Garner, *Reconstruction in Mississippi*, chap. iv; Fleming, *Reconstruction in Alabama*, 273 ff.

whites. The result was a marked acceleration of religious activity, the colored galleries of white churches standing empty while the freedmen organized their own congregations. But emancipation was also the signal for a series of revivals or emotional orgies, with shouting, praying and "trance sessions" which could be heard for miles, and with a plentiful accompaniment of pilfering and immorality. A camp meeting or baptizing attended by uproarious hundreds often laid the countryside bare.[1]

In the economic field, the Negro's first steps were extremely halting. In the first years he worked with hopeless irregularity. Many of the race were supported by rations from the army or the Freedmen's Bureau; many found that they could live in summer upon berries, green corn, and stolen pigs or chickens. "Spilin' de Egypshuns" was not accounted a sin, and the thefts became serious when, beginning in 1868, unprincipled dealers established crossroads stores where Negroes might exchange cotton, corn or other commodities for trinkets, groceries or liquor—no questions asked. Ingenious laws had to be devised to close their doors.[2] Shiftlessness among the colored folk was increased by the persistent legend that they would share in a distribution of their former masters' estates, a legend which inevitably led to friction with the whites. Of course, this hope for free farms was a mere dream, kept alive by demagogues and by swindlers who went so far as to sell the Negroes little red, white and blue sticks to peg out their claims.[3]

[1] Avary, Dixie after the War, 201 ff.; Fleming, Documentary History, II, 318 ff.; Washington, Up from Slavery, 82-83.

[2] For Negro criminality, see Fleming, Reconstruction in Alabama, 761 ff.

[3] Howard, Autobiography, II, 485-493. The Negroes did not even get lands fairly definitely promised them; see General Rufus Saxton, "Report," Senate Exec. Doc., 39 Cong., 1 sess., No. 27, 140 ff.

But in spite of all its handicaps and defects the race began to show evidence of definite progress even in the first three years after the war. As the months passed, more and more of them saw that they must work or starve, and heeded the admonition of General O. O. Howard and other Freedmen's Bureau officials to prove themselves industrious. The Bureau settled itself to the task of finding places for the blacks and encouraging them to sign contracts. Those who had skill, brains or unusual energy were not long in making themselves better homes than they had occupied in the slave quarters of the plantations. Showing a zeal for education that seemed positively abnormal, many felt that they could die happy if they could only learn to read the Bible; and tales of pickaninnies and grandparents learning to read from the same primer came North to warm philanthropic hearts. In 1866 some one hundred and fifty thousand were attending school, and the numbers continued to increase.

Every Southern state established normal schools for the race, and some even set up so-called universities for them. In Washington the school which later became Howard University was incorporated in 1867, with public-spirited residents of the capital as founders, and in the same year Atlanta University was chartered with funds from the Freedmen's Bureau and other sources. Berea College in Kentucky, for whites and blacks alike, Straight University in New Orleans and Shaw University at Raleigh, North Carolina, all came into existence shortly after the war. So did Fisk University at Nashville, which by 1870 was already doing much to supply Tennessee with a corps of colored teachers, and which became famous through its glee club, which delighted audiences all over the country by singing the fine old Negro melodies that Thomas Wentworth Higginson and others had discovered and begun to collect in book form.[1]

Most picturesque and original of all these institutions was the Hampton Normal and Agricultural Institute, a coeducational institution established in 1870 with the aid of the American Missionary Association.[2] Its founder, General Samuel C. Armstrong, was an officer of the Freedmen's Bureau. His experience as the son of a missionary to Hawaii and as a commander of Negro troops during the war gave him an insight into the problems of the colored South which few men possessed. From Booker T. Washington, who entered Hampton in the fall of 1872 with fifty cents in his pocket, we have the best short statement of Armstrong's statesman-like aims. First, he was eager to give the colored people a better conception of the dignity, beauty and civilizing power of intelligent labor with the hands. Secondly, he wished to lift labor out of drudgery by putting thought and skill into it. Again, he saw that through industrial education he could bring the two races closer to each other, for however vast the gulf between them in other respects, industrially their interests were identical. Finally, he wished to use the labor system at Hampton to build character as well as to give the poorer students a chance to pay for bed and board. Long before the end of the seventies, the Institute was not only supplying capable teachers for the Virginia schools, but was proving to the South that Negroes could become as expert in managing small farms or in the handicrafts as white men.[3]

[1] Holland Thompson, *The New South* (Allen Johnson, ed., *The Chronicles of America Series*, New Haven, 1918-1921, XLII), 167 ff.; Fleming, *Documentary History*, II, chaps. lviii-lix.

[2] J. E. Cooke, *Virginia* (*American Commonwealths*, Boston, 1884), 517.

[3] Edith A. Talbot, *Samuel Chapman Armstrong* (N. Y., 1904), 207.

The attitude of the whites, too, rapidly changed for the better. Many of them, embittered or discouraged, thought at first of expatriating themselves. Scores of families left the South for Europe, some, like Judah P. Benjamin, going to England, and others, including certain South Carolina Huguenots, to France.[1] Some more adventurous spirits, such as Henry W. Allen, the war governor of Louisiana, who had been badly crippled at the battle of Baton Rouge, set off for homes in Mexico, while a steady stream, particularly of ambitious young men, poured into the Northern cities. Both Lee and Jefferson Davis protested against abandonment of the section, but in vain. Equally futile was the tendency of many Southerners to cast about for some method of replacing Negro labor by white. They talked, with a certain traditional horror of free Negroes, of transporting the freedmen to Africa; a clamor went up for foreign labor, and men suggested bounties and direct steamship lines to the emigrant ports of Europe.[2] However, though thousands of immigrants arrived in New York every week, the high wages and the peace and prosperity of the North and West kept substantially all of them from going below Mason and Dixon's line.

This ill-natured and petulant spirit necessarily gave way before the realization by intelligent citizens that the future of the section must be carved out by a partnership of whites and blacks. Some states achieved a partial success with free labor at the very outset. For example, in Virginia and North Carolina and along the border the great majority of freedmen were placed at

[1] Pierce Butler, *Judah P. Benjamin* (*American Crisis Biographies*, Phila., 1907), chaps. xiii-xiv.
[2] B. C. Truman, "Report," *Senate Exec. Doc.*, 39 Cong., 1 sess., no. 43, 15 ff.; *Am. Ann. Cyclop.*, X (1870), 683. For Southern laws to encourage immigration, see, for example, *Laws* of Virginia, 1872-1873, 272; of Texas, 1871, 127; of Georgia, 1869, 26.

fairly regular work during 1865-1866, and the planters of Tennessee also employed most of the available hands.[1] In Louisiana free labor succeeded wherever the whites gave it a fair trial and had money enough to pay cash at frequent intervals. But in South Carolina, Georgia, Alabama and Mississippi the problem was more difficult, partly because of the higher proportion of Negroes and partly because of the general poverty. Everywhere, naturally, the former slaveholders soon showed themselves to be the best friends of the freedman. They needed him more, understood him better and did not fear his competition. In lowland Tennessee, for example, the planters gave the Freedmen's Bureau cordial coöperation, while the poor hill-dwellers of East Tennessee were malevolent. "I tell you what," one old Union adherent there said in 1866, "if you take away the military from Tennessee, the buzzards there can't eat up the niggers as fast as we'll kill 'em." In some sections the blacks were shamefully bullied or cheated by rascally farmers, while they were widely preyed upon by sharps, peddlers and rural storekeepers.

But real progress, little by little, was made toward a sound economic basis for labor.[2] Some Southerners tried renting their land for cash; some paid a money wage to their hands; and others rented out their land on the share system. Though each method had its advantages and disadvantages, powerful forces began to make the third the favorite. Most planters had little money to pay the Negroes, and the Negroes had even less to spend for rent. Negro wage-earners would frequently labor only half a day at a time; they were inclined to make preposterous demands; and when they received food and clothing in advance as an instalment of wages, they were likely to

[1] Howard, *Autobiography*, II, 248 ff.
[2] Trowbridge, *The South*, 239; J. S. Kiddoo, "Report," *Senate Exec. Doc.*, 39 Cong., 2 sess., no. 6, 144 ff.

complain later that they had been underpaid. The few Negroes who rented land for cash, providing their own labor, stock and machinery, usually failed disastrously within a few years.[1]

While the share system also remained on trial for a decade after the war, it steadily gained favor among the whites and was decidedly to the advantage of the Negroes as a whole. At the outset, in most places the planters furnished their tenants rations as well as tools and draft animals and took two thirds of the crop grown. Later it became more usual for the blacks to provide their own food, and the crop was often divided equally. Of course there were many complaints among the whites that the Negroes were negligent—that they let their fences sag into ruin, and that they were ready to drop their hoes when the weeds were thickest to attend a picnic or political rally. Inevitably, also, the Negroes complained, sometimes justly, that they were cheated in their contracts.[2] Yet the system did keep the white landowner's property at least partly productive, while it offered the Negro many advantages. He had a free cottage, free firewood, free pasturage for his livestock and free hunting and foraging. A few freedmen did very well indeed and there were profits of a thousand dollars a year reported. Many more fared poorly at first, but as their self-reliance developed began to prosper.[3]

It was the chief defect of the share system that it accentuated the devotion of the South to the production of cotton alone. Placing cultivation in the hands of untaught and unguided Negroes, it retarded the diversi-

[1] Garner, *Reconstruction in Mississippi*, 137 ff.; *Am. Ann. Cyclop.*, VII (1867), 518 ff.; Somers, *Southern States*, chap. xviii.

[2] Edward King, "The Great South," *Scribner's Monthly*, VII (1874), 136 ff. Somers thought the free Negro more efficient than the slave. *Southern States*, 58-59.

[3] A. A. Taylor, *Negro in South Carolina during the Reconstruction* (Wash., 1924), chap. iv.

fication of crops, the growing of a proper amount of livestock, the introduction of deep plowing and the making of physical improvements. The wretched crop-lien system became more deeply rooted than ever. The black renter almost invariably, and the planter landlord too frequently, had to obtain advances from the merchant, who took a mortgage on the harvest and who—since cotton alone was sure to bring ready money—usually insisted that cotton be planted. Moreover the planter was frequently in a position to bully his poor tenant; "It is more like a halfway slavery than any relation of capital and labor of an advanced type," wrote one observer. But we must remember that the Negroes would have fared badly anyway and that under the conditions of the day the crop-lien system was ineradicable. The great merit of the share plan was that it furnished a transition to independence. It constantly raised Negroes from the lowest rung to a position where they could rent land from the whites for cash and crop it themselves, or could even buy land.[1]

A revolutionary break-up of Southern plantations and farms into smaller units was certain under the new labor conditions. The Negroes during slavery had lived in compact "quarters" or rows of cabins, usually near the master's house; now each worker needed his individual corncrib, hogpen and mule stable, while it was convenient for him to be near his own land allotment. Little farmsteads sprang up by the dozen on what had been large single plantations, and a genuinely able body of colored farmers began slowly to emerge.[2] Their number, however, was very small compared with that of the

[1] Somers, *Southern States*, 84 ff.; Sir George Campbell, *White and Black* (London, 1879), 359 ff.
[2] Somers, *Southern States*, chap. xviii. One marked social result of emancipation was the tendency of many Negro women to refuse work in the fields.

new white farm owners. Poor men all over the South, whether they came from the Appalachians and the hill districts, from the ranks of the overseers and small shopkeepers, or from the small holders of the lowlands, found their opportunity in the high price of cotton and the low price of land. Cheap as good soil had always been, it was now far cheaper still, and for a time after the surrender, and again in the darkest Reconstruction days, plantations in some states could be had for a song. Many proprietors had to let part of their land lie fallow or to rent it free to anyone who would pay the taxes, and the constant foreclosure of mortgages helped to drug the land market.[1] We read of good land in the lower South selling just after the war at $3 to $5 an acre, one fifth or one sixth of what it had brought before 1860. A plantation three miles from Corinth, Mississippi, sold for thirty-five cents an acre.[2]

These low prices and the ensuing transfers marked the downfall of a ruling class. Nearly all the patrician families of the old South had been country gentlefolk and they suffered so heavily from the war that their names almost disappeared from public affairs for a generation. The Pickenses, the Allstons, the Mannings, the Middletons of South Carolina, the Carters, the Pages, the Tazewells, the Barbours of Virginia, the Forsythes and Cobbs of Georgia, represented a social stratum that was broken up and churned into the heterogeneous society of the new South.[3] The ambitious, hard-working middle class—farmers, lawyers, merchants, manufactur-

---

[1] Fleming, *Reconstruction in Alabama*, chap. v.

[2] The decline in land values was greatest in Louisiana, Alabama, Mississippi, Arkansas and South Carolina; it was least in Tennessee, Texas and Virginia. For exact statistics see Commissioner of Agriculture, *Report for 1879*, 147 ff. See also Garner, *Reconstruction in Mississippi*, chap. iv; Fleming, *Reconstruction in Alabama*, chap. v, sec. 1; and *Am. Ann. Cyclop.*, IX (1869), 12.

[3] Pike, *Prostrate State*, 117 ff.; Campbell, *White and Black*, 327.

ers—pushed forward to take their places. Poverty-stricken though the South was, it had its men of comparative wealth, for some had prospered by the rolling mills, foundries and factories of war time and some had made large profits by food speculation. By the spring of 1866 more than one thousand two hundred Georgians, who had been excluded from the general amnesty as being worth more than twenty thousand dollars, had received special pardons. Here was the nucleus of a new leadership. In *ante bellum* days the wealth and prestige of the South were in the hands of landed or professional men; now commerce received a large share, and city life gained in importance as compared with the country.[1]

The misfortune of the South seemed the opportunity of the North and the low land prices brought a notable influx of Northerners to engage in farming. A considerable colony of Ohioans was formed in Noxubee and Lowndes counties in Mississippi, and its glowing reports resulted in fresh arrivals.[2] Every other state had its fortune hunters, sure that they could show the indolent Southerner how to raise cotton at one hundred dollars a bale. Whitelaw Reid and General Herron of Iowa removed immediately after the war to Louisiana; John Hay invested in orange groves in Florida; and Colonel Henry Lee Higginson with two comrades went to Georgia and bought a plantation of about five thousand acres, thirty miles from Savannah, for twenty-seven thousand dollars. But three out of four of these self-confident Northerners failed ignominiously. Reid, dosing his ague with quinine in a damp cottage, met with one disaster after another—floods, the army worm and trouble with his one hundred and fifty Negro hands. Hay never re-

---

[1] Thompson, *Reconstruction in Georgia*, chap. v.
[2] Improved land could be had at from three dollars to five an acre. Garner, *Reconstruction in Mississippi*, chap. iv.

ceived a cent from his orange trees. Higginson and his comrades, after encountering heavy rains, insect plagues, labor difficulties and a vexatious lawsuit, sold their plantation for five thousand dollars and, returning North, found that their experience had cost them about sixty-five thousand dollars.[1] So the story went. Much more significant to the South than this Northern invasion was the vast migratory movement of both white and black farmers toward the Southwest. Energetic men of the old slave states, longing for a new chance, were drawn to Texas and Arkansas as by an irresistible magnet, and opened tens of thousands of fertile new farms there. The land was cheap, the soil productive, cattle-raising and mixed farming were easy, and the society was progressive. The rapid development of this region was one of the important factors in the emergence of the new South.[2]

Under these rapidly changing conditions of land tenure and labor, the dark skies above the South showed a roseate gleam of dawn in 1869. The cotton crop marketed in that year was so abundant and the price so good that Northern financial authorities estimated that it furnished the impoverished section with two hundred and fifty million dollars in currency, a sum swelled by easily fifty million dollars from the sale of sugar, tobacco, naval stores and other products. For the first time many planters felt comparatively independent.[3] Southerners made more purchases from the Northern cities than at any time since 1860 and paid for them more promptly.[4]

[1] Bliss Perry, *Life and Letters of Henry Lee Higginson* (Boston, 1921), 247 ff.; Royal Cortissoz, *Life of Whitelaw Reid* (N. Y., 1921), I, 123 ff.

[2] C. W. Ramsdell, *Reconstruction in Texas* (Columbia Univ., *Studies*, XXXVI, no. 1), 44 ff.; Bancroft, *Pacific States*, XI, 480 ff.

[3] *Com. and Fin. Chron.*, Feb. 6, 1869; *Am. Ann. Cyclop.*, IX (1869), 256 ff.

[4] *Com. and Fin. Chron.*, April 24, 1869.

New buildings were erected, houses were painted, worn out furniture was replaced, and exhausted fields were fertilized. The new stir of prosperity brought an enthusiastic industrial congress of seven hundred delegates together at Mobile. This feeling of buoyancy continued with the bountiful crops of the following years. The yield of 1871 amounted to the amazing total of 4,347,000 bales, one fifth again as great as the crop in the last year before the war. When cotton could be grown for ten cents a pound, as was coming to be the fact, and its average price was not far from twenty, such totals spelt new hope for the dejected Southern people.[1]

This increased production and higher prosperity were permanent, for they rested upon a remarkable and continuing growth in the number of farmers. The far-reaching revolution in the very basis of Southern agriculture was made startlingly evident by the census returns of 1870. Tennessee, with its large Northern immigration and mountaineer class, had 118,141 farms, against only 82,368 a decade earlier. In South Carolina the number increased from roughly thirty-three thousand to fifty-two thousand, in Mississippi from forty-three thousand to sixty-eight thousand, and in Louisiana from seventeen thousand to twenty-eight thousand, these being the states in which the great planters suffered most heavily. But not a single state failed to show a decided gain. All this, of course, meant a marked decline in the average acreage. The typical Louisiana agriculturist, for example, had tilled five hundred and thirty-six acres just before the war, and now held only two hundred and forty-seven, while even in North Carolina, where the small farmer had flourished from colonial days, the average farmstead fell from three hundred and sixteen acres

[1] *Am. Ann. Cyclop.*, IX(1869), 206.

to two hundred and twelve.[1] Frequently these so-called farms were mere patches of a few acres which Negroes had acquired, along with a mule and cabin, as the first step toward a larger property.[2]

Picturesque and far-reaching changes also resulted in the mercantile organization of the South. The great slaveholders had once bought goods for their entire retinue of hands. They corresponded, in the commercial world, to so many jobbers or extensive retailers, obtaining their supplies at wholesale from the nearest large city —Mobile, Charleston or Richmond. When the slaves became independent purchasers, all this was ended. A host of small stores sprang up throughout the South and Northern wholesale firms now made the acquaintance of customers in innumerable villages and crossroads stations. The Yankee drummer became familiar on Southern trains and goods suited to small farms, as distinguished from large plantations, came into demand.[3] Freedom meant a very substantial elevation in the living standards of hundreds of thousands of Negroes, and this also increased the retail market for widely assorted commodities sold in small lots.

In the method of selling Southern crops a similar change took place. Before the war the factor who took the produce of a wide plantation made but a single advance on the crop of a thousand acres. Now the same quantity of cotton was grown by the united efforts of perhaps a score of farmers, each of whom had to have his individual credit at the factor's, and a tribe of small money lenders sprang up and flourished. The great planters before 1861 had consigned their crops to commission men in the principal cities. Now most land-

[1] Commissioner of Agriculture, *Report for 1876,* 128-132.
[2] Somers, *Southern States,* 64-65.
[3] *Com. and Fin. Chron.,* Oct. 23, 1869.

holders did not know enough about marketing to ship so far, and sold their crops to the local dealers who, as the network of railways increased, constituted a more and more numerous class.[1] Economically the section was taking on a modern color; its commercial system was approaching that of the North and West.[2]

While agriculturally the South was struggling to its feet, politically the late sixties saw it plunged into the worst disorder and oppression since the war. We need not here review in detail the governmental history of Reconstruction, which interests us only in its social consequences; it is sufficient to say that Congress had taken control of the entire process and had done it in the vengeful spirit of a party triumphant after a desperate struggle. It had set up a military administration in the South, had declared the existing governments in the ten unreconstructed states illegal, and had arranged for constitutional conventions to erect new governments.[3] These acts had reduced the white citizens of the South to a condition of apathy or despair. The new constitutional conventions, guided in the main by Northern extremists, drew up instruments guaranteeing all races entire equality, political and civil. When the voters went to the polls in 1868 to decide the question of ratification, party ranks had for the first time been consolidated roughly along racial lines. The constitutions were supported by an ignorant, illiterate, emotional mass of freedmen, led by two groups, the hated Carpetbaggers from the North, and the still more detested Scalawags, a small body of native whites representing the war-time Unionists and

---

[1] C. W. Burkett and C. H. Poe, *Cotton, its Cultivation* . . . and *the Problems of the Cotton World* (N. Y., 1906), 72. For the gouging by loan sharks, see Somers, *Southern States*, chap. vii.

[2] But for the vicious one-crop system see Charles Nordhoff, *The Cotton States in the Spring and Summer of 1875* (N. Y., 1876), 108.

[3] W. A. Dunning, *Reconstruction, Political and Economic* (A. B. Hart., ed., *The American Nation*, N. Y., 1904-1918, XII), chaps, v-vi.

Columbia, S. C., after the passing of Sherman's army.

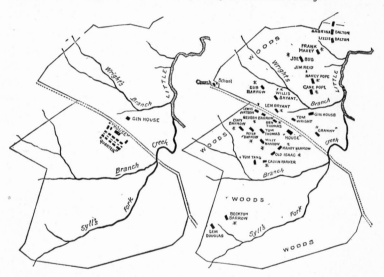

A Georgia Plantation—1860 and 1880.

The Negroes found new liberty in
the camp meeting.

Chivalry among the Southern
whites—a tournament.

the "reconstructed" ex-Confederates. The opposition
came from the "conservatives" or Democrats, composed
of the great majority of white voters and a thin sprink-
ling of Negroes.[1]

In every part of the South the old white ruling class
made a desperate struggle to preserve its control; it denounced in unmeasured terms the impending "lapse of
Caucasian civilization into African barbarism." Yet in
seven of the ten states—in South Carolina, North Carolina, Georgia, Florida, Alabama, Louisiana and Arkansas
—the new instruments were promptly adopted, assuring
Negro domination, and governors and legislatures elected
under them during 1868. In all of the seven except
Georgia, the Negroes and Carpetbaggers assumed a complete sway over the government. Most of the principal
officeholders, including ten of the fourteen senators and
four of the seven governors, were men who had come
from the North since Appomattox, while in the minor
offices the illiterate Negroes and the Scalawags were naturally a majority. In South Carolina the black members of the first legislature under the new government
numbered eighty-eight, and the whites only sixty-seven.[2]

Thus the North had gone far beyond the step of
merely granting the Negro a full participation in the
rights and duties of free society. It had taken the millions of former slaves, almost universally unlettered and
ignorant, the children of the Dark Continent and the
victims of slavery, and had placed them in charge of the
delicate and complicated mechanism of modern democracy, with power to deal with its laws and its courts,
its taxes and expenditures, its administrative system and
its public institutions, its thousand perplexing social and

[1] Dunning, *Reconstruction, Political and Economic*, chap. vii.
[2] Taylor, *Negro in South Carolina*, 153. Tennessee had wisely accepted the Fourteenth Amendment and hence escaped the hardest conditions visited upon the other states.

economic problems, just as their whims dictated. Nor had it been content to give them the state governments as they had existed before and during the war. It had insisted that new governments be instituted, with a multitude of innovations based upon Northern experience in the management of schools and charities, of the financial system, of the judiciary and of the instruments of local government. These far-reaching reforms were to be carried out by the Negroes. Inevitably the combination of fat offices, large revenues and an ignorant, inexperienced electorate attracted demagogues and place-hunters as carrion attracts vultures. The men most capable of governing, the able, experienced and well-educated whites whom the South had been wont in prewar days to place in office, were rigidly excluded from public affairs.[1]

According to the drastic scheme of Congress, the Southern whites were pushed brusquely to one side to make way for a class government. Their property, their institutions, their revered traditions were made the prey or sport of Northern adventurers. The Negroes, whom the North should have protected and helped forward one step at a time, were partly debauched by being made the participants in a corrupt and incompetent administration, in which lawless and selfish men stole the public moneys, bribed the legislatures, treated the dignity of office with ribald contempt and mismanaged every public trust. A surer method of delaying the Negro's preparation for the really stern tasks of self-government could hardly have been devised. The result, as might have been predicted, was an uprising by the angered white population of the South, which in its violence and force swept away much of what constructive work had been done. This uprising, beginning with the foundation of the Ku Klux Klan and culminating in the overthrow of

[1] See the *Nation's* caustic review, Dec. 7, 1871.

the Reconstruction governments, will be treated in a later chapter.

But the confusion and agony of the late sixties and the first years of the seventies should not be allowed to obscure the fact that beneath the surface a steady process of healing and growth was going on.   The social readjustment was surer and more continuous than the political readjustment.   The Negroes were establishing themselves as tenants or even small landowners, a considerable number of them were gaining a rudimentary education, and they were taking the first halting steps with their own schools, churches and social organizations. Agriculture, backward and unscientific though it was, began to respond to a few hopeful new impulses.   Robert Somers found Georgia in 1870 exhibiting "a great revolution" in methods of farming.   Agricultural societies had been formed in most parts of the state, the planting of Dickson's and other selected brands of cotton seed was increasing the yield, and many a plantation that some overseer had grossly mismanaged before the war was now intelligently conducted.[1]   All over the South, labor was steadily growing more dependable and energetic, a fact which was attested by the improvement in wages alone.   Three years after Appomattox a hand who hired out for the whole crop year could hardly expect more than eighty-three dollars with rations in Georgia, and one hundred and four dollars in Louisiana; ten years afterward he could demand one hundred and two dollars in the former state, and one hundred and thirty-six dollars in the latter.   Southerners, in discussing the recovery of their section, often expressed surprise that the cotton crops should so soon have overtaken the records made before the war; yet the reasons for this were plain to all who looked at the multitude of small farms and

[1] Somers, *Southern States*, 64.

the immense expansion of the cotton area in Arkansas and Texas. New resources, in lumber, marl, tobacco and naval stores, were being exploited.[1]

Little by little, traces of the conflict were being erased, and visitors to the South five years after Appomattox found Richmond, Atlanta and other cities already so well rebuilt that few marks of the war remained. Even Charleston showed the same bustle as of old. The cobblestones rang to the succession of carts hauling cotton and other produce down the river streets; the clang and wheeze of the cotton presses mingled with the shouts of the stevedores and whistles of boats; and the hotels, with their stately colonnades of white pillars and troops of ebony waiters, were full of visitors. The fine residences around the esplanade, long neglected, were being rapidly renovated. New quays and wharves and new lines of counting rooms had risen to meet fresh departments of trade. In cities like these could be caught the clearest glimpse of the new South that was destined slowly but irresistibly to rise to view.[2]

[1] See *Scientific American*, Oct. 1, 1870, on cotton; *Com. and Fin. Chron.*, Jan. 1, 1876, on cotton mills.

[2] Edward King, "The Great South," *Scribner's Monthly*, VI-IX (1873-1874), *passim*.

CHAPTER II

THE INDUSTRIAL BOOM IN THE NORTH

(1865-1873)

MEANWHILE the industrial North was pressing forward with a speed which seemed to leave all old landmarks behind and which year by year wrought new social changes. David A. Wells wrote in 1889 that to a generation whose memory covered only the years following 1860, "the recitation of the economic experiences and industrial conditions of the generation next preceding is very much akin to a recurrence to ancient history." [1] Economically the nation of 1865—a nation which had hardly advanced to the Missouri, which used iron alone, which had a modest railway system and but one and a half billion dollars invested in manufacturing—was a world away from the nation of 1878—a nation which had pressed to the Pacific, which was producing huge quantities of steel, which had the finest railway system in the world and which had invested nearly three billions in manufacturing. The impetus behind this stride was at its greatest in the years 1865-1873; Northern industry was booming when the war ended and the boom had eight years to run.

The victorious end of the war and the return of labor from the armies gave increased buoyancy to enterprise in every field. A leading Northern manufacturer, testifying under oath, said that his rate of profit in 1865 had been "painfully large;" and the special commis-

[1] D. A. Wells, *Recent Economic Changes* (N. Y., 1889), 65.

31

sioner of revenue reported at the end of the following year that the returns of business had been almost unprecedentedly high.[1] Scarcely a record in industry escaped being broken during the next five years. More cotton spindles were set revolving, more iron furnaces were lighted, more steel was made, more coal and copper were mined, more lumber was sawed and hewed, more houses and shops were constructed and more manufactories of different kinds were established, than during any equal term in our earlier history.[2] Moreover, the improvements in the quality of manufactures equaled the increase in quantity.

The high prices which war-time demands and the issue of greenbacks had brought about continued in nearly all markets. The elation of Northern victory, the feeling of recuperative power, the sense of enormous Western wealth waiting only to be unlocked, were reflected in industry. "The truth is," John Sherman wrote his brother in the fall of 1865, "the close of the war with our resources unimpaired gives an elevation, a scope to the ideas of leading capitalists, far higher than anything ever undertaken in this country before. They talk of millions as confidently as formerly of thousands." [3] Sherman himself thought of leaving politics to engage in railroading, banking or manufacturing in Ohio. The home market was steadily expanding, partly through the inflow of immigrants from Europe, partly through the rapid settlement of the Western prairies. The war had tended to break down the previous eco-

[1] Special Commissioner of Revenue, *Report* (Dec., 1869). See also *Scientific American*, Sept. 15, 1866: "There are more men in New York today whose annual incomes reach $100,000 than there were twenty-five years ago of those whose entire possessions amounted to as much."

[2] Special Commissioner of Revenue, *Report* (Jan., 1869).

[3] John and W. T. Sherman, *Letters* (Rachel S. Thorndike, ed., N. Y., 1894), 258.

nomic dependence upon Europe, and behind a high tariff wall a host of new manufactories were making articles formerly shipped from abroad. In 1859 there had been one hundred and forty thousand manufacturing establishments; in 1869 there were two hundred and fifty-two thousand with a commensurate increase in the number of employees.[1] A succession of foreign wars, beginning with the Austro-Prussian War of 1865-1866 and the coalition of Brazil, Argentina and Uruguay against Paraguay, also benefited American trade.

Although the modern steel age was born in 1856, when Henry Bessemer in England invented his process, it did not gain a real foothold in America for a decade. Till after the Civil War steel was rare and costly, used chiefly in cutlery and fine tools. The demands of the conflict gave manufacturers no taste or time for experimenting, so that not until 1864 was the Bessemer process first used, at a short-lived plant in Wyandotte, Michigan, and even in 1867 only two thousand six hundred tons of steel ingots were produced.[2] Then, steel making expanded with striking speed. The new process excited the wonder of all who witnessed it: the pouring of the molten iron into a great converter, the dazzling shower of sparks as the air was forced through the incandescent mass and the drawing off of the flaming metal as white-hot steel. The first steel king arose in the person of Captain Eber S. Ward of Detroit, who at the close of the war began making and selling steel under the American patents of William Kelly.[3] He soon found his chief

[1] *Abstract of the Census of Manufactures, 1919* (Wash., 1923), 13, table 3.

[2] C. D. Wright, *The Industrial Evolution of the United States* (N. Y., 1901), chap. xiv; H. U. Faulkner, *American Economic History* (N. Y., 1924), 574.

[3] V. S. Clark, *History of Manufactures in the United States, 1607-1860* (Carnegie Inst., *Contribs. to Am. Econ. Hist.*, Wash., 1916), 512 ff.

rival in Alexander M. Holley of Troy, New York, who had bought the Bessemer rights. Since neither could make steel satisfactorily without infringing upon the legal prerogatives of the other, Ward, who was growing old, surrendered his patents to Holley, a dashing young industrialist still in his early thirties, in return for a thirty-per-cent share in the consolidation. Holley thus for a time stepped forth as the leading steel-and-iron maker of America.[1]

Steel speedily became as cheap as cast iron and its cheapness created such a keen demand that by 1875 a dozen important Bessemer works had been established. Before the war the iron business of the nation had been widely diffused, with bloomeries and furnaces scattered from the Adirondacks and Berkshires to Virginia and Tennessee. Now the greatest steel works, including the Cambria Works, which Daniel J. Morrell established in Johnstown (1871), the Bethlehem Works (1873) and the J. Edgar Thomson Steel Works (1875), as Carnegie called his establishment near Pittsburgh, rose in Pennsylvania alone. When the first proposal came to Carnegie to use the Bessemer process, the young ironmaster demurred, saying that "Pioneering doesn't pay a new concern: we must wait until the process develops." But he soon afterwards saw it demonstrated in England, and hurried home to organize the firm of Carnegie, McCandless & Co., to develop the new methods with a capital of seven hundred thousand dollars.[2] Meanwhile smaller works were flourishing in Cleveland, Chicago and St. Louis. The American production of steel rose steadily to three hundred and seventy-five thousand tons in 1875 and nine hundred and twenty-nine thousand in 1879, even the Panic of 1873 producing little visible check.

[1] H. N. Casson, *The Romance of Steel* (N. Y., 1907), 1-60.
[2] Andrew Carnegie, *Autobiography* (J. C. Van Dyke, ed., Boston, 1920) ; Casson, *Steel*, 73 ff.

Hard on the heels of the Bessemer process came that of the open hearth, but its progress was slow, for it required more time and the more careful instruction of the steel workers. A Siemens regenerative furnace was installed by John Fritz at the Bethlehem plant in 1872, and about nine thousand tons of open-hearth steel were being made two years later.[1] Thousands of men found work and high wages in the steel plants, producing a commensurate development of the Michigan iron mines.[2] But the social importance of steel production lay beyond all comparison in its contribution to the improvement of transportation, engineering and building construction. The greater part of the steel went into rails, the output of which exceeded two hundred and ninety thousand tons in 1875 and nine hundred and fifty thousand tons in 1880. Their durability as compared with iron rails was an indispensable quality. The huge crops of the Middle West and the growing volume of manufactured goods from the Mississippi Valley could never have been carried without them.[3]

The years 1865-1873 also witnessed the emergence of the four factors whose combination made possible the development of the American meat-packing business upon an international scale. These were the tidal overflow of the plains by the cattle ranchers, the ramification of railways throughout the cattle country, the invention of refrigeration and the appearance of men as-

---

[1] John Fritz, *Autobiography* (N. Y., 1912), 166 ff.; J. M. Swank, *History of the Manufacture of Iron in All Ages* (Phila., 1884), chap. xvi.

[2] Mine owners raised their prices, whereupon some steel mills acquired their own mines. *N. Y., Eve. Post*, Aug. 21, 1873.

[3] Barbed-wire fencing became commercially important by 1874 when Joseph H. Glidden and Jacob Haish began a battle over patent rights; wire nails, in 1875 when Joseph Goebbles founded the Kentucky Wire Nail Works in Covington. Industrial Museum of American Steel and Wire Company (Worcester, Mass.), *Book*, no. 2.

tute enough to organize the distribution of livestock
and meats in an efficient way. In the first year of peace
the railway reached Kansas City, a cattle market and
shipping point was established at Abilene, and some
thirty-five thousand cattle were sent East from this
terminus. It was clear to farsighted men that the West
would shortly become one vast livestock range, crying
for a market

Already in Milwaukee and Chicago two of the great
packers of the future, Philip D. Armour and Nelson
Morris, had established themselves in readiness for this
rich opportunity.[1] Armour, an adventurous New
Yorker, had risen during the war to be partner in Jacob
Plankington's packing house in Milwaukee, then the
fourth largest of its kind in America. The business,
thanks to large war contracts and to Armour's careful
watch upon price fluctuations, expanded rapidly, throwing out branches in Chicago and Kansas City; and he
determined to head a firm of his own. A flood of cattle
and hogs had poured in war times into the Chicago
slaughterhouses, becoming so unmanageable that the Illinois legislature was compelled in 1865 to incorporate
the Union Stockyards, which on Christmas day of that
year opened its new facilities—three hundred and forty-
five rather swampy acres just south of the city limits—
to the livestock shippers. Two years later Armour and
Company, an enterprise in which Philip Armour was assisted by several able brothers, began meat packing in
Chicago, and it was not long before the Armour brand
was known in all parts of the world. Nelson Morris,
a young Bavarian Jew, had been even earlier in entering
the Chicago field. He went into meat packing at twenty-
two, in the first days of the Civil War, and had no

[1] R. A. Clemen, *The American Livestock and Meat Industry* (N. Y.,
1923), 149 ff.

difficulty in securing large army contracts. When the conflict ended his business was flourishing. By 1870 Armour and Nelson Morris in Chicago and Jacob Plankington in Milwaukee had emerged as the foremost Western packers, and were already taking the leadership from the older Eastern houses, like those of Jacob Dold in Buffalo and the Cordukes in Cincinnati.[1]

One Eastern packer possessed a driving energy equal to their own—Gustavus F. Swift.[2] A Cape Cod Yankee, Swift had risen so rapidly from the position of a local butcher that by the middle seventies he was conducting one of the largest dressed-beef businesses in New England. He knew that his natural sphere was the West and the year 1875 found him cautiously looking about for a site for a plant. In a very short time he had a large slaughterhouse in Chicago and was packing meats in competition with Armour and Morris. It was he who saw that beef might be fully dressed in Chicago and sent East, perfectly fresh, in refrigerator cars; and in initiating this fresh dressed-beef business on a large scale, he revolutionized the packing industry.[3] The industry now concentrated itself in a few great cities to an extent previously impossible, with large resulting gains in the cheapness and quality of the meat served on American tables. The local butcher, especially in the East, was thrust to the wall,[4] and even large Eastern slaughterhouses faced a competition from the Mississippi Valley

[1] F. W. Gunsaulus, "Philip D. Armour," *Am. Rev. of Revs.*, XXIII (1901), 167-176; A. Warren, "Philip D. Armour," *McClure's*, II (1894), 260; T. W. Goodspeed, "Gustavus Franklin Swift," *Chicago University Record* (new ser.), VII (1921), 96-116.

[2] Clemen, *Livestock and Meat Industry*, 159 ff.

[3] Commissioner of Agriculture, *Report for 1870*, 250 ff.; L. F. Nickerson, "Refrigeration," *National Provisioner*, III (1891), no. 8; L. D. H. Weld, *Private Freight Cars and American Railways* (Columbia Univ., *Studies*, XXI, no. 1), 16.

[4] Board of Health (N. Y. City), *Report of Sanitary Committee on Slaughtering for 1874.*

which they had difficulty in meeting. Kansas City, with her packing houses still closer than Chicago to the range, sent two carloads of refrigerated meats to New York and one to Boston in the fall of 1875, thus opening a business which increased steadily. By the end of the seventies a general effort was being made by Western packers, and with success, to develop an Eastern market for all the beef and pork they could dress.[1]

As the control of the meat-packing business passed to Chicago and Kansas City, simultaneously the seats of the milling industry were transferred to Minneapolis and in lesser degree to St. Louis and Chicago, with direct benefits both to wheat growers and customers. Its Western development heralded the ultimate extinction of the small gristmills scattered by thousands over the nation and it made possible the rapid settlement of Minnesota wheatlands and the overflow of farmers into the Dakota valleys. Here, too, we meet picturesque and aggressive figures in the persons of three Minneapolis millers: Cadwallader C. Washburn, Charles A. Pillsbury and George M. Christian. The two former were New Englanders by birth, Washburn being one of a group of Maine brothers who achieved a singularly varied eminence,[2] while Pillsbury had worked his way through Dartmouth College in the class of 1863. Christian was an Alabamian who came North after the war in search of opportunities lacking at home, and in 1869 was made a partner in Washburn's establishment.[3] With wheat fields, railways and water power all at hand in Minneapolis, these men were further aided by the introduction of new mechanical processes. They adopted the "gradual reduction"

[1] Clemen, *Livestock and Meat Industry*, chap. ii; Charles Winans, *Evolution of a Vast Industry* (Chicago, n. d.).

[2] Gaillard Hunt, *Israel, Elihu and Cadwallader Washburn, a Chapter in American Biography* (N. Y., 1925), *passim*.

[3] For biographies see *Northwestern Miller*, Sept. 10, 1924.

method brought to them in 1870 by a Minnesotan named Edward La Croix, which preserved much of the gluten previously lost with the bran. This process was of cardinal importance to the Northern wheat belt, for wheras previously winter wheat had made the best flour, now the hard spring wheat furnished as good a product. But men like Pillsbury were still not satisfied. Early in the seventies he and other Northwesterners went to Europe to investigate the milling processes of various nations, but particularly of Hungary, where for decades wheat had been reduced to flour by slowly passing it through a series of chilled iron rollers. In 1874 the Hungarian system was adopted, with modifications, in the Washburn and Pillsbury establishments and gradually extended to other American mills. The result was a fine flour which attracted every buyer by its snowy whiteness and made better bread than Americans had ever before eaten.[1]

Even more Aladdin-like was the development of the Pennsylvania oil fields. Petroleum was destined to be the foundation for a host of new industries, and though few of its uses were discovered between 1865 and 1878, these few were important in themselves and still more important for the vistas they opened up.[2] At the beginning of our period only six years had elapsed since Colonel E. L. Drake sank the first oil well near the village of Titusville in western Pennsylvania. In 1864 it was a district of more than four hundred square miles dotted over with derricks and producing during the twelve months more than two million one hundred thousand barrels. Already some of the uses of the new product, which a half-dozen years earlier had been a quack

[1] Hester M. Pollock, *Our Minnesota* (N. Y., 1917), 196 ff.; *Northwestern Miller*, March 12, 1924.

[2] Waldemar Kaempffert, ed., *A Popular History of American Invention* (N. Y., 1924), II, 83.

Indian medicine, were known through half the world. It lubricated machinery in Manchester and Lyons; Swiss peasants and English noblemen illuminated their abodes with its mellow rays; it was used to light mariners in the wild Indian Ocean and along the South American coasts. Many New Bedford mariners, reading the fate of their trade, had abandoned whale fishing to seek the oil fields.[1] There was no lack of a market, and the rapidity with which oil lamps sold in homes, rich and poor alike, assured it of a steady expansion.

The hold which petroleum had gained upon the popular imagination in the East was illustrated by the speculative mania of 1865, precipitated by the sudden opening in January of a new basin on Pithole Creek. Within six weeks an almost untouched sylvan district became the site of Pithole City and its ten thousand inhabitants, which steadily increased until it held five thousand more. The typical evolution of the mining or oil town was crowded into a few months: tents and shanties gave way to good frame residences, to long streets of restaurants, saloons, land offices and stores. For a time Pithole City, which not many years later reverted to an open wheat field, had a postal business outrivaling all cities in the state except Philadelphia.[2] Stimulated by the new discovery, a fever of speculation seized the large Eastern centers. The capital of the oil companies of public record, which had been computed early that year at three hundred and twenty-six million dollars, rose by midsummer to at least five hundred million dollars, with

[1] E. P. Oberholtzer, *United States since the Civil War* (N. Y., 1917-1926, in progress), I, 255.
[2] G. S. Montague, *Rise and Progress of the Standard Oil Company* (N. Y., 1904), 5. See also Andrew Cone and W. R. Johns, *Petrolia: a Brief History of the Pennsylvania Petroleum Region* (Walter Jones, ed., N. Y., 1870); G. W. Brown, *Old Times in Oildom* (Oil City, Penn., 1909); S. G. Bayne, *Derricks of Destiny, an Autobiography* (N. Y., 1924), 34-84.

new companies springing into life every hour. The rush of population lifted numerous hamlets almost overnight into small cities; the almost continuous loss of life due to carelessness and lawlessness proved no deterrent.

The chief initial difficulty of the industry, which despite constant vicissitudes and disappointments kept on growing, was to store and transport the oil. The expedients of the early days were picturesquely crude. Oil Creek had been navigable to the Allegheny in freshets and the desperate producers resorted for a time to artificial floods. That is, they repaired the old mill dams, collected water behind them and loosed it at prearranged hours, sweeping a crowded flotilla of oil boats—sometimes six hundred—down to the river. More commonly they relied upon teamsters who were as rough and undependable as the muddy roads.[1] Naturally it was not long before inventive men hit upon the remedy, and in 1865 the first extensive pipe line, carrying eighty barrels of oil every hour over a stretch of seven miles, was placed in operation despite the teamsters' protests. It was followed by others, and the price of delivering oil to the Allegheny River boats was reduced from two dollars and fifty cents or three dollars a barrel to one dollar or even fifty cents. At the same time the tank car, invented by Charles P. Hatch, began to take the place of ordinary cars loaded with barrels. Before 1870 long lines of wooden tank cars became familiar in Pennsylvania and Ohio, and soon afterwards these leaky and inflammable carriers were replaced by tubular iron cars.[2]

As the oil fields developed, a great new refining industry sprang up, offering work to thousands. By 1865

[1] Bayne, Derricks of Destiny, 66-67.
[2] Kaempffert, Invention, II, 93-94; Ida M. Tarbell, History of the Standard Oil Company (N. Y., 1904), I, chap. i.

there were a number of large refineries, producing benzine, gasoline, coal oil, paraffin and tar. Very shortly the refineries began to mass themselves at two points, Cleveland and Pittsburgh. The former city in 1865 had thirty such businesses and at the end of the following year sixty. For some time the two centers ran neck and neck, but at the beginning of the seventies the superior position of Cleveland became evident, for having the Great Lakes and Erie Canal as well as the New York Central, it lay upon competitive transportation lines, while Pittsburgh was completely dependent upon the Pennsylvania Railroad.[1] A centralization of the refining business was inevitable. The keen competition in refining methods, which were susceptible of great improvement, alone sufficed to drive many small manufactories from the arena.

It was at this moment that there appeared upon the scene the decisive factor in the sweep toward unification: a leader sufficiently astute, aggressive and merciless to drive it to its logical conclusion, the erection of a monopoly. In 1865 John D. Rockefeller, a young Cleveland commission dealer of twenty-six, launched into the oil trade under the firm name of Rockefeller & Andrews.[2] The Civil War had given him, as it did Armour and others, the capital needed for commercial undertakings on a large scale. Rockefeller saw that the necessary economies in refining were beyond the reach of any firm which had less than a half million in capital, and that the larger the unit the greater would be its efficiency. He pursued a policy of steady expansion. A second refinery was established. H. M. Flagler was accepted as partner, a New York office was opened, and one rival

[1] Tarbell, *Standard Oil Company*, I, 38 ff.; Montague, *Standard Oil Company*, 19.
[2] J. D. Rockefeller, *Random Reminiscences of Men and Events* (N. Y., 1909), gives an excellent impression of the oil magnate's personality.

manufactory after another was absorbed. In June, 1870, there appeared the Standard Oil Company of Ohio, with a capital of a million dollars and a position of towering strength in the industry. It was the largest company in the largest refining center of the country, with a daily output of one thousand five hundred barrels, or about one seventh of the whole production of Cleveland. Rockefeller's ambition, however, was far from satisfied.[1]

Thus the oil industry stood at a crucial point in 1870. Petroleum was being pumped from a large district of northwestern Pennsylvania, and wells were being sunk from West Virginia to Missouri in the hope of finding new fields. A business of which nobody had dreamed ten years earlier was giving the world more than five million barrels of oil annually, of which one hundred and fifty million gallons were going abroad, together with millions of gallons of gasoline, naphtha and benzine.[2] Hardly less than two hundred million dollars was invested in the business. The refineries had to keep pace with the oil harvest: Pittsburgh was now refining almost six thousand barrels a day, New York City more than nine thousand, the oil fields about nine thousand and Cleveland about twelve thousand.[3] The leading railways reaching the oil region, the Pennsylvania, New York Central and Erie, were keenly aware of the rich prize at stake and were bending every effort to gain the central stream of the traffic. It was under these circumstances that Rockefeller, who had already for two or three years insisted that the Erie and New York Central systems grant him secret freight rebates, planned a new

---

[1] Montague, *Standard Oil Company*, 6-7.
[2] See *Scientific American*, July 1, 1865, for beginnings of the coal-tar dye industry.
[3] Tarbell, *Standard Oil Company*, I, 51.

coup. This was nothing less than the formation of a great pool of refiners which, by using the weapon of discriminatory freight rates, should take control of the oil market. The story of this attempt, its temporary failure and eventual success, must be left to a later time.[1]

Meanwhile industries which could not be called new were exhibiting a large-scale standardization, involving also a concentration of capital, which gave them an appearance of entire novelty. In this roster the manufacture of men's clothing and of boots and shoes stood preëminent. During the Civil War a farsighted Scotchman, Gordon McKay, built up a huge business in supplying the army with machine-made shoes. Manufacturers East and West adopted the new machinery, which was rapidly improved, until it was hardly a fiction to say that leather was put in at one end and came out finished footwear at the other. Not only were shoes cheapened by the new process, but they were made more attractive and comfortable than the product of the ordinary artisan at the bench.[2] A single workman was able to turn out three hundred pairs in one day, and a single factory in Massachusetts was soon producing as many shoes as thirty thousand Paris bootmakers.

The manufacture of ready-made clothes had as striking a growth just after the Civil War. The first thought of the discharged soldier was to obtain good civilian clothes and this demand was sustained by the development of the West and the heavy immigration. Since it was difficult for garment cutters to keep pace with the sewing machines, inventors brought out mechanical cloth cutters, the first of which was made on Staten

[1] See chapter xiv.
[2] Andrew Carnegie, *Triumphant Democracy* (N. Y., 1887), 226-227.

Island in 1872.[1] Few sights struck foreign travelers so forcibly as the enormous piles of ready-made suits exposed in shop windows at surprisingly low prices.

But this consolidation of industrial enterprises was evident in almost every field of business. Not until the Civil War did any cotton mill have a hundred thousand spindles, or any iron furnace produce more than three hundred tons a week.[2] The success of the Waltham enterprise in making watches by factory methods instead of slowly and expensively by hand led to the establishment of the American Watch Factory at Elgin, Illinois, in 1865. The sewing-machine factory, the farm-implement factory, the piano and organ factory, all improved their processes, their subdivision of labor and their capacity for quantity production in these flush years. Many small businesses sprang into a hothouse life, for money was abundant,[3] but all the while the principal manufactories—those at the top—grew astonishingly. Less and less did the American people consume goods made in small and simple establishments managed by individual proprietors; more and more did they use goods from large factories managed by corporate boards.

A pronounced westward thrust of industry became evident quite apart from the birth of the meat-packing and flour-milling undertakings of the Northwest. Besides the Elgin watch factory and the Union Stock Yards in Chicago, the first year of peace saw large pottery works started at Peoria, woolen mills at Atchison, a farm-implement factory at Moline, and an important stove foundry at Quincy, Illinois.[4] Two years later

---

[1] Kaempffert, *Invention*, II, 395.

[2] Clark, *History of Manufactures in the United States*, 415, 456.

[3] See *Statistical Abstract of the United States, 1921* (Wash., 1922), 868.

[4] *American Annual Cyclopedia* (N. Y., 1861-1903), V. (1865), 432, 458.

George Pullman founded the Pullman Palace Car Company in Chicago. William H. Seward remarked of McCormick's reaper that through its use "the line of civilization moves westward thirty miles each year," and it was natural that the makers of agricultural machinery should move west too. McCormick's own factory stood on the north bank of the Chicago River. In Akron and Canton, Ohio, during 1865 about ten thousand mowing machines were made, though the price averaged one hundred and twenty-five dollars each. Two of the heritages of the war were a beet-sugar industry in Illinois and Wisconsin, and a flourishing tobacco industry in the latter state. Particularly interesting was the progress of the brewing business in St. Louis and Milwaukee, with their large German population, for the nation was beginning to appreciate the fact that beer was less harmful than ale or spirits, while the excise tax placed upon it was comparatively small. In 1865 Milwaukee, where the Schlitz and Pabst companies were active, was producing fifty-five thousand barrels of beer, while in 1873 the sale had risen to two hundred and sixty thousand.[1]

This westward march of manufacturing was plainly indicated by the census of 1870. It showed that in the nation as a whole the number of establishments had increased in the decade almost eighty per cent. But in Indiana they had more than doubled, in Illinois they had trebled, and in Missouri they had more than trebled. Before the war the great states along the upper Mississippi had been almost wholly agricultural and their cities had depended upon the trade of the farms; now the smoke of factory chimneys showed that they were definitely passing out of the pioneer stage. In the East,

[1] Frederick Merk, *Economic History of Wisconsin during the Civil War Decade* (State Hist. Soc. of Wis., *Studies*, I, 1916), 145, 154; F. F. Cook, *Bygone Days in Chicago* (Chicago, 1910), 196 ff.

the agglutination of industry in strategically placed centers interested every observer. Bridgeport, Connecticut, for example, was just rising to a place of prominence as the seat of the Wheeler & Wilson Sewing-Machine Company; the Simpson Waterproof Cloth Company, which had made trainloads of raincoats for the soldiers; the Hotchkiss Company, which had turned from shells to general hardware; and the newly established Mallory Hat Company.[1]

Financial institutions responded to the buoyant expansion of the time like vegetation to a tropical sun. The inflation of credit made banking a business which tyros could enter with success. The federal government having established a great new national banking system, between the fall of 1864 and the fall of 1865 the number of such banks rose from five hundred and eighty-four to 1,566.[2] But even more remarkable was the multiplication of savings banks. The workmen were enjoying what seemed high pay, and needed repositories for it. In Massachusetts there were ninety-three savings banks in 1862, and one hundred and eighty in 1875; in New York State in the same period the number increased from seventy-four to one hundred and fifty-eight. Costly offices were hired and fitted up, high rates of interest were promised and extravagant salaries were granted.[3] Insurance companies, many of them speculative ventures with insufficient capital, incompetent management and a shocking inattention to sound actuarial principles, rose on every hand. Until these years trust companies had been almost unknown in the United States, but now there sprang up a sudden realization

[1] *Scientific American*, July 8, 1865; *Compendium of the Ninth Census* (Wash., 1872), 796 ff.
[2] W. O. Scroggs, *Century of Banking Progress* (Garden City, N. Y., 1924), 203.
[3] *Commercial and Financial Chronicle*, April 25, 1874.

of their usefulness and opportunities, and between 1864 and 1875 no fewer than forty came into existence.[1] Many observers became alarmed by the disturbance of the former balance between production and consumption, pointing to the huge growth of all businesses of exchange—trade agencies, commission houses, brokerage, banking, retailing—as not wholly legitimate but in large part the forced fruit of inflation. When the census of 1870 was taken, it was found that while the population had been increasing twenty-two and one-half per cent, the trading classes, including those engaged in transportation, had increased forty per cent. Francis A. Walker computed that the nation was maintaining a useless array of middlemen and retailers equivalent to the standing armies of the British Empire and with a greater number of dependents.[2]

In answer to the heavy demands of industry upon the labor market, and to the alluring spectacle of prosperity, comfort and opportunity presented by American life, the stream of European immigration rose rapidly to a torrent. The Fenian movement and land troubles in Ireland, the panic of 1866 in England and the Austro-Prussian conflict gave tens of thousands of Europeans a special incentive to emigrate to the United States. For the first time American manufacturers combined in considerable numbers to send agents to Europe to stimulate emigration, and their efforts advertised the opportunities open to active men. The increasing speed and cheapness of transatlantic travel was also a factor of importance. In 1856 a mere handful of European newcomers, some five thousand in a total of one hundred and thirty-one thousand, had arrived in steamships, the others using

[1] *Com. and Fin. Chron.*, Aug. 3, 1878; H. W. Lanier, *A Century of Banking in New York, 1822-1922* (N. Y., 1922), chap. x.
[2] F. A. Walker, "Some Results of the Census," *Journ. of Soc. Sci.*, V, 71-97.

sailing vessels; but in 1865 the great majority were transported by steam. Not quite a quarter of a million immigrants were admitted in 1865, and thereafter the number rose year by year until in 1873 it reached the then amazing total of four hundred and sixty thousand.[1]

In this fresh surge of Old World population certain novel, interesting and valuable elements appeared prominently. When in 1850 Fredrika Bremer, the Swedish novelist, visited the Northwest, she found a large advance-guard of Scandinavians; now the central host was coming, and by 1870 there were almost forty-five thousand of them in Illinois alone. The first Swedish secular journal, the *Svenska Amerikanaren*, was established in Minnesota in 1866, edited by Colonel Hans Mattson who became known as an active agent in Europe to induce Scandinavians to migrate.[2] About one hundred and twenty-five thousand Scandinavians entered the republic in the first half of the seventies. Some Slavs, German-Russian Mennonites, and Bohemians also arrived. Decidedly more important was the accession of Italians from Sicily and Naples; for in the same half decade slightly more than a hundred thousand people of Latin blood, most of them Italians seeking work in the construction gangs on the railroads and other rough employment, were admitted. But it was the British, Irish and German immigration which continued the heaviest, these nationalities leading in the order named. The result of the inflow was that by 1875 the nation had about seven and a half million of foreign-born among its forty million people.[3]

---

[1] Philip Davis, *Immigration and Americanization* (Boston, 1920), 66, presents the figures by years. See *Com. and Fin. Chron.*, Sept. 1, 1866, for comment.

[2] R. E. Park, *The Immigrant Press and Its Control* (N. Y., 1922), 320; Pollock, *Our Minnesota*, 333.

[3] See *Am. Ann. Cyclop.*, XVII (1877), 386, for general review.

The building of railways, to which the nation turned with characteristic energy just after the war, was urgently needed. Not only was the meager Southern system now largely in ruins, but the railways from the East to the Middle West were quite inadequate. The produce of the Mississippi Valley had increased faster than the means of carrying it, and the corn growers of Iowa, the meat packers of Chicago and the oil shippers of Pennsylvania were especially vociferous in complaint.[1] The congestion on the trunk lines was accentuated by seasonal difficulties, for at the close of the war one third of the freight annually carried from the central valley to the Atlantic was still conveyed by the lakes and canals, and when they were frozen, the rail blockade often became disastrous. These transportation difficulties depressed the inland markets and kept land values unduly low. The need for new arteries grew steadily more acute, for every year a hundred thousand settlers poured across the Mississippi.

This task of construction was made the easier because railway profits had been high during the war and capital was easy to obtain, while the spirit of national self-confidence also played a large rôle.[2] At the close of the conflict the whole American system totaled about thirty-five thousand miles and had cost a little more than a billion. Then came an amazing leap forward, and by the end of 1872 the railway mileage had doubled.[3] Everyone looked upon this growth with rejoicing. It was estimated that the existing lines created more wealth each year than was absorbed by the cost of extensions and H. V. Poor concluded in 1868 that the gross earn-

---

[1] Sir S. M. Peto, *The Resources and Prospects of America* (London, 1866), 227, 278, 294.
[2] *Nation*, March 11, 1869.
[3] *Com. and Fin. Chron.*, Jan. 11, 1873.

ings of the railways amounted in a little over four years
to as much as their cost.[1]

The proudest achievement of the railway builders,
the completion of a transcontinental line, had everywhere
been regarded as an urgent task even before the fighting
ended. The Far West pointed to its farming possibilities, its mineral wealth, and to a world's commerce with
the Orient waiting only for the steel highway. Samuel
Bowles in his trip to the Pacific in 1865 found that the
one question of a yearning population was, "When will
the railroad be built?" [2] Eastern wealth wanted the opportunities for investment, Eastern labor wanted those
for employment. National leaders were apprehensive
lest a new generation should arise on the Pacific Coast
without any warm attachment to the Union; while some
social observers believed that the West was suffering from
the excessively rapid growth of communities far removed from the conventional and religious restraints
found in the rest of America and that the influence of
these communities upon American manners, letters and
politics was vulgarizing.[3] Every year the pressure of
goods and passengers upon the slender means of communication with the Far West became more excessive.

What were these means? The West in 1865 was
served beyond the Mississippi Valley railheads by a fast
growing network of freighter and stage lines, and already it boasted of one highly developed system, that of
Benjamin Holladay.[4] This system, which covered a dis-

[1] H. V. Poor, *Influence of the Railroads of the United States in the
Creation of its Commerce and Wealth* (New York, 1869).
[2] Samuel Bowles, *Across the Continent* (Springfield, Mass., 1865),
255 ff.
[3] *Nation*, Jan. 11, 1866.
[4] F. A. Root and W. E. Connelly, *The Overland Stage to California*
(Topeka, 1901); G. D. Bradley, *The Story of the Pony Express*
(Chicago, 1913); S. L. Clemens (Mark Twain, *pseud.*), *Roughing
It* (Hartford, 1872).

tance of three thousand three hundred miles in all, was a product of government patronage under a federal contract for the carriage of the transcontinental mails and included branch lines to such new mining towns as Virginia City in Montana and Boise City, Idaho. Though Holladay's rates were high (for the costs and risks were great), yet just after the war his stages were crowded with passengers who paid a fare of one hundred and seventy-five dollars from the Missouri River to Denver, three hundred and fifty dollars to Salt Lake City and from four hundred to five hundred dollars to California.[1] In answer to the constantly increasing demands there occurred in 1866 a general reorganization and consolidation of the Western stage lines. The Wells Fargo Company, with its huge capital, took over Holladay's stages, paying him two million five hundred thousand dollars, and also acquired the Pioneer Stage Company and all other stage and express properties between the Missouri River and the Pacific. It bought new coaches, improved their speed and opened fresh lines. Like Holladay himself, the company, with its chain of fortified storehouses, was not wholly popular and was frequently denounced as monopolistic.[2]

Though the stagecoach was a rude, uncomfortable and, at times, uncertain mode of travel, it served its purpose remarkably well and sometimes the speed attained was surprising. Schuyler Colfax, Samuel Bowles and Albert D. Richardson in 1875 covered the distance from Atchison to Denver, an arc-shaped route of six hundred and fifty-three miles, in four and a half days.[3] Bowles

[1] Holladay's investment was two million dollars. *Senate Miscel. Doc.*, 47 Cong., 2 sess., no. 19.

[2] F. L. Paxson, *The Last American Frontier* (N. Y., 1910), chap. xi.

[3] See letters of A. D. Richardson in *N. Y. Tribune*, June, July and Aug., 1865. For impressions by travelers see W. H. Dixon, *New America* (5th edn., rev., London, 1867), I, chap. iv; J. F. Rushing, *Across America* (N. Y., 1877), 150 ff.

tells us that he found the food at the early stopping
places better than that at the ordinary hotels and restaurants along the railway west of Chicago. On the stretch
between Denver and Salt Lake City, where hostile Indians had been troublesome, they were not so well fed,
the canned fruits and vegetables disappearing along with
the tablecloths, and antelope meat becoming the staple
dish. At every station fresh horses took the place of
the jaded teams with a delay of only from two to four
minutes, and every fifty miles a new driver climbed into
the box.[1]

The Union Pacific Railroad, begun during 1864, was
easily the greatest engineering feat that America had undertaken, and next to the Suez Canal and the Mont
Cenis tunnel, completed almost at the same time, it might
fairly have been rated the world's greatest engineering
achievement. Mountain gorge, umbrageous wilderness
and arid plain, amounting in all to one thousand eight
hundred miles from Omaha to Sacramento, had to be
traversed; and hostile Indians had to be fought back.
To house, feed and direct the thousands of laborers was
a formidable problem, for the railway passed through
only two small settled areas, Carson City and the Salt
Lake district, and near a third, Denver. Foundries and
machine shops had to be erected as the work progressed.
The Central Pacific—the western portion—gained at the
start, but when they met at Promontory Point in 1869,
the Union Pacific—the eastern line—had laid 1,086
miles against 689 by its rival.

Despite the difference in the amount of mileage laid,
the business enterprise displayed by the Central Pacific
was far superior to that of its rival.[2] The Californians

[1] Bowles, *Across the Continent*, letters 3-5, 14-17.
[2] H. H. Bancroft, *The Pacific States of North America* (San Fran.,
1882-1890), XIX, 543 ff.

who undertook this line were merchants past middle age who had acquired a generous competence without ever interesting themselves in railways. Leland Stanford, the foremost figure, had, after a brief career as a lawyer in Wisconsin, become a wholesale grocer in San Francisco, where he thrust himself forward in politics and in 1861 was elected governor. He was a man of great tenacity and strength of purpose, of imposing physique and masterful mien. Collis P. Huntington, a Connecticut Yankee who had established a large hardware business in California, was one of the keenest merchants in the West, cool, energetic and quick-sighted. Charles Crocker, a self-made man who had built up a large dry-goods trade, had shown himself an indefatigable pusher and an adroit manager of gangs of workmen. These three, all living in Sacramento in the early sixties, were converted to enthusiastic belief in the transcontinental railway by a promoter named T. D. Judah, the engineer of the Sacramento Valley and other rail lines. Their aim at first was simply to reach the rich Nevada mines and gain control of the Nevada trade; and in June of 1861 they had organized the Central Pacific Railroad Company, with Stanford as president, Huntington vice-president and Judah the chief engineer. When Congress authorized the transcontinental road, they hastened to accept the terms of the government for the western extremity. They did their own work, dismissing all sub-contractors and organizing the firm of Crocker and Company to secure all the profits from construction.[1]

A huge task it was. There was little white labor, and coolies were imported from China until by 1865 some five thousand were at work and in 1866 more than

[1] The standard general works on the Central and Union Pacific lines are: J. P. Davis, *The Union Pacific Railway* (Chicago, 1894), and Nelson Trottman, *History of the Union Pacific* (N. Y., 1923).

ten thousand. Iron, machinery, rolling stock and other supplies came by sea, a hazardous journey of months around Cape Horn or across Panama. The road had to traverse the Sierras at a height of more than seven thousand feet and in a space of sixty miles it passed through fifteen tunnels. Trestles, culverts, snowsheds, tanks and drainage systems must be built at enormous expense. Skeptics were loud in ridicule, yet the construction was rapidly and efficiently carried forward. In the first three years (1863-1865) about twenty miles were built annually; about thirty in 1866 and in 1867, when the state line was reached, forty-six miles. The company had long since resolved not to stop at the Nevada mines, but to push into Utah and meet the Union Pacific as far east as possible, perhaps at Salt Lake. Despite the hurry, the road was built for permanence.[1] Nor did it suffer from any scandal like the Credit Mobilier affair.

On the east, the Union Pacific met fewer difficulties. It had plenty of labor, the Irish workingmen available in 1864 being supplemented the next year by large bodies of discharged soldiers. With General G. M. Dodge as its chief engineer, the laborers had a semi-military organization as they crossed the Indian-troubled prairies, and more than once dropped their picks to deploy as skirmishers.[2] At the height of the undertaking, with more than twelve thousand men busy, the actual construction was a scene to quicken the pulse: the light cars bringing up the rails, the builders hurrying them into place, the gaugers, spikers and bolters following close behind and swinging to the grand anvil chorus of the sledge hammers. A city that Samuel

[1] Charles Nordhoff, *California for Health, Pleasure and Residence* (new ed., rev., N. Y., 1882), 32 ff.
[2] Slason Thompson, *A Short History of American Railways, Covering Ten Decades* (N. Y., 1925), 174 ff.

Bowles appropriately called "Hell on wheels" staggered forward with the railway across the plains—a terminal that every few weeks was packed upon a long string of freight cars, with houses, furniture, clothes, tents, gambling machines, bar equipment and rubbish, and transported to a new site.[1]

Almost before the nation knew it, the two iron bands met fifty-three miles west of Ogden, Utah. Here on May 10, 1869, while the entire country seemed to stand in expectation, the last spike was driven. As the smoke of the two engines facing each other mingled and the final three strokes went home, the telegraph in every city of the Union clicked off: "One, two, three—done!" East and West were joined and the frontier had begun to disappear from American history.[2] This iron girdle was, by modern standards, a precarious link. East of Ogden it was a hastily graded, ill-ballasted, poorly equipped railway of a single track, with few decent stations, shops or roundhouses; it had been built by the dizzy methods of the Credit Mobilier, and had cost three times as much as it should.[3] Yet it closed an old era and opened a new one.

East of this slight transcontinental thread a new network of lines spread rapidly throughout the Middle West. In Illinois alone the years 1870-1871 saw one thousand eight hundred and thirty-five miles of railway constructed, most of the routes running east and west across the state. The counties here and in other states were allowed to bond themselves heavily and sometimes foolishly in aid of railway enterprises. One railway

---

[1] J. H. Beadle, *The Undeveloped West* (Phila., 1873), 87 ff., pictures the rough town of Benton. See also W. A. Bell, *New Tracks in North America* (London, 1869), I, 17 ff.

[2] *Nation*, VIII, May 13. 1869.

[3] J. B. Crawford, *The Credit Mobilier of America* (Boston, 1880); Rowland Hazard, *The Credit Mobilier of America* (Providence, 1881).

after another, meanwhile, debouched from Illinois across Iowa or Missouri to tap the Great Plains.[1] The Chicago & Northwestern crossed the Mississippi at Clinton, Iowa, and pushed rapidly west till early in 1867 the first train rolled into Council Bluffs. The St. Joseph & Council Bluffs line, spanning northern Missouri, reached the latter town in December, 1867. Work at the same time was proceeding on the Chicago, Rock Island and Pacific, which had thrown the first bridge across the Mississippi at Rock Island as early as 1856, and which reached the Missouri at Council Bluffs in the early summer of 1869. The Chicago, Burlington and Quincy entered Nebraska in 1869, and in 1871 purchased a small railway which gave it a terminus in Omaha.[2] It was clear that Omaha and Kansas City would be the two great transportation centers west of Chicago, yet it was not until March, 1873, when the Union Pacific completed a two-thousand-seven-hundred-and-fifty-foot structure, that the Missouri River was bridged at the former point. Until that day all freight and passengers had to be carried across in ferryboats, against the uncertainties of a strong current and shifting bottom.[3]

The northern country, so recently a solitude, was now being pierced in every direction. In Wisconsin the railway mileage more than doubled in the years 1868-1873 inclusive, bringing the peninsular wilderness within sound of the locomotive whistle. Minnesota sent Edward Rice, whom it pleasantly called its Chesterfield for

[1] E. L. Bogart and C. M. Thompson, *The Industrial State, 1870-1893* (C. W. Alvord, ed., *The Centennial History of Illinois, Illinois Centennial Series, Springfield, Ill.,* 1898-1920, IV), 318 ff.

[2] A. C. Wakeley, *History of Omaha: the Gate City, and Douglas County, Nebraska* (Chicago, 1917), 252 ff.

[3] A. C. Wakeley, *History of Omaha and Douglas County,* 253; Alfred Sorensen, *Story of Omaha from Pioneer Days* (Omaha, 1889), chap. xxxi.

his fine bearing and genial manners, to London to obtain capital for construction, and by 1872 a web of lines was being spun over the southern and eastern sections. There was a two-hundred-and-seventeen-mile railway from St. Paul westward across the entire state to Breckinridge; there were lines southwest from Minneapolis to Faribault and southeast from Minneapolis to Winona; and a new railway of great value wound through forest and over ravine to connect the Mississippi at St. Paul with the Great Lakes at Duluth.[1] In Nebraska a railway was completed to the new capital at Lincoln in the summer of 1870, and two years later the Chicago, Burlington and Quincy formed a junction with the Union Pacific at Kearney. Branch lines were overspreading western Missouri and thrusting out into Kansas.[2]

Of especial importance was the commencement of a series of great new trunk lines roughly parallel to the Union Pacific. Only one of these lines lay to the north of Omaha and Denver—the Northern Pacific. As early as 1864 it had received a charter from Congress, the incorporators including many prominent Northern financiers and politicians; the route authorized lay from the head of Lake Superior to Puget Sound. Money was hard to obtain and until 1870, when Jay Cooke and his associates took up the enterprise, no actual construction was begun. But Cooke set to work with irresistible energy. By June, 1873, the railway had been extended four hundred and fifty miles westward to Bismarck on the Missouri River, and was giving a heavy impetus to Minnesota settlement. Then the Panic blasted the green plant, and its growth abruptly and totally

[1] E. P. Oberholtzer, *Jay Cooke, Financier of the Civil War* (Phila., 1907), II, 96 ff.; J. G. Pyle, *Life of James J. Hill* (Garden City, 1917), I, 103 ff.
[2] Secretary of the Interior, *Report for 1875*, 113.

stopped.[1] Similarly unfortunate was the history of the Southwestern Pacific, or Southern Pacific, which was extended from a point near St. Louis southwest to Vinita in Indian Territory when the Panic of 1873 caused it to default and ended construction. The ambitious Texas & Pacific hardly became more than a mere paper railroad, though under John C. Frémont it sufficed as a foundation for much gilded and rather reprehensible speculation.

Happily, some other trunk lines did far better. One was the Missouri Pacific, pushing from St. Louis to Kansas City. Another was the Kansas Pacific, which cut westward from Kansas City through the new towns of Wichita and Topeka to Denver, which it reached in the summer of 1870. Most interesting of all the great southwestern lines was the Atchison, Topeka and Santa Fé system, which flourished like a green bay tree between 1868 and the Panic. Following the old Santa Fé trail, this railway, under the guidance of an indefatigable free-soil pioneer and promoter named Cyrus L. Holliday, reached Emporia in the summer of 1871, and by the close of the following year a furious spurt had carried it across the Colorado boundary. The shock of the Panic arrested it at Pueblo, at the foot of the Rockies, but the road opened various Kansas branches, and the Centennial year found it one of the important trunk arteries of the nation. Other railways whose names have long since become familiar, such as the Missouri, Kansas and Texas, and the Denver and Rio Grande, were being prosecuted in these years with greater or less success.[2]

[1] Oberholtzer, *Jay Cooke*, II, chaps. xv-xvi.
[2] Stuart Daggett, *Railroad Reorganization* (*Harvard Economic Studies*, IV), chaps. vi, ix; M. S. Snow, ed., *History of the Development of Missouri, and particularly of Saint Louis* (St. Louis, 1908), II, 332 ff. For Texas railway building, see Bancroft, *Pacific States*, XI, 570 ff.

Was all this feverish railway expansion really healthy, well-planned or profitable? The element of speculative mania was evident to everyone. Thousands of miles of railway were being constructed in advance of real need and by the most questionable financial methods.[1] With six or eight lines planned to cross the continent from east to west and as many more to connect the Great Lakes with the Gulf, the investing public was being fed by roseate dreams of an utterly unrealizable character. Altogether too much was being made of the supposed ability of any railway to create traffic in a virgin district. The competition among the lines tapping the West was growing keener and keener and was certain ultimately to force down their receipts. The stock of many companies had been recklessly watered; and the frequency with which dividends were declared in stock and scrip, not in cash, suggested that earnings were small. Year by year the method of financing new railway lines seemed to grow worse.[2] At first the companies constructing them had sold for cash sufficient stock to pay for the work; but later the promoters had found a way of lining their pockets well by appropriating most or all of the stock to themselves and juggling it to high levels, while they paid for the road by reckless bond issues.

Even where financial operations were well-intentioned, the recklessness was often astounding. Jay Cooke's Northern Pacific railway was a comparatively well-managed enterprise, yet some of his methods of

[1] For a thorough discussion of financial aspects of the "railmania," see *Com. and Fin. Chron.*, March 11, 1869. The astonishing activity in building and rebuilding Southern railways is set forth in the *Com. and Fin. Chron.*, Aug. 10, 1867; Dec. 19, 1868; Jan. 18, 1869. By the close of 1868 there were nearly five thousand miles under construction in this section.

[2] See the *Nation*, VI, May 21, 1868, for a vivid characterization of dishonest methods of railroad financing.

pushing it would now be deemed fantastic, if not insane. The first step of his firm was to organize a gigantic lobby to obtain the patronage of the government. Governors of Pennsylvania and Minnesota, congressmen, financiers and politicians were enlisted; money was used freely, and shares in the project were discreetly bestowed upon leaders who wanted *douceurs*; while Cooke himself argued with several refractory representatives. An enormous selling campaign was organized. Schuyler Colfax was offered a lucrative position if he would resign the vice-presidency; agents were granted territorial districts; squads of lecturers were organized and advertising was undertaken on the costliest scale. The road was bitterly attacked as a fraud and a thievish raid upon the public lands and Cooke spared no expense in replying to these assaults. As for the bonds, they bore an interest rate of seven and three tenths per cent, and the selling agents were to receive a commission of six per cent in cash and ten per cent in stock. In this manner was a golden millstone hung about the neck of the infant Northern Pacific.[1]

So long as the country enjoyed its flush of after-war prosperity, the roads which were thus being built paid. For a time the profits of some seemed magnificent. Thus in 1867, fourteen of the leading lines of the nation showed aggregate earnings of more than sixty-five million dollars, and in the next year of almost seventy million dollars. The gross revenues of the railways of the whole country in 1867 were about twenty-seven per cent of their cost.[2] The generosity of the federal and state governments in land grants and cash subsidies assured at least a temporary affluence to a majority of the

[1] Oberholtzer, *Jay Cooke*, II, 225 ff.
[2] "Our existing railroads are computed to create more wealth every year than is absorbed for the construction of new railroads." *Com. and Fin. Chron.*, Jan. 11, 1873.

new railways. Even in the devastated South the roads
returned to a dividend-paying basis with astonishing
celerity. During 1867, for example, it was found that
one thousand three hundred and thirty-three miles of
railway in Georgia earned five thousand two hundred
and eighty-seven dollars gross for every mile, which was
more than one tenth of the cost of the lines and which
permitted dividends of from two and a half to ten per
cent.[1]

Yet all the while there were ominous indications of
the probable inability of many great railways to weather
such a storm as burst in 1873. The chief of these was
perhaps the difficulties into which the Union Pacific fell
within a few years after its completion.[2] It and the
Central Pacific charged excessively high rates on transcontinental freight, reaching at first ten or eleven cents
in gold for every ton-mile: they demanded all that the
traffic would bear. The same tea that was shipped
from China to New York for two cents a pound by
sea was carried from San Francisco to New York by
rail for thirteen cents. To carry a ton of flour from
San Francisco to Chicago cost one hundred and twenty-
six dollars, while to transport it from Chicago to New
York, a distance one third as great, the charge was only
ten dollars. Passenger rates, which at the outset were
almost equally exorbitant, were later reduced to a more
tolerable level.[3] While the Central Pacific, carefully
built and financed, flourished, the Union Pacific, waste-
fully built and recklessly financed, languished. It was
burdened with interest payments on seventy four million
dollars in bonds and, if any thing were left, dividend

[1] *Com. and Fin. Chron.*, Oct. 3, 1868.
[2] Anna Youngman, *The Economic Causes of Great Fortunes* (N. Y.,
1909), chap. iii.
[3] Oberholtzer, *United States since the Civil War*, II, 482-483.

payments on thirty-six million dollars in stock.   Moreover, the Credit Mobilier scandal struck a heavy blow at
its prestige.[1]   By 1872, when it was in the hands of a
coterie headed by Commodore Vanderbilt's son-in-law,
Horace F. Clark, it was in sore straits.

The land-grant railways naturally made every effort
to people their wide holdings and the colonizing activities of the Santa Fé furnish an interesting example of
the work of nearly all Western roads in scattering the
seeds of future millions.[2]   It held alternate sections in a
ten-mile strip on each side of the main Kansas line.   In
1870 the railway established a land department and
invited the editors of between three hundred and four
hundred newspapers to come to Kansas, transportation
free.   Homeseekers were carried at half rates, and if any
man bought land, his whole fare was refunded.   Sometimes European agents of the railway recruited homeseekers in large groups, which were discharged from the
trains at a suitable station, so that there was soon a community of Swedes at one spot, Englishmen at another,
and Irishmen or even Russians at a third.[3]

Not less important than the new railway construction
was the establishment of long-distance trunk lines by the
amalgamation of short railroads, the building of extensions or the conclusion of leasing arrangements.   Hitherto travel from New York to Chicago had meant the
use of eight or a dozen independent lines with repeated
changes.   In the East the New York Central led the
way.   In 1868 Commodore Vanderbilt combined the
New York Central and the Hudson River railroads, furnishing a single road from New York to Buffalo; it was
a logical step to arrange with the Lake Shore and Michi-

[1] See pages 188-190.
[2] Cy Warman, *Story of the Railroad* (N. Y., 1898), 113 ff.
[3] W. E. Miller, *The Peopling of Kansas* (Columbus, 1906).

gan Southern for through service to Chicago and in
1873 he made this line an integral part of the Central
system.[1] Not merely that, but as early as May, 1870,
he came to terms with the Rock Island and the Chicago
& Northwestern, so that he could advertise an uninter-
rupted carriage of New York passengers as far west as
Omaha. The Vanderbilt group of railways thus held
control of four thousand five hundred miles of track and
a capital of not less than a quarter billion dollars. The
Pennsylvania, one of the most powerful lines in the
country, having for years monopolized the traffic between Philadelphia and Pittsburgh, was hardly behind
in the race; its shrewd head, J. Edgar Thomson, used
the Pennsylvania legislature as he needed it. Turning
westward he reached Chicago by an agreement with the
Columbus, Chicago and Indiana Central; at the same
time he prevented the Erie from making a connection
with the Western metropolis.[2] Jay Gould, however,
did shortly obtain a direct and unbroken communication
between New York on the east, and Cleveland, Cincinnati and St. Louis on the west. In April, 1869, the
Erie was able to advertise: "1,400 miles under one management; 860 miles without change of cars; the broad-
gauge, double-track route between New York, Boston,
and New England cities and the West." This made
three main routes between the coast and the Middle
West, and when the Baltimore & Ohio reached Chicago
in 1874, there were four. Competition for passengers
and freight was keen.

In the Mississippi Valley a similar consolidation took
place under pressure of the demand for through trunk
lines joining Chicago with the transcontinental roads

[1] Daggett, *Railroad Reorganization*, 2 ff.
[2] E. H. Mott, *Between the Ocean and the Lakes; the Story of Erie*
(N. Y., 1899), 173, 177.

built or planned to the Pacific. The Chicago & North-western, under the presidency of William B. Ogden, the greatest figure in Western railway affairs, was one of these lines; the Rock Island and the Chicago, Burlington & Quincy were others.[1] The Illinois Central lost no time after the conflict in completing a through route, nine hundred and fifty miles almost as the crow flies, from Chicago to the Gulf. At the South also the tendency toward the formation of long trunk highways was irresistible. The organization of the Chesapeake and Ohio in 1868, a direct line from Norfolk to Cincinnati, furnished the shortest route from the Ohio Valley to tidewater. Both Norfolk and Charleston were joined at the same time with the Tennessee railways, so that they enjoyed easy communication with Memphis. The South, it should be said, was building railways rapidly during these years—more than twelve hundred miles of track in 1870, more than one thousand in 1871, and in 1873, nearly thirteen hundred miles.[2]

One result of the tremendous railway expansion of the time was a sharp check upon the commerce of the Great Lakes and the inexorable conquest of much lake and canal business in grain carrying. Lake transportation had flourished during the war, coming out of the conflict with a great fleet of more than six hundred thousand tons; yet its essential weaknesses were evident.[3] During the winter months the vessels were icebound and idle, their capital charges meanwhile steadily mounting.

[1] Slason Thompson, *Cost, Capitalization and Estimated Value of American Railways* (3d edn., Chicago, 1908), 187; J. W. Cary, *The Organization and History of the Chicago, Milwaukee, and St. Paul Railway Company* (Milwaukee, 1892) ; W. H. Stennett, *Yesterday and Today; History of the Northwestern Railway System* (Chicago, 1910).

[2] *Com. and Fin. Chron.*, Feb. 15, 1873; J. L. Ringwalt, *Development of Transportation Systems in the United States* (Phila., 1888).

[3] C. R. Fish, "Some Phases of the Economic History of Wisconsin," Wis. Hist. Soc., *Proceeds.*, LV, 204-216.

Moreover, ships from Milwaukee and Chicago had to round the Michigan peninsula, an indirect and wasteful route, and transfer charges added to the cost. The railways struck hard at these weaknesses through their ability to make long continuous hauls in all seasons. Almost as important was the development just after the war of "through freight" or "fast freight" companies, owning large numbers of freight cars, which, by contract with the railways, they sent express from shipper to consignee in every part of the nation.[1]

Slowly but surely lake vessels were being driven out of existence, and many of the shipping centers of the Great Lakes felt their prosperity threatened. Chicago, already one of the greatest railway centers of the world, was quite safe; but Buffalo, at one extremity of the lakes and Milwaukee at the other, with Detroit and other ports between, were in grave danger. In 1869, through a convention of the boards of trade of all the principal lake ports, they took steps to meet the situation. Their plan was to enable the captains of all the lake freighters to offer lower rates, by reducing the transfer and terminal charges and by getting the marine insurance companies to cut their premiums. To a noteworthy extent they realized this program. Buffalo, Oswego and Toledo sliced their transfer charges by one half or three fourths, and the railway companies running between Lake Michigan and the Mississippi River struck one half off their charges for wheat and flour; while, as the most important stroke of all, the New York legislature in 1870 reduced the tolls for wheat on the Erie Canal from six to three cents a bushel.[2]

The stubborn tenacity of the owners of the schooners, the new screw steamers and the steam barges not only

[1] Merk, *Economic History of Wisconsin*, 384.
[2] Merk, *Economic History*, chap. xv.

conserved the prosperity of the Lake cities, but was of indispensable value to the Middle West as a competitive check upon the railways. Whenever they could avoid this competition, the trunk lines shamelessly gouged the farmers and other shippers. Year after year they shoved up their freight rates, as soon as November came and ice closed the ports, by from one third to two thirds; and year after year they reverted to an honest competitive level when April released the vessels.[1] The war between the two transportation agencies steadily continued, and though the rail rates never reached so low a point, in general, as the water rates, the quickness and safety of land transit gave it an advantage. Finally, by 1875, a fair balance had been reached. By that year the carriage of ores had attained a volume which gave the lake vessels a great new field of employment.

Much more complete was the railway conquest of the Mississippi.[2] Before the war ten million bushels of Western wheat had been annually shipped from New Orleans, while millions of dollars of Western corn, pork and beef went down the river to be sold in Southern markets. In those years St. Louis often showed the visitor a solid mile of steamboats lying in two or three tiers. The scene at New Orleans was one never to be forgotten. Now these days were as utterly gone as those of the Roman triremes. Mark Twain, crossing under the shadow of the mighty Eads bridge at St. Louis early in the seventies, saw only a half-dozen inert steamboats, a mile of empty wharves and a drunken Negro. From

[1] These were also the years in which sailing ships were being steadily crowded out by steam vessels. J. C. Mills, *Our Inland Seas* (Chicago, 1910), 158.

[2] For river steamboating see G. B. Merrick, *Old Times on the Upper Mississippi* (Cleveland, 1908) ; same author, "Joseph Reynolds and the Diamond Jo Line of Steamers, 1862-1911," Miss. Valley Hist. Assoc., *Proceeds.*, VIII, 217-261; E. W. Gould, *Fifty Years on the Mississippi* (St. Louis, 1889).

the long reach of plank wharves at New Orleans the steamboats had almost vanished.[1] In the sixties the tonnage plying the Mississippi fell from 468,210 to 398,-296, and it became far more largely than before a commerce of the upper river, not of the entire channel from Dubuque to New Orleans. The river boats acted merely as local carriers, distributing their cargoes to the railway terminals scattered along the banks. The river, in other words, became a mere feeder to dozens of railways. With some exaggeration Mark Twain summarized the contrast between the old days and the new:

Boat used to land . . . captain on hurricane roof . . . mighty stiff and straight . . . iron ramrod for a spine . . . kid gloves, plug tile, hair parted behind . . . man on shore takes off hat and says: "Got twenty-eight tons of wheat, capt'n . . . be great favor if you can take them." Captain says: "I'll take two of them . . ." and don't even condescend to look at him. But nowadays the captain takes off his old slouch, and smiles all the way round to the back of his ears, and gets off a bow which he hasn't got any ramrod to interfere with, and says: "Glad to see you, Smith, glad to see you—you're looking well—haven't seen you looking so well for years—what you got for us?" "Nuth'n," says Smith; and keeps his hat on, and just turns back and goes to talking with somebody else.[2]

For years the old-time interests nourished by Mississippi commerce refused to accept the doom which had fallen upon them. They declared that all would be well if the rapids near Keokuk were overcome and the silt bars at the mouth of the river cleared away; they persuaded Congress to dredge and light the channel as

[1] S. L. Clemens (Mark Twain, pseud.), *Life on the Mississippi* (Hartford, 1874), chap. xxii.
[2] Mark Twain, *Life on the Mississippi* (N. Y., 1911), 433.

never before, and it spent millions on the Eads jetties. St. Louis even erected elevators on the river and established a barge line to New Orleans. Several powerful corporations were formed to place large fleets upon the river and to handle them with all the economy of large-scale management. Among these were the famous "Diamond Jo" line, organized by Joseph Reynolds near the close of the sixties, and the Northwestern Union Packet Company, which came into existence in 1866 through the exertions of Commodore William F. Davidson. But the position of all these lines was essentially weak and even the barging business was more and more heavily invaded by the railroads. The Mississippi by 1873 had ceased to be a great highway.

It would be expected that the position of labor, in this period of thriving industry, would be one of great prosperity; and viewed superficially, this seemed the fact. Work was abundant and wages were firm or rising. Men talked with wonder of the high pay which skilled employees were receiving. Rumor exaggerated the returns obtained by labor, while employers, as ever in flush periods, had much to say of the money the working class spent on liquor, fine clothes, jewelry and parlor organs.[1] But when investigators looked beneath this bright surface they found a very different state of affairs. It can be summarized in Commissioner Wells's succinct statement at the close of 1866 that while the average wage had risen about sixty per cent since 1860, the increase in the cost of commodities was about ninety per cent, while in computing the cost of living a still greater rise in house rents had to be considered. Wells found that only a single working group, the copper miners, enjoyed the advantage of doubled wages in fac-

[1] N. Y. Eve. Post, July 13, 1865; Am. Ann. Cyclop., IX (1869), 260 ff.

ing a doubled cost of living. Innumerable workmen—
the ready-made clothing workers, the farm laborers of
the North and West, and so on—obtained only half
again as much as before the war.[1] Nor was this a
merely transient pinch. Two years later, when a momentary depression was making business men uneasy,
it was still more evident that the workingmen had actually suffered a loss from the economic changes produced
by the war. For all their apparently enhanced reward,
skilled employees could be found living in shabbier and
less sanitary homes than formerly—sometimes eating
plainer fare. Commissioner Wells again asserted that
the great majority of wage-earners were worse off than
in 1860.[2]

Ordinary workmen of intelligence in the larger cities
were glad to get $2 a day. The whistles everywhere
sounded at seven a.m., at noon an hour was allowed
and at six in the evening the ten-hour day was finished.
In some trades the hours were a little shorter, but in
others a good deal more. Thus in New York the
drivers of horse cars and stages labored, in blazing heat
or biting cold, twelve or even sixteen hours a day for
two dollars, while hotel or livery drivers toiled an equal
period for from ten dollars and fifty cents to twelve
dollars a week. The lot of women employees was often
bitterly hard. When peace came, New York had not
less than fifteen thousand working women whose weekly
pittance did not rise above three dollars and fifty cents
or four dollars. They were employed in shops, factories and large stores and they had reason to count
themselves happier than the thousands of wretched
women, sisters to Tom Hood's slaving seamstress, who

[1] Special Commissioner of Revenue, *Report for December, 1866,*
14 ff.; *N. Y. Eve. Post* and *N. Y. Herald,* Jan. 4, 1867, for comment.
[2] Special Commissioner of Revenue, *Report for December, 1868;*
Nation, IX, July 15, 1869.

carried materials home and made shirts and overalls for
seventy-five cents a dozen. Girls in the drygoods
stores of the great Eastern cities, where civilization was
proudest of its achievements, toiled from seven thirty in
the morning till the closing hour of nine or ten, without
seats, without rest rooms or facilities for a quiet lunch,
without more consideration than dumb animals received;
and for this health-ruining drudgery many were paid
five dollars a week.[1]

It was therefore no impulse of perversity, as some
employers suggested, which led at once to a concerted
movement for shorter hours and better pay. Ira Stew-
ard, a self-educated Boston machinist, indignant at the
overwork he saw all about him and imbued with the
ideas of John Stuart Mill, became the foremost apostle
of a widespread agitation for an eight-hour day.[2] Eight
Hour Leagues were formed in various states, a national
congress met at Baltimore in 1866, and labor pressure
carried through six legislatures laws which established
eight hours as the legal day, unless other hours were
agreed upon. These statutes proved futile, but the
movement, by calling forcible attention to some of the
grave abuses which labor endured, had its decided value.
Another expression of the growing labor discontent lay
in the vigorous movement for distributive coöperation
on the Rochdale plan, an outgrowth of Socialistic and
Fourieristic philosophy. Coöperative stores were set up
to sell groceries, meat, drygoods and footwear to workmen, while many workers, in the years 1866-1869, tried
to open small factories and produce wares coöperatively.

---

[1] N. Y. Eve. Post, July 13, 1865.
[2] J. R. Commons and Associates, History of Labour in the United
States (N. Y., 1921), II, 87 ff.; 124 ff., 138-139; F. T. Carlton,
The History and Problems of Organized Labor (N. Y., 1921), 63;
J. R. Commons and others, Documentary History of American Industrial
Society (Cleveland, 1910-1911), IX, 26.

Bakers went into the breadmaking business; coach makers combined to make and sell vehicles; coal miners, shipwrights, glass blowers, hat makers, tailors, printers and many others embarked in business for themselves. Most important of all were the coöperative stove foundries established in Rochester, Troy, Pittsburgh, Louisville, Cleveland, Chicago and other cities in 1866-1867 under the leadership of William H. Sylvis, president of the Molders' International Union.[1] Some of these undertakings were financially successful, but the basic difficulty was that they tended to turn into old-style capitalistic enterprises, the owners hiring new workmen on a wage basis.

The best weapon of underpaid, overworked labor was after all, not legislative action nor coöperation but a trade union powerful enough to call an effective strike. Though by 1870 there were more than thirty national unions with a total membership of perhaps three hundred thousand, and though the year 1866 witnessed the formation of the National Labor Union as a result of Sylvis's efforts, there was still little militant labor action. Strikes were few in number, frowned upon by public opinion, and for the most part abortive. Many organizations fell into quick decay, the National Labor Union going to pieces in the years 1870-1872.[2] In many respects the most impressive of the bodies formed in the first decade after the war was the Knights of St. Crispin, the shoemakers' organization. It was a natural response to the introduction of the factory system into the shoe industry and its chief initial object was to pro-

[1] J. C. Sylvis, *The Life, Speeches, Labors and Essays of William H. Sylvis* (Phila., 1872); Commons and Associates, *Labour in the United States*, II, 111.

[2] Mary Beard, *A Short History of the American Labor Movement* (N. Y., 1920), 72 ff.; Commons and Associates, *Labour in the United States*, II, chap. iv.

tect the skilled journeyman against the competition of green hands and apprentices. Established in Milwaukee early in 1867, it spread like a prairie fire before a gale, until by the spring of 1872 there were no fewer than three hundred and twenty-seven lodges. The Crispins for a time conducted strikes with impressive success, waging a series of victorious battles in Lynn, Worcester, Philadelphia and San Francisco; but after an unsuccessful strike at Lynn in 1872, the order was gradually beaten back by the employers.[1] Throughout these years the organization of unions and the conduct of strikes were grievously hampered by the inrush of immigrant workers, many of them skilled and all ready to accept employment under conditions which American labor found unsatisfactory.

This sullen discontent on the part of a great mass of workers, these attempts to seize upon one remedy after another—of one, the organization of the Knights of Labor in 1869, we shall hear a great deal more [2]—represented part of the dark reverse of the bright shield of industrial prosperity and expansion. Another gloomy aspect of the business rush and whirl lay in the frequent dishonesty, the sharp manipulation and the ever-growing tendency toward speculative excesses, which accompanied it. Still another lay in the private extravagance, the relaxation of moral standards and the vulgarization of taste which it encouraged from Boston to Omaha. The war, which had done so much to create the era of inflation and abounding prosperity, had also introduced many elements of confusion and recklessness into American life and thrown off old restraints. But for the time the great body of Americans, intent upon dipping their

[1] D. D. Lescohier, *The Knights of St. Crispin, 1867-1874* (Univ. of Wis., *Econ. and Pol. Sci. Series*, VII, 1910, no. 1).
[2] See pages 393-394.

cups into the golden stream, overlooked all this. They thought only of the humming mills, the smoking factories, the magic birth of new cities and towns all over the West, the throng of immigrants from Europe, the atmosphere of optimism and cheer. The nation had never seemed so busy, its future never so bright. There was faith everywhere; but after the stunning disasters of 1873, so suddenly to follow, men wondered how they could have been so credulous.

CHAPTER III

URBAN LIVING AND ROUTES OF TRAVEL

A NATURAL consequence of the great industrial prosperity of the time, with its multiplication of mills and
railways and its growing stream of European immigrants, was the rise of the city to a new importance in
American life. East of the Mississippi an ever larger
proportion of the population lived in towns. New
York in 1870 had almost a million people, Philadelphia
nearly three quarters of a million, Chicago three hundred thousand and Cincinnati two hundred and sixteen
thousand.[1] All of these centers were expanding at a
rate which pressed painfully upon their housing accommodations. Meanwhile, the greater ease and swiftness
of communication made urban modes and manners much
more widely influential, while the abundance of money
bred in every Northern community a desire for urban
luxuries and conveniences such as the American people
had never before known. The cities were full of wealthy
newcomers of rural antecedents, like W. D. Howells's
sterling but crude Silas Lapham, who was so proud of
his magnificent new residence on the water side of Bea-
con Street, and who boasted to his friend Corey: "Yes,
sir, give an architect money enough, and he'll give you
a nice house every time." [2] More and more the texture of
American civilization was becoming urban in character,
though the great transformation was not to occur until
later in the century.

[1] *United States Statistical Abstract, 1910* (Wash., 1911), table 23.
[2] W. D. Howells, *The Rise of Silas Lapham* (Boston, 1884), 75.

75

The large-scale industrialization of the North would alone have assured a multitude of the changes characteristic of city, as distinguished from country, modes of life. Clothing was altering to conform with the exigencies of a machine civilization. The ordinary man still had his best suit tailor-made of sooty broadcloth, but for everyday wear his suit was ready-made and his shoes and congress gaiters came from the factory. As the seventies wore on, Americans grew used to meats sent from Chicago, canned salmon from Oregon and canned tomatoes from Maryland; they learned, especially after the Centennial Exhibition gave popularity to Vienna rolls and other hard-crusted breads, to patronize the commercial bakeries. Invention played its part in the introduction of novelties. Washing machines, still regarded by many people as a failure when the war closed, were rapidly improved—fifty patents were granted in the latter half of 1868—until they sold in enormous numbers. Sewing machines were being distributed by a half-dozen manufactories of national repute, like Singer, Wheeler and Wilson, Wilcox and Gibbs, and Grover and Baker, in addition to many smaller firms; and several sewing-machine millionaires were as well-known as the petroleum capitalists. At the end of 1866 sewing machines were being made at the rate of one thousand a day, and were selling for an average of sixty dollars apiece. Though half were exported, American shops and homes were absorbing one hundred and eighty thousand annually, and their busy whir was heard in every prosperous household throughout the land.

Kerosene brought in its train a wide array of new lamps, and the ground glass globe was as characteristic of the ordinary American home as the base-burner with red coals shining through its mica windows; the more pretentious dwellings had Argand gas lamps. The two objections to kerosene were the frequency of explosions, which led to legislation to regulate the quality of the oil, and the readiness with which the glass chimneys cracked. As the use of anthracite coal increased with the marked development of the Pennsylvania fields, cooking ranges and heating stoves were rapidly improved. The large office buildings and flats of the seventies had to be heated by steam radiation, and the hot-water furnace in the late seventies was making its way into many of the finer city homes. Refrigeration and artificial ice were becoming well-known in many quarters; New Orleans in 1871 boasted an ice factory which was making seventy-two tons daily from distilled water and which had reduced the price, to the dismay of Northern ice importers, from forty dollars or even sixty dollars a ton to fifteen dollars. Even at that price its large profits were encouraging the formation of similar companies in other Southern cities.

While the urban household was becoming a much more comfortable abode many minor innovations were contributing to the convenience of business life. Thus the earliest safety-deposit vaults came into use just after the war. Henry Lee Higginson, who had gone into business in Boston with his father, conceived the idea of excavating the first vaults of that city under the building in which his firm had its offices. For half a century they were the principal depository for securities in Boston and have been described as the models from which others were forthwith built elsewhere. Meanwhile the use of the passenger elevator, first designed for an exhibition tower adjacent to the Crystal Palace in London in 1853, was becoming common. It was indispensable for such comparatively tall structures as the new Bryant Building and the Lord and Taylor department store in New York, and in all the great cities it permitted contractors to raise their buildings first to eight and then to ten or even more stories.[1]

The best hotels, like the Tremont House in Boston, the Astor House in New York and Willard's in Washington, had long been the most elaborately fitted in the world, and they maintained their high standards, but though they impressed everyone by their size and magnificence, their service was not always equally good. The novelist Trollope found that the clerks were frequently inattentive, that the "extras" cost too much, and that the meals, brought on all together in their flock of bird-bath dishes, were greasy and badly served. In New York some striking improvements were embodied in the great Park Avenue Hotel, which A. T. Stewart began late in life with the aim of erecting a house fireproof, possessing a homely comfort, and yet with magnificent public rooms. It was a quadrangular edifice of seven stories, with a spacious courtyard upon which the interior rooms opened; and the stonework and broad arches bore witness to its noninflammable character. The Hoffman House, which was finished just as the war closed, became famous for its grand banquet hall, sixty feet square, and its art gallery.[2] In many cities the hotels tried to fill a larger civic purpose and devised more ambitious entertainments. The Fifth Avenue Hotel in New York was well known for its political meetings and banquets to public figures; the Grand Pacific Hotel, in Chicago served annually a game banquet to invited guests, turning its dining hall into a miniature forest, crowding its tables with stuffed animals and beautifully arranged birds' nests, and placing every meat and fowl

[1] J. H. Jallings, *Elevators* (Chicago, 1915), 7 ff.
[2] H. C. Brown, *The Last Fifty Years in Old New York* (N. Y., 1926), 100.

of the West, from bear to reedbird, on the generous menu.[1]

All the cities of the country, new and old, were busy carrying through what then seemed astonishing public improvements. It will suffice to instance Chicago, "the great Babylon of the West," as an illustration of the transformation being wrought.[2] By the close of 1870 the Illinois metropolis could boast of more than three hundred thousand people, almost sixty thousand buildings, sixty miles of cedar-block pavement and a network of horsecar lines. Numerous structures were built of limestone or marble, and the city took special pride in the eight-story Palmer House and the six-story Sherman House. Concrete sidewalks appeared, and Wabash and Michigan avenues were broadened into fine drives with their residences threatened by the expanding business district. The streets were lighted by two thousand five hundred gas lamps, making them brighter than those of most Eastern centers. The level of the city was being raised twelve feet above that of the surrounding prairie. Early in the seventies the swamp along the lake front, between Michigan Avenue and the Illinois Central tracks, was filled in and converted into a park, while with far-sighted energy the city was intent upon creating other breathing spaces. Well outside the municipal limits to the south, on the edge of the little town of Hyde Park, the city engineers had already laid out what are now Jackson Park and Washington Park, with the Midway between. Many people thought the enterprise foolish, but others saw how insatiably the town was growing down the lake front.[3] During the year 1871 more than

[1] Moses King, ed., *Handbook of New York City* (Boston, 1892).
[2] See the unsigned article on "Chicago," *Atlantic Monthly*, XIX (1867), 325-345.
[3] *N. Y. Tribune*, June 30, July 8, Sept. 8, 1865.

twelve thousand ships came into the port, which the federal government had improved with piers and breakwaters. Factories were sending out trainloads of farm implements, vehicles and harness; grain from the West poured like a golden torrent into the tall elevators lining the Chicago River; vast yards were filled with lumber. Every second block on the river had its swinging bridge, yet the jam of boats was so incessant that the city had to build two tunnels in rapid succession under the stream. A ceaseless flow of emigrants to the West crowded the hotels in spite of extortionate rates, and many of them, seeing the bustle and opportunities, decided to stay in Chicago.[1] It was a great city and its people had illimitable dreams for the future—though no brighter than the residents of many another booming town.

Some of the outstanding feats of engineering conducive to municipal growth or convenience quite surpassed anything attempted before the war. The most striking was unquestionably the Brooklyn Bridge planned by the engineer John A. Roebling, a native of Prussia who had just finished a fine suspension structure across the Ohio at Cincinnati. The first caisson between New York and Brooklyn was sunk in the winter of 1866-1867, but unfortunately the designer had little time to supervise the work; two years later he received an injury from which he died, and the bridge fell under the direction of his son, Washington A. Roebling, who prosecuted it with stubborn vigor throughout the seventies.[2] Other noteworthy bridges rose in the West, where the new railways were converging upon the rivers. In 1869 the first bridge over the Missouri was finished

[1] E. P. Oberholtzer, *A History of the United States since the Civil War* (N. Y., 1917-1926, in progress), I, 231 ff.

[2] *Scientific American*, August 7, 1869; *Commercial and Financial Chronicle*, May 24, 1879.

at Kansas City, and early in 1872 the long bridge between Omaha and Council Bluffs was opened. But the most important and costly of the Western structures was the great bridge which James B. Eads built across the Mississippi between 1867 and 1874. The superstructure, which was mainly steel, was supported by four granite and limestone piers, resting on the rock bed of the river, to which in one instance the stonework had to be sunk through one hundred and twenty feet of sand.[1] A highway for carriages as well as one for railroads was carried sixty feet above the water, and the edifice towered almost as impressively over the Mississippi as Roebling's high piers and web of cables did over the East River. Mention should be made, also, of the two-mile tunnel which Chicago built under Lake Michigan in 1866 to obtain a supply of pure water, a work compared by Chicagoans with the Croton Aqueduct in New York.[2]

Yet not all the problems presented by urban growth were so successfully solved; and the population which demanded these changes was content to endure an extraordinary amount of inconvenience and inefficiency in some of its municipal arrangements. Without exception the cities still depended upon horsepower for transportation. In some instances this elementary means of transit was highly developed. The New Yorker, for example, had at his disposal in 1866 some fourteen hundred hackney coaches; seven lines of omnibuses, employing perhaps three hundred vehicles on regular routes; sixteen separate lines of horse railway, with eight hundred cars and not far from eight thousand

[1] *Am. Ann. Cyclop.* (N. Y., 1861-1903)), XIII (1873), 520; M. S. Snow, *History of the Development of Missouri* (St. Louis, 1909), II, 343 ff.
[2] *N. Y. Eve. Post,* July 27, 1865; C. R. Fish, *The Rise of the Common Man* (*A History of American Life,* VI), 104.

horses; and a few hansom cabs.[1] Yet the slow-moving
horse vehicles crowded the main thoroughfares of the
largest cities to suffocation, they littered the pavements
with dirt and cruelly overtaxed many dumb beasts. So
limited was their range that the outlying districts remained totally undeveloped while the central streets
were congested. Thus in New York the most desirable
parts of the island, the sections abreast of and above
Central Park, were largely given up to pigs, ducks,
shanty squatters and filth, while lower Broadway was
so jammed that a man in a hurry almost lost his
reason.[2]

Only in New York were the beginnings of a reform
effected. Here, after much talk of sunken railways, sub-
ways and elevated lines running over the housetops, construction of an elevated railway on pillars was actually
begun in 1867. The fiercest of fights was waged
against it. Horse-car interests and property holders
brought suits; its charter was attacked as unconstitutional. Business men declared that the noise would kill
trade, that the unsightly structure overhead would ruin
the city's appearance, and that the moving trains would
frighten horses. But the railway was finally completed
from the foot of the island up Ninth Avenue to Thirtieth Street in 1870, and within a short time was being
operated with such success that its immediate extension
and the building of another on Sixth Avenue were called
for.[3]

The cities were equally patient with the wretched
street paving of the time, though they recognized its
inadequacy and the New York press spoke wistfully of

[1] *Nation*, V, July 25, 1867.
[2] *Scientific American*, April 3, 1870.
[3] *Com. and Fin. Chron.*, May 31, 1879; *U. S. Tenth Census* (1880),
XVIII, 557.

Scene from "The White Fawn,"
New York City.

"Two Sides of the Way

Broadway
Swell.

Left: The fi

Right: Th

Below:

1865—Glim

on *Fifth Avenue, New*

*Section of the carnival pageant, Louisville,
Kentucky.*

*Philadelphia
Quakers.*

sleeping car.

railroad.

the fire.

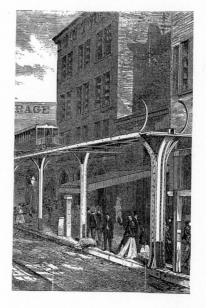

ities—1878.

the day when all thoroughfares might be as smooth as a
specially laid section of concrete on Nassau Street. The
close of the seventies found surprisingly little done.[1]
Philadelphia, with nine hundred miles of paved streets
at this date, had five hundred miles of cobblestones,
rough, noisy and impossible to clean. Most of the remainder was rubble stone and broken stone. New York
paved the greater part of its streets with stone blocks,
which were uneven, held mud and dust in their cracks
and were ruinous to vehicles, while for the rest, macadam
and cobblestones were used. Boston had resort to
cobblestones, trap blocks and broken stones, though in
the late seventies by far the greater part of her ways were
merely graveled. Many cities used wooden blocks, especially in the West, where stone was scarce, lumber was
cheap and the subsoil was favorable. Washington spent
more than five millions in laying chemically treated
blocks in the early seventies, so that by the Centennial
year it was called the best paved city in America.
Everywhere the really best materials were neglected.
Asphalt was extensively used in Paris after 1854, and
in London after 1868, and was there found smooth,
durable and clean; but an opinion prevailed in the
United States that it was too costly and that stone remained the best of all pavements. Even by the close
of the seventies Boston, Philadelphia and New York
did not have ten miles of asphalt among them.[2] But
happily concrete sidewalks were coming steadily into
favor.

A far graver failure of the cities was their neglect to
insist upon fire-resisting buildings. *Harper's Weekly*
pointed out after the war that the dense masses of
wooden houses and offices in New York invited a repeti-

[1] *U. S. Tenth Census* (1880), XVIII, 812.
[2] *Popular Science Monthly*, VII (1875), 80 ff.

tion of the disastrous conflagration of 1835.[1] When Portland, Maine, suffered her terrible fire of July 4, 1866, which began with a match tossed into a boat-builder's shop, a cry of warning was raised.[2] But these voices went unheeded. Until 1871 Boston made no attempt whatever to regulate the construction of buildings, while Chicago was equally negligent. Both paid a memorable penalty.

Chicago's great fire of 1871 burned over an area in which many buildings were fondly believed to be fire-proof, reducing them to ashes and fragments. The conflagration, originating in a small wooden barn in De Koven Street on a Sunday night in early October, was driven by a strong wind through the squalid shanties of that quarter and gained momentum in the large lumber-yards on the Chicago River. Leaping eastward across the stream, the flames swept north into the main business district, closely built up with structures of stone, brick and iron. No Chicagoan would have believed that they would yield to the fire like tinder, but they did.[3] The flames pushed through this section from the southwest, eating a path a mile wide, and then debouched upon the scattered buildings farther north. Banks, theaters, newspaper offices, hotels, grain elevators, the court house and the waterworks all disappeared in the holocaust. The deafening roar of the flames and the overpowering heat made the scene an inferno. When Frederick Law Olmsted visited the ruins three weeks later, he found that a man standing on an omnibus could see people walking three miles distant across what had been the densest, loftiest and most substantial part of the city. This destruction of 17,450 buildings, leaving almost

[1] *Harper's Weekly,* March 17, 1866.
[2] *Nation,* III, July 12, 1866.
[3] *Nation,* XIII, Oct. 19, 1871.

one third of the population homeless, was an unforgettable object lesson in the necessity for fuller safeguards against fire.[1]

The much smaller fire in Boston a little more than a year later also swept the business section, and destroyed hundreds of brick and granite buildings which the people had supposed entirely safe. Here the fierceness of the flames owed much to the mansard roofs, which along the narrow streets burst into an instant blaze, and were inaccessible to the firemen, while, as in Chicago, the fire department lacked discipline and its apparatus proved imperfect.[2] The shock produced throughout the country by these conflagrations caused a powerful movement in favor of fire-resistant materials, and laws were passed which forced the question of safety upon the attention of architects and builders. One innovation after another aided the movement. Concrete buildings were unknown in America just after the war, though Napoleon III had used concrete in the erection of workmen's houses in Paris and it had been employed in business edifices in England. But within a few years concrete was exciting keen interest in all parts of the United States and in 1870 the first dwellings of that material were erected in Bellville, New Jersey. Plate glass at this time was just coming into general use in stores and offices, and it did away with the necessity of much wooden-sash work. Most of it was imported though by 1870 there was one American factory which produced unpolished plate glass.[3] Asbestos, too, began to be known in the late seventies after large mines were discovered in Canada. Above all, the manufacture of steel by the Bessemer process made it possible to use it in place of

[1] *Nation*, XIII, Nov. 9, 1871; *Am. Ann. Cyclop.*, XI (1871), 393 ff.
[2] *Nation*, XV, Nov. 14, 1872.
[3] *Scientific American*, Sept. 25; Oct. 23, 1869.

wrought iron for buildings and prepared the way for the coming era of fireproof steel construction.

The multiplication of cities and towns and the increasing congestion of population within industrial areas furnished new problems in communication. These were years in which the nation and the planet seemed to shrink perceptibly in size. It need hardly be recalled that the first successful transatlantic cable was laid by Cyrus W. Field in 1866 and that it wrought an immediate alteration in men's outlook upon all intercontinental affairs. Bankers and brokers rejoiced in having the opening quotations for London securities upon their desks when they arrived for work in the morning; the Associated Press almost immediately had the speech of King William of Prussia to his parliament transmitted at a cost of $5,790 in gold; and Napoleon III used the cable in communicating with the Emperor Maximilian in Mexico.[1] Thus in the broad fields of business, of news and of diplomacy the new link with the Old World instantly proved itself invaluable; and men within a few years accepted as a matter of course the intimate contact with European events.

Meanwhile the mileage of American telegraph lines was trebled within a few years and far-reaching improvements were made in the postal service of the nation. City after city was adopting the free-carrier service which Congress had authorized in 1863. The urgency of the need was best illustrated in New York, where some six thousand boxes had represented thirty thousand names, and the sorting clerks had to be able to recall and associate any one of these names with the proper box on the instant. Carrier delivery, which Europe had

---

[1] Success was won with the cable only after twelve million dollars had been spent. H. N. Field, *The Story of the Atlantic Telegraph* (N. Y., 1892), 386.

long employed, led for the first time to the extensive directing of letters to streets and numbers. By 1871 there were fifty-one cities with carrier service, and though the work of the postmen did not yet command universal confidence, it was rapidly improving.[1] Two years later the postal card was introduced from Europe. Thomas A. Edison, the future magician of light and sound, was soon at work improving the telegraph and using it to print stock quotations.

Yet nothing did more to expedite communication than two widely different inventions upon which in the early seventies two modest geniuses were laboring all unnoticed—the typewriter and the telephone. Each answered a strong, though ill-realized, social demand, and each did much to change important phases of business and urban life.[2] The telephone was the work of a mercurial young Scotch-American named Alexander Graham Bell who at the outset of the seventies was conducting a school for deaf mutes in Boston and laboring over the dream of a musical telegraph. The typewriter we owe chiefly to a middle-aged printer of Milwaukee named C. L. Sholes, a dreamy, erratic man who just after the war was giving his spare hours to a device for numbering serially the pages of a book. Each was led step by step to an achievement far beyond his first ambitions.

Sholes had completed his device for printing numbers when his attention was called to an article by Alfred Beach in the *Scientific American*, expatiating on the value which a practical typewriter would possess. The

[1] Postmaster General, *Report of 1868*, 24 ff.; same author, *Report of 1869*, 18; same author, *Report of 1870*, 16; same author, *Report of 1872*, 36. The government at the same time was establishing a national weather service, of great value to farmers, mariners and the general public. *Am. Ann. Cyclop.*, X (1870), 797 ff.

[2] Waldemar Kaempffert, ed., *A Popular History of American Invention* (N. Y., 1924). For the history of the typewriter, see I, 264-285; for the telephone, I, 286-317.

immense growth of business and official affairs, Beach pointed out, had made letter writing and record keeping by pen deplorably inadequate; the time was ripe for a quicker, clearer, more permanent method.[1] Sholes set to work in his dingy two-story machine shop and with the help of several friends, notably Carlos Glidden, made by the autumn of 1867 a machine which would write with a fair degree of accuracy and rapidity. One of the letters written by his typewriter fell into the hands of a business man of Meadville, Pennsylvania, named James Densmore, who was so interested that he asked to buy a share in the invention. It was Densmore who, pointing out that the machine was full of the gravest defects, insisted that they must be corrected. Between 1867 and 1873 Sholes, Densmore and Glidden built model after model, each showing some improvement, until in the latter year the device was deemed good enough to be manufactured for general sale. We find Mark Twain in December, 1874, composing a letter upon a machine which had cost him $125 and explaining its many virtues. "I believe it will print faster than I can write," he declared. "One may lean back in his chair and work it. It piles an awful stack of words on one page. It don't muss things or scatter ink blots around. Of course it saves paper." [2]

The same year 1874 saw Bell laboring in his basement workshop in a Salem dwelling with the idea of speech transmission by wire ever more prominent in his mind but with the means still quite unforeseen. He took a long step forward when, with the advice of a friendly surgeon, he began experimenting with an apparatus of which a dead man's ear formed a part.[3] He

---

[1] Herkimer County Historical Society, *The Story of the Typewriter, 1873-1923* (Herkimer, N. Y., 1923), 30 ff.

[2] A. B. Paine, *Mark Twain, A Biography* (N. Y., 1912), I, 537.

[3] H. N. Casson, *The History of the Telephone* (Chicago, 1910), 26.

noticed how the delicate eardrum set the heavy bones behind it to vibrating. "Why," he asked, "should not a vibrating iron disk set an iron rod or electrified wire into vibration?" It was on a hot June afternoon in 1875 that, patiently toiling over the complicated mechanism which he and his assistant, Thomas A. Watson, had set up, he heard a feeble sound, a faint twang, come over the wire from a similar machine in the next room. It was the birth cry of the telephone. While Sholes in 1875 was slowly marketing his first crude typewriters, Bell was puzzling out the mechanical details which made his invention workable. It was to be only a few years until in every city office the two most familiar noises would be the ring of the telephone bell and the click of the typist's key.

The process of urbanization operated with highly uneven results in different cultural fields. It was of decided benefit to the stage, for the growing number of large cities and the improvements in transportation gave increased vigor to the theater and particularly to the star system as represented by such figures as Modjeska, Joseph Jefferson and Mary Anderson. On the other hand, it had as yet accomplished singularly little for architecture or for music. The architect of the period whose work demands the warmest praise, H. H. Richardson, a Louisianian by birth who began his career immediately after the war and who died in 1886, stands out as an almost unique figure, surrounded by cheap jerry-builders and ignorant engineers. Richardson found his stride in 1872, when he was commissioned to build Trinity Church in Boston, and for the next fourteen years he sowed America with admirable examples derived from the Romanesque style. He had a few compeers of importance, like Richard Morris Hunt, and a distinguished group was soon to arise; but as yet the great mass of

Americans thought it quite unnecessary to call in a skilled architect when they planned a public building or church, and were content to let a treasury politician named Mullett design scores of hideous federal structures, many of them to be eyesores for generations. City planning, despite the rough object lesson given by "Boss" Shepherd in Washington, was virtually unknown. As for music, which an urban society would seem naturally to demand, it was producing only a few eminent organizers and pioneers and they were almost without exception foreign-born. This was the period of Grau, Maretzek and Mapleson (an Englishman) in opera, and of Theodore Thomas and Leopold Damrosch in the symphony field; the German *saengerbund* was to be found scattered from Brooklyn to Topeka, and German opera was about to overthrow the long sovereignty of the Italians in that field. But the native American stock brought forth neither musicians, composers nor musical organizations of distinction.

The larger American cities were as yet far from standardized in institutions, outlook and manners. Though pulsing with new activities of a kindred sort, they still seemed cast in highly individual molds. New York was of course distinguished among them all by its contrasts of weath and poverty, splendor and sordidness, philanthropy and vice. The war contracts and postwar inflation and speculation had made it a city of riches upon a new scale; by 1868 securities to the value of three billion dollars were being dealt with on the exchange, and the establishment of stock tickers in 1867 was one indication of the increased importance of stock trading. So great was the diffusion of riches that a hundred thousand New Yorkers now made some pretense to "fashion." The old Knickerbockers, who combined family, culture and wealth in a unique pride of caste, held themselves aloof.   There was a much greater body of fashionable folk who made no claim to lineage, but who had some intellectual distinction as well as inherited wealth.   They patronized the opera, Wallack's and the classical concerts of Theodore Thomas; they were the figures most sought after at Newport and Long Branch, and they held agreeably democratic receptions at which appeared authors, artists and journalists.   But the most picturesque element among the rich were the *parvenus*. It was they who flashed oftenest at the opera in Irving Place or at Pike's Opera House, who had the finest brown-stone palaces on the monotonous Fifth Avenue, and who cut the boldest dash at Jerome Park.

The richest New Yorkers were representative and national figures.   Cornelius Vanderbilt, the typical railway reorganizer of the time, had an office in Fourth Street—a tall, hale old gentleman with white hair, ruddy face and flashing black eyes who might be seen any fine afternoon driving in Central Park.   William B. Astor, the foremost among those winning fortunes from the rise in real estate, was to be found almost constantly at his desk in Prince Street in a one-story brick office looking like a village bank.   He, though also past seventy, was fond of walking to business from his old-fashioned brick house in Lafayette Place, adjoining the Astor Library, and his six-foot frame, coarse, cold features and small eyes were familiar to New Yorkers.   The third figure in the great triumvirate of New York wealth was Alexander T. Stewart, representative of the department-store business to which men like John Wanamaker and R. H. Macy were giving fresh vigor.[1]   His huge building overlooking City Hall Park housed one of the largest

[1] W. A. Croffutt, *The Vanderbilts and the Story of Their Fortune* (Chicago, 1886); James Parton, *Life of John Jacob Astor* (N. Y., 1865); *Obituary and Biographical Notices of A. T. Stewart* (scrap-book in N. Y. Public Library).

wholesale trades in America, his new retail establishment on Tenth Street, a structure covering two acres, was the largest of its kind in the world, and on Fifth Avenue he was building a white marble residence costing more than two million dollars. He was a slight, sandy, commonplace-looking Scotch-Irishman, but a man of unresting energy and industry. Each of these three capitalists had a fortune estimated at from fifty to seventy-five million dollars.

In regarding such notorious figures as Jim Fisk and Daniel Drew, we are likely to forget that the really typical business men of the metropolis, such as those whose portraits now adorn the Chamber of Commerce, were of an utterly different stripe. One was Peter Cooper, whose rise from the position of coach-maker's apprentice had given him that keen appreciation of the needs of aspiring youth which led him to endow Cooper Institute, with its evening classes, its school of design and its free reading-room. Another was Jackson Schultz, who had amassed a fortune as a leather dealer, and was one of the city's most public-spirited leaders— president of the health board and director and helper in many benevolent institutions. Of like intent was Abiel A. Low (the father of Seth Low), whose house was foremost in the Oriental trade. Another business man whose son rose far higher, and whose death in 1878 was lamented by the press as an irreparable loss to the city, was the elder Theodore Roosevelt.[1]

As always New York was a rather gay municipality. It counted a transient population of about fifty thousand, which gave some of its hotels a markedly sectional air. The St. Nicholas was patronized by Middle Westerners, the New York by Southerners, the Metropolitan by visitors from the Far West and the Clarendon, with

[1] *Nation*, XXVI, Feb. 14, 1878.

its memories of Thackeray and the Prince of Wales, by Britons. These outsiders furnished much of the audience for such attractions as the "Black Crook," or the Parisian ballet which for seventeen months crowded Niblo's Theater, and realized profits of two hundred thousand dollars. Western visitors censured New York for allowing the appearance of stage girls who seemed to wear nothing but satin slippers and a few roses in their hair, but they attended.[1] With a German population of almost two hundred thousand, New York was naturally full of beer gardens and *rathskellers,* three or four thousand in number. The best known came to be the Atlantic Garden, which under one roof offered room for twenty-five hundred people, a shooting gallery, billiard tables, an orchestrion and a band. Oyster houses and chop houses abounded; cycloramas of battle scenes competed with the Eden Musée; bowling clubs and rifle teams were at their apogee, and there was archery in Central Park. Much alarm was excited in Puritanic quarters by the sudden rise, not only in New York but in other cities, of the "concert-saloon," with its pretty waitresses. The first of them opened on Broadway and the Bowery, and with their illuminated transparencies, jangling music and painted girls, made an instant success. They multiplied with astonishing rapidity; by 1869 it was said that New York had six hundred. The best of them, like the Louvre and the Olympic, were gorgeously fitted up and maintained a certain decorum, but in Chatham Street and the Bowery were dens of a baser kind, which needed a better police supervision than they got. Coney Island abounded with side shows, roulette wheels, and hot-corn vendors, while the Sheepshead Bay races were an annual attraction.

Philadelphia was still a sober city where, even in 1870,

[1] Brown, *The Last Fifty Years in Old New York,* 67-106.

Quaker bonnets, dove-colored gowns, shad-bellied coats and broad-brimmed hats remained a frequent sight.[1] Social position depended largely upon whether a man was born above or below Market Street. Though the Arch Street Theater was justly renowned for its stock company, the population as a whole took a prudish and conservative attitude toward all the arts. Fairmount Park was still for the most part new and was the chief pride of Philadelphians, who showed a great taste for outdoor amusements—picnicking, fishing on the Wissahickon, drives to Lemon Hill, and beyond, and regattas on the Schuylkill. The people were more comfortably homogeneous than New York's, the Anglo-Saxon and the German elements of long residence controlling the city's life. They enjoyed a fairly high level of comfort with few gilded millionaires and no large slums. By virtue of its abundance of trees, lawns and gardens, the town retained a pleasantly rural appearance in many districts. On its outskirts were numberless staid homes like that which Joseph Hergesheimer has described as his grandfather's. Here could be found a victoria for pleasure, a "Germantown" for marketing, a rock garden, a library with Dickens, Thackeray, Bulwer, Cooper, and Scott in stiff sets, aunts in heavy corsets and cut jet, card packs whereon fruit replaced the customary wicked symbols, and the piety which accorded with a family pew at the First Presbyterian Church.[2]

Visitors to Boston found the city in the Indian summer of its cultural effulgence, with the Irish flood that was changing its whole character now setting in strongly. It was still half the Boston of Holmes's "Autocrat," priding itself upon being "the thinking center of the continent." Its best society was based on the old families

[1] James Huneker, *Steeplejack* (N. Y., 1920), I, chaps. i-viii.
[2] Joseph Hergesheimer, *A Presbyterian Child* (N. Y., 1923), *passim*.

—families which represented generations of education and position and upheld traditions which ran back to Tudor days. Wealth counted for comparatively little, as Henry Cabot Lodge tells us, and a hundred thousand dollars was looked upon as a very handsome property.[1] Though Henry Adams was grieved to find that people no longer dined at two, or skated on the Back Bay, which was being rapidly reclaimed, he declares that the city still seemed simple and less restless-minded than ever.[2] The Saturday Club still brought together a New England group of such intellectual distinction as could scarcely have been surpassed in any country. With only a quarter of a million people in 1870, Boston had genuine personality. It was very decidedly growing, for the population increased about seventy-five thousand in the decade of the sixties, new suburbs were spreading out and the Massachusetts Institute of Technology (1865), Boston University (1869) and the Museum of Fine Arts (1870) were being founded; but at heart it was the old Boston still. Not even the *parvenus* who were pushing the gentle old families to the wall could change its essence.

Social life in Washington just after the war was only moderately florid and glittering. It had Southern geniality still and a Yankee observer tells us that the gay round "went on excellently well without houses, or carriages, or jewels, or toilettes, or pavements, or shops, or *grandezza* of any sort." The entertainments, numerous but not elaborate, were affected by the presence of many political figures of hazy social and cultural background. Even while President Johnson and Congress were at swords' points, many dinners, dances and receptions were held. General Benjamin F. Butler cele-

[1] H. C. Lodge, *Early Memories* (N. Y., 1913), 208.
[2] Henry Adams, *The Education of Henry Adams* (Wash., 1907), 241.

brated the debut of his daughter in a house transformed
into a bower by thousands of camelias; and crass, pushing men like Butler and John A. Logan represented
the social norm of the capital.[1] Among the eligible
young men were Henry Adams, who would have spared
half his Boston culture to have reversed better in waltz-
ing, Moorfield Storey, and a handsome young naval officer named George Dewey. When Grant became president there was more splendor than before, for Grant had
the heartiest respect for wealth, while Nellie Grant and
Secretary Fish's daughter Edith added much to the animation of evening affairs.[2] Even then, however, champagne was not considered indispensable. As the years
passed during Grant's administration, the element of
coarseness in political affairs was more and more felt in
society. The woman lobbyist was seen everywhere,
making the streets and hotels disreputably gay, while
everybody despised the numerous tribe of venal congressmen. "You can't use tact with a Congressman!" burst
out one cabinet member; "A Congressman is a hog!
You must take a stick and hit him on the snout!"[3] Not
until the advent of President Hayes, his irreproachable
cabinet and the Puritanical tone which Lucy Hayes gave
to administration entertainments, did the social atmosphere improve.

The changes in urban life were not the only evidences
of the increasing luxury of American life. Equally
striking were the improvements in the comfort and
safety of long-distance traveling. When an American
entered a railway car at the beginning of our period,
he could seldom find a window that opened easily, a

[1] Mrs. John A. Logan, *Reminiscences of a Soldier's Wife; an Autobiography* (N. Y., 1913), 247 ff.
[2] Helen Nicolay, *Our Capital on the Potomac* (N. Y., 1924), 387 ff.
[3] *Education of Henry Adams*, 261.

stove that warmed his body, or a seat secure from the
tobacco juice and talk of rowdies.[1] The railway waiting rooms were usually small, dirty and insufferably
close with no more facilities for comfort than a police
station. A pleasant restaurant was nowhere to be
found; instead, the passenger who entered the hot, noisy
"refreshment saloon" had to lift himself to a high stool
and bolt the viands which, badly cooked, were literally
thrown at his plate. Once embarked on a train, no
matter how long the journey, he could have no food
save stale pop corn, apples and candy.

But within the space of a half-dozen years first-class
travel was completely transformed. The agent who
produced this change was an enterprising young New
Yorker, still in his early thirties, named George M. Pullman. He had carried an unusual eye for opportunities
into his business as cabinet maker and contractor and had
given some attention to the refitting of ordinary railway
cars with berths. As the war was ending, he invested
more than twenty thousand dollars in building in Chicago the first Pullman car, a sum four times as great as
had ever been spent upon a railway coach.[2] The "Pioneer" possessed improved rubber-bearing trucks, was a
foot wider and two and a half feet higher than any other
car, and showed resplendently ornate furnishings. The
dimensions of railway platforms and bridges would not
permit its passage over any existing line, but the needed
changes on two routes were hastened by the request that
it be attached to Lincoln's funeral train and be used to
carry General Grant from Detroit to Galena. Pullman,
confident that the public would welcome the innovation,
asked only that the railway superintendents give his cars

[1] G. M. Towle, *American Society* (London, 1870), II, 175 ff.
[2] Joseph Husband, *The Story of the Pullman Car* (Chicago, 1917),
32.

a fair trial. This was first done on the Michigan Central, where several of the new cars were attached to trains together with the old-style sleeping cars, the charge being two dollars a berth on the one, and one dollar and fifty cents on the other. The success of the Pullmans was immediate. Lines competing with the Michigan Central found that many travelers preferred the railway which had the Pullmans and hastened to install them.[1]

As the number of Pullman cars multiplied, their designer prepared to bring forward fresh luxuries and innovations. In 1867 he introduced the first "hotel car" or rudimentary diner, a sleeping car with a built-in kitchen from which meals were served at tables placed in the sections. When in that year the gauge between New York and Chicago was standardized by the addition of a third rail to the Great Western, and the first "through" train ran between the two cities, the hotel car was coupled to the train.[2] Others were soon running between Chicago and Boston or New York; and the dining car proper, devoted exclusively to restaurant purposes, followed in 1868.[3] Later still came the drawing-room cars and the reclining-chair cars. Pullman had laid the foundation for a huge business which, carried on at first in shops in several cities, was in 1879 to be centralized at the town of Pullman, near Chicago.

Not only did the American travel more comfortably; he traveled more safely. In 1866 George Westinghouse, a shrewd young New Yorker, had his attention

---

[1] Husband, *Pullman Car*, 42 ff.

[2] *Detroit Commercial Advertiser*, June 1, 1867, quoted by Husband, 49.

[3] See W. F. Rae, *Westward by Rail* (London, 1870), 28, for transcontinental accommodations. He is enthusiastic about the splendor of the cars; but, actually, most of the early Pullmans, with carved wood, heavy upholstery and silver plate, were vulgarly ornate.

directed by a railway wreck near Schenectady to the difficulty of stopping trains in motion, and began working at a power brake. A magazine article on the use of compressed air in driving rock drills on the Mont Cenis tunnel gave him a brilliant idea, and the result was the air-brake patent issued to him early in 1869 when he was not yet twenty-three.[1] Westinghouse's invention, which included a steam pump on the locomotive to compress air to about seventy pounds a square inch, was first tested near Pittsburgh in the fall of 1868. His train had not emerged from the city when a drayman was espied on the track just ahead and the engineer applied the new brakes with an abruptness which hurled all the guests to the floor. The train made demonstrations throughout the country, and orders at once came in. Almost immediately young Westinghouse became president of an air-brake company capitalized at a half-million dollars, with leading railwaymen of the country, such as A. J. Cassatt of the Pennsylvania system, as directors. He continued zealously to perfect his invention, patenting (1872) an automatic air brake, which was so constructed that when the train broke in two the brakes set of themselves upon the detached cars. By 1876 nearly two fifths of all the locomotives and passenger cars of the country were equipped with his appliances.[2]

Nor were Westinghouse's devices by any means the only contribution to railway safety and convenience. Just after the war Miller's car platform, coupler and buffer, the first noteworthy improvements in this equipment, were adopted on all passenger trains. They brought the

---

[1] H. G. Prout, *A Life of George Westinghouse* (N. Y., 1921), 26 ff.; F. E. Leupp, *George Westinghouse, His Life and Achievements* (Boston, 1918), 18 ff.

[2] Prout, *George Westinghouse*, 32.

platforms into close contact, thus minimizing the jolt in starting and stopping trains and lessening the danger of telescoping.[1] Meanwhile steel or steel-capped rails were fast being substituted for iron, and iron bridges, Carnegie's first large business venture, for wooden structures. Wood was used as fuel upon important trunk lines of the East, even near the Pennsylvania coal fields, until after 1870, and one of the improvements which Jay Gould wrought upon the Erie lay in the introduction of coal in adequate quantities. A highly important step in railway safety, the invention of the automatic railway signal, came early in the seventies, when David Rousseau's device was brought into use on the New York Central.[2] Every wreck in these years—for example, the great Revere catastrophe upon the Eastern Railroad of Massachusetts in the summer of 1871, which revealed astounding negligence—was seized upon by the press as the text for an argument in behalf of the new safety appliances.[3] By 1878 it could be said that railway travel in the United States had passed out of the stage of fumbling youth into that of sophisticated young manhood. The American rightly boasted that he could travel with less discomfort and greater safety than anyone else in the world.

[1] E. H. Mott, *Between the Ocean and the Lakes: the Story of Erie* (N. Y., 1899), 140.
[2] *Am. Ann. Cyclop.*, XVI (1876), 516.
[3] C. F. Adams, jr., "The Revere Catastrophe," *Atlantic Monthly*, XXXVII (1876), 92-103.

CHAPTER IV

THE TAMING OF THE WEST

(1865-1873)

THE building of the transcontinental railway, the filling in of a great transportation network behind it and the rapid advance of settlement, all pronounced the doom of the wildest West—the West of hostile Indian tribes, enormous bison herds, unexplored mountain ranges and unnavigated rivers. There were approximately three hundred thousand Indians in the United States when the war closed, of whom thirty-two thousand lived in the region east of the Mississippi (including Minnesota) and forty-eight thousand upon the Pacific slope.[1] The tribes with which we are most concerned are those which made their homes on the Great Plains west of the Mississippi or in the Rocky Mountain territories—about two hundred and twenty-five thousand in all. In numbers they were not formidable, but being scattered over a vast extent of territory, much of it difficult of access, they could harry the thin van of the oncoming white population almost at will. The northern Indians on the Great Plains numbered more than sixty thousand and included four nations of the first importance, the Sioux, the Crow, the Northern Cheyenne and the Arapahoe. Of these the Crow, like the Pawnee, were always friendly to the whites; and they were enemies of the fierce and warlike Sioux and furnished many scouts to the government. But the other

[1] Secretary of the Interior, *Report for 1872*, 402 ff.

101

three nations needed the most tactful and generous treatment. The southern tribes of the plains included not only the peace-loving and industrious Cherokee, Creek and Choctaw, well-settled on reservations in what is now Oklahoma, but the Kiowa, the Comanche, the Southern Cheyenne and the Southern Arapahoe, all of them roving and totally uncivilized. They were tinder for any blaze of hostilities and they numbered about eighty-five thousand in all.[1]

Certain main characteristics stamped the life of these plains Indians. They were physically of fine stature, strong and active. They lived by the hunt, and their habitat, their government, their social institutions and their beliefs were affected, above all other factors, by the buffalo. Agriculture played a comparatively small rôle in their economy.[2] Their chief elements of wealth consisted of their herds of ponies and of their weapons and ammunition, while they were quite unable to understand the desire of the white man to monopolize any part of the earth.[3] Their government was simple and, in a sense, democratic, consisting in a leadership of chiefs who attained their primacy by skill and courage and whose sway was most stringently exercised in time of war or other emergency.

These proud, stern, and really formidable peoples, who had many faults but whose courage and fortitude touched even their enemies to admiration, were now

[1] *American Annual Cyclopedia* (N. Y., 1861-1903), VII (1867), 403.

[2] The Secretary of the Interior in 1872 classified all the Indians of the United States as follows: civilized, 97,000; semicivilized, 125,000; utterly barbarous, 78,000. He reported that about 180,000 had treaties with the government, 40,000 more were without reservations but more or less under the control of agents, and 55,000 were totally uncontrolled. Secretary of the Interior, *Report for 1872*, 402 ff.

[3] Livingston Farrand, *Basis of American History* (A. B. Hart, ed., *American Nation, a History*, N. Y., 1904-1918, II), chap. ix.

caught as in a gigantic vise. The Missouri frontier and the Pacific frontier, shaped like a pair of parentheses, tended constantly to contract. On the east the advance of the settlers had by 1872 crept up to the semiarid region of the Texas, Kansas and Nebraska cattle range, where tillage was difficult; on the west, it pressed up to the Sierras.[1] A marked restiveness developed among most of the plains tribes during the Civil War—a restiveness not the result of Confederate machinations, as many observers believed, but of the irresistible thrust of settlement. From 1865 to 1870 there was almost constant war and long after 1870, when the West had been fairly subdued and policed, there were sporadic outbreaks of a bloody nature. The Indians would have been tame indeed had they not revolted. Their food supply in the herds of elk and buffaloes was being cut off, their reservations were reduced, they were constantly shifted to less desirable territory, and individually they were often cheated and maltreated. The almost universal testimony along the border was that the only wise policy toward them was extermination, and even so liberal an American as Samuel Bowles could say that if this policy alone was feasible, the sooner and quicker it was carried out the better.[2]

Moreover, the government's plans for their disposal were weak and fluctuating. Up to 1851 the whole immense region between the Missouri and the Rockies had been officially recognized as an Indian domain; but the successive gold discoveries in California and in Colorado, with the rush of prospectors and other emigrants across the plains, had caused the tribes to be partitioned off into ever smaller and more barren districts. In 1861 the

[1] F. L. Paxson, *The Last American Frontier* (N. Y., 1910), chap. xxii.
[2] See General Halleck in 1866 on the Apache: "They must be hunted and exterminated." Secretary of War, *Report for 1866*, 31 ff.

restive Cheyenne and Arapahoe of the south agreed by treaty to restrict themselves to a region along the Arkansas River and the northern boundary of New Mexico.[1] In return, the United States was to protect their lands, pay thirty thousand to each tribe annually for fifteen years and supply them with stock and farm implements. Finding themselves in a poor and inhospitable region, their discontent was immediate. Meanwhile, the Sioux to the northward had driven the Crow into the Montana country and had taken sole possession of the area between Montana and the Missouri, with parts of Minnesota. But this was not so wide a range as they desired. They felt irritated and alarmed. So did the Northern Cheyenne and Arapahoe, who in large numbers during the summer of 1864 took the warpath, harried the emigrants and ranches of Nebraska and Colorado, and brought on general hostilities.[2]

The second cardinal error of the government lay in tolerating a vague division of authority over the Indians between the war and the interior departments. Western military officers accused the agents sent out by the Indian bureau of sentimentality, weakness and criminal acquiescence in redskin atrocities; the bureau accused the army of gross barbarity and of a policy of organized murder.[3] Unquestionably many of the men at the Indian agencies were corrupt, and stole large sums, a fact which the army officers noisily advertised. Unquestionably, on the other hand, many Westerners wished to see the Indian country controlled by the army because the garrisons were a profitable source of revenue for tradesmen—General Sherman said as much. To

[1] H. H. Jackson, *A Century of Dishonor* (N. Y., 1881), chap. iii.
[2] G. B. Grinnell, *The Fighting Cheyennes* (N. Y., 1915), *passim*.
[3] See successive issues of the Indian Office, *Reports*, and *Reports for 1861-1868* of the Secretaries of War—especially General Sherman in the *Report for 1865*, 188 ff.

add to the confusion, both the army officers and the agents had to regard the Indian chiefs as responsible sovereigns with a treaty-making power, whereas many of them had but the weakest control over their braves.[1]

While still predominantly savage, the tribes had been subjected to important social changes by white contact and several contained an element that was now half-civilized. Among the Sioux of southwestern Minnesota, for example, many individuals just before the war had been induced to cut their hair, don the white man's garb and take up land allotments.[2] However, the great majority remained "blanket Indians," and the savages learned far more of the vices than the virtues of their neighbors. For instance they fell a ready prey to the whisky seller. The system of government annuities made them beggars, and whenever the government bounty failed or fell into arrears, they were needy, distressed and angry. A large half-breed population was the result of the contact of whites and redskins, and these half-breeds were usually an undesirable element, dissipated, cruel and lazy.[3] The outbreak of 1862 began when some Sioux who had been waiting for delayed annuity payments fell into such straits for food that they dug up bitter roots and devoured their corn uncooked like so many wild animals.[4] The Indians of Utah at the close of the war were in such wretched plight, with the white man holding their best pastures and wild game growing rare, that in the depth of winter they went starving and almost unclad, sleeping in

---

[1] Jackson, *A Century of Dishonor*, chaps. iii, v.
[2] W. W. Folwell, *History of Minnesota* (S. J. Buck, ed., Minnesota Hist. Soc., *Publs.*, 1921-   ), II, 220.
[3] T. J. Galbraith, in Indian Office, *Report for 1861*, 93.
[4] Folwell, *Minnesota*, II, 287 ff.

the snow and sleet with no covering but capes of rabbits' fur and moccasins lined with cedar bark.[1] Needy, smarting under a sense of wrong, the Indians naturally undertook forays, and the splitting of the tribes into small units made it difficult to learn who was guilty of a given outrage.

The first hostilities on a general scale were inaugurated by the Cheyenne uprising in 1864. They began in August, with an attack upon Ben Holladay's stage and freight line east of Denver, and with raids upon scattered farms, ranches and stagecoach stations. For three hundred and seventy miles every ranch but one along Holladay's route was deserted; the frontier was reduced almost overnight to a state of abject terror.[2] At this juncture occurred the barbarous Sand Creek massacre, throwing a lurid illumination upon the attitude of most Westerners and military men toward the savages. Colonel J. M. Chivington at the head of nearly a thousand Colorado volunteers suddenly fell upon between five hundred and six hundred harmless, unsuspecting and friendly Cheyenne and Arapahoe, mostly women and children, and slaughtered them with sickening barbarities.[3] When news of the massacre reached the East, a passionate wave of indignation swept all humane circles. But in the West, where the Indians were hated like serpents, Chivington received general applause.[4] For the moment, as the news spread, the whole frontier was ablaze.[5] The Platte route was raided from a point near Denver almost to the Missouri; telegraph lines went

[1] N. A. Miles, *Serving the Republic* (N. Y., 1911), 115; General Pope, in Secretary of War, *Report for 1866*, 23 ff.

[2] P. E. Byrne, *Soldiers of the Plains* (N. Y., 1926), 140.

[3] *Senate Reps.*, 39 Cong., 2 sess., no. 156.

[4] Committee on the Conduct of the War, *Report*, III (massacre of the Cheyenne Indians).

[5] Commissioner of Indian Affairs, *Report for 1866*.

down; trains were captured and men and women killed. For six weeks no mail passed east or west.

At the close of 1865, after a summer of arduous campaigning, the state of Indian affairs was dismaying to all observers. Not fewer than twenty-five thousand troops were in the field against the tribes. They were employed along the frontiers of Minnesota and Dakota, in the Black Hills and the Powder River country, all over the Nebraska plains and along the Smoky Hill route in western Kansas and in New Mexico and Arizona. This large army was performing important services to American civilization. It was holding open the great central and southwestern mail routes; it was protecting two thousand miles of the navigable Missouri above Kansas City; it was keeping the overland telegraph from Omaha to the Carson Valley uncut; and under the shield it raised, emigrants were thronging toward the West.[1] Nevertheless, the question arose whether this tremendous outlay of capital and appreciable expenditure of blood was necessary or even justified. Secretary Harlan of the Interior estimated that every regiment thrown upon the plains to fight the Indians cost the treasury two million dollars a year and that all the campaigns of the preceding twelvemonth had not wiped out more than a few hundred braves.[2]

It was plainly cheaper, not to say more humane, to feed the Indians than to kill them. But was it necessary to do either? Could not the Indian Territory be made a really inclusive reservation; could not treaty stipulations be honestly fulfilled and the trade in Indian supplies fairly conducted; could not justice be enforced against the ruffianly white man and the murderous In-

[1] *Nation* (N. Y.), II, Jan. 11, 1866.
[2] Sherman testified that hunting Indians was like hunting the *Alabama*. Secretary of War, *Report for 1867*, 31 ff.

dian alike? Under pressure of these considerations, the government made an earnest effort to deal constructively with the problem. There was a congressional inquiry; two peace commissions were dispatched westward in 1865, one to bargain with the Southwestern Indians and the other to make a treaty with the Sioux and their allies.[1] Agreements were actually concluded and the Cheyenne and Arapahoe gave up their reservation along the Arkansas in return for the privilege of ranging the unsettled plains for buffalo. But none of the deeper causes of the Indian hostility were removed or even softened. The savages felt crowded on the south by the new Kansas and Nebraska settlements and on the east by the steady thrust from Iowa and Minnesota, while they saw a new stream of white migration strike across their best northern hunting range to the mines of Montana and Idaho.

In the next two years, 1866-1867, hostilities shimmered like heat lightning here and there over the plains. The sharpest fighting occurred with the Sioux along the new Powder River Road to Montana, which the troops were trying to hold open by establishing Fort Reno, Fort Phil Kearny and Fort C. F. Smith. A series of bloody border clashes led up, as the year 1866 closed, to the massacre of seventy-nine cavalrymen under a rash captain named Fetterman just outside Fort Phil Kearny.[2] Encouraged by this stroke, the Sioux redoubled their activities and were joined by fresh recruits from other tribes.

Intelligence of the Sioux uprising spread at once to the savages of Nebraska and Colorado, causing great excitement. Many small tribal units, facing imminent

[1] Commissioner of Indian Affairs, *Report for 1865*, 699 ff.
[2] *Senate Exec. Docs.*, 39 Cong., 2 sess., nos 15-15; G. B. Grinnell, *The Fighting Cheyennes*, 220 ff.

starvation, were stung into desperation. By late spring the news of widespread Indian depredations, raids and murders came from both north and south of the projected Union Pacific line. It was necessary to make a powerful military effort, for as General Sherman testified, fifty Indians could often "checkmate" three thousand soldiers.[1] General W. S. Hancock was soon fighting the Indians in Kansas, General C. C. Augur in western Nebraska, General A. H. Terry on the route from Minnesota to Montana, and General Crook in Idaho and Oregon. The struggle, marked as always by deplorable barbarities on both sides, was denounced by humane people of the East while it was cheered on by the realistic pioneers of the West. Two pitched battles against the Sioux were fought and won during August, while Hancock, with artillery and a pontoon train, made a glittering military parade to Fort Dodge on the Arkansas. But the Eastern demand for a more constructive handling of the situation was persistent and it bore fruit when Congress in July, 1867, provided for a new peace effort.[2] The result was a series of treaties which pushed the Indians away from the railway lines, and placed most of them on two great main reservations, one in the north, the other the Indian Territory in the south.[3] Long lines of Cheyenne and Arapahoe, with ponies, dogs and children, were soon wending their dusty way to the Cherokee Outlet region in the southwest part of Indian Territory, while the Kiowa and Comanche accepted a reserve not far distant. The Sioux were more difficult to satisfy. Red Cloud demanded and obtained the dismantling of the forts in the Powder River Valley and

[1] Secretary of War, *Report for 1867*, I; Commissioner of Indian Affairs, *Report for 1867*, 95 ff.; art., "Indian War," *Am. Ann. Cyclop.*, VII (1867).
[2] *U. S. Statutes at Large*, XV, 17.
[3] Secretary of the Interior, *Report for 1868*, 464 ff.

the closing of the road there. It was then arranged that the Sioux should occupy a great part of western Dakota, with the Missouri on the east, the Powder River range on the west and the Black Hills in the heart of their lands.[1]

These treaties of 1867-1868 (including compacts which placed the Indians just west of the Rocky Mountain divide on suitable reservations) opened the way across the continent for the railroads. They also ushered in a fresh and more permanent Indian policy, replacing the old uncertainty of aim and the ugly bickering between the war department and the Indian bureau.[2] Hereafter there was no question, so long as the savages dwelt peacefully on their reservations, of the civilian jurisdiction. The government realized, too, that their subsistence must be carefully provided for, that they could not be left without food and fuel in the December snows. Finally, the element of graft and incompetence in the Indian bureau had to be dealt with sternly. For this object Congress in 1869 authorized the president to appoint a board of Indian commissioners, who, acting with the secretary of the interior, should exercise joint control over the expenditure of all appropriations by the Indian bureau.[3] Corruption, though not stamped out, came to occupy a less important place.

The life of the military forces which ranged and policed the Western plains during these years was rich in interest and excitement. The letters and memoirs of Custer and Miles, two generous rivals and close friends, furnish us glimpses of the hardships and compensatory joys of their campaigns.[4] Safety was purchased only

---

[1] F. M. Hans, *The Great Sioux Nation* (Chicago, 1907), chap. xxxvii.
[2] H. B. Whipple, *Lights and Shadows of a Long Episcopate* (N. Y., 1899), 124 ff., 523 ff.
[3] *U. S. Statutes at Large*, XVI, 566.
[4] G. A. Custer, *My Life on the Plains* (N. Y., 1874): Miles,

by unremitting vigilance. A moment's relaxation of watchfulness, or a display of recklessness in wandering from the safety of a fort or a main column, and the soldier would be stretched naked on the prairie, his body filled with arrows and bullets. Frequently at dawn a sudden chorus of yells and fusillade of shots would rouse the camp to a defense against the redskins, circling rapidly at close range on their ponies. The captive was tortured with refinements of cruelty that varied with the tribe. If he brought his wife with him to the plains, he did so with the knowledge that her fate, if she fell into the Indians' hands, would be far worse than death. Day after day the troops were forced to shake themselves awake at four, snatch some bacon and coffee and march on under a burning sun and brazen sky, amid the stifling alkaline dust, with scanty rations of water, till at nightfall their legs utterly failed beneath them. Sometimes this exhausting routine endured for weeks and then culminated in a desperate desert battle. After fighting through the Civil War, Miles said that he had never witnessed such suffering as his men endured in a running twenty-mile engagement on the Llano Estacado.[1]

The life of the soldiers, however, was enlivened by a hundred incidents—now coursing wolves with stag hounds; now the rescue of a white woman, her mind unhinged by the sufferings she had endured; now the necessity of killing hundreds of Indian ponies, captured in a single herd; now the loosening of a teamster's wagon stuck in the quicksands; now an encounter with a picturesque, malodorous encampment of friendly savages. Men of the most varied types made up these Western commands. Some units were composed of for-

---

Serving the Republic; Frederick Whittaker, *Life of General George A. Custer* (N. Y., 1876).

[1] Miles, *Serving the Republic,* 124.

mer Union and Confederate soldiers, fighting side by side; in most of them were mingled officers from patrician Eastern families and Westerners who had fought their way to command by rough ability. Attached to Custer's command was Wild Bill,[1] a tall, lithe frontiersman, who, though one of the mildest-mannered men in his camp, had slain many an antagonist and who was dismissed following a saloon affray with lawless soldiers in Hays City. The best known of all was a scout enlisted for a short time under Miles, who called him one of the handsomest men he had ever seen—Buffalo Bill, or William F. Cody.[2] Such men showed the Western pride in individualism of bearing and personality; they were the legitimate descendants of Daniel Boone and "Davy" Crockett.

While the Indians were being thrown back from the country which the white newcomers wanted, the destruction of the great buffalo herds was being relentlessly organized. Of all the wild quadrupeds that have ever lived the bison marshaled the greatest numbers.[3] Our most careful estimates place the number of buffaloes in the trans-Mississippi West just after the war at fifteen millions.[4] A single herd seen by Colonel R. I. Dodge on the Arkansas River in 1871 has been estimated to have contained at least four millions. Their range lay between the Canadian plains on the far north, and the Gulf on the south, and they swept back and forth in spring and autumn as the line of pasturage advanced and receded. The building of the Union Pacific separated the bison into northern and southern herds, and

---

[1] Elizabeth B. Custer, *Following the Guidon* (N. Y., 1890), chap. xii.
[2] Miles, *Serving the Republic*, 145.
[3] W. T. Hornaday, "Extermination of the American Bison," Smithsonian Museum, *Report for 1887*, 367 ff.
[4] F. A. Root and W. E. Connelley, *The Overland Stage to California* (Topeka, 1901), chap. ii.

other railways stretched rapidly into the most populous buffalo regions. Coincidentally there arose a general demand in the East for buffalo robes and hides, while the armies released a host of men with new and accurate breech-loading rifles and fixed ammunition.[1]

The destruction of the southern herd, ranging south of the Union Pacific and east of Pueblo, came first. By the building of the Santa Fé, the Kansas Pacific and shorter lines, every part of the buffalo range was made easily accessible. Railroad workers, teamsters, professional hunters, trappers, guides and unemployed men turned out to share in the harvest of free hides and free meat and during the years 1870-1874 buffalo killing became one of the chief industries of the Southwestern plains.[2] The first large shipments from the Western terminals were bales of buffalo skins, and at Dodge City at one time there were to be seen one hundred and twenty cords of them in a single corral. Prominent among the hunters were sportsmen from the East and Europe. The youngest son of the Czar Alexander III, the Grand Duke Alexis, with a large entourage, traveled across the plains in 1871-1872, and for his benefit a grand buffalo chase was arranged on the plains of western Kansas under Buffalo Bill, General Custer and General Sheridan.[3] The approved commercial party consisted of four men: one shooter, two skinners and an assistant who stretched hides and cooked. It has been carefully estimated that in the four years 1871-1874 three million seven hundred thousand buffalo of the southern herd were slain, and

[1] See unsigned article on the "Destruction of the Buffalo," *Popular Science Monthly*, IX (1876), 377.
[2] R. I. Dodge, *The Plains of the Great West and their Inhabitants* (N. Y., 1877), 134 ff.
[3] See G. A. Sala, *America Revisited* (London, 1883), II, 174, and W. A. Bell, *New Tracks in North America* (London, 1869), II, 233, for foreign views of conditions.

that of the total more than three million one hundred and fifty thousand were killed by professional white hunters.[1]

By the end of the hunting season of 1875 the herd passed out of existence, utterly annihilated as a body, though a few vestiges had fled to remote parts of the range. So overstocked was the market for robes that by 1875 the hunters received only sixty-five cents each for an ordinary buffalo-bull's skin and one dollar and fifteen cents for a cow's. The consequence was that whenever it became difficult to skin an animal, it was simply left in its tracks. According to Colonel Dodge, each buffalo skin which reached the East represented five slain buffaloes in 1871, three in 1872 and one and a fourth in 1874. Though the meat might have fed hundreds of thousands of people, little of it was preserved. Probably no great American resource has ever been quite so wantonly and completely destroyed within so brief a time.[2] The main northern herd was smaller, and in its greater isolation it persisted somewhat longer. It was not until the opening of the Northern Pacific in 1880 that its fate was sealed. Within a few years thereafter almost the only surviving bison were those on the cold Canadian plains. The American people had all the buffalo robes they needed for sleighing; buffalo heads had become a commonplace ornament of homes and public buildings. But one of the most picturesque and impressive forms of wild life the world has ever seen was left virtually extinct.

Meanwhile the new policy of keeping the Indian tribes within bounds and laboring to civilize them was yielding encouraging results. By 1871 the board of Indian

---

[1] Colonel Dodge computed that 5,500,000 bison were shot in the three years 1872-1874. *Plains of the Great West*, 142-144.

[2] Bitter winters slew many buffalo. J. H. Beadle, *The Undeveloped West* (Phila., 1873), 436.

An attack on the Overland coach.

Shooting buffalo from the train.

The Invasion of the West.

commissioners was able to describe "the remarkable spectacle seen this fall, on the plains of western Nebraska and Kansas and eastern Colorado, of the warlike tribes of the Sioux of Dakota, Montana and Wyoming, hunting peacefully for buffalo without occasioning any serious alarm among the thousands of white settlers whose cabins skirt the borders of both sides of these plains." [1] The tribes had greatly improved in temper and docility, even if they did not advance greatly in civilization and Christianity.   Another step of great importance was taken this year, when Congress passed an act ordering that no more treaties with Indian tribes should be made by the president and Senate.[2]   The fiction that the Indian chiefs held a sovereign treaty-making power was thus abandoned and Congress as a whole, not the Senate alone, assumed jurisdiction over the entire field of Indian administration.   Henceforth the West gradually lost all apprehension of another general Indian war; the tribes were too widely scattered and weak, while the railways made it easy to throw troops into vital positions.   The Cheyenne of the South and some of the remoter Sioux still showed a great deal of turbulence and the Apache were almost utterly intractable.   But a good many of the Arapahoe were already engaged in farming; in Nebraska the Pawnee and Omaha had made encouraging progress; and with the extinction of the buffalo from the plains, it was believed that nearly all the tribes would settle down in earnest to agriculture.[3]   Unfortunately, corruption was allowed to persist among the agents on distant reservations, and Congress refused

[1] For Indian dependence on the buffalo, see G. B. Grinnell, "The Last of the Buffalo," *Scribner's Mag.*, XII (1892), 267-286.

[2] *Senate Exec. Docs.*, 48 Cong., 2 sess., no. 95.

[3] U. S. Commissioner of Indian Affairs, *Report for 1872*.   Extracts from this report are reprinted in Jackson, *A Century of Dishonor* (rev. edn., 1886), 411.

to make the appropriations needed to teach the savages and equip them with livestock and farm implements. Now that they had ceased to be feared they were treated with indifference.[1]

As the Indians were pushed aside and pacified in the period from 1865 to 1873, the stream of migrants to the trans-Missouri region steadily increased in size. During the summer river towns like Kansas City, Leavenworth and Omaha were scenes of bustling confusion as crowds of settlers prepared to face the perils of the long journey into the farther West. An Eastern newspaper man who traveled on horseback across the plains in 1866 found that though the prairie might be solitary, the trails were as busy as Eastern highways.[2] He was scarcely ever out of sight of long ox teams or shorter mule teams, and in one week after leaving Leavenworth, passed six hundred and eighty creaking vehicles. Samuel Bowles remarked the same procession of heavy wagons and carts, going east empty or rolling west full of emigrants and the supplies needed by ranchers and miners. Covered with dirty white cloth, the separate trains frequently stretching from one quarter to one third of a mile, they looked at a distance like Oriental caravans. At night the wagons were drawn into a circle as a protection against Indians or storms, and the animals turned loose to graze.

An effort might be made to exhibit the growth of population graphically on the motion-picture screen by showing the West as it became peppered with spots representing a thousand people. We would see the spots

---

[1] E. E. Sparks, *National Development* (*The American Nation*, XXIII), 275-276. For the operations of the spoilsmen of the "Indian Ring," see W. H. Carter, *The Life of Lieutenant-General Chaffee* (Chicago, 1917), chap. xii.

[2] J. F. Meline, *Two Thousand Miles on Horseback* (N. Y., 1867), 8-10.

first appearing sparsely at railheads and the intersection
of trails and streams; then following the ramifications
of the railways; and finally stippling the prairie lands.
As they move westward, they push before them the
black and sinuous frontier line, from Dakota to Texas.
Upon the map of Minnesota for 1870 we may fancy
four hundred and thirty-six such spots massed largely in
the south and east, an agglomeration of thirty representing St. Paul and Minneapolis.[1] Though only a third of
Iowa's farm land was under the plow and the northwest
corner was yet unsettled, that state would show one
thousand two hundred spots. It was already one of the
chief agricultural units of the nation—the fourth state
in corn production, the fifth in wheat and the sixth in
livestock. Kansas was hard on the heels of Minnesota,
with about three hundred and eighty spots, growing
sparser and sparser toward the west.[2] Western Missouri
shared in the influx of new settlers brought by the railways; thus Jackson County, in which lay Kansas City,
would show twenty-three spots on the screen for 1860,
and fifty-five for 1870.

Despite the war and the bushrangers, Missouri increased her population by eighty-three per cent in the
decade, and emerged from it with more than two million people, the fourth state in the Union—and St.
Louis the fourth city.[3] There were hardly more than
twenty-five thousand people in Nebraska at the beginning of the war, but when the transcontinental line was
finished, there were almost if not quite that many in
Omaha alone. The territory clamored to enter the
Union, and when admitted in 1867, had about eighty

[1] *Am. Ann. Cyclop.*, IX (1869), 447 ff.
[2] W. E. Miller, *The Peopling of Kansas* (Columbus, O., 1906),
passim; *Am. Ann. Cyclop.*, X (1870), 421.
[3] It was proposed shortly after the Civil War to make St. Louis the
federal capital. *Nation*, IX, Sept. 2, 1869.

thousand white inhabitants.[1] So rapidly did it grow
that by the census of 1870 the population exceeded
one hundred and twenty-three thousand. Yet Nebraska
was the laggard state of the Middle West, handicapped
by drought, grasshoppers, Indian wars and the earlier
start of Kansas.

Where did this tide of population get its homes?[2] The
public lands had been thrown wide open to settlers by
three great enactments during the Civil War: the homestead act, the Morrill land-grant act and the act giving the Union Pacific a princely domain. While Grant
was preparing to move upon Vicksburg the earliest
homesteaders had made their entries and after the war
the entries increased rapidly. During the fiscal year 1871-
1872 nearly six thousand homesteads passed into the
possession of settlers; during 1872-1873 more than ten
thousand, and in 1875-1876 no fewer than twenty-two
thousand five hundred and thirty.[3] The public lands
were, for the most part, occupied by families with no
spare cash, who built their sod houses or frame shanties
and toiled like slaves, saving every penny to obtain stock
and machinery. Those settlers who wished to buy land
from private owners found it abundant and cheap. Under the Morrill act each state had received, for the endowment of colleges of agriculture and the mechanic arts,
thirty thousand acres for every member in Congress, with
the result that New York, for example, had nine hundred and ninety thousand acres to sell or rent. And
enormous though the railway land grants of the fifties
had been, they were now far surpassed. All the great

[1] *Am. Ann. Cyclop.*, IX (1869), 473 ff.; A. K. McClure, *Three
Thousand Miles Through the Rocky Mountains* (Phila., 1869), 37 ff.
[2] For an excellent contemporary answer, see L. P. Brockett, *Our Western Empire* (Phila., 1880), chap. iii.
[3] Between 1860 and 1880 almost 470,000 applications for homesteads
were filed. Thomas Donaldson, *The Public Domain* (Wash., 1884), 208.

transcontinental lines—the Union Pacific, the Santa Fé, and the Southern Pacific—received twenty sections a mile on each side within all territories traversed and ten sections within all states, while other railways were given lesser amounts. The last railway land grants were made in 1871, the year in which the outburst of Western hostility to grasping rail corporations resulted in the "Granger legislation" of Illinois. But by this date the whole area thus given away by the government had reached the colossal total of one hundred and twenty-nine million acres, an area three times the size of New England.[1]

Nearly all the grantees were eager to dispose of their land holdings. Thus the Illinois Central, given two and a half million acres by the state, which had received it in turn from the federal government, sold all but a third of a million acres before 1871, at an average price of ten dollars and sixty-one cents an acre. Up to November 1, 1872, the Union Pacific reported land sales of six hundred and fifty thousand acres, at an average of four dollars and seventy-two cents an acre, while it was widely advertising its unsold area of almost eleven million five hundred thousand acres.[2] A skilled mechanic in the cities, discontented with his lot and eager to own his own farm, could earn the equivalent of an acre of land in a day. The Burlington and Missouri River Company began selling its grant in 1870 at from ten to thirty dollars in Iowa, and from one to ten dollars in Nebraska. Its agents were busy scattering circulars and buttonholing purchasers in New York, London, Liverpool and Glasgow as well as in the Western cities. All the railways understood the wisdom of developing an immediate freight business by selling land to farmers rather than to

[1] B. H. Hibbard, *A History of the Public Land Policies* (N. Y., 1924), chap., xiii.

[2] Hibbard, *Public Land Policies*, 254-255; *Commercial and Financial Chronicle*, Dec. 14, 1872.

speculators and were seldom inclined to cling to their acreage for the unearned increment. The average price of the huge volume of railway lands disposed of before 1881 was only four dollars and seventy-six cents an acre.[1] Unfortunately, the land departments of the transportation systems, with glowing promises and advertisements, often induced inexperienced colonists to push into spots remote from neighbors or markets, or to buy poor land. The destitution and semistarvation suffered by farmers along the Republican and Solomon rivers in Kansas early in the seventies was blamed in large part on the Kansas Pacific Railroad. But, on the whole, the lines played an invaluable part in Western farm development.[2]

Nearly all the tillable lands went to small holders— to war veterans, Eastern clerks and artisans, German and Scandinavian immigrants and farmers' sons, all men of limited capital. Some few large farms were acquired by rich men. There was an eight-thousand-acre estate in Bureau County, Illinois. Much more famous was M. L. Sullivant's seventy-thousand-acre farm a short distance to the east in Champaign County, the owner of which employed from one to two hundred laborers and lived as on a manorial estate.[3] In the Northwest large holdings were more common. As southern Minnesota became settled, it contained one farm—the property of the Rock County Company—with fifty thousand acres, and others of from two thousand to seven thousand acres. Near Fargo, in the Dakotas, was the forty-thousand-acre farm of J. L. Grandin, nearly three times the area of Manhattan Island. But such concentrated holdings,

---

[1] Hibbard, *Public Land Policies*, 261.
[2] W. B. Hazen, "The Great Middle Region of the United States," *North American Rev.*, CCXLVI (1875), 1-34.
[3] *Scientific American*, June 30, 1866.

apart from the large ranches of the cattle country, were rare until the failure of Jay Cooke in 1873 threw large tracts of Northern Pacific land into the hands of the security holders, some of whom kept them intact for farming. They required altogether too much capital for operation, and as the lands increased in value the interest charges on the investment became excessive.[1] All the Western states made strenuous efforts to attract immigrants of more limited means. Thus Minnesota in 1868 appropriated ten thousand dollars for the use of an immigration board, printed pamphlets in a half-dozen tongues, inserted advertisements in the Irish press and maintained agents in Milwaukee, Chicago, New York and Germany.[2] Everywhere was heard the strident voice of the booster.

Cities sprang up as if by magic on the central plains, the waving prairie giving way in a half-dozen years to blocks of stone and brick structures and fine residences. Some of these thriving communities were made by the government, most of them by private energy. Lincoln, Nebraska, and Wichita, Kansas, will serve as examples, both of them towns which were nonexistent when Grant's administration began and well-known to every American when it ended. In 1867 legislative commissioners, searching for a capital site for Nebraska, pitched upon the little settlement of Lancaster, consisting of ten crudely built stone and log houses almost a hundred miles distant from the nearest railway. For their initial task the commissioners had to sell enough lots to provide at least fifty thousand dollars for a capitol building, which the law required to be ready in a little more than a year. The first two days' sales at Lincoln, with a meager crowd

[1] W. G. Moody, *Land and Labor in the United States* (N. Y., 1883), 63 ff.

[2] For the increase of foreign-born in the Northwest, see *U. S. Tenth Census* (1880), I, xl.

and many scoffers, were so dismal a failure that the commissioners saw their plans collapsing. In a spasm of energy they mustered all their friends and ready cash and sold thirty-four thousand dollars' worth of lots on the third day. A later auction at Nebraska City netted ten thousand dollars. With this money they found a contractor, imported skilled labor from the East and hauled all the material by teams for from forty to sixty miles. The capitol was finished on time and the next legislature met in it. Thereafter Lincoln grew by a series of rapid leaps.[1]

Wichita took its origin in the prosaic activities of land speculators.[2] The organizers found a natural site formed by the junction of the Arkansas and Little Arkansas, where a cholera-stricken Indian village had stood in the shade of some scraggly cottonwoods. In 1868 plats were made, lots sold, and the few settlers who lived there were reënforced by a steady stream of newcomers. Early in 1871 it became the center of the Texas cattle trade, rivaling Abilene as a market for steers, and by 1874 it was shipping about seventy thousand cattle a year. When the cattle trade decayed, fortunately the surrounding country filled with wheat growers, and Wichita was soon able to boast itself the greatest inland wheat market in the world. The town took on more sobriety and prosperity; a thousand-foot bridge was thrown across the Arkansas; public institutions of various kinds were founded; and in 1872 Colonel M. M. Murdock established the *Wichita Eagle,* which chanted the bright destinies of the city.[3]

When the Panic year began, the frontier had crept up

---

[1] See *Lincoln Illustrated* (1887); J. S. Morton, Albert Watkins and others, eds., *Illustrated History of Nebraska* (Lincoln, Neb., 1905-1906).

[2] Wichita Daughters of the Revolution, *Early Wichita* (Wichita, 1914), *passim.*

[3] Victor Murdock, *Folks* (N. Y., 1891), 68-69.

to central Minnesota and the semiarid region of central Nebraska and western Kansas.[1]   This filling up of the plains meant an increase in wheat production which was very shortly to upset the markets of the world.   Even more remarkable than the swift settlement of the prairies was the rapidity with which the people succeeded in re-establishing the essentials of the civilization they had left behind them.   They demanded churches, schools, newspapers, smart clothing and the newest novels. "They want to hear Froude lecture," said the *Nation*, "would like a chance of listening to Lucca, and wonder what the Emperor of Austria will think of the Illinois schoolhouse at the Vienna exhibition." [2]   The little sun-baked, blizzard-chilled hamlet that was talking of Indian raids one day might be talking of the *Atlantic Monthly*, the suffragist lecturer and Paris fashions the next.   University towers began to catch the bright ray of the future.   By 1873 the University of Minnesota had two hundred and seventy-eight students, the agricultural college in Iowa had graduated two classes, and several scores of young men were studying in the halls which Nebraska had hastened to erect at Lincoln.

[1] *Am. Ann. Cyclop.*, XIV (1874), 586; XV (1875), 412.
[2] *Nation*, XVII, July 31, 1873.

CHAPTER V

THE WEST AT WORK

(1 8 6 5 - 1 8 7 3)

STOCK breeding and agriculture were the two chief concerns of the settlers in the region between the Mississippi and the Rockies. The rise of the cattle range, one of the most romantic chapters of American history, occurred simultaneously with the building of the transcontinental lines, the birth of cities like Wichita and Cheyenne, the destruction of the buffalo, and the suppression of the hostile Indians. The whole wide expanse where the bison had ranged became, save where the homesteader invaded it, a great cattle region. It was admirably adapted to the purpose. The dry winter climate of the Northern plains permitted the snow to be blown off the hillsides to expose the dead grass, the coulees and ravines gave shelter during the blizzards, and the bunch grass covering most of the country offered nutritious pasturage. Shrewd Texas cattlemen perceived, as soon as the plains were opened up by the railwaymen and infantry, that the northern ranges were superior to their own;[1] and furthermore the war had left them heavily overstocked with cattle.[2]

Hence there sprang up a great annual northward drive of cattle, following well-beaten trails to the feeding grounds along the railways and to sections farther north.[3]

[1] *American Annual Cyclopedia* (N. Y., 1861-1903), VI (1866), 442.
[2] F. L. Paxson, "The Cow Country," *Am. Hist. Rev.*, XXII, 65-86.
[3] Emerson Hough, *The Story of the Cowboy* (N. Y., 1897), 30 ff.

As early as 1856 large Texas herds had been driven through Missouri to St. Louis to find a northern market. When nine years later the railway system reached Kansas City, the drive was made shorter still. But the first decisive step toward developing the upper range country came with the opening of a great cattle market and shipping point at Abilene, Kansas.

The news that an outlet had been established there spread as by electricity through the Southwest. The first year, 1867, some thirty-five thousand cattle were driven into Abilene and thence shipped east over the new Kansas Pacific, which had been persuaded to make favorable rates and furnish yards.[1] Thereafter, as the rival railways pushed west, new markets, or "cow-towns" were established from point to point—Newton, Wichita and, later, the picturesquely vicious Dodge City, on the Santa Fé; Ellsworth, on the Kansas Pacific; and Baxter Springs, on the Fort Worth and Gulf. Of course some Texas cattle were sent to market from the coast, while others were driven to points on the Red River, whence they could be dispatched north by steamer and rail. But the great majority were driven, in numerous independent herds ranging in number from a few hundred to ten thousand each, into Kansas, Nebraska and Colorado.[2]

So profitable was the business that by 1870 the livestock industry showed an activity never before witnessed in Texas. Men scoured the country, contracting for herds of longhorns to be delivered in time for the next spring drive, buying horses and hiring cowboys, while numerous companies were formed to obtain capital for

[1] J. G. McCoy, *Historic Sketches of the Cattle Trade of the West and Southwest* (Kansas City, 1874).

[2] R. A. Clemen, *The American Livestock and Meat Industry* (N. Y., 1923), 192 ff.

investment.[1] During the early seventies the northern
herds grew rapidly. The possibilities of gaining wealth
were so tempting that adventurous men came flocking
from the East and Southwest. Young cattle could be
bought cheap, driven to the plains at very little expense,
matured on "free air," as free grass and water were
called, and sold in favorable seasons for four or five times
the original cost. The stream of Texas cattle driven
northward increased as steadily as did the herds bred
and fattened on the upper plains. In the year 1871
more than six hundred thousand cattle crossed the Red
River for the northern markets that were opening up all
along the transcontinental lines. In the decade 1869-
1879, the golden age of the cattle drive, not fewer than
four million beeves were driven up, an annual current
that slackened only in the years 1874-1875 when the
financial panic checked it.[2]

The main paths of this drive naturally shifted to the
west. At the outset they led through the eastern part
of the Indian Territory (colloquially called the "Nations") to southwestern Missouri, while a little later the
Chisholm Trail from Texas to Wichita was the most
famous. Some years afterward, under the constant pressure of the railways and farms, a new channel for the
drive was established up the Pecos River Valley of New
Mexico into Colorado. There arose at one time a demand for congressional protection of a fixed right of
way from south to north, but this was impracticable.[3]
The drive was always an adventure, sometimes a very

[1] J. S. Gould, "Texas Cattle Disease," *Journ. of Social Sci.*, I, 56-71;
J. M. Hunter, ed., *The Trail Drivers of Texas* (2 edn., rev., Nashville,
Tenn., 1925), I, 20 ff.
[2] Hough, *Story of the Cowboy*, 6 ff.; Clemen, *American Livestock and
Meat Industry*, 177 ff.
[3] H. H. Bancroft, *Pacific States of North America* (San Fran., 1882-
1890), XXVI, 720 ff.

dangerous one. From southern Texas the start would be made about the first of March, the riders or "brush-poppers" usually gathering together cattle of many brands, for which they gave a very loose accounting. Later on a system of state inspection of trail herds at different points before the Texas boundary was crossed made the division of proceeds more careful. The men toiled incessantly, sometimes going for several days with scarcely a wink of sleep when wind and rain made the cattle uncontrollable. They had to fight roving Indian bands, ford great rivers like the Red and Arkansas at flood, check night stampedes that meant many a fall and broken limb, and encounter desperadoes and rustlers.[1]

Let us look at a typical ranch of the southern range —a ranch which centered about a roughly built log house of generous size, set in some sheltered nook with shade and abundant water.[2] This house contained a single large room lined with bunks; its furniture was a table or two and a few stools or broken chairs; and the men's clothing hung on wall pegs or was stuffed under the bunks. The rough domicile was unfinished and open to the weather at a hundred cracks, but comfortable in its rude masculine way. An open front passage infested by the numerous dogs used for wolfing led to the cookhouse, where the men ate hurriedly at a long pine table, seated on two or three wooden benches. Branding pens stood near, stables for the horses and a woodpile. The grub wagon, with the cook busy about it, might be seen making ready for a trip. Sometimes the ranch bore the owner's name—the Keith or Martin Ranch; sometimes the name of his brand—the Diamond

---

[1] J. H. Cook, *Fifty Years on the Old Frontier* (New Haven, 1923), 106, gives a vivid first-hand description of a cattle stampede during a thunderstorm at night.

[2] P. A. Rollins, *The Cowboy . . . His Part in the Development of the West* (N. Y., 1922).

Ranch or Bar-4 Ranch. At such a ranch house the stranger, whether hunter, traveler or fleeing horse thief, received unquestioning hospitality. Sometimes the ranch, especially in long-settled parts of lower Texas, would be more elaborately equipped.[1] In addition to the cowboys' bunk house, there would be a frame dwelling for the owner—a long, low, one-story structure with large airy rooms, a wide hall to keep it cool, and comfortable furniture. Farther to the southwest, in the vast region between the Pecos and Rio Grande where the Spanish civilization of Mexico had left an enduring imprint, the Mexican or American ranchero would have an adobe dwelling with walls three or four feet thick.

The central buildings of a Northern ranch were even more varied in character.[2] The house might be a mud dugout or a log shack of timbers planted upright in the ground. It might be a sod house on the semi-arid plains, where the unresting summer wind seared the skin with its alkaline touch. More frequently it was a commodious, well-built structure of hewn oak or cottonwood, far more nearly wind-proof than the ranch houses of the South. For the bitter winter weather there would be both a huge fireplace and a big "cannon" stove, stoked red-hot. Here, too, bunks would line the walls, but buffalo robes as well as blankets would be everywhere in evidence, while the floor would be overlaid with furs and skins.[3] Only Easterners, like Roosevelt on the Elkhorn Ranch, would insist upon a separate bedroom and an easy chair.

North or south, a ranch might cover a million acres, of which the ranchman perhaps held legal title to a sin-

---

[1] James McIntyre, *Early Days in Texas* (Kansas City, 1902), 45 ff.; Mary J. Jaques, *Texan Ranch Life* (London, 1894).

[2] Theodore Roosevelt, *Hunting Trips of a Ranchman* (Sagamore edn., N. Y., 1886), chap. i.

[3] Hough, *Story of the Cowboy*, chap. iii.

gle quarter section. To maintain the ownership of his huge herds he relied primarily upon branding and secondarily upon "out-riding" by his employees. Daily the cowboys went out to "ride sign" around the territory recognized as their special range and to turn back any cattle that seemed to be wandering from it. Every spring, after the grass had grown lush and the calves were large enough, there was a round-up for branding which might last for weeks.[1] Naturally, upon a range that was common property for many ranchers, this was a coöperative enterprise. By a general agreement—for as the industry developed, the state or territorial cattle associations divided the range into round-up districts— a group of cowboys selected from the various ranches met under a captain who ruled the work like a czar. The cattle, perhaps two or three thousand in all, were driven together in a tumultuous mass in some valley or corral, the cows bellowing, the calves bawling and the horses whinnying amid a thick cloud of dust. When a little order had been restored and the mothers had found their calves, the work of cutting the calves out, dragging them to the fire, and marking them with the brand and perhaps the knife began.[2]

The cowboys had a remarkable homogeneity, as if the West had put the same stamp upon them all. Those of Texas possessed the reputation of being the most fearless riders, the keenest masters of the ways of half-wild cattle and the best users of the rope; but they were inclined to drunken, boisterous conduct.[3] The northern cowboys seldom developed equal skill and dash, but were more trustworthy. All were hardy, muscular, self-

[1] Hough, *Story of the Cowboy*, chap. ix.
[2] Clark Stanley, *Life and Adventures of the American Cowboy* (Providence, n. d.), 82 ff.
[3] Roosevelt, *Hunting Trips of a Ranchman*, 19.

reliant, daring to the point of recklessness, and though sometimes noisy and truculent in groups, as when amusing themselves in a rough frontier town, were rather taciturn and self-contained with strangers. Their ranch life developed a fairly standardized garb, varied by certain sectional differences. The high-pommeled saddles, weighing from thirty-five to fifty pounds, half covered the ordinary cow pony. The big-brimmed hats were required as a shield from the scorching sun, the wind-blown sand and the mud thrown by flying hoofs. The big handkerchief about the neck was also a needed protection and not an affectation, while the buckskin clothes withstood the wear and tear of the saddle better than cloth and turned the thorns of cactus and mesquite. The cowboy was a picturesque and apparently eccentric figure, yet his chief peculiarities of dress and aspect were simply a product of his environment.[1]

If the cowboy had his rough traits, it was because he had to have them; for the social life of the Western range was pitched to a key of conflict.[2] There was conflict between the rival cattle barons, particularly in the lawless Southwest; conflict between the cattlemen and sheep herders, whose flocks destroyed the range grass and tainted the water; conflict between honest ranchers and the "rustlers;" conflict with the Indians; and conflict, finally, with the irresistible current of homesteaders or "nesters," whose barbed-wire fences [3] turned back the roving cattle and whose irrigation ditches robbed the ranches of water. The face of the West changed from year to year, and every element in that change produced

[1] Cook, *Fifty Years on the Old Frontier*, 112 ff.; Rollins, *The Cowboy*, chap. vi.

[2] Rollins, *The Cowboy*, 55.

[3] Competition among manufacturers reduced barbed-wire prices by 1874 to twenty cents a pound. H. U. Faulkner, *American Economic History* (N. Y., 1924), 409.

friction. Desperadoes sometimes gathered in gangs in sparsely settled regions and with a dozen rifles swept before them every herd of cattle not safely corralled. Many a rancher saw his whole property driven away before his eyes and, if he resisted, was shot dead. Sometimes the range witnessed a dramatic feud waged for years, like the famous "Lincoln County War" of the seventies in the Pecos Valley of New Mexico—a contest between two violent factions, one led by a powerful rancher named John Chisholm, and the other by a great supply firm called Murphy and Dolan, which embroiled a third of the territory and required the use of federal troops under General Sherman to restore order.[1] It was in the course of this affair that there sprang into prominence the notorious man-killer "Billy the Kid" (William Bonney), a desperate youth who perpetrated sickening outrages—his gang once killed seven inoffensive Mexicans "to see them kick"—before an officer of the law hunted him from lair to lair and finally shot him dead.[2] Raw towns of the "cow country," like Newton, Kansas, and later Dodge City, were haunts of shameless vice; saloons, gambling dens and dance halls sheltered a dissolute and desperate set of men who preyed on the cowboys as they came in from the ranches.[3] The term "stiff"

[1] See President Hayes's proclamation, J. D. Richardson, ed., *Messages and Papers of the Presidents* (Wash., 1896-1899), VIII, 489.
[2] F. R. Bechdolt, *Tales of the Oldtimers* (N. Y., 1924), 61 ff.; C. A. Siringo, *A Texas Cowboy* (Chicago, 1885), chap. xxvii.
[3] See R. M. Wright, *Dodge City, the Cowboy Capital* (Wichita, 1913), chap. viii, for a vivid picture of a border town where twenty-five men were killed the first year. Railway corporations and other interests which needed gunmen used to recruit them in Dodge City. Wild cowboys, buffalo hunters, "bullwhackers" and "mule-skinners" (freighters) made the town a hotbed of violence till the decent element chose a city marshal ready to use his buffalo rifle with effect. See G. D. Bradley, *The Story of the Santa Fé* (Boston, 1920), for the towns filled with saloons, brothels and gambling dens. Notorious outlaws became so well-known by nicknames that their real appellations were forgotten—Scarface Ike, Bullwhack Jones, Coach Joe. For the wickedness

for a corpse is said to have been invented in Dodge City, and its main cemetery was significantly called "Boot Hill." But with comparative rapidity vigilance committees and law officers brought in the regime of law and order.

The ranchmen and cowboys were essentially transitory occupants of the plains. They utilized its wealth in pasturage while it was waiting for the farmers who should put it to more profitable employment. It was evident to everyone that a more intensive use of the soil was desirable, yet the ranchers yielded only after a bitter struggle. Homesteaders in the semiarid regions naturally sought to preëmpt sufficient water for irrigation, and frequently they would construct irrigation ditches serving a whole tier of farms. Little by little the tillers of the soil seriously interfered in many sections with old-style ranching.[1] The enraged stockmen used threats, tore down the farmers' fences and occasionally killed stubborn men; but the homesteader had the government behind him, and his enclosures steadily crept snakelike around the watercourses while his irrigation ditches dried up the running streams. Sections like that north of Great Bend in Kansas were settled by farmers who, when they obtained a land claim, would simply plow a furrow about it; and since the state law declared this a fence, heavy damages were invariably claimed against drovers whose cattle crossed it. Western and central Nebraska became dotted over with farming communities which the ranchers had to avoid. "Free air" steadily contracted and the open tracts that were left became more and more congested, though in many parts the old-style ranching managed to survive into the eighties.

of Newton, Kansas, see T. A. McNeal, *When Kansas Was Young* (N. Y., 1922), 37.

[1] F. W. Rolt-Wheeler, *The Book of Cowboys* (Boston, 1921), 364; J. M. Hunter, ed., *The Trail Drivers of Texas*, II, 25.

One of the services which the range performed for American life can never be forgotten: it created a unique, picturesque and extraordinarily hardy type of manhood in the cowboy, and furnished a spectacle of free and fearless activity with horse, rifle and lariat that had a powerful influence upon the national character. From the boodling, extravagance and financial recklessness seen in Eastern cities we can turn to no more refreshing contrast than the wild West that Owen Wister and Frederic Remington have celebrated. It had its faults, but even these were often healthily different from the corruptions wrought by ease and wealth. Here American virility appeared as nowhere else since the battlefields of the Civil War. "We felt," the greatest of cowboys has said, "the best of hardy life in our veins, and ours was the glory of work and the joy of living." [1] In time the range country developed a lore and a balladry all its own. The cowboy songs, composed around the camp fire or in the ranch house, recalling the daily routine or the thrilling events of the cow country, or trolled in minor key to soothe the steers on the march, were a distinct addition to the folk literature of the American people; and they help keep alive the flavor and spirit of an heroic interlude that is almost as dead as Atlantis. [2]

If farming and ranching were the chief interests of the region lying east of the Rockies, mining may be regarded as the great magnet that drew settlers into the farther West. The main foundation of the mountain and Pacific states had been laid by a series of mining rushes, of which the California gold rush in 1849, the Comstock Lode rush during 1858-1859 in what became Nevada, and the Montana gold rush just after the war were typi-

[1] Theodore Roosevelt, *An Autobiography* (N. Y., 1914), 95.
[2] J. A. Lomax, *Cowboy Songs* (N. Y., 1910).

cal. As the successive mining fevers died away, the immigrants would perceive the rich farming or stockraising opportunities about them. But the distance of the Far West from the main centers of population and the inadequacy of its transportation facilities retarded agricultural development prior to 1873. Outside of California, Oregon and Utah the Far West was exploited only for minerals, with the prospector always in the van. This meant that it had a jerky, wasteful and, in striking degree, an evanescent development, without much direct profit to the territories involved. The hectic gold or silver rush commonly resulted in drawing an excited mass of men to a single barren spot, where a rough and vicious town rose like magic, where money was spent like water in digging shafts and installing machinery, where get-rich-quick companies flourished and whence for a time a stream of bullion flowed to the world outside. The precious metal did very little for Nevada or Montana or Idaho; almost none of it stayed in the district where it was produced.

Colorado's history just after the war illustrated the frequent barrenness and unsatisfactoriness of the mining craze as an impetus to permanent growth. Busy gold and silver camps had sprung up just before and during the war at Oro City (now Leadville), at Boulder, along Clear Creek near Denver and along the Arkansas beyond Pueblo. Denver, which became the territorial capital and thrived on the freighting trade to the mines, was a town of five thousand people when the conflict ended and five years later, when it was doing an annual business of ten millions, had eight thousand inhabitants.[1] The hotels handed their guests bills of fare which read precisely like those of New York, and the fine drives were remarkable-

[1] *Am. Ann. Cyclop.*, V (1870), 710 ff.; A. D. Richardson, *Beyond the Mississippi* (Hartford, 1867).

A cattle shoot at Abilene, Kansas.

Gold and silver mines in a Colorado mountainside.

Work in the Far West, 1865-1878.

for their flashing equipages.[1] But the territory was slow
in finding its feet; the federal census of 1870 showed less
than forty thousand residents, a growth of only about
five thousand in ten years. Part of the blame could be
placed upon the disastrous Indian wars and part upon
the grasshoppers which for several years ravaged the
crops near Denver. The chief reason, however, was that
as fast as new mining camps were established the old
ones declined. Moreover, Colorado was not a region in
which the miner with no capital could prosper; the richest deposits lay in quartz lodes, requiring heavy machinery and a large financial outlay to reach and reduce.
Speculation became a rage and swindling promoters
found that there was more profit in organizing big corporations at fancy stock prices than in legitimate mining.
In a single day's ride from Denver to Idaho City in 1867
Colonel A. K. McClure saw idle mills, machinery and
shafts representing twenty millions in capital, and he
found the mining districts filled with an array of ill-con-
ceived, badly managed, unsuccessful undertakings.[2]

But it was Nevada which best exhibited the mining
boom in its spasmodic phases. Here in 1865 the new
golcondas were the wonder of the world. Five years
earlier the region had been a desert; but the discoveries
at Virginia City, Austin and in the White Pine district,
assisted by Lincoln's need for political support in Congress, had brought it into the Union in 1864 as a full-
fledged state. Nowhere in the West were the social conditions and results of the rush for wealth better exhibited
than in these three centers, the first of which will forever
be remembered as the site of the Comstock Lode, one of

[1] A. K. McClure found it a more orderly city than Omaha. A. K.
McClure, *Three Thousand Miles through the Rocky Mountains* (Phila.,
1869), 82. See also J. C. Smiley, *History of Denver* (Denver, 1903),
chap. xlii.
[2] McClure, *Three Thousand Miles*, 91 ff.

the globe's richest mines. They made Nevada, but they did not make it a populous, stable, steadily-growing community.[1]

Virginia City affords perhaps the best illustration of the indomitable energy with which the miners flung themselves against the difficulties in the path of their operations. In the winter of 1866 the towns and mills along the Comstock Lode were using two hundred thousand cords of wood for fuel, while the time soon came when eighty million feet of lumber a year went down into the chambers and drifts. Since the mountains about were naked rock, flumes had to be built from the forested slopes of the Sierras, and by 1880 there were ten of them with an aggregate length of eighty miles. The town's water supply presented an ever increasing problem, until in 1873 a gigantic siphon was completed from the high Sierras at a cost of two millions.[2] The Gould & Curry, the largest mine, had by 1865 invested almost a million dollars in its stamp mill alone, and when it exhausted its first vein, it boldly sunk a new tunnel and shaft a thousand feet into the mountain to find another. Most stupendous of all was the great undertaking known as the Sutro Tunnel, the conception of Adolph Sutro, who owned a quartz mill on the Carlson River. He saw the practicability of constructing a three-mile tunnel into the mountain side to intersect the Comstock Lode at a depth of one thousand six hundred feet, draining all the mines to that level, and affording an economical means of carrying the ores to the river, where cheap water power and abundant fuel were available. In 1866 he obtained contracts from twenty-three of the principal mining companies on the

---

[1] Bancroft, *Pacific States*, XXV, chaps. v-vi.
[2] C. H. Shinn, *Story of the Mine as Illustrated by the Great Comstock Lode of Nevada* (N. Y., 1896), 101-103, 118 ff.

lode, binding them to use the tunnel and pay for its services; and after incessant effort, in which any man of less
marvelous pluck and energy would have failed, he raised
sufficient capital to begin the project.   In 1869 he broke
ground for the tunnel and set a corps of drillers upon
the task that was to occupy them for eight weary years.
It was the labor of a giant.[1]

The nation gazed upon Virginia City after the war
as one of its chief marvels.[2]   In the twenty-one years
between 1859 and 1880 the various Comstock companies extracted a mass of bullion valued at three hundred and six million dollars.   The Belcher mine alone
produced a gross yield of twenty-six millions and the
Crown Point of twenty-two million dollars.   During
the eight flush years after the war the average annual
production exceeded twelve million dollars.   These
were days when elated stockholders walked the streets
of Virginia City as if pacing the roof of an inexhaustible
treasure house.   A superintendent of one mine filled his
water-tank with champagne for his guests at a wedding;
another mining magnate fitted his entire house with
door handles of solid silver; and mansions luxurious
enough for an Oriental monarch studded the raw Nevada hillsides.[3]

California, not Nevada, reaped the richest profit of this
vast output of wealth.   Most of the original capital invested was Californian, most of the managers came from
California and the seat of control for most of the companies was San Francisco, the natural center for trade in

[1] Adolph Sutro, *The Mineral Resources of the United States*. . . .
with Special Reference to the Comstock Lode and the Sutro Tunnel
(Balt., 1868), describes the project.   See also Bancroft, *Pacific States*,
XX, 141 ff.

[2] See Mary McV. Mathews, *Ten Years in Nevada* (Buffalo, 1880), for
a picture of life in Virginia City.

[3] Shinn, *Story of the Mine, passim.*

their stocks.[1] Not a single promising city, no counter-
part of Denver or Sacramento, was created in Nevada
by the whole wealth of the Comstock, whose flush paled
in the western sky like a brief sunset. When the seventies
ended, the magical history of the lode was almost over.
The stock of its mines, which had been valued in 1875
at more than three hundred and ninety-three million
dollars, had sunk in the spring of 1880 to less than seven
millions. No approach was ever again made to the discoveries of early days, and the population slowly ebbed
away. Nor did the other mining camps in Nevada, such
as the gold fields at Austin and the strange community
in the White Pine region, where a city of twenty thousand leaped into brief existence on the harshest of mountain sides, accomplish anything more for the state.[2]

The regions which are now Idaho and Montana fared
better because agriculture could gain a firmer footing and
ranching became profitable soon after the first flare of
excitement over gold and silver had died down. Between 1860 and 1866 a series of discoveries brought
into Idaho a motley population of thirty thousand, the
majority of them poor fortune hunters.[3] Montana received a still greater impetus, its population rising to
forty thousand just after the war.[4] But the flush times
in both territories quickly ended with the exhaustion of
the placer deposits. A disillusioned resident remarked
that Montana's mining camps consisted of ophir holes,

---

[1] Bancroft, *Pacific States*, XX, chap. x.
[2] For the Austin camp, see Samuel Bowles, *Across the Continent*
(Springfield, Mass., 1866), 141 ff.; for White Pine, W. F. Rae, *Westward by Rail* (London, 1870), 203 ff.; anon., "Up in the Po-Go-Nip,"
Overland Monthly, II (1869), 273-280; *Am. Ann. Cyclop.*, VIII
(1868), 534 ff.
[3] F. L. Paxson, *History of the American Frontier* (Boston, 1924),
451 ff.
[4] Bancroft, *Pacific States*, XXVI, chap. vi.

gopher holes and loafer holes. The census of 1870 revealed something very like the collapse of a boom. Virginia City had only eight hundred and sixty-seven people, and Helena, which had recently been described as
possessing more solid men and more gamblers, more fast
boys and frail women, than any other mountain town,
had only 3,713.[1] The whole white population of Montana was little more than twenty thousand, and that of
Idaho not quite fifteen thousand. With the pricking
of the bubble, however, truer and broader sources of
wealth were found. Many turned from mining to settle upon land claims, investing their gold in livestock
and implements. The irrigable valley lands in particular produced lavishly, while the bunch grass, which
was green until August and then dried into excellent
hay, made it an admirable region for ranching. The
baser minerals began to receive attention and yielded
encouraging results.

The surest road to wealth in the mountain region was
demonstrated by men like William A. Clark of Montana, whose rise from teamster and itinerant peddler to
multimillionaire and senator contains so much that is
characteristic of his time. An ill-educated youth of
Pennsylvania birth, Clark became discouraged after two
years of placer mining and turned in 1865 to the mercantile business, bringing supplies from Salt Lake City
to the Montana settlements. He was soon doing a wholesale trade in groceries and frequently doubled his investment on every commodity sold. One opportunity followed another. He obtained federal contracts for carrying the mails, opened a bank in Helena, and steadily increased the number of his small stores. Then early in
the seventies he purchased important properties in the

---

[1] See Bancroft, *Pacific States*, XXVI, 638 ff., for frontier disorders
and justice.

placer-mining districts at Butte, where gold and silver were being obtained in large quantities. There was copper mixed with the silver ore, and Clark, building the first copper smelter in the region, found his road to fortune clear before him, though it was not till 1881 that the great Anaconda mine was opened at the town of that name.[1] Clark's career could easily be paralleled by many others.

These jerry-built, evanescent mining towns, filled with a reckless, excitement-loving population, were hot-beds of vice. Not even the levee district of St. Louis could show scenes of debauchery comparing with those of Virginia City, Nevada, at its fastest. Here was the community in which the traveler found a living counter-part of Bret Harte's Roaring Camp and Poker Flat— where French Pete and Kanaka Joe shot each other dead, where Oakhurst the gambler fleeced rough miners like Kentuck, and where women like Mother Shipton and the Duchess plied their trade. Saloons flourished in rows and at one time a majority of the men seemed to be gamblers. As late as 1876 there were sixteen faro games, all at the rear of leading saloons.[2] The mining camps of Colorado, Montana and Idaho were similarly lurid centers.

The combination of mountain solitudes and valuable freighter lines inevitably produced sets of "road-agents" or highwaymen, and some of these became famous. Perhaps the best known was the gang of Henry Plummer of Bannack, a "gentleman," legislator, robber and murderer, whose followers wore their neckties in a sailor knot, shaved their beards down to goatees and cast off one member for being a drunkard. The

[1] G. F. Redmond, *Financial Giants of America* (Boston, 1922), II, 179 ff.
[2] *N. Y. World*, June 19, 1876.

only certain remedy, when these desperadoes became intolerable, was to organize vigilance societies, which sometimes overspread a whole territory and relentlessly hunted down their marked men.[1] Yet as the plains produced the cowboy, the mountain states produced their own heroic figure in the prospector. These sturdy adventurers roamed the ranges of the Far West, braving privation and danger in the dream of some rich pocket or lode. They spied out the land, they blazed trails and discovered passes, and their indomitable labors carried the seeds of thriving communities far into the mountains.

When we turn to the other commonwealths of the Far West, we meet with agricultural rather than mining communities. Even California learned during the seventies that the riches locked in her mountains were as nothing beside those obtainable from her fertile plains and valleys. Lincoln had called Utah "the treasure-house of the nation," yet after the war Utah was known preeminently as a farming population.[2] Indeed, Utah gave the West by far the best example of the farsighted development of a new land. This was due principally to the fact that the people had to be self-sufficing and to the fortunate circumstance that their destinies were guided by a real statesman, Brigham Young. Theirs was essentially a Mormon state, peopled and ruled by members of that faith; of the one hundred and twenty thousand people estimated to be living there in 1866, only a handful were "Gentiles." Salt Lake City was the metropolis, though it contained fewer than twenty thousand of the well-diffused population. Here travelers

---

[1] McClure, *Three Thousand Miles*, 229 ff. For the most famous of the rough-and-ready officers of the law on the Western frontier, see Frank J. Wilstach, *Wild Bill Hickok, The Prince of Pistoleers* (Garden City, 1924).

[2] L. E. Young, *The Founding of Utah* (N. Y., 1923), chap. xiv.

found, in a matchless physical setting between lake and mountains, the largest city between St. Louis and San Francisco. In addition to the overland telegraph it had stage lines plying in every direction. Indians and Mexicans jostled with prospectors laying in supplies and with eager converts fresh from Europe. With its wide and symmetrical streets, its flashing streamlets running down the gutters, its fine public buildings, its shade trees and bright gardens, the capital was one of the most attractive cities to be found anywhere in the nation.[1]

This self-contained theocracy had an efficient and highly centralized economic system. All the great business enterprises of Utah were in Brigham Young's hands.[2] He kept a close control of the medium of exchange, confining most transactions among his people to a virtual system of barter. The payments he made for the innumerable services rendered him or the church were calculated in dollars, but actually granted in orders on the tithing office, where all the necessities of life, from firewood to potatoes, were to be had. Mechanics and farmers found it easy to obtain every comfort, but very difficult to accumulate funds for a rainy day, or for emigration. As long as the community grew food and made simple wares for its own use alone this system served well; but with the springing up of mining camps all over the Rockies, where the Mormons sold their products, it began to weaken. When the transcontinental railway arrived its doom was clear. Gentile shopkeepers and middlemen crowded into Salt Lake City, and as a desperate measure to prevent trade with them, Brigham Young incorporated in 1869 the Zion Coöperative Mercantile Institution, to which almost all the retailers in

[1] A. D. Richardson, *Beyond the Mississippi*, 338 ff.
[2] Bowles, *Across the Continent*, 98 ff.; Justin McCarthy, "Brigham Young," *Galaxy*, IX (1870), 178-187; Mrs. T. B. H. Stenhouse, *The Rocky Mountain Saints* (London, 1882).

the territory were forced to sell out. But such steps were futile.[1]

The Mormon state presented its most attractive side in the attention it paid to cultural institutions. The three hundred and eighty thousand settlers who dwelt in Kansas in 1870 could boast no prouder list of educational and artistic undertakings than the population, only one third as great, of Utah. Elementary schools flourished under wise territorial laws and town patronage. Congress had appropriated five thousand dollars for a library which was duly sent out from New York; a university, fifteen years old in 1865, had gained some vigor. No architectural achievement of the time beyond the Mississippi equaled the Tabernacle, erected between 1864 and 1868—a huge structure in the shape of an oval, two hundred and fifty feet long and seventy feet high, the interior presenting one of the largest unsupported arches in the world.[2] Yet there were two markedly depressing factors at work in this strange Mormon society—the tyrannical centralization of Brigham Young's administrative system, which had a paralyzing influence, and the institution of polygamy. Young's will was law, and it was impossible to obtain needed reforms for which he lacked sympathy. Social conditions favored an absolute rule, a large proportion of the community being poor, ignorant and industrious foreigners. But the absolutism was carried too far. A citizen who incurred the enmity of his Mormon rulers had no choice but to flee Utah, for once he was excommunicated, Mormons were forbidden to associate with him or to succor him. As between Mormon and Gentile, the administration of justice was utterly lacking in

[1] M. R. Werner, *Brigham Young* (N. Y., 1925), 437; W. F. Rae, *Westward by Rail*, 110 ff.

[2] Young, *Founding of Utah*, 435 ff. Pages 295-372 deal in detail with cultural institutions.

fairness. Worst of all for the territory, individual initiative was sorely hampered by the rulers.[1]

As for polygamy, it was both a divisive and a deteriorating influence. Two thirds of the Mormons, the "Orthodox Saints," were devoted to Brigham Young and his elders and accepted it; one third, the "Hickory Mormons" or Liberals, opposed it.[2] "Will Brigham Young fight?" asked Schuyler Colfax of Elder Stenhouse in 1869. "For God's sake," answered the elder, "keep the United States off. If the government interferes and sends troops, you will drive the thousands back into the arms of Brigham Young who are ready to rebel against his one-man power." Even those women who lived in plural marriage very generally detested the practice; one journalist was told by a Mormon wife that she would rather see her daughter dead than married to a polygamist. Only religious fanaticism and self-abnegation of the rarest kind enabled many women to endure the practice, and then with open lamentation.[3] The most prominent among its evil effects were the degradation of women, the brutalization of men and the ruin of all the finer side of family life. Jealousy and discord filled many households to such a degree that the wives lived completely separate existences. But not all of its consequences lay upon the surface. Its opponents asserted that its economic effects were bad, for it made the number of women and small children, all nonproducers, excessively large. Certainly few men were able to support many wives well, and polygamy offered numerous instances of large families

[1] Werner, *Brigham Young*, 418 ff. Woodbridge Riley, *The Founder of Mormonism* (N. Y., 1902), is a psychological portrait of Young.

[2] J. H. Beadle, "Social Experiments in Utah," *Pop. Sci. Mo.* IX (1886), 479-490.

[3] Bowles, *Across the Continent*, 114; Mrs. T. B. H. Stenhouse, *An Englishwoman Among the Mormons* (London, 1880).

living in extreme poverty. The statement of Mormons that their church-state had no vice—Salt Lake City long permitted but two drinking saloons—was vigorously contradicted.[1]

The advent of the railway brought Utah face to face with an entirely new set of conditions, social, political and economic. The *New York Herald* remarked that "railroad communications corrupt good Mormons," and the thin stream of Gentiles seeking employment steadily altered the character of the territory.[2] The Union Pacific altered also Utah's economic status. Before its completion the whole territorial trade, imports and exports, had seldom exceeded twelve thousand tons a year; now it quickly rose to eighty thousand tons in 1871, and to an average of one hundred and twenty-five thousand a few years later. Had it not been for the exorbitant freight rates charged by the railroad, Utah would have produced a much larger surplus of farm crops and fruit for shipment. But even without this, the filling up of the territory, the needs of the railway workers and the market offered by the mining towns introduced new commercial methods and ways of life. The age of barter was ended. Meanwhile, a marked stiffening of the attitude of the federal government toward the little theocracy became evident. One federal governor after another made it plain that Brigham Young was no longer the ruler of the region. The Nauvoo Legion, or Mormon militia, was disbanded under federal pressure. Finally, in 1871, a prominent elder was convicted of adultery, on the complaint of his first wife, and given a heavy sentence; the mayor of Salt Lake City was held in bail on a charge of murder; and Brigham Young himself

[1] G. A. Sala, *America Revisited* (London, 1883), II, 289 ff.; McClure, *Three Thousand Miles*, 439.
[2] *Am. Ann. Cyclop.*, X (1870), 710 ff.

lost a suit brought by a woman who charged that he had failed to account for certain trust moneys. These were all tokens of a new day.[1]

Picturesque as Utah was, California presented a civilization far more varied, active and full of historical and racial color. Here the conquest of 1846-1847 and the gold rush of 1849 had superimposed an American culture upon the old Spanish culture of Mexican days. With a population approaching a half million, already in 1865 California was one of the great states of the Union. The casual visitor was surprised to find towns and cities full armed in the paraphernalia of civilization, wanton with the luxuries of the East, rich in social amenities, supplied with colleges and libraries, and even affecting high art. The state was a most striking example of the rapidity and completeness with which Americans could colonize a new land, organize its society and provide themselves with comforts and superfluities.[2]

The Western slope had yet but one metropolis and did not dream of the day when Los Angeles would rival San Francisco. With one hundred and fifty thousand residents in 1870, "Frisco," as it was already called, sprawled irregularly for several miles over the bare, brown-white sand hills above the bay. The scene was one of strange contrasts and rapid changes. In the background was a line of rocky heights—Telegraph Hill, once the site of a criminal settlement; Nob Hill, where the mining and shipping magnates were building their mansions, and Pacific Heights.[3] In the foreground

[1] *Nation*, VIII, Nov. 2, 1871; Bancroft, *Pacific States*, XXI, chap. xxiv.

[2] Josiah Royce, *California from the Conquest of 1848 to the Second Vigilance Committee in San Francisco* (*American Commonwealth Series*, Boston, 1886), is an admirable short history of California to the Civil War.

[3] For a description of San Francisco in this period see B. E. Lloyd, *Lights and Shades of San Francisco* (San Fran., 1876).

the tumbled dunes and slopes were being steadily altered as men cut streets through the bluffs and sliced the tops of hillocks away. The business district was shooting far out into the old residential area; dignified mansions overlooked the "tin-can" houses of the Chinese— wooden shanties roofed with beaten-out tin cans; and transportation facilities were being outgrown.[1] So- cially, the city exhibited a strange combination of hard- headed industry and speculative extravagance. There were no more farsighted and sagacious men of affairs anywhere than those who built up the machine shops of Pacific Street, the great banking firms, the Wells-Fargo Express, the Pacific Mail Line and the California Steam Navigation Company. Yet the optimism and reckless- ness of the frontier were present also, as was demon- strated by a succession of real-estate and mining crazes.

Despite the exhaustion of the rich placer deposits, California's mining just after the war was still the most important industry and chief source of wealth; for the output of the quartz mines was steadily growing, and enabled the state to assert in 1866 and again in 1867 that its gold yield exceeded twenty-five million dollars.[2] But by the commencement of the Panic year agriculture, stimulated by the transcontinental railway, had defi- nitely emerged as the leading California interest.[3] The cosmopolitan character of California's population, the varieties of soil and climate and the tendency of each newcomer to experiment with the crops he knew best, insured a singularly diversified agriculture in specialized farms.[4] For some years grain and livestock, which

[1] A. B. Paine, *Life of Mark Twain*, I, chaps. xlvi-xlvii; H. H. Ban- croft, *Retrospection Political and Personal* (N. Y., 1912), 203 ff.

[2] *Am. Ann. Cyclop.*, VI (1866), 64; VIII (1868), 86.

[3] During the decade 1860-1870 a heavy surplus of wheat was pro- duced for export. E. J. Wickson, *Rural California* (N. Y., 1923), 75.

[4] *N. Y. Tribune*, May 4, 1866.

required comparatively little labor and capital, were the main products. Meanwhile, fruit-growing developed steadily.[1] Canning and preserving flourished as the production outstripped home needs, while dried fruits of fine appearance appeared and by 1868 large shipments East were being made. In the first year after the war the orange orchards near Los Angeles were already supplying San Francisco with two hundred and fifty thousand oranges. California wine, though still in the experimental stage, with the vine planters "prospecting" for a soil that would bring forth a Clos Veugeot or Lafitte, was hopefully regarded. By 1867 the state could boast that some of its vineyards rivaled the largest in Europe, with thirty million vines set and more than six million gallons of wine produced. Hock, port, sherry, champagne and other varieties were all sold in the East.

In California everything seemed on a larger scale than elsewhere; and because great areas were purchasable at low rates from the holders of Mexican titles, the number of extensive ranches was a marked feature of the state's agriculture. Some which were partly tilled covered thirty thousand acres, and a traveler could hear a farmer mention casually that he was holding one hundred and twenty tons of wheat for a rise in the Liverpool market.[2] Half a dozen years after the war there were one hundred and twenty Californians who possessed five million three hundred and forty-seven thousand acres in tracts of from twenty thousand to three hundred and thirty-five thousand acres apiece, and two hundred and thirty-one owners whose holdings ranged between five thousand and ten thousand acres. At this time it was supposed that such large areas, even for farm-

[1] Wickson, *Rural California*, 162 ff., 282.
[2] Rae, *Westward by Rail*, 266 ff.

ing, paid better than moderate units intensively cultivated, an opinion that was soon to be decisively refuted.
Meanwhile, the existence of these huge ranches retarded
the process of bringing the best California lands under
the plow.[1] In the aridity we meet another factor which
delayed the development of farm lands, for the right
principles of irrigation were not understood till about
1870, and this hindered the use of the vast interior
plains and mesas from which California's distinctive
products now chiefly come.[2]

That same rich flow of investment-seeking capital
from the mines which fertilized farming gave a steady
stimulation to manufacturing. Easterners approaching
San Francisco through the Golden Gate were surprised
to see the lower town enveloped in dense smoke, pouring
out in volumes from tall chimneys burning Mount
Diablo coal. The isolation from the East and the variety of natural products fostered a wide array of enterprises. Thus the fine malts and hops, and the difficulty
of shipping beer in good condition, encouraged local
breweries; the fruit and salmon led to the establishment
of canneries; the proximity to Hawaii's raw sugar gave
birth to refineries. An Englishman in 1870 found saw
factories which rivaled those of Sheffield and locomotive
and steam-engine works comparable with Philadelphia's
and Newcastle's.[3]

For reasons not hard to find, the state, a little world
in itself, had a distinctive culture at a date when the new
prairie commonwealths had none. It was blessed with
wealth; it was fortunate in possessing a society not only
markedly cosmopolitan and hence stimulating, but

[1] *Am. Ann. Cyclop.*, XIII (1873), 82.
[2] Wickson, *Rural California*, 304 ff.
[3] J. S. Hittell, *Resources of California* (San Fran., 1863), is full upon
this subject. See also Bancroft, *Pacific States*, XIX, 70.

drawn from the higher intellectual ranks of Europe and America. The long and dangerous transcontinental journey was undertaken only by men of energy, brains and, for the most part, education.[1] The greatest newspaper of the coast, the *Alta California*, compared favorably with all but a few Eastern journals. Mark Twain contributed to it in the days when, living in Portsmouth Square, he wrote *Roughing It*, and as its correspondent in 1867 he collected the material for his *Innocents Abroad*. The *Overland Monthly*, founded the next year with Bret Harte as first editor, was sweeping into its pages all the new writers of the West.[2] Charles Warren Stoddard was in San Francisco, a young man fresh from the experiences which enabled him to write *South Sea Idylls*. Across the bay in Berkeley the College of California was gathering strength and was succeeded in 1869 by the University of California, to which Joseph LeConte the geologist was early called as a professor. The spring of 1868 saw a thin, black-bearded young man named John Muir, still wan from a sharp attack of fever in the South, arrive in San Francisco, and startle one of the first men he met on the street by inquiring "the nearest way out of town to the wild part of the state."[3]

The one alien, unassimilable and socially barren element in California life was the Chinese population, which by the close of the war presented a harsh but by no means baffling problem, a problem of the sort that American heedlessness is always letting arise. Fifty thousand or more Chinese were scattered through the

---

[1] Edwin Markham, *California the Wonderful* (N. Y., 1914), 328 ff.

[2] T. E. Pemberton, *Bret Harte, A Treatise and a Tribute* (London, 1900).

[3] W. F. Badé, *Life and Letters of John Muir* (*Sierra edn.*, Boston, 1923-1924), I, 177.

large towns and mining regions, and more were arriving. Comparatively few were coolies, the great
majority being a sturdy peasantry from near Canton
and Hong Kong.[1]   They were busied in mining, railway building, farming and fishing and as cooks and
house servants; they made nine tenths of the cigars,
almost monopolized the laundry business and furnished
many hands for the woolen factories.   In short, they
were highly useful, if not actually indispensable.   The
Chinese evinced an orderliness that was never ques-
tioned; yet their rapidly growing numbers made their
presence a sharper and sharper irritant.[2]

This irritation was chiefly economic, for the workmen
of the state resented their willingness to labor long hours
for perhaps three fifths of a white man's pay.   They
had no families to support, no children to educate, no
desire for the luxuries and refinements that white men
crave, and no interest in the higher aims of life.[3]   They
obstinately remained Chinese in dress, diet and ways of
thought; and the Christian missionaries were resentful
because they could not convert them from their cheap,
showy idolatry.   Some repugnant vices they unquestionably had: they were addicted to gambling, their
opium dens were numerous and foul and they imported
many prostitutes.   They were also accused of treach-
erous murders.   Yet three fourths of the agitation
against them was artificial and false, being very largely
the work of demagogic politicians appealing to a set of
bar loafers and hoodlums.   "The people who actually
earn the bread they eat," wrote a New York journalist,
"do not persecute the Chinese."   Discriminating taxes

[1] G. F. Seward, *Chinese Immigration in Its Social and Economical
Aspects* (N. Y., 1881), 10 ff.; Richardson, *Beyond the Mississippi*, 389.
[2] *Senate Rep.*, 49 Cong., 2 sess., no. 689.
[3] George McNeill and others, *Labor Movement in America* (Boston,
1887), 454.

were laid upon them, and before they were found unconstitutional, they largely benefited the treasury. Indeed, from 1850 to 1870 about half the state's income came from the anti-Chinese levies.[1] They were forced to live in the most squalid quarters of the large towns, and in San Francisco particularly they occupied, for the most part, a set of decayed rookeries that would have disgraced the Five Points in New York.[2] Fortunately, the Chinese problem was far less serious and intricate than it often seemed and the irrepressible growth of the state alone did much to solve it.

Farther north, in Oregon and Washington, there was growth also but without the varied social background that distinguished California. Most of the population was collected in a few fertile valleys: the beautiful Willamette Valley in southern Oregon, the Columbia Valley, the Walla Walla Valley in eastern Washington, and the Grand Ronde.[3] Of these the Willamette, with its neat towns of Salem and Portland, was easily the most important. The leading element, the clergy, teachers, traders and professional men, was largely of New England blood; the Sabbath was kept in Portland as in the staid Connecticut Valley, and academies and colleges thrived in this region as in the East.[4] In the far Southwest, on the other hand, growth was comparatively slow, though there was a steady drift of Southerners into New Mexico after the war. The migration of the American settlers into New Mexico and Arizona accentuated a dramatic social conflict with the old Mexican

[1] Mary R. Coolidge, Chinese Immigration (N. Y., 1909), 80.

[2] Charles Nordhoff, Northern California, Oregon, and the Sandwich Islands (London, 1874), chap. v.

[3] For the paucity of women in the Far Northwest see Harper's Weekly, X, Jan. 6, 1866.

[4] For economic development, see Joseph Schafer, A History of the Pacific Northwest (N. Y., 1905), chaps. xviii, xix; E. S. Meany, History of the State of Washington (N. Y., 1909), chap. xxviii.

order. Possessing more capital and energy than the Spanish-speaking aristocrats and quite as determined, arrogant and quick on the trigger, the newcomers rapidly seized the government and the best of the wide areas devoted to semifeudal ranches.[1]

No treatment of the Far West of this period would be complete without some reference to the psychological effect which the mere existence of this vast, romantic, half-known treasure house had upon the remainder of America. It was a porch opening upon wide free vistas. It gave national life a sense of spaciousness and adventure that it would otherwise have lacked. Men listened with wonder to Major Powell's story of the first perilous voyage down the Grand Canyon, to Clarence King's descriptions of the Sierras, to Custer's narrative of his campaigns. They could feel that the age of almost boundless opportunities in America had not yet come to an end. Stagecoach and immigrant train, mining rush and cattle round-up, Mexican mission and salmon fishery, Chinatown and Indian agency, made up a varicolored panorama that added breadth and brightness to the American scene. They, and the kaleidoscopic bustle that was month by month altering the face of the huge region, were a constant stimulus to the imagination and energy of Americans whose lives were narrowed into parlors and countingrooms thousands of miles away. And beyond the passing day, the social contrasts of the Western scene, its types and incidents, were destined to become a lasting part of American folklore, influencing the mind and enriching the fancy of the nation for many generations to come.

[1] U. S. Commissioner of Agriculture, *Report for 1870*, 308; *Am. Ann. Cyclop.*, X (1870), 710 ff.; J. F. Meline, *Two Thousand Miles on Horseback* (N. Y., 1867), chap. xvii.

CHAPTER VI

THE REVOLT OF THE FARMER

(1868-1874)

As every year showed more decisively, the decade after the war was the period of the rise of the Middle West to agricultural dominance.   Grain growing which in 1860 was confined to eastern Iowa and southeastern Minnesota had spread a decade later over virtually all of Iowa, nearly all of southern Minnesota, and the eastern third of Kansas and Nebraska.   By 1870 more than one third the farm population of the nation was in the North Central region, and its products constituted a still larger portion of the whole.   As against more than two million people engaged in agriculture in the North Central states, there were only one half as many in the North Atlantic group; and while the rural population of the latter section remained at a standstill, that of the Northwest during the next decade increased by seven hundred thousand. It is an eloquent fact that the population of the four great new grain states and territories—Minnesota, Dakota, Nebraska and Kansas—rose from three hundred thousand in 1860 to nearly a million in 1870, and to nearly two and a half million in 1880.[1]   This shift of tillage carried tremendous social and political implications.   Never in the nineteenth century had so large a part of the farm population lived under pioneer or semi-pioneer conditions, facing frontier hardships and deprivations.   Never had the number of those engaged in

[1] *U. S. Tenth Census* (1880), I, 4.

agriculture risen so rapidly; it was clear that, if once stirred to action, the farming elements could wield formidable power.

Rural life in the eastern part of the Mississippi Valley, though still laborious and bare, was by now possessed of many social and material advantages. Even in Wisconsin and western Illinois the amenities of life were cultivated and comforts began to abound.[1] To be sure, the farms were new, the houses ugly frame structures; the furniture was cheap and worn, the clothing coarse and ill-fitting. The women performed the drudgery of carrying water, cutting wood and helping in the fields. In winter the home was likely to be so ill-heated that for comfort's sake the family cooked, ate and lived in a single room. Salt pork was the year-long staple of the farm table. But year by year more attractive houses were built, more farmers bought washing machines and sewing machines, and the children were better clothed. There were gay dances to "Money Musk," "Napoleon's March" and "The Devil's Dream," revivals by itinerant exhorters, and county fairs. Many families had a shelf of books—Porter's *Scottish Chiefs, Ivanhoe* and Headley's *Lives of the Presidents*—while the well-chosen selections of McGuffey's *Readers* (Professor W. H. McGuffey died at the University of Virginia in 1873) inculcated respect for the best British and American authors. An academy or high school somewhere in the county was within reach of families with money and ambition. Such a genius as John Muir had no difficulty in attracting attention and making his way to the state university.[2]

[1] See Hamlin Garland, *A Son of the Middle Border* (N. Y., 1917), and Herbert Quick, *One Man's Life* (Indianapolis, 1925), for pictures of farm life in this period.

[2] W. F. Badé, *Life and Letters of John Muir* (*Sierra edn.*, Boston, 1923-1924), I, 77 ff.

Lonely as farm life usually was, it had its compensating moments of bustle and crowded human intercourse. The old-fashioned threshing, with a J. I. Case or Buffalo Pitts separator operated by five teams of horses pulling long levers, brought farmers from the whole countryside, "changing work" with each other. The threshing supper, with neighbor women helping, was an occasion of rough merrymaking. There were four great public holidays: the Fourth, the Grange picnic, the circus and the county fair. Some communities which the Granges did not reach had neighborhood picnics under another name—"Old Settlers' Day" was common. Here were the whinny of horses, the smell of crushed grass, the farmers pitching horseshoes, the feasts of cold fried chicken, the courtships and the speech making, usually carefully nonpartisan. All country youths knew the pleasures of nutting along the wooded creeks, of going camping, of hunting rabbits and quail over the snowy fields, and of box suppers in the country schoolhouses. It was by no means a life of unrelieved drudgery.[1]

Moreover, outside the more primitive areas certain general tendencies were making for a distinct improvement of the farmers' lot. Scientific ideas were spreading steadily. Before the war the practice of manuring was confined almost wholly to the Eastern and Middle Atlantic states, but a few years afterward both this method and deep plowing had spread into the Middle West and the South. The necessity for crop rotation was becoming generally understood in the North.[2] Fruit culture was spreading with wonderful rapidity, and one nurseryman advertised fifty million grapevines for sale. The

[1] For good fictional studies of farm life, see Margaret Wilson, *The Able McLaughlins* (N. Y., 1923), and Herbert Quick, *The Hawkeye* (Indianapolis, 1923).
[2] *Prairie Farmer*, April 4, 1868; *American Annual Cyclopedia* (N. Y., 1861-1903), VII (1867), 13.

American Agriculturist boasted a circulation of almost two hundred thousand copies.   Even in the newer parts of the upper Mississippi Valley the change was striking. The early Minnesota settlers had grown nothing but wheat—no other grains, no vegetables and not even pork.   They had neglected the fertility of their soil, had wintered their stock at the open strawstacks, and had lived in cold, uncomfortable, rudely furnished shacks of one room.   But by 1868 they were found to be rotating their crops; they had organized farmers' clubs; they had well cultivated gardens, and were giving thorough care to blooded stock; they were subscribers to one or more agricultural journals.[1]

Still more important was the advance attributable to improved machinery.   A swift revolution in grain harvesting was taking place in these years.   First there appeared the self-rake reaper, generally used in the West, which dumped the grain in bundles on the ground to be bound; then came the harvester—a reaper on which two men stood and bound the grain as it came over the bullwheel by an endless apron and was dropped on a table between them.[2]   Briars cut their hands, the balls of their fingers became raw, the sun beat down inexorably, and the rust stung their raw flesh like vitriol; but still they had to keep pace with the endless stream of grain— ten acres a day.   It was with general relief that farmers hailed the advent of the self-binding harvester shortly after the Civil War.   A young farm hand and soldier, John F. Appleby, perfected the contrivance, which was promptly taken up by a manufacturer of harvesters named William Deering.   It did more labor with one man than a half dozen had formerly accomplished and

[1] *Prairie Farmer*, April 25, 1868.
[2] A. H. Sanford, *The Story of Agriculture in the United States* (Boston, 1916), chap. xiii.

as the seventies wore on it came into wide use.[1] The steam engine, applied to threshing as early as 1860, steadily usurped the place of the clumsy treadmill and horse sweep. The modern windmill, which was developed almost simultaneously, grew so cheap that a fair machine could be had for twenty-five dollars; the invention of the vane that turned the wheel into the wind (the device of a Wisconsin missionary named Wheeler) occurred immediately after the war. The harrow became much more efficient about 1870, when the teeth were made so as to be adjustable to any desired angle.

Far more important was the invention of the chilled iron moldboard for plows by an immigrant Scotchman named James Oliver, of South Bend, Indiana, in 1869. Previously all moldboards had been rough because of the blowholes made by escaping gases when the plowshares were cast, but Oliver turned out shares that cut the stickiest soil cleanly. He became one of the richest men in Indiana, but the wealth he gave to American agriculture defies computation.[2] Although grain drills had been known a quarter century earlier, it was not till just after the war that the expiration of patents permitted their manufacture in quantity. Two-horse cultivators for corn came in at the same time. Everywhere the tool shed of the farmer who possessed capital was being widened to make room for mowers, corn planters, horse rakes and corn shellers, with all that they meant in release from back-breaking toil. When Fillmore became president, the total value of farm implements

---

[1] H. W. Quaintance, *Influence of Farm Machinery on Production and Labor* (Am. Econ. Assoc., *Publs.*, ser. 3, IV, no. 4).

[2] Waldemar Kaempffert, ed., *A Popular History of American Invention* (N. Y., 1924), II, chap. vii. For the growing use of Pitts' thresher, McCormick's reaper, the Buckeye dropper and other implements in Virginia, see U. S. Commissioner of Agriculture, *Report for 1870*, 278 ff.

manufactured for the year was $6,842,611; by 1870 it was, in gold, $42,653,500.[1]

But on the whole the comforts of the Middle Western farmer, even in well-settled regions, were meager, and in the newer belts of settlement, pushing west over the plains, life was harsh indeed. Homesteaders came by thousands in almost penniless estate, with few tools, little household furniture and no conveniences. Many lived for years in dugouts, an excavation perhaps a dozen feet wide in the side of a hill, roofed with lumber and sod, and walled with sod, logs or stone. Frequently an entire house was built of sod, and fitted for the most part with home-made furniture; sometimes a little frame structure was erected with a few loads of lumber. Those used to neighbors found the life intolerably cheerless. On every side the treeless plains stretched away with depressing monotony; within the cramped dwelling, which was frequently hot in summer and cold in winter, the slightest comforts were lacking.[2] From one year's end to another the isolated farmer might see only a dozen faces; and in winter especially, each family was pent within its little farmhouse as in a prison. An excursion to town, where the ill-dressed farmers and their wives might gather timidly in the stores for a chat, became a rare adventure.

So much for the mere deprivations; but the positive perils, vexations and worries made up a list to dismay the stoutest heart. The danger from the Indians, whose sudden attack might end in the massacre of men and the outraging of the women, was till the middle seventies a source of recurrent anxiety. Prairie fires frequently caused loss of property and life; terrible blizzards men-

[1] See H. U. Faulkner, *American Economic History* (N. Y., 1924), 234.

[2] E. V. Smalley, "The Isolation of Life on Prairie Farms," *Atlantic Monthly*, LXXII (1893), 378-382.

aced the livestock and sometimes overwhelmed unwary wanderers. In 1874 Kansas and Nebraska suffered a fearful devastation from the plague of locusts, later repeated on a less extensive scale.[1] More disastrous than even the locusts were the recurrent droughts, which drove thousands of families in the more arid parts of the West back in utter dejection. The bitterest tragedy was concealed beneath those grimy wagon covers, slowly crawling eastward, upon which the ruined pioneer had in bravado chalked, "Going back to our wife's folks," or "In God we trusted, in Kansas we busted."[2]

The pioneer farmers suffered these perils in the hope of a generous reward; and when this was denied them, they were tinder for the flame of revolt. The occupation of the plains resulted in disastrous overproduction. Between 1854 and 1868 the receipts of flour at Chicago increased tenfold, and those of wheat fivefold. For a time after the war prices remained, on the whole, at a high level, and the year 1867 was one of marked prosperity. Then the first harsh blow to the grain growers came late in 1868 with a heavy fall of breadstuffs in the foreign and Eastern markets, followed by a piling up of wheat and other grains in the shipping centers of the West.[3] The Western farmers and middlemen waited for higher prices, but the drop continued. By the spring the decline had reached such a point that wheat and flour brought little more than half as much as a year earlier. A confused uproar of distress and indigna-

[1] The United States Entomological Commission, created by Congress (1877), published a *Report* on the locust.

[2] See art. "Kansas," *Am. Ann. Cyclop.*, XIV (1874), XV (1875).

[3] For prices, see files of *Prairie Farmer* and *Commercial and Financial Chronicle*. Just after the war, in the winter of 1865-1866, corn dropped in some North Central states to ten cents a bushel and was a cheaper fuel than wood. E. L. Bogart and C. M. Thompson, *The Industrial State* (C. W. Alvord, ed., *The Centennial History of Illinois*, Springfield, Ill., 1918-1920, III), 384.

tion came from the prairies.   Eastern merchants in turn were hard hit, complaining of difficulty in making their collections in the West, and finding the demand for goods unexpectedly limited.   The prices of manufactured wares fell in turn.   Yet after a slight rally during the summer, the depression of farm prices grew worse still.   During August of 1869, no. 2 spring wheat sold on the Chicago exchange for one dollar and forty-five cents; in January, 1870, when the new crop was in, it sold for seventy-six cents, a fall of almost fifty per cent, and a rate that meant actual bankruptcy to thousands of hard-working farmers.   Worst of all, the two main causes—a glut in the world markets, and a fall in the value of gold, unsettling all credit—seemed likely to be permanent.[1]

A temporary relief was at hand in the Franco-Prussian War.   Lasting for eleven months of 1870-1871, the conflict caused a marked advance in the prices of breadstuffs, bringing no. 2 spring wheat in the New York market back to one dollar and fifty-three cents in April of 1871.   Three months later there was another heavy decline, and the best spring wheat was down to one dollar and thirty-one cents in New York, which meant about a dollar in Chicago.   For the next few years the price remained uniformly low in these markets and the rate paid at remoter points was much less still; it actually cost twenty cents a bushel to transport wheat merely from Dubuque to Chicago.[2]   The falling price of wheat spelt despair to tens of thousands of farming

[1] See *Com. and Fin. Chron.*, July 10, 1869, for the flood of grain.

[2] We have an accurate official record of the December quotations of wheat in the St. Paul market, as follows: in 1866, $1.60; in 1867, $1.40; in 1868, 95¢; in 1869, 75¢; in 1870, 85¢; in 1871, $1.10; in 1872, 85¢; in 1873, 95¢; and 1874, 82¢.   This shows graphically just why a wave of rebellion surged up among the grain growers of the West.   J. D. Hicks, "Origin and Early History of the Farmers' Alliance in Minnesota," *Miss. Valley Hist. Rev.*, IX, 203-226.

families. It meant a lapse from comparative prosperity to grinding poverty. It meant that the farmer dressed in denim trousers and cheap cotton shirts, and his wife in faded calico; that furniture was reduced to the barest necessities; that the children could not be sent to high school. The farmer lived from half-year to half-year in fear that he could not meet the payment on his mortgage, and that foreclosure would ruin him. In contrast with his own lot he pictured the enviable position of the Eastern business classes in the flush years before 1873, with their carriages and comfortable homes, their assured income from an ever more prosperous trade. There has never been an Anglo-Saxon population which would endure such conditions without revolt, and the bitterness of the Middle Western farmer rapidly ripened into open rebellion.

This rebellion was the more direct and purposeful because it could be directed against flagrant evils. Intelligent farmers knew that one cause of their hardships lay in the simple fact that they were producing more wheat, corn and pork than the world would consume at a profitable price; but they also saw other causes rooted in private and corporate injustice. These were the extortions practised by railways and middlemen, the abuses resulting from the disturbed currency and the iniquitous tariff, and the injustices of an unscientific and unfair tax system. These evils produced an exasperation which quickly became explosive.[1] The railways were a particular object of the farmers' wrath. The great rail corporations were intrenched in a position which to many executives justified an arrogant attitude toward the small shipper. When the question of supervision was broached, the astute presidents declared that the un-

[1] S. J. Buck, *The Granger Movement* (*Harvard Hist. Studies*, XIX), is the best study of this revolt.

restrained competition made this unnecessary, and that the decision in the Dartmouth College case many years before showed that it was unconstitutional. So much did the public want new lines that it acquiesced in this view.[1] Yet the exorbitant nature of railway tariffs and the gross discrimination practised in adjusting them became clearer year by year. The *Prairie Farmer* complained in 1867 that it cost eight or ten times as much to transport shelled corn from Iowa to Liverpool as the farmer could obtain for the grain at his local elevator.[2] Freight rates on cattle were then so high that many Illinois farmers had driven their stock to Chicago rather than pay them. To carry a bushel of grain from the Mississippi to the seaboard cost in 1869 not less than fifty-two and a half cents, of which forty cents went for carriage, and the remainder for transfer and toll charges. The lines between the Misisisppi and Chicago, where there was no water connection, asked 20 cents a bushel for two hundred miles or less, a clear example of profiteering. Such rates meant that when corn was 70 cents a bushel in the East, it might be 15 cents in the local market in Iowa or central Illinois.[3] Moreover, the farmers nearest the Eastern markets had an enormous advantage of position. Thus, in Iowa and Nebraska in the midsummer of 1873, corn was valued at 25 or 30 cents a bushel, and wheat at 90 cents, while the Michigan farmer rejoiced in 60 cents for his corn and $1.32 for his wheat.[4]

To fortify their privileged position, the railways tried to maintain an improper influence over the legislatures. They issued free passes to important public officials,

[1] E. R. Johnson, *American Railway Transportation* (N. Y., 1908), 351.
[2] *Prairie Farmer*, Nov. 30, 1867.
[3] *Com. and Fin. Chron.*, May 8, 1869.
[4] *Com. and Fin. Chron.*, Aug. 16, 1873.

while bribery flourished both openly and in such other forms as the sale of stock below market levels. They chose governors and sent their picked servants, like W. B. Allison of Iowa, to the Senate. They curried favor with important interests by their discriminatory rates. This discrimination in charges was practised between towns—higher tariffs being charged at intermediate points than at junction points where the competition by other agencies applied a brake—and also between private shippers, large firms being granted secret rates or rebates. It raised up enemies but it also raised up friends, and it was a power which intimidated many patrons. Meanwhile the railways continued their brazen stock watering, which was worst on the three great lines of the East, the Erie, the New York Central and the Pennsylvania, but was also bad on such Western lines as the Rock Island and the Chicago and Northwestern. To show the startling proportions of this evil, a financial journal in 1869 cited twenty-eight railways which in less than two years had raised their combined capital from $287,036,000 to $400,684,000, or by forty per cent.[1]

The farmer's resentment of abuses by the middlemen almost equaled his anger against the railways. The local grain dealers and stock buyers frequently took an unjust advantage of the producer.[2] They seldom had any real competition; they could watch the markets far more closely and expertly; and they possessed storage facilities which enabled them to make the most of fluctuations. It was stated in 1870 that the middlemen's charges made to and in Chicago reached, as a rule, half the value of every bushel of grain sent to the Atlantic. The actual cornering of the market to the great disadvantage of the

[1] *Com. and Fin. Chron.*, May 15, 1869.
[2] Buck, *Granger Movement*, 14 ff.

farmer was repeatedly attempted and sometimes accomplished. Sentiment throughout the West developed rapidly between 1865 and 1870 against what was called "the livestock ring" of Chicago. Almost all the capital of the Union Stockyards was at first secretly held by nine Western railways, and railway heads and commission men were constantly attempting an artificial manipulation of the market. They were able at times to make enormous marginal profits upon meats while the stockmen received an unjustly low price. In 1868, when wheat had been at least three times partly cornered, corn and barley twice, and rye and oats once, a corner in pork resulted in a drop in prices which shocked and angered farmers all over the West.[1]

If the farmer often felt cheated by the price he received for his produce, he felt outraged by the charge he had to pay for many necessities of life. Farm machinery, sewing machines and other patented goods were in many instances to be bought only through agencies which sold them on a commission basis, and this commission was excessive. A still greater grievance was the high cost of capital, for the Western grain growers necessarily had to buy much on credit. In the expansive days of the war and just afterward, when money rolled in like a Pactolian flood, the farmers made lavish purchases and ran into debt. They believed that their quarter sections would rise in value, and that in the meantime their crops would carry the interest payments.[2] But when the Hessian fly destroyed the wheat or the elevator offered only fifteen cents for corn, the farmer had to sign another note. A growing burden of mortgages weighed like a millstone around the Western farmer's neck; and

[1] A. C. Cole, *The Era of the Civil War* (*The Centennial History of Illinois*, III), 384-385.
[2] Buck, *Granger Movement*, 18-19; Sanford, *Story of Agriculture*, 227.

the interest rates were atrocious, reaching fifteen or twenty per cent. Here again a grasping middleman was partly at fault, for the prairies were infested with loan agents who procured money from Eastern capitalists, found hard-pressed farmers who had to accept the iniquitous terms, and grew fat on the "service" they rendered. Hamlin Garland's story of the piratical mortgage holder who foreclosed without allowing the toil-worn tenant a cent for the many improvements which he had put on the land was not an exaggeration.[1] The South felt the same burden with equal keenness.

So much for the abuses committed by private interests; but there were others for which the government was held responsible. The disturbed state of the federal currency and the jerky deflation which followed the war bore with great severity upon the farmers. The burning financial question of the day was whether the great volume of paper money called forth by the conflict should be contracted with a view to the resumption of specie payments. The uncertain position of the currency was a main cause of the high interest rates, while, affecting the exchange rates adversely, it helped cause the low European prices for farm products.[2] As the value of the greenbacks in gold slowly increased, the farmers who had contracted debts immediately after the war found they had to pay their obligations in money worth far more than they had received. Pressure from the West in 1868 peremptorily stopped the contraction of the currency begun by Secretary McCulloch, and the "greenback question" became acute. The Greenbackers argued against deflation on the ground that it would reduce prices; would compel the government and the

[1] Hamlin Garland, "Under the Lion's Paw," in his *Main-Travelled Roads* (Cambridge, Mass., 1891).

[2] D. R. Dewey, *Financial History of the United States* (A. B. Hart, ed., *American Citizen Series*, N. Y., 1902), 332 ff., 372.

debtor classes to pay in a dearer currency than they had borrowed; would lower the rate of foreign exchange, and thus decrease the exports to Europe; and would deprive the country, enlarged by the reconstructed South and the new West, of a supply of currency plainly needed for its growth. In great degree this was a sectional issue between the money-lending East and the money-borrowing West and South.[1]

Other grievances of the farmer against the government grew out of the tariff and the tax system. The Morrill tariff act of 1864, passed at the instance of manufacturers, raised duties enormously and indiscriminately. When peace came, the tariff should have been drastically revised at once, but it was not touched until 1872 and then only slightly reduced. It cost the farmer heavily upon a hundred articles of constant use, from sugar upon his table and blankets upon his bed to the plowshare in his field.[2] As for taxation, it was its inequalities rather than its weight, though it was very heavy, which aroused the ire of the agriculturists. Both the internal revenue taxes and the custom duties pressed with especial severity upon persons of small means. And when it came to state taxes, the struggling farmers had a grievance peculiarly their own. They saw the prosperous city men concealing their assets while their own possessions were carefully appraised by the tax collector. Their indignation led to a powerful demand for the local taxation of government bonds. Immense amounts of wealth were invested in national securities, and while the mechanic's house and the farmer's land paid heavy levies, these securities escaped scot free. Yet the bondholders had bought their bonds at low rates, they were paid a

[1] *Chicago Tribune*, June 15, 1877.
[2] Special Commissioner of the Revenue, *Report for 1869*, 48 ff.; F. W. Taussig, *Tariff History of the United States* (7th edn., N. Y., 1923), 185.

high rate of interest, and this interest was in gold, which commanded a premium. A lurid contrast could be drawn between the farmer or the laborer, toiling to meet the demands of the tax collector, and the wealthy banker, clipping his untaxed coupons.[1]

The first warning rumble of the storm gathering in the West came in an attack of the Illinois farmers upon the railways and the alleged monopolists of the Chicago markets. When the railways tried to crush certain independent grain elevator companies in Chicago by refusing transportation to them, the agriculturists instantly forced the passage of the famous warehouse act of 1867. This provided for the strict state inspection of all warehouses and elevators and penalized heavily any refusal to deliver grain to the warehouse to which it was consigned. An ineffective attack was made at the same time upon trading in futures. As prices fell and the abuse of the big corporations persisted, the indignation in the rural districts mounted. It came to a head in the Illinois constitutional convention of 1870, which decided, after a fierce debate, to lodge the power of railway rate-making in the hands of the legislators.[2]

Under the authority thus conferred, the farmer-controlled legislature of 1871 passed a comprehensive and complex railway law. This levied a heavy blow at rate discrimination, provided that there should be no special favors in handling or storage, and fixed maximum rates for freight and passengers. A commission of three was appointed to enforce the law. When the railroads refused to obey, the farmers took enforcement into their own hands. Parties of them would board trains, offer the maximum fare stipulated by the law and refuse to

---

[1] Buck, *Granger Movement*, 20-21.
[2] E. L. Bogart and C. M. Thompson, *The Industrial State* (*The Centennial History of Illinois*, IV), 19-20.

pay an additional cent. When trainmen tried to eject them they even drew revolvers and bowie knives and repulsed the attack. Meanwhile the commission sought to punish the Chicago & Alton for rate discrimination, and the state supreme court in 1873 declared the statute a violation of the state but not the national constitution. The result was a new act for rate regulation passed the same year, much more radical and effective. Other states, their farmers rallying to the fight, rapidly followed in the footsteps of Illinois. Ohio aimed a blow at discriminating freight rates in 1872,[1] and Iowa fixed maximum passenger rates the following year.

As the farmers thus engaged in a duel with powerful corporate interests, there occurred the sudden rise of a rural organization, partly economic, partly social and partly political—the Grange. This astonishing society was founded in 1867 by a few government employees in Washington led by O. H. Kelley and William Saunders.[2] These men had been impressed by the complaints of poverty, depression and injustice reaching the government from every farming region and by the need for some agency of relief. It occurred to them that a secret organization, like the Odd Fellows, might accomplish much. A constitution was drawn up and Saunders set forth early in 1868 as an organizer with no funds except a ticket for Harrisburg, Pennsylvania, and two dollars and fifty cents in cash. In rapid succession he founded granges in Harrisburg, Fredonia, New York, Columbus, Ohio, and Chicago, and a few weeks later was at work in Minnesota, where he established six more. But thereafter the growth of the Grange, or Patrons of Husbandry, was halting. The North Central states proved chillingly indifferent; in neither 1869 nor 1870

[1] *Com. and Fin. Chron.*, July 20, 1872.
[2] *Am. Ann. Cyclop.*, XIII (1873), 622 ff.

were so many as forty branches added. However, the following year a period of amazing growth began, with more than one thousand one hundred branches established in 1872 and about eight thousand four hundred in 1873. By the spring of 1874, six years from the day Saunders had set forth, the membership was not less than one million five hundred thousand, the number of local granges had risen to almost fifteen thousand, and every week brought a host of new recruits.[1] The rising power of the order was causing profound alarm in various quarters.

Social conditions made it inevitable that the Grange should gain its greatest vigor in the Middle West and the South. It first rose to maturity in Iowa, Minnesota, South Carolina and Mississippi. The Eastern farmers held back because they had long felt the Western agriculturists to be menacing rivals. The virgin soil of the prairies, tilled in large units, produced crops far more cheaply than the smaller, thinner farms of the East; and under the stress of this competition, the Yankee did not care to help his Illinois brother lower the freight charges. Moreover the East suffered less from mortgage foreclosures and did not require new capital at the exorbitant rate prevailing. Yet the organization was in the fullest sense national, and by the end of 1873 only four states were unrepresented. One of its proudest boasts was that it admitted women to full membership, and this was one of the features which did most to give the granges vitality. Even in the South it became an organization of immense influence, with six thousand four hundred local granges by the end of 1875.[2] From the presence of this feminine element grew a wealth of social fea-

[1] S. J. Buck, *The Agrarian Crusade* (Allen Johnson, ed., *Chronicles of America Series*, New Haven, 1918-1921, XLV), chap. iii.

[2] Holland Thompson, *The New South* (*Chronicles of America Series*, XLII), chap. iii.

The Western Farmer.

Above: A dugout on the Kansas plains.

Below: A Grange meeting in an
Illinois schoolhouse.

tures: festivals and picnics, concerts, general lectures and the provision of libraries. What would otherwise have been a rough business organization, devoid of any interest not connected with the pocket, became a means of lighting up the drab life of lonely farm communities.

Sometimes honestly, sometimes with tongue in cheek, the Grange leaders emphatically disclaimed any intention of using the organization in politics. Their official objects embraced a wide range of activities: to enhance the comfort of farmers' homes, to increase crop diversification, to reduce expenses and to attack the mortgage system. They advocated agricultural education and assailed all forms of political corruption. But chief among their purposes stood the legislative regulation of freight charges and the promotion of coöperative effort. "We propose meeting together," declared the Grangers in their St. Louis convention of 1874, "talking together, working together, buying together, and in general acting together for our mutual protection and advancement as occasion may require." This was a direct warning to commission men, jobbers and retail dealers that coöperative farm organizations would shortly begin a drastic competition.[1]

Coöperation was, indeed, the weapon nearest at hand in the farmers' grim fight against poverty and hardship. The railways could be reached only through the legislatures and could turn to the courts as a refuge; the middlemen, bankers and merchants who were victimizing the producers could be reached direct. Grange leaders at once began educating the farmers to the benefits involved in paying cash for supplies and in pooling their buying power. Every farmer wanted more machinery, and when they joined to make purchases in large quantities, they found they cut the prices amazingly—some-

[1] A. E. Paine, *The Granger Movement in Illinois* (Univ. of Ill., *Publs.*, I, no. 8).

times in half. Illinois granges were able to buy for $175 the reapers for which middlemen had charged $275, while they brought down the cost of small threshers from $300 to $200, wagons from $150 to $90, and sewing machines from $75 or $100 to $40 or $50.[1] Some corporations, like the McCormick Company, yielded little to the Granger demands; but many firms seized upon the opportunity to cater to them. Grangers' supply houses sprang up everywhere. An immediate fruit of the movement was the birth of the great mail-order business which for decades was to act as an increasing check upon retail prices in rural communities.

Montgomery Ward & Company in 1872 opened in Chicago the first mail-order house "to meet the wants of the Patrons of Husbandry." [2] Indorsed by the National Grange, it was soon driving an enormous trade. We don't pay forty thousand dollars a year rent, the firm announced; we don't sell goods to country dealers on six months' time; we don't hire agents; we buy for cash and sell for cash. Within a few years the house was boasting—and justly—that it had saved the consumer millions merely by forcing local dealers to sell their wares at fair prices. For a time it even undertook to sell grain and seeds on consignments, charging a cent a bushel as commission. Meanwhile the farmers, with an enthusiasm that stopped at no obstacles, were organizing not only their own purchasing and selling agencies but even their own factories. The Iowa grange bought the Werner harvester patent, and during the summer of 1874 built and sold about two hundred and fifty machines for half the prevailing price; but money losses and threatened patent suits caused it to give up this enterprise. At one

[1] A. E. Paine, *The Granger Movement in Illinois*, 40.
[2] Montgomery Ward & Company, *Catalogs*, vol. 1, no. 11 (see prefatory matter).

time the Iowa grange had three factories at Des Moines
making plows and controlled three large establishments
in other parts of the state.[1] Thirty grain elevators
were owned by local Iowa granges and run by salaried
superintendents. The *Chicago Tribune* early in 1874
was able to give nearly three columns to a description
of the economic activities of the Grangers, with a list
of coöperative enterprises which included insurance, elevators, factories, gristmills and pork-packing establishments. In California even banking was attempted.[2]

To anyone who realizes the innate individualism of
the American farmer, the reluctance and suspicion with
which he always approaches group activities, this sudden efflorescence of Grangerism is eloquent of the evils
which he felt himself to be suffering. And if any men
thought that he would stop with mere economic action,
they knew little of the nature of agrarian movements in
America. Broad and sane though the Grange's program was, it failed to satisfy all shades of opinion among
the farmers. To some the Grange seemed too radical,
to some its secret ritual and its seven orders appeared a
mere hocus-pocus; to many it seemed too conservative.
The consequence was the emergence of various rival organizations, of which the most important were various
farmers' clubs which at once thrust the rural power into
politics. These clubs, at first independent but soon forming state organizations, were most vigorous in the Middle West.[3] In Illinois their origin antedated that of the
Grange, and elsewhere the two bodies in the early seventies grew up side by side. The Grangers of Iowa and

[1] F. E. Haynes, *Third Party Movements since the Civil War with
Special Reference to Iowa* (Iowa City, 1916), 85 ff.

[2] *Chicago Tribune*, April 25, 1874. See also Bogart and Thompson,
The Industrial State, 88.

[3] Buck, *The Agrarian Crusade*, chap. iii. See also *Nation*, XIX, July
2, 1874.

Minnesota circumvented the clause forbidding any political activities by the simple device of calling meetings "outside the gate."

This political flare-up, like the revolt against the railways, first became violent in Illinois. When the state supreme court held the railway law unconstitutional in 1873 the farmers sprang to arms. Their candidates made almost a clean sweep in the judicial election that summer. During the fall, in county after county— more than half the state—they met in picnics, listened to a reading of the so-called Farmers' Declaration of Independence, and named farmers' tickets for county offices. All but a few of these counties were triumphantly carried. With the rapidity and fierceness of a prairie fire the movement spread west and north.[1] Nascent farmers' parties appeared the same year in Minnesota (the Anti-Monopoly party) and Wisconsin (the Reform party) and took a triumphant part in the state elections. As a result, both Wisconsin and Iowa prescribed maximum freight rates in 1874, while Minnesota established a commission empowered to do so. The picturesque leader in Minnesota was Ignatius Donnelly, a hot-headed, keen-witted agitator of Irish blood, who marshaled the farmers so effectively that he came within about five thousand votes of winning the governorship. In Wisconsin the Democrats joined the new Reform party in taking control of the lower legislative chamber. In Kansas also the reformers and the Democrats gained such a grip upon the legislature that they were able to send to Washington the first senator representing the Mid-Western farm revolt, ex-Governor James M. Harvey. Even as far west as California the agrarian spirit blazed up during the critical year 1873. For almost a decade the farmers and the press had been assailing the preposterously exorbitant

[1] Haynes, *Third Party Movements*, 54 ff.

charges and the discriminatory rates of the Central Pacific, and in 1873 the insurgent movement, led by Governor Newton Booth, suddenly shot into power. The fall election gave the antirailway party control of the legislature, and after a contest in which the Central Pacific spent money like water, Booth was sent to the Senate.[1] Three years later California passed a drastic railway regulation law.

At the close of the year 1874 it was possible to point to independent agrarian parties in nine prairie states and in Oregon and California. Men like Donnelly and Booth were becoming national figures. The *Chicago Tribune* declared that "if there is any healthier political organization anywhere than that which the farmers have originated in the West, we do not know what name it is called by." In fact, it had completely upset the politics of a half-dozen Western states, carried doubt and consternation among the politicians in as many more, and even threatened a revolt in conservative Eastern communities.[2] In Illinois that fall the farmers' party elected four members of Congress, in Wisconsin three, and in Iowa one. It is interesting to note that in Missouri an emphatic declaration was made against currency contraction, in Kansas a plank was adopted for the election of the president and senators by popular vote, and in Nebraska a demand was made for the congressional regulation of interstate commerce. The radical farmers were reaching out for the progressive issues of the future.[3]

The fight was carried into the courts on a broad scale, and in 1876 the Granger legislation won a decisive vic-

---

[1] *Am. Ann. Cyclop.*, XIII (1873), 83 ff., 362 ff., 378 ff., 393 ff., 506 ff.; H. H. Bancroft, *History of the Pacific States of North America* (San Fran., 1882-1891), XIX, 64 ff., 625 ff.

[2] *Nation*, XVIII, Jan. 22, 1874.

[3] Holland Thompson, *The New South*, chap. iii; Haynes, *Third Party Movements*, chap. xxx.

tory in the case of Munn *v.* Illinois.[1] Interpreting the
Fourteenth Amendment, the Supreme Court declared
that state legislatures had the power to restrict the rates
charged for the services of any public utility.   The
Granger movement attained its climax in both the economic and political fields during the dark years 1873-
1874.   The Grange factories, stores and coöperative
agencies were still for the most part flourishing, though
their results were not as great as their promoters hoped.
Politically, the farmers were achieving their main goal,
state railway regulation.   The laws which one legislature
after another were passing were by no means as sober and
scientific as the economic complexities of the situation required, but they marked the end of a *laissez faire* régime
which the farmers had found intolerable.   Never again
would the public carriers be allowed to practise any ex-
tortion they pleased unchecked.   The crusading farmer
had opened a new era in the relations between government and industry.[2]

With the achievement of these initial railway laws,
and the advent of an economic period in which manufacturing was depressed, prices fell and the farmer might
count himself comparatively better off than before, the
expansion of the Grange ceased.   Yet the effects of the
farmers' revolt persisted.   It marked a new phase in the
old clash between the frontier and the Eastern capitalists;
it had proved that the agricultural interests of the nation
could organize to make themselves respected.   The embattled wheat growers contributed powerfully to a much
needed socialization of politics just after the war; men
had been concerned with governmental and constitutional questions, and it was necessary to bring economic

[1] 94 U. S., 113.   See R. A. Brown, "The Function of Courts and
Commissions," *Harvard Law Rev.,* XXXVIII, 149.

[2] See J. R. Commons and others, *A Documentary History of American
Industrial Society* (Cleveland, 1910-1911), IX, 49.

and social issues to the front. The farmers' new measures, however erratic, showed an instinctive sense for a
real and half-hidden peril to the nation in the growth
of corrupting monopolies. Even in the South, where
the Grangers accomplished less than in the Middle West
—though by 1875 there were more than ten thousand
local granges in the South—the revolt helped to develop
a class consciousness among farmers, to direct attention
to such economic evils as the crop-lien system, and to
implant the idea that legislation might be a valuable
weapon against poverty and injustice.

CHAPTER VII

THE MORAL COLLAPSE IN GOVERNMENT AND BUSINESS

(1865-1873)

THE two elements dominant in social life just after the war—confusion and unsettlement on the one side, a hurried, aggressive growth on the other—united to give birth to an alarming public and private corruption. Obviously much of the shocking improbity was due to the heavy war-time expenditures. A wealth of contracts was let, speculators and jobbers waxed fat on government money, the collection of federal revenues offered large opportunities for graft, and the grant of bounties was a fertile source of corruption. Under the stimulus of greenback inflation, business ran into excesses and lost sight of elementary canons of prudence. Meanwhile it became clear that thievery had found a better opportunity to grow because the conscience of the nation, aroused against slavery, had neglected what seemed minor evils. Now that the preoccupation with the struggle was over men felt in the predicament of Cromwell at Marston Moor, who returned from routing the main body of the enemy to find its other wing holding the field and plundering his baggage trains.[1] Yet another cause was that the war broke the cake of custom as never before; certain sections and classes lost their power and wealth, and other hands seized both. The *nouveaux riches*, the thousands who had rushed into speculations which they

[1] *Nation* (N. Y.), VI, May 14, 1868.

178

had no moral right to risk, the pushing, hardened men brought to the front by the turmoil, observed a coarser, lower standard of conduct.

Equally important, if less obvious, were two reasons connected with the process of national expansion. The "West," with its unschooled, unpolished inhabitants, had now spread over a wide belt, while its influence upon the older regions was communicated with unprecedented activity and vigor. In Grant it may be said to have given the country a president who was painfully blunt in his ethical perceptions.[1] But much of the trouble lay in the immense growth of national wealth unaccompanied by any corresponding growth in civic responsibility. A generation earlier, when bank charters had been almost the only prize which made it worth while to bribe a legislature, the granting of such charters had been a source of flagrant state corruption. Now the increase of capital and corporate activity had given state legislatures the power of conferring glittering privileges, and had enabled men like Jay Gould to spend a hundred thousand dollars in bribes where their predecessors could not spend a thousand.

Corruption had been far from unknown before the war; yet the impetus which the conflict gave to evil tendencies was alarming. Parton's account of New York misgovernment in the *North American Review* of 1866 led the *Nation* to indulge in a prophecy which was signally vindicated: "What is our shame and misfortune today will, if some remedy is not applied, be in a few years the shame and misfortune of Boston, of Philadelphia, of New Haven, of Rochester, of Cincinnati, and San Francisco."[2] Two years later the same weekly burst

[1] See Goldwin Smith, *The United States: an Outline of Political History* (N. Y., 1893), 203-204.
[2] *Nation*, III, Oct. 18, 1866.

out: "there is hardly a legislature in the country which is not suspected of corruption; there is hardly a court over which the same suspicion does not hang." [1]   The *New York Tribune* in 1867 published a series of Albany letters showing that votes at the capital were as openly bought and sold as meat in the market and that few bills could be passed without purchasing a considerable proportion of both houses.   Some members, moreover, had begun to raise money by blackmail—that is, by introducing outrageous bills which, if enacted, were sure to ruin some vested interest.   The up-state farmers, lawyers and merchants were as bad as the Tammany Irish.   The legislature of 1870 was corrupt beyond all precedent, money being spent like water by "Boss" Tweed.   Six of the leading Republican senators were authentically reported to have received twenty thousand dollars each for their obedience to his wishes.   Evidence was at one time produced indicating that Governor Fenton himself accepted twenty thousand dollars from Jay Gould for his signature to the bill legalizing the acts of the Gould directors in the "Erie War."   The state judiciary in New York was almost as disreputable as the legislature.   There were judges who were known to be as much the thralls of certain capitalists as Gurth was of Cedric the Saxon. [2]   The most notorious of these was Barnard, who first appeared in New York as a dissipated California loafer. When he was convicted of corruption in 1872 upon twenty-six counts, removed from the bench and disqualified for office, the public rejoicing was impressive.

Bad as Albany was, men agreed that if she should be destroyed by fire from heaven, Harrisburg might well fear the same fate. [3]   Simon Cameron, after his discredit-

[1] *Nation*, VI, May 14, 1868.
[2] *Harper's Weekly* (N. Y.), XIV, Feb. 19, 1870.
[3] *Commercial and Financial Chronicle* (N. Y.), March 26, 1870.

able Civil War record, continued the political ruler of Pennsylvania until in 1877 he resigned from the national Senate, naming his son Don as his successor.[1] Meanwhile another personage had appeared on the scene—Matthew S. Quay who had got himself elected to the legislature in 1865. "Cameron made the use of money an essential to success in politics, but Quay made politics expensive beyond the most extravagant dreams." With such men as these in power, and with such corporations as the Pennsylvania Railroad and the coal companies insisting on glaring special privileges at the cost of the public, corruption was unescapable.

Yet in the Western states the record was almost as bad. In Illinois the legislative session of 1867 was signally corrupt, and in 1868 there was a veritable orgy of boodle legislation. Governor John M. Palmer tried the following year to stem the tide by vetoes, but proved almost impotent in the face of a lobby which spent fortunes. Ten or twelve million dollars were declared to have been voted in 1867 into the pockets of corporations, contractors and speculators. In 1869 a powerful lobby assembled, special legislation was jammed through, and about seven hundred acts of incorporation were passed in defiance of the constitution, while the press again rang with charges of wholesale bribery.[2] Wisconsin saw an unscrupulous railway lobby crush all unfriendly bills between 1865 and the Panic year, while during 1873 a veritable wave of scandals ran through the West. In Iowa, which was so moral a state that the governor once ordered a company of militia to Council Bluffs to pre-

[1] See S. W. McCall, *Thaddeus Stevens* (J. T. Morse, jr., ed., *American Statesman Series*, Boston, 1889), 311; S. P. Orth, *The Boss and the Machine* (Allen Johnson, ed., *The Chronicles of America Series*, New Haven, 1918-1921, LXIII), chap. vii.

[2] A. C. Cole, *The Era of the Civil War* (C. W. Alvord, ed., *The Centennial History of Illinois*, Springfield, Ill., 1918-1920, III), chap. xix.

vent a prize fight, the funds of the State Agricultural
College were found to have been stolen. In Minnesota
the state treasurer was impeached and removed, though
he was a much more honest man than some of his predecessors. In Missouri the legislative balloting to fill a
senatorship brought to light a brazen attempt by one
candidate to use fifteen thousand dollars in bribery.[1]

But the most dramatic revelation of the year occurred
in Kansas. Here the arrogant Senator Samuel C. Pomeroy, who had represented the state for twelve years, was
backed by a staunch Republican machine and felt sure of
reëlection. But the supporters of an aggressive young
attorney named J. J. Ingalls laid plans to beat him.
There was a profound sensation when a member named
York arose, pale and trembling, and placed on the
speaker's table seven thousand dollars which he said
Pomeroy had paid him for his vote. Everyone knew
that he spoke the truth. For once the courage of Pomeroy's supporters was broken, and they dared not deny
the accusation. Ingalls, who was known for some bril-
liantly caustic articles on state politics, was promptly
chosen in Pomeroy's stead, and the Granger forces at once
seized upon the scandal as text for a demand that the
corrupt use of corporation and machine money be done
away with.[2] Meantime, as we have seen, in the South
the same sordid drama was being played out in state
after state, against a background of racial antagonism
and ill-planned federal efforts at reconstruction.

Between state corruption and municipal corruption
there existed a close connection. The Tweed Ring in
New York City could never have flourished and produced the most colossal scandal in the history of our cities

[1] *American Annual Cyclopedia* (N. Y., 1861-1903), XIII (1873),
394 ff., 379, 506, 523 ff.
[2] W. E. Connelley, *Ingalls of Kansas* (Topeka, 1909), 141.

but for the connivance and aid of the legislature. Just before the war a bargain had been made between the Tammany Democrats and the Seward-Weed Republicans for a division of the spoils, whereby Tammany managed the city vote, A. Oakey Hall drew up the laws which the combination needed to carry out its purposes, and Thurlow Weed and his lobbyists had them passed by the legislature. This corrupt alliance between city Democrats and up-state Republicans passed through various permutations, but it steadily retained substance.[1] By the municipal election of 1868, which made Hall mayor, Peter B. Sweeney chamberlain, and Richard B. Connolly comptroller, the Tweed Ring placed itself in a position to scrape the last coins from the city coffers. These three were able to work effectively under the boss-ship of Tweed, whose control of the county supervisors was highly useful. They were assisted by the city charter, which the legislature had so framed that no effective responsibility for abuses could be enforced and no check kept upon peculations. Tweed went to the state senate in 1869 to labor there for the Ring.[2]

The leading personalities of the Tweed Ring are so characteristic of the place and period that they deserve momentary attention. Tweed himself, a familiar figure in the city of a million people, was a tall, bulky person, his apparent ponderosity belied by his firm, swift step and his piercing eyes, grim lips and sharp nose. His untiring activity, his imposing physique and his union of cruelty, shrewdness and audacity had raised him in fifteen years from the position of chair maker to that of multimillionaire dictator of the city. He had begun as a member of the rough volunteer fire department, then

---

[1] Allan Nevins, *The Evening Post: A Century of Journalism* (N. Y., 1922), chap. xvi.
[2] See the excellent historical article in the *Nation*, XIII, Nov. 9, 1871.

an important instrument in the gang politics of New York and Philadelphia; he had become the grand sachem of Tammany.[1] His lieutenant Sweeney was later described by a reform committee as "the most despicable and dangerous, because the best educated and most cunning, of the entire gang." Thomas Nast's pencil in *Harper's Weekly* made the most of his villainous appearance—his low forehead, heavy brows, thick lips and bushy hair.[2] Neat and suave, "Slippery Dick" Connolly was the most respectable in appearance, but he was, in reality, an ignorant accountant who contributed to the Ring plenty of low cunning and a complex quadruple-entry system of bookkeeping. Oakey Hall, a debonair clubman and man about town, was the most reputable and least active member of the four, a mere tool of the others.

Their methods were those which the city boss has since made familiar from Boston to San Francisco. The Citizens' Association found in 1871 that, of about one hundred and thirty thousand voters, Tweed could control or influence half by the agencies at his command— offices, contracts, employment on public works, licenses, untried indictments, suspended sentences and so on.[3] A heavy stratum of the population was composed of ignorant, credulous immigrants, for seventy-seven thousand or nearly two thirds of the electorate were foreign-born. They had no comprehension of the elaborate mechanism by which New York was governed, and no sense of the true aims of municipal administration. But

[1] Samuel J. Tilden, *Letters and Literary Memorials* (John Bigelow, ed., N. Y., 1908), I, 272 ff.; John Foord, *Life and Public Services of Andrew Haswell Green* (N. Y., 1913), chap. viii.

[2] A. B. Paine, *Th. Nast, His Period and His Pictures* (N. Y., 1904), 135-205.

[3] *Nation*, XXI, Nov. 4, 1875; XXV, Aug. 16, 1877; XXVI, Feb. 14, 1878.

A Nast cartoon on the Tweed Ring.

they had a lively appreciation of Tweed's distributions of coal, flour and money, of the ward politician's help in obtaining jobs and of the machine's assistance to poor fellows "in trouble" with the law. They liked the hearty grip and voice of the Tammany heeler; they thronged to the gay din of ward picnics; they knew that if the cupboard was empty Tammany would always help them earn a few dollars. If they ever thought of the Ring's frauds and thefts, they regarded them as a rightful fleecing of the rich and Tweed as a type of modern Robin Hood.[1] With such popular support behind them the bosses astonished honest men by their audacity. Parton described in 1866 the impudence with which the looting was going on. Eighteen corrupt councilors in City Hall laughed at the six who were honest. They rented buildings at twice the proper cost; they allowed a contractor twenty-five thousand dollars for removing dead animals, and the contractor gave the politicians sixty thousand dollars for the position; they sold appointments and overloaded payrolls; they disposed of a gas franchise on terms that robbed the public for twenty years to come. All this was known to everybody; and Tammany's answer to the charges was more false registration and more illegal naturalization of voters.[2]

The scale of the stealing and the fierce intensity of the final storm of anger have made the Tweed Ring memorable beyond all rivals. Enough money had been taken by 1866, said the *Nation*, to have made New York one of the most beautiful cities in the modern world, the richest in works of art, fine buildings and conveniences. Yet the worst had not yet begun. The period of com-

[1] Gustavus Myers, *History of Tammany Hall* (rev. ed., N. Y., 1920), 302 ff.

[2] James Parton, "The Government of the City of New York," *N. Am. Rev.*, CIII (1866), 413-468.

plete Ring control comprised the years 1869, 1870 and 1871, until the overthrow of the Tweed régime in November. Street openings, paving contracts, public printing, sewers, parks, all yielded their contributions. By midsummer of 1870 the percentage of graft which the Ring extracted from public contractors had been shoved up to eighty-five per cent. By the fall of 1871 the Ring was generally credited with the theft of twenty million dollars.[1] The greatest single source of gain was the courthouse, which was planned in 1868 to cost not more than two hundred and fifty thousand dollars and which swallowed up more than eight million dollars without reaching completion. The aggregate of the fraudulent bills certified by the Ring's members, sitting as a board of special audit, on the single day of April 5, 1870, was nearly fifteen and three quarter million dollars; and of this more than fourteen millions was sheer plunder. For the remainder of 1870 the total of fraudulent bills was twelve million two hundred and fifty thousand dollars, and for 1871 it was three million four hundred thousand dollars.[2]

We need not rehearse here the story of the final exposure and violent disruption of the Ring. Only two significant facts interest us. The first was the difficulty and slowness with which even the better citizens were aroused. The repeated and concrete charges of the reformers met no response. In the fall of 1870 three of New York's best-known business men, John Jacob Astor, Moses Taylor and Marshall O. Roberts, let the Ring hoodwink them into making a cursory six-hour inspection of the city's doctored books and publishing a statement that its finances were being correctly ad-

[1] *Nation*, XIII, Nov. 9, 1871.
[2] C. F. Wingate, "An Episode in Municipal Government," *Il. Am. Rev.*, CXXI (1875), 137 ff.

ministered. The *World* consistently defended the Ring, while the *Sun* proposed a statue to Tweed.[1] In the end only a lucky accident, the fatal injury of the county auditor in a sleighing mishap, and the consequent installation of one of Tweed's enemies in the county book-keeper's office, made the exposure possible. The second fact was the vigor and intensity of the uprising which ensued. Decent opinion in New York was stirred to the depths as never since the firing on Sumter, and there came to the helm a group of men, including Samuel J. Tilden, Andrew H. Green and Charles O'Conor, who made the victory complete.[2]

But New York City by no means stood alone in requiring purgation. Across the East River Brooklyn was simultaneously in the grip of a ring of its own.[3] The municipal corruption of Philadelphia was as deep-seated and pervasive as that of New York, but it did not express itself in such spectacular robberies, while it was more difficult to attack because of the intrenched position of the Republican party. During 1871 a defaulting city treasurer cost Philadelphia four hundred and seventy-eight thousand dollars. In Chicago the fire burnt up a promising ring, one member of which, an unsuccessful candidate for mayor, was accused of large thefts.[4]

Men who were shocked by the crimes in city and state government rejoiced for a few years after the war that the federal administration was not grossly tainted; but only for a few years. Railway lobbyists spent money lavishly in Washington, the Union Pacific alone disbursing fully a half million by the middle of 1868.

[1] F. M. O'Brien, *The Story of the Sun* (N. Y., 1918), 271-274, charitably treats this as an example of Dana's peculiar sense of humor.
[2] Foord, *Life and Public Services of Andrew Haswell Green*, chaps. vii-x.
[3] *Nation*, XV, July 4, 1872.
[4] *Nation*, XIII, Nov. 15, 1871.

From the beginning it was recognized that the internal-revenue system was honeycombed with corruption. The war taxes on tobacco, cigars, and, above all, on distilled spirits were openly evaded. After two years of peace a congressional committee was able to report that few if any of the large American distilleries were doing a legitimate business and that at least seven eighths of the spirits escaped taxation.[1] The internal-revenue laws, like the tariff acts, bred the practice of blackmail by carrying a heavy fine and a provision for giving a small share to the informer. Thus the manufacturer who defrauded the government of fifty thousand dollars lost twice that amount, one hundred thousand dollars; but the informer got only five thousand dollars, and hence it was much more profitable for him to demand ten thousand dollars of the manufacturer. A horde of spies sprang up in the large cities, paying regular weekly or monthly visits to men whom they suspected of engaging in revenue evasion, and receiving large stipends for their silence. This became a thoroughly organized business and the hush money amounted to millions.[2] When later the federal corruption became appalling, many traced its vigorous inception to the revenue laws which had fostered a spirit of boodlery.

The first important scandal to develop was the Credit Mobilier affair.[3] The controlling stockholders of the Union Pacific had formed the Credit Mobilier to obtain for themselves the fat profits on the construction of that railway. In 1867 these financiers, with Oakes Ames, a congressman from Massachusetts, at their head, awarded to themselves, under the name of the company,

[1] *N. Y. Eve. Post*, Feb. 26, 1867; *Com. and Fin. Chron.*, Feb. 14, Feb. 21, March 14, 1874.
[2] *Com. and Fin. Chron.*, March 26, 1870.
[3] Rowland Hazard, *Credit Mobilier of America* (Providence, 1881); J. B. Crawford, *The Credit Mobilier of America* (Boston, 1880), 100 ff.

the contract for building and equipping most of the road on terms which gave them almost all the proceeds from the stocks and bonds created by the Union Pacific. That is, the cost of construction would exhaust the resources of the line and leave it mortgaged to its full value, stripped of the rich endowment provided by the federal government. The men who devised this scheme wanted to make sure that Congress would not interfere; and Oakes Ames hit upon the obvious method—a gentlemanly *douceur*. In the winter of 1867-1868 he sold to various members of the House and Senate shares of the Credit Mobilier, charging them only the par value, although the stock was understood by its owners to be worth at least twice that much. Ames stated in his letters that he wanted the shares distributed "where they will do the most good to us;" he declared that "there is no difficulty in inducing men to look after their own property."

Such members of Congress as Blaine, Boutwell, Bayard and Conkling were too circumspect to touch the proffered shares, but a large number of others, including some of the most influential men in public affairs, gratefully accepted them. There was the usual sequel; in 1872 one of the Credit Mobilier stockholders named McComb had a sordid quarrel with Ames, and published in the *New York Sun* a series of letters throwing a glaring light over the whole discreditable set of transactions. When Congress opened that fall there was an immediate inquiry under Representative Luke S. Poland of Vermont. This investigation brought forth facts which fell with ruinous force upon Ames, who was recommended for expulsion from the House, upon Vice-President Schuyler Colfax, who had bought twenty shares to be paid for out of dividends, upon Senator Patterson of New Hampshire, and upon James Brooks. The revelations were damaging, though not permanently so, to James A. Garfield, William B. Allison, William D. Kelley and others.[1] One feature of this scandal has a social significance that is worth noting. This was the difficulty of making many participants realize that they had done anything culpable. A number of men calmly avowed that they had felt no suspicion of what was virtually a free gift. Representative B. M. Boyer of Pennsylvania, for example, who had accepted seventy-five shares for his wife, declared that it was "a legitimate stock operation" and that his sole regret was "that it was no larger in amount."

Quite apart from governmental corruption, probably no period in our history has seen our commercial morality quite so widely debased as just after the war. During the summer of 1865 the country was shocked by repeated defalcations on a large scale, the chief being the flight of Edward B. Ketchum of the New York firm of Ketchum, Son and Company after stealing securities worth about two million five hundred thousand dollars, and forging gold certificates for one million two hundred and fifty thousand dollars more.[2] When the following spring an adventurer named John Ross was proved to have defrauded various men and banks to the extent of almost a half million dollars, the leading financial organ of the country pointed to the main cause of such events. "The reign of paper money," it exclaimed, "is always fertile in fraud, peculation, embezzlement, as well as in prodigality and extravagance."[3] But there was actually less outright defalcation than observers troubled by the epidemic of speculation expected. A far more serious rent in the moral garment of business was visible in the

---

[1] *House Rep.*, 42 Cong., 3 sess., no. 77.
[2] *Com. and Fin. Chron.*, Aug. 19, 1865.
[3] *Com. and Fin. Chron.*, May 5, 1866.

epidemic of wildcat stock selling, in stock watering, in
railway wrecking and in other schemes for plucking
the public.

The novelty and glamour of the resources opened
after the war, the inexperience of the public in investment and the total lack of regulatory laws, all produced
a natural consequence. The oil fields of Pennsylvania
were the first rich hunting ground for adepts in fraud.
Lured by the bait of a few glittering fortunes made by
lucky investments, hundreds of thousands poured a large
part of their means into the fields. As a matter of fact,
more men grew rich in "Petrolia" through speculation
and misrepresentation than through the actual yield of
oil.[1] Railway construction was equally fertile in schemes
to trap the unwary. One line after another promised
investors ten per cent or more, "security undoubted;"
and the purchaser found too late that the shares were
unsalable. The railway which James G. Blaine helped
promote in 1868-1869, the Little Rock and Fort Smith
line, was representative of a host of dubious enterprises.
It began nowhere, it led nowhere, its only hope of becoming profitable was to be made part of a Southern
transcontinental system. After Blaine had urged its
bonds upon possible customers and had gone to such
lengths in promising the use of his official position in its
behalf as to jeopardize his whole political future, it
finally involved him in serious monetary loss.[2] The
swindling stock companies of the mining regions, already mentioned, had their noted figure, too, in General
Robert C. Schenck, an Ohio ex-congressman who, after
serving with credit in the war, had been sent in 1870

[1] William Wright, *Oil Regions of Pennsylvania* (N. Y., 1865), 218 ff.;
Com. and Fin. Chron., Oct. 1, 1865.
[2] Edward Stanwood, *James Gillespie Blaine* (*American Statesmen*, ser.
2, Boston, 1905), 145 ff.; *Cong. Record*, 44 Cong., 1 sess., 2124 ff.

as minister to England. Known as the author of a treatise on poker, journals which considered him too rough and uncultivated for the place derisively referred to him as "our literary ambassador." While in England he virtually sold his name to the promoters of the Emma Mine for fifty thousand dollars in stock, with eighteen per cent interest guaranteed; and when the mine failed, English investors held Schenck morally responsible for their losses. They felt that he had given it virtually an official indorsement.[1]

Indeed, one of the chief features of interest in these swindles is the readiness with which eminent men lent their names to ventures which a little sober inquiry would have proved disreputable. When the Blaines and Schencks were so careless, what could be expected of those with no high reputation to maintain? Another aspect of equal social significance is the extraordinary gullibility of the public. Both find a partial explanation in the general belief, produced by victory, inflation and the industrial boom, that the nation had entered upon a golden age in which everyone could have wealth for a mere bold venture. Yet sometimes, as in the great diamond swindle which was revealed in San Francisco in the fall of 1872, both are difficult to comprehend. This attempted fraud was one of the boldest ever attempted in a wealthy, sophisticated community. Beginning in midsummer, rumors of a great discovery of diamond and ruby mines cropped out in the Pacific press.[2] Several of the shrewdest and richest men in California, with S. L. M. Barlow and General George B. McClellan in New York, formed the San Francisco and New York Mining and Commercial Company with a nominal capital of ten millions and the object of exploiting a diamond field

[1] *Nation*, XX, Dec. 5, 1875.
[2] *Nation*, XV, Dec. 12, 1872.

of extraordinary richness, the exact site of which was as yet unrevealed. Then just as the bubble was rising to impressive dimensions, it was neatly pricked. Clarence King, acting for the United States geological survey, showed that diamonds and rubies had been planted in a region utterly barren of gems. McClellan was left looking very foolish; so was Congress, which had been induced just before adjournment to pass in hot haste a placer-mining act so worded as to cover diamond mining. Yet McClellan meant no wrong, just as Grant meant no wrong when later he gave his name to aid the schemes of an unscrupulous partner who ruined him and many other men.[1]

But while mines, oil wells and other physical properties were natural pawns in the games of dishonest speculators, the absence either of careful statutes or of a well-established code of business ethics made manipulations of a subtler kind all too easy. In the life-insurance field the losses to the public reached an appalling total.[2] In the eight years beginning with 1870, no fewer than twenty-eight life insurance companies went out of business in New York. Some of them failed, others were amalgamated to save them from receiverships. Even in the latter event the policyholders were likely to lose, for their insurance was often deliberately extinguished by the process called "freezing out." The net total of nominal insurance represented by the twenty-eight companies was one hundred and fifty-nine million dollars, of which by far the greater portion was lost by the men and women who had paid for it. "The whole chapter," said the country's leading financial journal, "is so dark a record of betrayal of corporate trust—incapacity being so blended with dishonesty that it is impossible to sepa-

[1] L. A. Coolidge, *Ulysses S. Grant* (Boston, 1917), 556 ff.
[2] *Nation*, XII, Jan. 26, 1871.

rate them—that if we had the space and the data, we should not have the desire to expose its details." [1]   It was no darker, however, than the history of certain savings banks of the day. Early in 1872 the decent financial community of New York was hot with indignation against three, the Market, the Bowling Green and the Bowery savings banks, which had just failed under scandalous circumstances. Upon the poorest depositors, whose little accumulations might easily have been replaced out of the personal wealth of the bank officers, the blow fell with cruel violence. A wave of distrust swept the public and within a few months more than twenty million dollars was withdrawn from the remaining savings banks. The failure was followed, in bitter winter weather, by long delays in the distribution of assets. [2] Intelligent men who watched this distressing drama saw that here, as with insurance, some effective measure of state supervision was an urgent necessity, while there was also a demand for a law making the officers liable.

The most lurid light upon the rudimentary commercial morals of the period and the legal defenselessness of the public was that thrown by the great railway freebooters, whose operations were well launched before Grant took office. Daniel Drew, Jay Gould and Cornelius Vanderbilt, three New Yorkers, battled with an unscrupulousness previously unknown in American finance. All three men had risen from the humblest estate to positions of financial might, under circumstances that had taught them little of the responsibilities imposed by wealth. Drew was born on a small farm in Putnam County, where he began life as a cattle drover; Gould, the son of a farmer in Delaware County, was

[1] *Com. and Fin. Chron.*, April 19, 1869.
[2] *Com. and Fin. Chron.*, Jan. 27, 1872.

successively a clerk in a country store, a surveyor and a
tanner; while Vanderbilt, a native of Staten Island, had
gained his first capital by running a ferry to Manhattan.[1]
Drew, now a very old man but as energetic and unscrupulous as ever, was no better than a sharper though he
maintained a snuffling piety. Whenever he had been un-
usually fortunate in plucking trustful men, he salved his
conscience by a grant to some philanthropic object; it
was he who founded the Drew Theological Seminary
in New Jersey with promised gifts totaling a million,
most of which was never delivered. Gould was a cold-
hearted corruptionist who never hesitated to debauch a
newspaper, prostitute a legislature or make city officials
his pawns. As for Vanderbilt (called "the Commodore" from his success in building boats), he maintained
an air of high respectability and public spirit, but he
never forgot his pocket interests.[2]

Vanderbilt's effort in the late sixties to wrest control
of the Erie from Drew and Drew's associate, Gould,
brought on a veritable battle of the giants in which all
thought of public rights and all considerations of decency
were lost. The "Commodore" played a lone hand.
Drew not only relied heavily upon the cunning Gould,
but enlisted also the extraordinary figure known as "Jim"
Fisk. Fisk had begun his career as a peddler in Vermont, had been the manager of an itinerant circus and
had finally made a profitable place for himself among the
New York stock gamblers. He became distinguished as
a fat, flashy, boastful voluptuary who kept a harem of
mistresses, maintained a costly opera house, and lived a
life of gilded luxury.[3] This triumvirate not only out-

[1] Bouck White, *The Book of Daniel Drew* (N. Y., 1910), is an in-
cisive semifictional study of these three men.
[2] G. F. Redmond, *Financial Giants of America* (Boston, 1922), 75 ff.
[3] See Willoughby Jones, *James Fisk, Jr., the Life of a Green Mountain
Boy* (Phila., 1872).

played Vanderbilt, but employed methods that shocked the whole nation as a revelation of business corruption run wild.

For example, they used their power as officers of the Erie to print enormous quantities of stock, with which they broke down Commodore Vanderbilt's efforts to effect a corner of the railway's securities, and which they dumped on the market at the cost of still further weakening its credit. When Vanderbilt went to the notoriously venal Judge Barnard for an injunction, the trio appealed to a venal judge in Binghamton for a counter writ.[1] The warfare of the two circuit courts ended in a drawn battle. But when Judge Barnard issued a process against Drew, Gould and Fisk for contempt of court, making them liable to arrest, they hastily bundled up the millions they had received for their newly issued stock, fled across the Hudson, and took refuge in a railway hotel in Jersey City where they fortified themselves against any possible attack from ruffians who might be hired by Vanderbilt. The legislature being in session at Albany, the combat was immediately transferred from the courts to the capital, and a bill in the interests of Drew, legalizing the ten-million-dollar stock issue just printed, was introduced. Had the legislature been honest, it could never have been passed, but the session was thoroughly corrupt.[2] Gould was dispatched to Albany to act as a lobbyist and carried a trunk full of greenbacks; votes were openly for sale, and ordinary senators were paid fifteen thousand dollars apiece, while one man accepted seventy-five thousand dollars from Vanderbilt and one hundred thousand dollars from Gould, voting with the latter. It was said later that some rural districts felt humiliated

[1] For the corruption of bench and bar by these men, see Tilden, *Letters and Memorials*, I, 299 ff.
[2] *N. Y. Senate Doc.*, 1869, no. 52.

because their assemblymen sold themselves for less than
the ruling quotation.[1]   In the end the bill passed, and
the governor signed it.   The result was a treaty of peace
between Vanderbilt and Drew, a financial adjustment of
their quarrel and the cession of the plundered hulk
of the Erie railway to Gould and Fisk as managers,
Drew remaining their associate but keeping in the background.

The "Erie War" would seem to have sounded the lowest depths of commercial dishonesty; yet there was still
a bottom to be plumbed.   Gould and Fisk showed themselves to be apt pupils of Drew by their skill in plundering a property which any ordinary observer would have
decided was almost worthless.   They started the printing
presses again, and between June and October, 1868, increased the capital stock of the railway from thirty-four
million two hundred and sixty-five thousand dollars to
fifty-seven million seven hundred and sixty-six thousand
dollars, without consulting the board.[2]   The shares were
secretly and rapidly sold for cash, bringing a supposed
return of about ten million and plunging the stock down
to a preternaturally low point.   But the drop was not
sufficiently great to enable Gould and Fisk to repurchase
all the shares they had sold without compelling a sharp
increase in prices.   It was necessary to undertake a bolder
stroke, and to serve their speculative ends they and Drew
proceeded to prostrate a large part of the nation's business by a coup even more characteristic of the period than
that which the next year precipitated the panic of Black
Friday.

The readiness with which a badly controlled and operated financial system lends itself to buccaneering was

[1] *Nation*, XX, Feb. 18, 1875; Gustavus Myers, *History of Great
American Fortunes* (Chicago, 1910), II, 155 ff.
[2] White, *Book of Daniel Drew*, 325 ff.

never better illustrated.[1] Their scheme was simply to produce a money panic. The national banking act made it necessary for the national banks of New York to hold a reserve, in greenbacks and other legal tender, amounting to twenty-five per cent of their indebtedness to depositors and other creditors. These reserves usually declined in the fall under the pressure of crop movements; and in the event of a sharp money pinch the banks had to call in three dollars of loans for every dollar of greenbacks they paid out. The fact that the banks had to make a statement to the government early in each October and were hence likely to call in loans in order to place their affairs in a conservative condition held out a temptation to speculators to produce an artificial stringency. This had actually been done upon several occasions, compelling holders of stock to sell at ruinous prices to raise money to meet their obligations. The Drew-Fisk-Gould alliance resolved to repeat the stroke on a new scale.[2]

Taking the ten million dollars which they had realized from stock sales and four or five millions from other sources, the Drew-Fisk-Gould group deposited it in the city banks. At the critical moment they demanded payment of the whole amount in greenbacks and thus produced in a single day a dangerous reduction of the legal greenback reserves. The result was a hurried calling in of loans by all the banks, an almost unprecedented tightness of money, a frenzied rush to sell stocks and bonds to realize cash, and a shocking decline in the price of all securities. Trade throughout the United States ground sharply toward a standstill. Banking facilities almost failed the mercantile world, hundreds of men were ruined and thousands involved in grievous losses. Many hold-

[1] See *Com. and Fin. Chron.*, Oct. 10, Nov. 14, 1868.
[2] *Hunt's Merchants' Mag.*, LIX (1868), 344.

ers of good stocks and bonds had to sell them at one half
or one third their value; prices of goods declined from
ten to thirty per cent; even government bonds fell five
or six per cent almost overnight. Over the whole scene
of confusion and despair Drew, Fisk and Gould stood
triumphant, buying back Erie and other stocks at
enormous profits.[1]

But this was only half of their plan of campaign. The
conspirators at once employed their immense gains to
buy large amounts of gold, which had been depressed in
price along with all other values; and they then with-
drew the entire stock of gold they owned from the market. The metal immediately became so scarce that the
price advanced four per cent in two days, and one-per-
cent interest was paid upon it, while the whole export
and import trade of the nation felt the same profound
shock that internal trade had just suffered. The foreign
exchanges shook and many foreign merchants lost all
or part of their property. By now, too, the effects of
the first blow which the Erie speculators had struck at
the nation's commercial life had been felt by agriculture.
The money that should have flowed South and West to
pay for the incoming harvest was frozen tight, the crops
were immobilized, and the farmers were thrown into
straitened circumstances, numbers of them losing their
homes. From the Mississippi to the Danube this whirl-
wind raid through the stock and the gold markets was
felt with disastrous effect.[2]

One reassuring evidence of a basically sound business
life buried somewhere beneath such disturbances was
the storm of anger and denunciation with which this
foray was received. It was plain that the robbers could
not be attacked through the criminal courts; for as soon

[1] White, *Book of Daniel Drew*, 325 ff.
[2] *Nation*, VII, Nov. 26, 1868.

as August Belmont obtained an injunction against them, it was learned that they had taken the precaution to enlist Judge Barnard on their side and to obtain from him court orders nullifying any possible stroke of their enemies.[1] But the press was outspoken in its condemnation. Thus the *Nation* declared that no matter how the fortunes thus acquired were spent, "all good men should unite in treating the owners as infamous." The *Springfield Republican* asserted that "nothing so audacious, nothing more gigantic in the way of real swindling has ever been perpetrated in this country." Its other comments led Fisk to bring a libel suit for fifty thousand dollars, which was not pressed, but which enabled Fisk's partners in the Tammany Ring to seize suddenly upon its editor, Samuel Bowles, when he visited New York in December, 1868, and throw him into jail for a night.[2] The comments of the *Evening Post* maintained the pungency that had already led Barnard to declare from the bench that Bryant was "the most notorious liar in the United States." The *Commercial and Financial Chronicle* was blistering in its attacks.[3]

The same emphatic condemnation by every agency of public opinion followed Black Friday, when Gould and Fisk audaciously tried in September, 1869, to effect a corner of the gold supply of the nation and were defeated by the government's sale of four million dollars in gold.[4] All Wall Street rushed upon the pair, and they showed

[1] White, *Book of Daniel Drew*, 314 ff.
[2] Richard Hooker, *The Story of an Independent Newspaper* (N. Y., 1924), 105.
[3] See Henry Adams, *The Education of Henry Adams* (Boston, 1918), 271-272: "The worst scandals of the eighteenth century were relatively harmless by the side of this, which smirched executive, judiciary, banks, corporate systems, professions, and people, all the great active forces of society, in one dirty cesspool of vulgar corruption."
[4] For Black Friday, see G. S. Boutwell, *Reminiscences of Sixty Years in Public Affairs* (N. Y., 1902), II, chap. xxxv.

a new side of their utter unscrupulousness by refusing to pay a dollar of the funds they had borrowed. This was done by a flat repudiation through Fisk's responsible partner Belden. Fisk was asked by a congressional committee what had become of all the money involved in that disastrous coup. "It has gone," he replied, "where the woodbine twineth." Two years later the chorus of editorial denunciation was heard in its most impressive tones when Fisk was fatally shot in the Grand Central Hotel in 1872 by a business and amatory rival, Edward S. Stokes. His body lay in state in his Grand Opera House, the Tammany administration paid him every honor, and his funeral cortege included the Ninth Regiment and a band of two hundred pieces; but his career was made the theme for a thousand condemnatory sermons.[1]

The constant outcropping of violence in American life in these years was also disquieting, though much of it was a natural result of the spirit of ruffianism engendered by the Civil War and of the recklessness of the frontiersman and the ignorant alien. Both Cole and James Younger, and Jesse James, who organized notorious gangs, had been with Quantrell's Confederate guerrillas during the conflict and, when peace came, were left smarting under a sense of persecution. For ten years they conducted their intermittent raids over a wide territory, looting banks in Missouri and Kentucky, holding up stagecoaches in Arkansas and Texas, and wrecking trains in Iowa and other states. Jesse James's most spectacular exploit was his descent upon the Kansas City Fair on Sept. 26, 1872, when he escaped with ten thou-

[1] E. H. Mott, *Between the Ocean and the Lakes; the Story of Erie* (N. Y., 1899), 489. It is a fact of some social significance that Stokes escaped with four years in jail, was allowed to keep his carriage and pair at Sing Sing, and lived to be socially popular as the owner of the Hoffman House in New York.

sand dollars in gate money.[1] But there were other gangs
as well throughout all the border territory from West
Virginia to Arkansas, while for a short time after the war
even upper New York, Ohio and Indiana had troublesome rural organizations of robbers. The gangsters and
ruffians of New York City committed innumerable outrages, and in the bloody Orange Riot of July 12, 1871,
the work of the same immigrant element which had
played the chief part in the draft riots, had to be sup-
pressed by the state militia.

Another disquieting fact of these years was the prevalence of gambling from New York to Sacramento. New
York City after the war was said to have two thousand
gambling houses. All the way from the Battery to
Thirtieth Street were scattered hidden gaming parlors,
placed in the upper stories of business buildings—luxurious resorts with velvet rugs, gleaming sideboards well
laden, soft lounges and a general air of wealth. At a
famous game between John Morrissey and Ben Wood, in
which the latter won one hundred and twenty-four thousand dollars, a well-known judge watched the entire evening and lent Wood the money he needed to continue
playing. In other cities the gamblers were a numerous
and wealthy tribe, while the Louisiana lottery, placed on
a new footing by the Reconstructionists, flourished. Yet
while the manifold evils of the time gave rise, among
thoughtful observers, to much pessimism, it was not
tinged with despair. Many of these evils were superficial, and for those which were deep-seated a surgeon's
knife, sharp and painful, was already at hand in the
Panic of 1873 and the sobering depression which followed.

[1] Robertus Love, *The Rise and Fall of Jesse James* (N. Y., 1926).

CHAPTER VIII

THE EVERYDAY LIFE OF AMERICANS

AMERICAN life between the war and the Panic of
1873 was characterized throughout the North, except
for the depressed rural districts and some underpaid labor
groups, by a decidedly greater prosperity and comfort
than ever before. The Panic, of course, brought grinding economy and privation into millions of homes, but
this burden was gradually lightened and the old level
restored. Taking the period as a whole, the real wealth
of the population attained a higher average than before
the conflict. The heavy production of cheap foodstuffs,
the progress of invention, the application of factory
methods of manufacture, all brought increased ease and
well-being to the public. In what we may call the
typical American town or city home, the dwelling of a
fairly well-to-do clerk or shopkeeper or business man,
there was better food, better furniture, better clothing
and more books and magazines. The domestic economy
of the time offers much that now appears stuffy, tasteless and repellent, but in part these very qualities grew
out of a higher standard of living. Men had money to
spend without knowing very well how to spend it.[1] In
this period the late Victorian modes and manners came
into their full bloom, and they make a curious study.
There have been few decades in which ugliness so

[1] "Who knows how to be rich in America?" demanded Godkin.
"Plenty of people know how to get money; but not very many know
what best to do with it. To be rich properly is indeed a fine art. It
requires culture, imagination, and character." *Nation* (N. Y.), II,
March 8, 1866.

prevailed in the building of houses as that just before the Centennial Exhibition; yet it was an ugliness that spoke of wealth and that was associated with comfort. Jay Cooke's huge mansion called "Ogontz" was not untypical of many rich men's residences.[1] A vast gloomy pile of granite, one hundred and seventy-five feet long, with seventy-two rooms, it cost two million dollars; and the *Art Journal* rightly dismissed it as "inharmonious, heavy, and confusing."[2] Bayard Taylor's Italian villa at Kennett Square, also near Philadelphia, showed how badly a literary man building a costly house quite beyond his means could do. An Italian villa, its main body square and ugly, it possessed a tall tower, with spire, dormer windows and a veranda in it.

Yet the artists themselves proved no better. Albert Bierstadt built a house on Haverstraw Bay, on a fine commanding site overlooking the widest part of the Hudson, that in its weird medley of towers, turrets and jigsaw work in iron and wood was an atrocity. It did not quite equal, however, the residence of the painter F. E. Church on the same noble river.[3] This in a bastard "Persian" style, with four towers, several minarets, Moorish arches, much glaring mosaic work in red, yellow and black bricks, and a glittering crescent above all for a weathercock, was an outrage upon taste that could hardly be parallelled in the East. When men of distinction indulged themselves in such architectural nightmares, it is hardly surprising that the ordinary American with money to spare lived in an altogether tasteless

[1] Described in E. P. Oberholtzer, *Jay Cooke* (Phila., 1907), II, 33, 447. *Sloan's Homestead Architecture* (Phila., 1866), an architectural guide compiled by Samuel Sloan, highly recommended architectural monstrosities of the kind described in the text; its popularity is evidenced by the fact that it was already in its second edition in 1867.

[2] *Art Journal*, III (1877), 260 ff.

[3] *Art Journal*, II (1876), 45, 247.

This Solid Walnut Centennial Italian Marble Top
Chamber Suit, three pieces, viz.: Double Bedstead,
Marble Top Bureaus, and Marble Top Washstand, $47.

An "Italian" villa.
Bayard Taylor's house.

A Rogers group.

A typical American
courthouse.

In the best taste of the period—the Roosevelt parlor, New York City.

house. Only at the close of this period did new tendencies show signs of driving the mansard roof, the heavy ornaments and the rococo lines into the past.

The interior of the typical urban home of the North was somber, crowded and deficient in simple refinement, but quite comfortable to the occupants. Floors were usually covered to the edges with carpets, nailed down tight with straw beneath, and swept with heavy brooms till worn out. The *Nation* tried to convert housewives to the European fashion of throwing a few rugs loosely upon hardwood floors, but with slow results. Visitors at the Centennial contrasted the American carpets, poor in material and design but protected by a high tariff, very unfavorably with the imported Axminster and Indian carpets. Late in the seventies a new floor covering, linoleum,[1] was being extensively advertised. The great majority of homes were of course still heated by stoves or fireplaces, and even Franklin stoves survived here and there. In the cities most of the better houses were warmed by hot-air furnaces, with pipes leading to large iron registers in the floor; but the public had begun to apprehend an unhealthfulness in this system and to demand steam heat. Even in small towns many newly built houses were now supplied with gas and running water. One observer of the wealthier classes tells us that by 1869 it was unusual to find a town home without a comfortable bath room; but the bathtub was certain to be a zinc-lined structure of black walnut or pine.[2] The fine pictured wall papers of the past had been universally displaced by cheaper and gaudier print papers of questionable design.

[1] *N. Y. Times*, March 6, 1876. The *Times* noted a growing protest against mansard roofs, a new interest in simplicity, and an increasing taste for Oriental rugs. See also *Appleton's Annual Cyclopedia* (N. Y., 1861-1903), XV (1876), 262 ff.

[2] G. M. Towle, *American Society* (London, 1870), I, chap. xviii.

The furniture of these homes tended to be elaborately decorative. The Atlantic states were filled with the work of a New York cabinetmaker named Marcotte and his imitators, who produced ornamental curving tables covered with chocolate-hued marble, while fashionable people bought the much better square-patterned pieces called the Eastlake, with incised lines of gilt tracing elaborate figures.[1] A happy influence that grew stronger in the seventies was that of the Englishman William Morris, who had established furniture workshops in 1861 on the principle that "decoration involving rather the luxury of taste than the luxury of costliness will be found to be much less expensive than is generally supposed," and whose designs were known in America ten years later.[2] Most people felt that a parlor was incomplete without a Rogers group of statuary, and a popular anecdote of a later day told of a tramp who assured his benefactress, "You can realize how poor we were, ma'am, when I tell you that my parents could never afford to buy Rogers's 'Weighing the Baby.'" Wealthier householders used, instead, an ornamental bowl of alabaster called a "tazza." But everyone delighted in the portière, the lambrequin, the whatnot, the antimacassar and Berlin wool work; everybody thought it proper for daughters to learn to decorate china or paint on a brass plaque or on crimson plush; and in the late seventies nearly everyone deemed iron statuary on the lawn a mark of taste and means.[3] Crocheting was a constant feminine employment, and crocheted match holders and dog muzzles were not unknown. Plush albums were universal. Even the White House had its hand-painted china with fruit, fish

[1] M. F. Egan, *Recollections of a Happy Life* (N. Y., 1924), 66-67.
[2] *Nation*, XII, March 2, 1871. See Oscar Wilde's denunciation a little later of American horsehair furniture and of stoves with funereal urns on top.
[3] Helen Nicolay, *Our Capital on the Potomac* (N. Y., 1924), 403-404.

or poultry portrayed on each dish. Late in the eighteen-seventies came the "aesthetic movement" from England, bringing gilded chair legs, vases filled with cat-tails, embroidered "throws," and Japanese fans tacked to the walls.

The remoter the communities the more likely they were to be filled with excruciating household materials. Mark Twain in 1874 described with rare gusto the typical well-to-do Southern home as it still survived, scattered in towns and villages along the Mississippi.[1] Here was the parlor with its ingrain carpet, its mahogany center table, its polished airtight stove with a pipe passing through the painted board which closed a discarded fireplace, its piano with a beribboned guitar tilted against it, and its pyramidal whatnot in a corner. Tupper, Ossian and a copy of *Friendship's Offering* represented literature, the current number of *Godey's Lady's Book*, with painted fashion plates as double-page illustrations, showed an interest in periodicals; and the piano was piled with such selections as "The Battle of Prague," "The Last Link is Broken" and "Long, Long Ago." On the walls were hung a variegated array of drab steel engravings, Landseer being especially popular, lithographs, amateurish crayon drawings, a family group in oils and a pious motto done in faded grasses. The bric-a-brac included shells with the Lord's Prayer or a carving of Washington, several alum baskets of various colors, a pair of bead moccasins from some relative who had crossed the plains, several daguerreotypes spread open in folding covers, and under a glass dome a large bouquet of wax flowers. Somewhere in the house, if not in this sacred parlor, would be a number of horsehair chairs and a slippery horsehair sofa.

Such homes continued to exist in diminishing num-

[1] Mark Twain, *Life on the Mississippi* (Hartford, 1889), 295-299.

bers down to the end of the century, and a few may be found today.[1]   Naturally they were most numerous in the conservative South, the section which actually found diversion after the war in holding what it called "tournaments," after the model of that described in *Ivanhoe*. Crowds gathered at these entertainments to watch young men who were dressed in fantastic costumes and who called themselves "disinherited knights" or "knights of the sword," tilting at a ring to win a prize offered by some young woman who was styled the "queen of love and beauty."

In New York City an important innovation just after the war was the construction of many "French flats" or modern apartment houses of which the first was erected in 1870 at 142 East Eighteenth Street by the architect Richard M. Hunt.[2]   It was said to be better than most of those in Paris and, at rentals of from one thousand dollars to one thousand five hundred dollars a year, offered sixteen suites of six rooms and a bath.   G. P. Putnam, the publisher, and other men of means lived here. The demand for these convenient homes, with their saving in servant hire, rapidly increased.   They filled a keenly felt need, for previously all well-to-do New Yorkers had known but two modes of residence: they must either take a full single house or consent to live in a dismal boarding house.   Builders vied with each other in putting up costlier and better equipped buildings.   A block of flats was shortly overlooking Central Park from the east at Sixty-eighth Street, and gave each tenant eight rooms and a bath, black-walnut floors, elevator service and his own kitchen range and hot water heater for from

[1] For an excellent picture of a well-to-do Indiana home in the seventies, see the first pages of Booth Tarkington, *The Magnificent Ambersons* (N. Y., 1922).

[2] Henry Holt, *The Garrulities of an Octogenarian Editor* (Boston, 1923), 125, 170.

seventy-five dollars to one hundred and fifty dollars a month.[1] By 1874 the *Evening Post* thought that the new apartment houses "may now be considered almost perfect," and by the close of the following year the *World* could state that there were one hundred and ninety-eight of them in New York, accommodating about three thousand families.[2] The Haight Building, at Fifteenth Street and Fifth Avenue, offered flats renting for from two thousand dollars to three thousand dollars, with an elevator, an internal telegraph and a restaurant. Among the notables living there were Henry M. Field, the traveler; Colonel W. C. Church, editor of the *Galaxy*; E. L. Youmans and the Spanish consul.

Across dress, as across architecture, the meretricious splendor of the Second Empire threw its influence even after the empire had fallen into ruins. Eugénie invented, or at least revived, the crinoline skirt which became universal in the sixties and which Anthony Trollope found far more vulgarly excessive in size in New York than in Europe. She also gave vogue to the horizontally striped stocking which appeared in all its gayety in 1865 and was soon followed by solid colors.[3] There were Empire bonnets and hair was dressed in the Empire style, while zouave jackets were much in fashion, and the "robe impératrice" also showed the French influence. In the late seventies came the bustle and the barber-pole skirt, while throughout the decade the sealskin coat was the height of elegance. Women cultivated the absurd posture called the Grecian bend, while the chignon and waterfall—the latter a heavy bag of hair which most girls were sensible enough to lay aside

[1] Allan Nevins, *The Evening Post* (N. Y., 1922), 368-369.
[2] *N. Y. World*, Dec. 18, 1875; Jan. 24, 1876.
[3] See the files of *Godey's* and *Demorest's*, 1865-1866.

on hot days—were familiar everywhere. A powder called "golddust" was frequently sprinkled on the hair for evening parties.[1] Shawls were much used by women, but men had dispensed with them. All well-dressed little boys appeared in kilts and in boots with black tassels, while little girls wore Garibaldi suits. Men's clothing still tended to the somber in color and in cut, black broadcloth being the approved material for everyday business wear, and bright waistcoats having faded from the scene. Full dress, which included tight "doeskin" trousers and a stovepipe hat, was regarded as merely a matter of choice at even very formal evening gatherings, while it was not infrequently worn at other times of the day; at the famous breakfast in honor of Holmes's seventieth birthday in Boston in 1879, served at noon, a few guests appeared in evening garb.[2] Men pomaded their hair, and regarded trouser creases, a sign of the store shelf, with distaste. It was the era of universal, luxuriant and variegated beards.

The American diet altered but slowly. One of the principal changes was the more and more general introduction of oatmeal, called "grits" or "Irish oatmeal," as a breakfast dish. It tended to lighten that repast, which still usually comprised not only fruit, coffee and rolls but steak, chops, or ham and eggs, and frequently in addition fried potatoes. Even Emerson, as we wonder now to learn, habitually ate pie for breakfast. Through large parts of the North men found it hard to rise from breakfast without a stack of buckwheat cakes, while New Englanders retained all their old fondness for baked beans and pork on Sunday morning.[3] This heavy meal betrayed the persistence of rural habits. So,

[1] *Valentine's Manual of Old New York* (new ser., N. Y., 1923), 4 ff.
[2] G. C. Eggleston, *A Rebel's Recollections* (N. Y., 1875), 177.
[3] Towle, *American Society*, I, chap. xviii.

too, did the prevalent habit of making dinner the mid-
day repast and the fact that most prosperous American
families thought that two dishes of meat, or one of
meat and one of fish, were none too many. A half-
dozen vegetables were frequently served. Supper, or
tea, was a much simpler refection, and was served early,
for the English fashion of eating after 7:00 P.M. was
followed only in a few highly fashionable circles.
Nearly every family still made its own bread, and the
hotels usually had a baking establishment of their own.
Among the novelties of the seventies were oleomargarine
and butterine, which appeared soon after the establishment of meat packing as a highly centralized industry
and which within a few years found a large export
trade.[1]

As for drinks, wine was seldom served except upon
ceremonial occasions and even then was frowned upon
by good American families. It was practically unknown on the table of city hotels, where it was customary for men to repair to the bar for a drink or two of
spirits before or after eating. In some private houses
there was a genial practice called "taking the oath,"[2]
which meant finding a little bourbon and ice water in the
recesses of a bookcase or behind a statuette of Powers's
"Greek Slave;" but outside the large cities spirits were
regarded with stern disapproval. Beer was no longer
treated as a foreign beverage; the war record of the Germans, as well as the low excise tax already mentioned,
commended it to growing numbers. In Milwaukee, the
home of the Schlitz, Best and Pabst breweries, its production thrived so well that the output rose from thirty-

[1] C. D. Wright, *Industrial Evolution of the United States* (N. Y.,
1901), chap. xiv.
[2] But for the more convivial, artistic and literary circle of New York,
see Egan, *Recollections*, 107 ff.

six thousand barrels in 1860 to two hundred and sixty thousand barrels in 1873.[1]

The rigidity of private morals and the primness of convention were still striking. Sunday was generally observed with strictness throughout the Northern and Middle states. No theaters could open their doors; all liquor sales were forbidden though evasion was frequent; and businesses were tightly closed, even drug stores sometimes falling under the prohibition. The British journalist G. A. Sala found that the observance of the day was "more than Scotch in its severity" and felt fortunate in Baltimore that he could hire a carriage for a drive.[2] The rural South was even more rigid, but in some Southern cities such light refreshments as tobacco and confectionery were purchasable, and in New Orleans the fish market was open for an hour or two on Sunday morning to dispose of its perishable wares. Even charitable work for the poor was often considered a desecration of the Sabbath, and Maurice Francis Egan found that sewing in their behalf would have created a scandal in the Washington of 1875.[3] At least two states, Vermont and South Carolina, were so straight-laced that throughout these years they had statutes making church attendance compulsory. Still, steady inroads were being made upon the bleak Puritan Sunday, for men were beginning to realize that the toiling masses in the cities needed the day for unfettered relaxation.[4]

The utmost regard was paid in the better social circles to the proprieties. Among many families of the Eastern cities chaperons were considered indispensable, and in

[1] Frederick Merk, *Economic History of Wisconsin during the Civil War Decade* (State Hist. Soc. of Wis., *Studies*, I, 1916), 152 ff.

[2] G. A. Sala, *America Revisited* (London, 1883), II, 58 ff.

[3] Egan, *Recollections*, 65.

[4] J. H. Ward, "The New Sunday," *Atlantic Monthly*, XLVII (1881), 526-537.

Philadelphia young men like James Huneker found that
for a girl to go alone with her suitor to a theater or ball
would have riddled her reputation.[1] Elsewhere young
people were allowed a freedom based on a complete and
justified confidence that the rules of good behavior would
be instinctively observed. The novels of Charles Reade
were regarded as shocking, and *A Terrible Temptation*
was denounced by press and pulpit as "carrion literature." Swinburne and Whitman were declaimed against
with equal fervor, and Whitman's removal from his
clerkship in the interior department in 1865 on the
ground that he had published improper poetry was a
deplorable example of moral rigidity pushed to Pharisa-
ism and intolerance. Throughout the seventies John
Burroughs and other devoted friends had to champion
Whitman against the running attacks of journals like the
New York Tribune.[2] Such family magazines as *Scribner's* and *Harper's* never printed a word which could be
considered objectionable by the most prudish taste; and
Howells in the seventies commenced a series of novels so
dominated by a respect for what "nice" people wanted
that their realism totally neglected the uglier aspects of
American social life.

Much was said about what Mrs. Lynn Linton in
England called "the girl of the period," who was
thought then, as always, a little faster than her
mother; much was said about the corroding effect of
prosperity and luxury upon morals. But sexual morality was still, as Rhodes declares it was in the fifties,
kept at a high level.[3] To be sure, the great cities had

---

[1] James Huneker, *Steeplejack* (N. Y., 1920), I, 92.
[2] Clara Barrus, *The Life and Letters of John Burroughs* (Boston,
1925), I, 133, 182. The *Atlantic* would have nothing to do with
Whitman, and *Scribner's* returned his poems with insulting notes.
[3] C. L. Brace, *Gesta Christi* (N. Y., 1888), 307 ff. *Cf.* Don C.
Seitz, *The Dreadful Decade* (Indianapolis, 1926), 213 ff.

scandals enough; those feminist crusaders, Victoria and Tennessee Claflin, published a weekly which for a time specialized in exposures of double life in New York. But the nation as a whole met fairly rigid moral standards.

This was partly because of the force of public opinion and rooted Anglo-American standards; partly because men worked hard; and partly because marriage came early and home life was well protected. It is true that observers still commented upon the popularity of the boarding house and residential hotel. Even in the Far West many a young couple began their life together in this wise. E. L. Godkin thought it worth while in 1868 to fulminate in the *Nation* against the married couple who, though able to own a home, deliberately boarded to save trouble, as citizens who were "enemies of society and deserve clerical reprobation in almost equal degree with the purchasers of Indiana divorces." [1] It was not the mere chilly aridity of the boarding house that made it objectionable. It was accused of leading to indolence, promiscuous friendships, a disregard for family ties and immoral relations between the sexes. J. D. Burn wrote that, from his observation, "I have no hesitation in saying that many of these houses are hotbeds of vice and every species of immorality." However, the extent to which Americans patronized the residential hotel and the restaurant was greatly exaggerated by the foreigners who were entertained in many such institutions and in few private homes. Their patronage represented in the main a transitory mode of life until a family could find permanent occupation and a settled home. American boarding houses were, as a native commentator said, chiefly asylums for bachelors, spinsters, widows and young couples who longed ardently

[1] *Nation*, VII, Dec. 3, 1868, 453.

for love in a c...   ...reover, they were typical of
the great cente...   ...nan of the smaller cities.

The health...   ...icity of Americans was, in fact,
unquestionabl...   ...ne old usage of early marriage continued, though of course not so early as in colonial times,
and we are assured by Von Glosz that the ages of twenty-
three for men and seventeen for girls were regarded as
perfectly normal for contracting a union.   As a French-
man put it, before the young Americans had passed
twenty they were "thinking of establishing themselves,
taking a wife, founding on their own account a banking
or mercantile house, and of quitting the temporary hospitality of the paternal roof."   Sir George Campbell
formed a decided impression in the late sixties that
Americans married earlier and trusted more to their wits
to support a family than did the British.[2]   Some Americans took a different view; but the Nation's editorial of
1868 on "Why is Single Life Becoming More General?"
referred primarily to New England and to the upper
tenth there.[3]   As for divorce, there was as yet very little
of it though it was increasing.   In the year 1867 there
were 9,937 divorces in the whole nation, and we have
evidence that the number rose with great uniformity to
16,089 in 1878.   This was an increase of more than
sixty per cent.[4]   But when it is realized that in 1867
there were only twenty-seven divorces in the country
for every one hundred thousand people, it will be seen
that the situation was far from disquieting.   Divorce
has its beneficent side in that it reflects a higher independence and self-respect among women and is preferable

[1] Towle, quoted by A. W. Calhoun, Social History of the American
Family (Cleveland, 1917), III, 183.
[2] George Campbell, White and Black (London, 1879), 283.
[3] Nation, VI, March 5, 1868.
[4] U. S. Commissioner of Labor, Rep. on Marriage and Divorce in the
United States, 1867-1886 (Wash., 1889).

to a jangling and loveless marriage. Nations with little divorce are commonly nations with numerous irregular establishments and in which the domination of the husband overrules any incompatibility. With the drift toward the cities, where couples had less neighborhood disapproval to fear if they separated, with the growing economic independence of women and with the restless movement of the population, it would have been astonishing if divorce had not increased.[1]

In only two states, Connecticut and Indiana, was the legislation governing divorce liberal to the point of laxity, and here it was gravely censured by the rest of the Union. The statutes in Connecticut allowed the dissolution of a marriage for "any such conduct as permanently destroys the happiness of the petitioner, and defeats the purpose of the marriage relation," but public opinion compelled its repeal in 1878. It was to Indiana that divorce hunters usually proceeded, as at a later date to Nevada. A year's residence qualified for a petition, the case could be tried thirty days after a published notice, and the defendant was often ignorant of the proceedings. W. D. Howells in *A Modern Instance* gives a vivid picture of an Indiana divorce trial and of the frustration of a wife-deserter's effort to procure his release by perjury.[2]

Americans after the war were keenly interested in all forms of amusement. The growing urbanization of the country brought summer resorts into increased favor and caused the rapid multiplication of seashore cottages. Newport in 1866, a city whose permanent residents numbered only fifteen thousand, had about three thousand

---

[1] See Jennie L. Wilson, *The Legal and Political Status of Women in the United States* (Cedar Rapids, Iowa, 1912).

[2] W. D. Howells, *A Modern Instance* (Boston, 1881), chap. xxxi, *passim*.

summer visitors who took cottages, six or seven thousand who stayed at hotels and boarding houses, and tens of thousands who came for one-day excursions.[1] Here, north of Boston and at other watering places, the crowds were so great that many, disgusted by the heterogeneous company at hotels, erected their own villas. This new departure was most evident at Long Branch where the many summer houses were supplemented by hostelries of an exclusive type. When Grant became president, he began spending the hottest weeks in Long Branch, building two modest cottages, one of which he rented; and taking his horses with him the second year, he spent hours in driving.[2] The popularity of the White Mountains grew rapidly, and in 1866-1869 a railway on the cogwheel principle was built to the summit of Mount Washington, making possible the erection there of a comfortable inn called the Summit House. Saratoga, after suffering a temporary loss of prestige and gayety through the absence of the Southerners who had given it so much life before the war, made a steady recovery.[3] Meanwhile, increasing crowds were seeking the Rockies and the South. Denver became a place of resort for tourists and pleasure seekers as soon as the Indian hostilities died away, while Colorado Springs at the foot of Pike's Peak, boasting a climate better than that of Davos, was founded in 1871. By 1874 the population of several Florida cities, notably Jacksonville, was doubled every winter.[4] The summer vacation, which before the war had been largely an indulgence of the well-to-do, now rapidly became general

[1] *N. Y. Eve. Post*, July 12, 1865.
[2] Hamlin Garland, *Ulysses S. Grant, His Life and Character* (N. Y., 1898), 398. Ocean Grove and Asbury Park were founded soon after the war, primarily for Methodist visitors.
[3] *N. Y. Times*, editorial, Oct. 7, 1876.
[4] E. King, "The Great South," *Scribner's Monthly*, IX (1874), 1-31.

among nonmanual workers.[1] In the Northeastern states the practice of summer camping in the woods was noted in 1873 to be on the increase, having the advantage of cheapness as well as the opportunity to live close to nature.

Everyone commented on the popularity of the theater in Eastern cities just after the war. In 1866 it was estimated that the total receipts of the New York playhouses were between two million dollars and two million five hundred thousand dollars—Niblo's Garden alone took in nearly three hundred and fifty thousand dollars.[2] The opera flourished, with its fashionable audience arrayed in decorative opera cloaks and gay rich dresses, with jeweled fans and marvelous chevelures. Even New Orleans, it must not be forgotten, had its opera. It had also its great Mardi Gras festival, which toward the close of this period annually drew strangers by thousands from the entire lower South, but especially from Alabama. Henry Adams was a little depressed by a new postwar Boston in which fortunes of four millions did not seem extraordinary; but it was, above all, in New York that, as one observer put it, the social type was "that of a brilliant, ostentatious, sprightly, pleasure-seeking kind." Here the desire was keenest to outdo one's neighbors, to have the most gorgeous drawing-rooms, equipages and dinners, and to follow an unceasing round of glittering gayety.[3] The newcomer found that the more *recherché* his manners, the more piquant his conversation, the purer the breed of horses he drove, the more fashionable his criticism of pictures, books and music, the better he was liked; but above all it was money that was indispensable.

[1] *Nation*, XVII, Aug. 7, 1873.
[2] *N. Y. Eve. Post*, Aug. 31, Sept. 8, 18, 1865.
[3] Towle, *American Society*, I, chap. xix, gives a good description of a fashionable evening party in New York.

Immediately after the peace, racing attained a new popularity and dignity, chiefly because it was taken up by the leaders of fashion in New York. The American Jockey Club, founded by Leonard W. Jerome, W. R. Travers, August Belmont and other wealthy sportsmen, purchased a beautiful site of two hundred and thirty acres in Westchester County, which was named Jerome Park, and in 1866 built there a grandstand accommodating eight thousand people. The sale of liquors was prohibited and everything done that money could effect to give the place an air of gentility fit for ladies.[1] At the opening races General Grant was present. The towns north of New York promptly built a fine broad drive to this race course, so that rich citizens could trot their pacers over the Harlem River and through the green country. Belmont and others set themselves to horse breeding with great assiduity, and racing was soon intrenched as a pastime of the best society. Very shortly that newspaper prince, James Gordon Bennett, jr., was introducing polo into the United States at Newport.

It was due to the war that outdoor sports showed in the late sixties a vigor never before approached. Baseball, a popular pastime in the camps, promptly established itself as the national game.[2] Club after club was formed until hundreds were represented at the annual convention of the National Association of Baseball Players. The meeting of 1867 showed fifty-six in Illinois alone, and forty-two in Iowa; while in the Eastern cities great crowds gathered throughout the summer to watch the matches. Young men of future distinction on the diamond were emerging—A. G. Spalding of Rockford, Illinois, Adrian C. Anson of Marshalltown, Iowa, and

[1] N. Y. Eve. Post, May 7, 1867.
[2] See A. G. Spalding, *America's National Game* (N. Y., 1911), chap. viii.

James White of Sutton, New York. It was not long before intersectional contests were arranged. Arthur Pue Gorman of Maryland, a crack player whose executive talents later placed him in the Senate, helped to arrange a triumphant Western tour of the National Club of Washington in 1867; and three years later Spalding's club of Rockford made a trip through the East, winning fifty-one games out of sixty-five played. At first an effort was made to keep the sport on a thoroughly clean amateur basis; but amateur standards quickly collapsed as betting on games became prevalent and players were bribed to "throw" matches. City clubs arranged to give coveted small-town players high-salaried positions in commercial and industrial enterprises, and we find Spalding early in his career offered forty dollars a week, ostensibly to clerk in a wholesale grocery in Chicago, but really to be a member of the Excelsior Club there.

The public began to lose its former confidence and to grumble. The result was that the Red Stockings of Cincinnati took in 1869 a revolutionary step, frankly turning themselves into a professional team under the management of a veteran player named Henry Wright. That summer they made an Eastern tour, the first tour of a professional club, in which they won every game. It demonstrated at once and decisively the superiority of a team chosen, trained and paid for the work they did over any set of amateurs brought together for mere exercise and amusement. Professional baseball immediately overspread the whole nation, and names now long familiar to every lover of the sport became for the first time well-known: the Chicago White Stockings, the Philadelphia Athletics, the Washington Nationals. In 1871 ten such clubs entered a championship contest.[1]

[1] F. L. Paxson, "The Rise of Sport," *Miss. Valley Hist. Rev.*, IX, 143-168.

1869

1866   *Divorce*   *1877*

On the road to the Jerome Park races.

The Grant family at Long Branch.

Costumes for lawn tennis—1878.

But while the important teams were thus being professionalized, and the way paved for the organization in 1876 of the National League of Professional Baseball Players, an agency which dealt severely with the evils of betting, game-throwing and contract-breaking, purely amateur teams were multiplying everywhere. Every town and every school had its nine; all young America learned to play. Year by year the game was improved in its rules and its material. At first a very "live" ball was employed, which bounced erratically and led to the running-up of enormous scores; then the other extreme, a very "dead" ball, and finally a happy medium. Gloves and masks were introduced and the swollen hands of the early catchers became a thing of the past, while bats were perfected. In 1865 the New York press had thought it a matter for some wonder that five thousand spectators frequently gathered for a match at Hoboken, but now tens of thousands collected at the games.[1]

Cricket, which in 1865 was played by various New York and Philadelphia clubs and by teams at Newark, Bridgeport and other small cities, was naturally stunted and thrust to the wall by the overwhelming success of baseball.[2] But meanwhile football was developing slowly but steadily. One of the first of all intercollegiate matches was that played in the fall of 1869, with very uncertain rules, between Princeton and Rutgers. A modification of the English Association game was fairly well-known to all boys of the period, and early in the seventies a code was drawn up to govern it. But the real birth of the sport dates from the middle seventies, when the Rugby game, imported from Canada to Harvard and other colleges, assumed the leadership.

[1] The first college league for baseball was formed in 1879. See R. H. Barbour, *The Book of School and College Sports* (R. D. Paine and others, eds., N. Y., 1904).

[2] *N. Y. Eve. Post*, July 1, 1865, describes its extent.

Harvard and Yale held their first contest in 1875, and
their game, with modified Rugby rules, was soon a spectacular feature of the college year.[1] Both also had
rowing crews, and in 1878 they began their famous
series of races on the Thames above New London.
There was an enthusiastic demonstration in the same
year when a Columbia crew returned from England
after defeating Oxford, Cambridge and Dublin.

The college youth could no longer be a mere grind,
whose only outdoor recreations were walking and swim-
ming. Nor, for that matter, was youth anywhere left
in the deplorably unathletic position of the fifties. The
organization of Young Men's Christian Association
branches all over the country gave an impetus to organized sports, outdoor and indoor, for their city buildings
contained gymnasiums and their directors taught gym-
nastics after the German model. Moreover, the growing wealth of the cities, the emergence of a large class of
men with leisure, and the needs of sedentary life led to
the systematic establishment of athletic clubs. The
great leader and prototype in this field was founded in
1868 in New York. This, the New York Athletic
Club, rented a field for games at Mott Haven, on the
Harlem River, which soon became famous. It grew
and flourished for almost twenty years on the stern regimen of athletic games alone; its boathouse, track and
field becoming centers of general sport, while its annual
contests for young athletes furnished an array of records
that was an incentive to emulation the nation over.[2]

All in all, the nation took a very different attitude
toward sports after the war from that before. No
longer could a man like Edward Everett deplore, as he

[1] Walter Camp and L. F. Deland, *Football* (Boston, 1896); A. A.
Stagg, "Touchdown," *Sat. Eve. Post*, Sept. 18, 1926.
[2] F. L. Paxson, "The Rise of Sport," *Miss. Valley Hist. Rev.*, IX,
143-168.

did in 1856, the almost complete inattention to "manly outdoor exercises, which strengthen the mind by strengthening the body." No longer could Holmes assert that "society would drop a man who should run round the Common in five minutes." The whole country watched with bated breath the efforts of the English yachtsmen who brought over the *Cambria* in 1870 in the vain hope of capturing the *America's* cup, a trophy closely guarded by the New York Yacht Club, and the later equally unsuccessful attempts of the *Livonia* (1871) and the *Countess of Dufferin* (1876).[1] It watched lawn tennis become a sport of such importance that a few years later it had its national association. It saw organized field "meets" begin in the colleges—the earliest one at Yale in 1872—and outside, the first great amateur handicap meet taking place in New York in 1876. What Charles Kingsley called "Muscular Christianity" was coming into its own.

Twice during this period the country was conquered by sudden popular crazes in recreation: the first time by croquet, the second by the velocipede or bicycle. "Of all the epidemics that have swept over our land," the *Nation* exclaimed in the summer of 1866, "the swiftest and most infectious is croquet."[2] Every lawn from the Atlantic to the Mississippi seemed to be impressed into service. Expensive English sets of balls and mallets found a large sale. Four years later the bicycle had become an equally universal passion. It was as yet a crude vehicle of locomotion, one variety having a very high front wheel fitted with pedals, a low rear wheel, solid tires, and a seat so placed over the large wheel that the rider was likely to be pitched over the handlebars if he

[1] R. F. Coffin, "The History of American Yachting," in F. S. Cozzens, ed., *Yachts and Yachting* (n. p., 1887), 11-100.
[2] *Nation*, III, Aug. 9, 1866.

met even a slight obstacle. Schools opened for instruction in the large cities. At one in New York, according to the *Scientific American,* the visitor could see every evening "upward of a hundred and fifty gentlemen, doctors, bankers, merchants, and representatives from almost every profession, engaged preparatory to making their appearance upon the public streets." [1] The craze subsided, only to be revived a decade later. Improvements were rapidly introduced, tricycles and ladies' bicycles were devised, and late in the seventies wheelmen's clubs began to be formed in large numbers. But for the average American of sedentary habits the chief outdoor amusement, as in earlier years, was driving. The most prominent social line was that which parted the family with a carriage from that which had none. The sleigh was as prominent in winter as the wheeled vehicle in summer, and in city, town and village it was seen in every variety—shell-shaped, basket-shaped and box-shaped. [2]

During these years also the circus attained its mature stature as an American amusement. Shortly after the war the business genius of P. T. Barnum lifted it to a new scope and popularity. [3] He formed in 1871 a traveling tent circus which offered many more attractions than any predecessor, including wax works, dioramas, Swiss bell ringers, a new Cardiff Giant, [4] dwarfs and monstrosities, and among many other beasts, a real giraffe—still a rarity in the United States. In 1872 he showed his acumen by two additional innovations.

---

[1] *Scientific American,* Jan. 9, 1869.

[2] Towle, *American Society,* II, 30 ff.

[3] See P. T. Barnum, *Struggles and Triumphs: or Forty Years Recollections of P. T. Barnum. Written by Himself* (Buffalo, 1882), for a remarkable self-revelation.

[4] For this famous imposture, see C. R. Fish, *The Rise of the Common Man* (*A History of American Life,* VI), 149.

One was the introduction of a second ring, a development soon imitated by his rivals, but making his claim to "the greatest show on earth" doubly secure. The other was the transportation of the circus by rail instead of by wagon, thus by long trips eliminating all towns where the receipts did not promise to reach five thousand dollars. The details were so perfected that the establishment could be carried one hundred miles in a single night, could give a street parade in the morning, and present an afternoon and evening performance before packing up again for travel. Since a much larger show could be carried over a much greater extent of country, for the first time the circus became a really national institution. Financial success crowned Barnum's experiment, and in the first season with the railroad the receipts exceeded a million dollars.[1] It is an indication of American tastes and character in this era that Barnum heavily emphasized the wholesome and ethical element of his circus. It was always advertised as "Barnum's Great Moral Show;" clergymen as well as editors were given passes.

Whatever can be said against the manners and morals of the time, it was a larger, fuller life that people of the North and West lived after the war. Education was better diffused, the conflict had given birth to new ideas, and the growth of wealth purchased new refinements.[2] Americans, shrewdly remarked Godkin, "are far less raw and provincial than their fathers; they have seen more, they have read more, they have mixed more with people of other nationalities, they have thought more and had to think more, they have spent more for ideas and given more away."[3] They were also beginning to travel far more. It is interesting to note how many of these years

[1] M. R. Werner, *Barnum* (N. Y., 1923), 309-311.
[2] Egan, *Recollections*, 68.
[3] *Nation*, VI, Jan. 30, 1868.

a long list of our literary men—Bryant, Bayard Taylor, Lowell, Charles Eliot Norton, Mark Twain and others —spent in Europe; and it is significant that the first overseas tour of an ex-president, Grant, occurred in the seventies. Increasing colonies of American expatriates were to be met abroad, including such distinguished figures as W. W. Story and Henry James, and it will be recalled that James's fine novel *The American*, with its picture of a Western business man who had made a small fortune and gone to Paris to imbibe culture, appeared in the seventies.[1] Directly or indirectly, the daily life of the American people was thus achieving a greater variety and breadth; and yet the very rapidity of its expansion bred some glaring defects. Its greatest fault was its lack of depth, of cultivation and of established canons of taste, permitting the frequent display of what Godkin aptly called a "chromo civilization." There was something recurrently flashy and cheap in its activities, which only a more thorough culture could eradicate.

This cheapness was due less to the effects of the war than to the crude, aggressive growth of the republic and its defective social organization.[2] The West, with its heterogeneous population busy with the rough work of subduing the country, was peculiarly liable to a relaxation of standards. The great Eastern cities also, melting pots of Irish, Germans, Italians and other races, with a froth made up of grasping business men and newly rich families, suffered from similar tendencies. The belief that a twenty-five dollar plaster statuary group representing the "Courtship in Sleepy Hollow" was fine art was a mark of a "chromo civilization." So was the insistence upon equipping every hotel and steamboat

[1] See J. R. Lowell on Europe and America in his *Letters* (C. E. Norton, ed., N. Y., 1893), II, 112-113.
[2] See *Nation*, XIX, Oct. 22, 1874, on frontier and other influences.

with a gilt monstrosity called a bridal suite. So was the devotion of boulders, cliffs and barns to glaring advertisements of Rising Sun Shoe Polish, Schenck's Pulmonic Bitters and Dr. Brandreth's pills.[1] A distinct mark of a "chromo civilization" was the action of the Plymouth Church in Brooklyn, on the day Henry Ward Beecher came to trial for his alleged intimacy with Mrs. Tilton, in sending flowers to decorate the courtroom; like placing wreaths, said Godkin, about the open manhole of a sewer. Only a "chromo civilization" could have produced the expansive people who, in 1876, could not see that Blaine's railway transactions, even if admitted, were to his discredit. "He showed his smartness in it," they said, "and that is just the smart man we want."[2]

Nevertheless, despite passing maladies, despite grave scandals, the life of Americans at this period was fundamentally wholesome, progressive and fruitful. Its chief faults were less of quality than of tone, less of structure than of finish. James Bryce's arraignment of our national weaknesses a few years later was substantially valid.[3] We wished, he said, to keep abreast of the best thought of the world and to achieve much in art and letters; but we also showed an excessive fondness for bold and striking effects. Lacking refinement of taste, we were disposed to regard anything brilliant as superior to really admirable work in a quiet style. We demanded quick, showy results and constantly tended to identify bigness with greatness. Fortunately, however, there were countervailing tendencies at work which were steadily growing in vigor and usefulness. These conditions and influences it will now be instructive to examine.

[1] See *Nation*, XX, May 20, 1875, for the rapid spread of advertising.
[2] See *Nation*, XX, Feb. 4, 1875, on the Beecher trial; and XXII, June 29, 1876, on Blaine.
[3] James Bryce, *The American Commonwealth* (London, 1888), III, chaps. xcv, cvii, cviii.

CHAPTER IX

THE BROADENING OF AMERICAN CULTURE

INTELLECTUALLY, a new maturity was stamped upon the country by the grim struggle for the Union and the stern problems which had to be solved after it was over. Millions of people, the fighters and their families, were left with a deeper sense of the values of life, a wider interest in national affairs. This ripening process was assisted by the new cultural breadth which came with the conquest of the Far West and the vigorous emergence of the Middle West. Intellectual interests which had been focused before the war in comparatively small groups in New England and the Middle Atlantic states —in the literary circles of Boston and Concord, New York and Philadelphia, the faculties of Harvard and Yale and a few other centers—now played over a wider field. What was in some respects the most alert and progressive university was found as far west as Ann Arbor.[1] Among authors, Mark Twain, Edward Eggleston and W. D. Howells suddenly came forward from the Middle West, Bret Harte and Joaquin Miller from the Pacific, and G. W. Cable and Miss Murfree from the South.

For a brief period after the war, before these new impulses had had time to appear, there seemed a pause in the nation's cultural life. The colleges, chilled by poverty and the blow that recruiting had struck at class enrollments, hesitated to plunge into the bold innova-

[1] See A. D. White, *Autobiography* (N. Y., 1905), I, 266-287.

tions that were to re-create many of them. Literature seemed to produce nothing original. Hawthorne died at the close of the war; Bryant was seventy-one, Longfellow nearly sixty, and Emerson, sixty-two.[1] It seemed an evidence of the palsying effect of the conflict that the best poets turned to translation, and within a half-dozen years after 1866 the country was given Longfellow's, Norton's and T. W. Parsons's translations from Dante, Bayard Taylor's from Goethe, C. P. Cranch's from Virgil, and Bryant's Homer. Not a novel of importance appeared in the four years following the war. Although Lowell and Holmes produced some enduring literature, and the patriotic odes and "Democracy" of the former seemed to catch the new note of the period, it was not until the year 1869 brought *Innocents Abroad* and 1870 Bret Harte's *Luck of Roaring Camp* that the fresh era could be said to have commenced.[2] In science, also, the changed outlook did not come till at the opening of the seventies E. L. Youmans established the *Popular Science Monthly,* and John Fiske devoted himself to propagating the doctrine of evolution.

There was a crying need for fresh impulses, for the intellectual sway of the great New Englanders and Victorians, which belonged to the prewar period, was still dominant. Rebecca Harding Davis speaks of the pride in Emerson especially, as an American prophet, which in the sixties pervaded the nation.[3] "In the West and South there was no definite idea as to what truth this Concord man had brought into the world. But in any event it was American truth and not English." Holmes

[1] W. P. Trent and others, eds., *Cambridge History of American Literature* (N. Y., 1917), III, chaps. xi-xiii.

[2] A. B. Paine, *Mark Twain; a Biography* (N. Y., 1912), I, chap. lxxxi.

[3] Rebecca Harding Davis, *Bits of Gossip* (Boston, 1904), 47 ff.

was equally popular. "Everybody who cared for books, whether in New York clubs, California ranches, or Pennsylvania farms, loved and laughed with 'the little doctor.' " Howells has told how, returning in the late sixties from Cambridge to Ohio, he stopped overnight at Hiram, and was sitting with Congressman James A. Garfield and speaking of his Cambridge friends, when Garfield interrupted him. "He ran down into the grassy space, first to one fence and then to the other at the sides, and waved a wild arm of invitation to the neighbors who were also sitting on their back porches. 'Come over here!' he shouted. 'He's telling about Holmes and Longfellow and Lowell and Whittier!' and at his bidding dim forms began to mount the fences and follow him up to his veranda." [1] All of the West settled by New England stock sat at the feet of these writers with especial fervor; and Hamlin Garland's thrill when he first found the train carrying him over the Massachusetts boundary was felt by thousands of Western travelers. [2]

Since the moral tone of the American reading public was perfectly assimilated to that of the English, the sway of the eminent Victorians was even more powerful than that of the New Englanders. There was a Dickens worship abroad in the land. Sets of his books and Scott's and Thackeray's were to be found in the remotest hamlets. Dickens's second visit, in 1867, though it did not evoke the callow, unbalanced demonstrations of 1842, was a prolonged ovation. [3] In Boston the demand for tickets to his readings was so great that Harvard undergraduates could not obtain a single seat; in New York,

[1] W. D. Howells, *Literary Friends and Acquaintances* (N. Y., 1911), 209; same author, *Years of my Youth* (N. Y., 1906), 205.
[2] Hamlin Garland, *A Son of the Middle Border* (N. Y., 1917), 273.
[3] John Forster, *Life of Charles Dickens* (London, 1872-1874), bk. x. See *Nation* (N. Y.), XVII, March 12, 1874.

where people stood all night in the December cold, there were two lines nearly a mile in length when the box office opened, and speculators hovering near the head offered twenty dollars for anybody's place. His earnings during a tour that did not take him outside the East amounted, after the deduction of forty thousand dollars for expenses, to one hundred thousand dollars. The year of his visit saw thirty-one different editions of Dickens's collected works published.[1] Wilkie Collins was paid seven thousand five hundred dollars each by Harper for his successive books *The Moonstone* and *Man and Wife*. Of Disraeli's *Lothair* (1869) eighty thousand copies were sold in America. Charles Reade commanded five thousand dollars for so poor a novel as *A Woman Hater*, and in 1867 the same sum was paid for Trevelyan's *Macaulay*. Such remuneration, above the reach of any American author, attested the prestige of English works.[2] Besides the great British writers, Turgenev, Hugo, Björnson, Auerbach and others of equal merit were laid in translation before discriminating Americans.

From its four years' preoccupation with the war the younger public turned eagerly to ideas and doctrines that had already become familiar abroad. In 1865, says Henry Holt, "I got hold of a copy of Spencer's *First Principles,* and had my eyes opened to a new heaven and a new earth."[3] Charles Francis Adams, jr., coming out of the army a colonel, tells us that he chanced one day upon a copy of John Stuart Mill's essay on Comte. "My intellectual faculties had then been lying fallow for nearly four years, and I was in a most recipient condition; and

---

[1] *Nation,* IV, May 16, 1867; *American Annual Cyclopedia* (N. Y., 1861-1903), VII (1867), 430 ff.

[2] J. H. Harper, *The House of Harper* (N. Y., 1912), 114, 393, 446.

[3] Henry Holt, *The Garrulities of an Octogenarian Editor* (Boston, 1923), 46.

that essay of Mill's revolutionized in a single morning my whole mental attitude." [1]   For the first time, he, with millions of others, heard of Darwin.   Carlyle was receding into the past, his voice less potent than in the fifties; Mill, succeeding him, was the chief influence for a few years until Darwin, Spencer, Tyndall and Huxley as leaders of the new scientific movement, and Arnold, in criticism and theology, took his place.   Thinking Americans were about to pass from the theological stage into the scientific.

Popular literary taste, which of course reached no such lofty level, continued to be remarkable for the vogue it gave to authors who combined commonplace entertainment with a rigidly Victorian code of morality.   The *Nation* remarked upon the immense number of families which had just five secular books on their shelves: Abbot's *Napoleon,* Headley's *Washington and His Generals,* Ingraham's *The Prince of the House of David,* an illustrated giftbook on the Orient, and Tupper's *Proverbial Philosophy.* [2]   The same audience wanted popular didacticism offering no such difficulty as Emerson.   Dr. J. G. Holland, under the pseudonym of Timothy Titcomb, obtained a wide reputation by truisms insipid enough for a young ladies' boarding school and religious enough for the most bigoted sectarian.   All together, nearly a half-million copies of the Titcomb letters were sold.   His long narrative poem *Katherina* (1867) enjoyed a similar vogue, selling thirty-five thousand copies in its first three months and soon passing its fiftieth edition.   Holland's novels were rivaled in circulation by the moral tales of E. P. Roe, who studied at Williams College, served as a chaplain in the war, and until 1874 was a minister in a Hudson River village.   His first

[1] C. F. Adams, jr., *An Autobiography* (Boston, 1916), **179.**
[2] *Nation,* II, June 15, 1866.

novel, *Barriers Burned Away*, with its topical interest growing from the Chicago fire, made him famous among semieducated readers who enjoyed a love story weighted with a religious purpose; and thereafter a new book appeared almost yearly till his death in 1888. Three popular didactic essayists of the day were Carl Benson, Fanny Fern and Gail Hamilton.

It was creditable to American society that Motley's *United Netherlands,* the third and fourth volumes of which appeared in 1868, should within a year sell more than fifteen thousand copies; it was creditable that Parkman's books were eagerly hailed.[1] But looking at the people as a whole several minor authors were more truly characteristic. The Reverend Dr. Henry M. Field, a circumlocutory writer with some talent for description, catered to the taste for the "instructive." Elizabeth Stuart Phelps, of an equally able New England family, expressed several tendencies in postwar fiction. Her *Gates Ajar,* with its glimpses of Paradise, comforted many who mourned dead soldiers, and her *Silent Partner* dealt in a philanthropic spirit with the wrongs of New England working people. T. S. Arthur continued to deal out tracts in fictional form with astonishing success.[2] There were thousands who supposed E. P. Whipple a great critic, Noah Porter a great moral teacher, and J. W. Draper a great thinker, and even in the pages of the *Atlantic* there was asserted a comparison between Macaulay and James Parton. Such saccharine nonsense as Theodore Tilton's novel *Tempest Tossed* (1874), the tale of a family which lived for twenty-six years on a calm-bound but fortunately food-stocked ship in the South Atlantic, and which came ashore just in time to

[1] J. S. Bassett, *The Middle Group of American Historians* (N. Y., 1917), 314.
[2] See C. R. Fish, *The Rise of the Common Man* (*A History of American Life*, VI), 266.

give the young daughter a romantic marriage, found an eager audience.[1]

Worse still, the managers of the Boston Public Library in 1872—Boston!—named as the most popular authors of the day Mrs. E. D. E. N. Southworth, Carolina Lee Hentz and Mary J. Holmes, while Mrs. A. D. T. Whitney was a close competitor in the suburbs.[2] Indeed, when the *Publishers' Weekly* four years later asked the bookstores of the country to state which works of fiction were most salable, such titles as *St. Elmo, The Wooing O'T, Infelice, My Wife and I, Barriers Burned Away* and *The Opening of a Chestnut Burr* crowded out all but a few really good novels, like *Jane Eyre* and *The Scarlet Letter*.[3] And when in 1879 the libraries of three representative New England cities reported on the circulation of various novelists, the showing was equally unpleasant to lovers of the classics. In Bangor, Mary J. Holmes, Mrs. Southworth and Charles Reade were first in the order named; in Lawrence, Mrs. Southworth stood first and Dickens third; while in Quincy, where Mrs. Southworth's trash was excluded, Mrs. Whitney held second place, against fifth for Dickens.[4] Most of the novel reading, it is clear, was done by the women of the country—and college women were almost unknown. Some of the books imported from abroad were of the same stripe: this was the period of Louisa Mühlbach and Ouida. In 1868 the sale of the romances of the former outstripped all competitors—Henry Ward Beecher's *Norwood*, Rebecca Harding Davis's *Dallas Galbraith*, Reade's *Foul Play* and Auerbach's *On the*

[1] *Nation*, XIX, July 2, 1874. The really excellent juvenile stories of Louisa M. Alcott and J. T. Trowbridge should be mentioned on the credit side of the ledger.
[2] *Nation*, XIV, May 23, 1872.
[3] *Publishers' Weekly*, May 20, 1876.
[4] *Nation*, XXVIII, March 5, 1879.

Heights. The novels of Spielhagen were also popular. If he and Miss Mühlbach were approved because they taught history, the stories of the Reverend George Mac-Donald, such as his portrait of an ideal Calvinist philanthropist in *Robert Falconer,* achieved a wide circulation for their moral and religious tone.[1]

One curious phenomenon of popular taste deserves a word. The Civil War had given a remarkable vogue to the dime novels published in New York by Beadle and Company, which the soldiers passed from hand to hand in literally millions of copies. Erastus Beadle, the astute head of the firm, had at first directed his corps of writers—not all of them hacks, for Mayne Reid and Edward S. Ellis were active—to themes from Eastern pioneer life and the Revolution. Now he turned to the Far West, enlisted the pens of numerous Western explorers, Indian fighters and plainsmen, and began issuing enormous numbers of "yellowbacks" which bore such titles as *Deadly Eye,* by William F. Cody, *Idaho Tom, the Young Outlaw of Silverland,* by Oll Coomes, and *Spitfire Saul, the King of the Rustlers,* by Joseph E. Badger. Among the contributors were Captain "Bruin" Adams, Major St. Vrain, Captain Jack Crawford and others whose years of personal knowledge and actual adventure were woven into their volumes. Adult Easterners looked upon these lurid tales as dangerous trash, and youngsters who devoured them in secret were taken to the woodshed if caught. Nevertheless, many of the volumes possessed genuine merit as a presentation of the Wild West of the explorer, cowboy and prospector, and their picture of pioneer life and character is more accurate and vivid than that of many a formal historian. The books, too, were ethically sound, the authors inculcating lessons of manliness, and avoiding scenes of vice.

[1] *Am. Ann. Cyclop.,* XIII (1873), 523.

Beadle, in his tens of millions of dime, half-dime and quarter-dollar publications, covered a large field, from songbooks to popular biographies, and shortly had a flattering number of imitators.[1]

Then, as afterwards, the masses were nourished chiefly upon periodical literature. Robert Bonner's *New York Ledger* was the great bourgeois success of the time, able with its high prices to capture poets like Longfellow and divines like Beecher. It paid three thousand dollars for "The Hanging of the Crane," and maintained an adroit mixture of eminent names with tales of the "Demon Cabman" and the "Maiden's Revenge." *Hearth and Home,* a languishing periodical, was revived early in the seventies by Edward and George Cary Eggleston, who also compounded religion and thrilling stories according to an infallible formula. *Godey's Lady's Book* still pursued its blithely decorous way, the indispensable feminine magazine, but it lost vigor in the late seventies. As earlier, a prominent place in American life was occupied by the atrociously moral and gossipy family weekly of religious tendencies. The best of the religious publications, because the broadest in interest, was the *Independent,* which in political opinions lived up to its name, and which a succession of men—Beecher, Tilton, Edward Eggleston, William Hayes Ward—edited with ability.[2]

One of the factors to be marked in considering the literary culture of the day was the bad organization, evinced chiefly in two defects, of the book trade. There was no systematic method of distributing new volumes from publisher to retailer, and a spring book sale in New

---

[1] N. Y. Public Library, *The Beadle Collection of Dime Novels* (N. Y., 1922), 3-17.

[2] See Washington Gladden, *Recollections* (Boston, 1909), 182 ff., for the *Independent.*

York and other centers still partly took the place of modern methods. Retail buyers crowded to the auction rooms on lower Broadway, where each publisher sold his stock on consignment, not at a fixed trade discount. In 1867, with a good attendance and spirited bidding, three hundred copies of Whittier's *Snowbound,* worth one dollar and twenty-five cents at retail, brought eighty cents a copy, and two hundred copies of Reade's *Griffith Gaunt,* worth one dollar and fifty cents, the same sum.[1] Not till the eighties did the book auction die. Another indication of weakness was the success of the subscription plan of publication, reduced to a secondary rôle in the eighties by better methods. The leading house in this field for some years was the American Publishing Company of Hartford, which sold thirty-one thousand copies of Mark Twain's *Innocents Abroad* within five months at three dollars and fifty cents or more, paying him five-per-cent royalty. At the end of the year the total sales had reached sixty-seven thousand. For *Roughing It* Clemens obtained better terms, seven-and-one-half-per-cent royalty; and again there was a heavy sale, nearly forty thousand copies in three months.[2] But even the old-established publishers, in order to reach the public in great areas bare of bookstores, used the subscription plan. Thus Appleton had Bryant edit a superb two-volume collection of steel engravings of scenes in the republic, called *Picturesque America*—published in portfolio parts—of which nearly a million sets were sold. The firm of Ford and Company in New York brought out Greeley's autobiography, and Bryant's *Library of Poetry and Song,* which within nine years, though costing five dollars in its cheapest form, had sold eighty thou-

[1] *N. Y. Eve. Post,* April 3, 1867.
[2] *Am. Ann. Cyclop.,* VIII (1868), 408 ff.; Paine, *Mark Twain,* I, lxxxiv.

sand copies. The subscription system flourished not only because of the lack of retailers and good book advertising, but because it lent itself to a species of "star system" in literature; yet a method which gave Mark Twain financial independence and a large audience was not wholly a bad method.[1]

Prominent among the agencies which contributed to the general broadening of culture was the lyceum, of which the thirteen years after the war witnessed the spectacular reorganization and decline. It was James Redpath, an able journalist of English birth, who took the chaotic lecture system of prewar days, and in 1867 opened a central booking office through which local lecture committees might engage the speakers they wanted.[2] For a ten-per-cent commission he assured the lecturers ample remuneration while saving them troublesome correspondence, and at the same time he was able to offer lyceum managers programs of a high character. Under Redpath's influence the whole character of the lyceum steadily altered, becoming commercialized and of wider popular appeal. Taking charge of John B. Gough, he enabled that temperance orator to clear forty thousand dollars for the year 1871-1872, and thirty thousand dollars or more in succeeding years. Redpath paid Beecher a thousand dollars for a single Boston appearance in 1872. A number of men whose fees had formerly been fifty or one hundred dollars now discovered that they could command two hundred and fifty or even five hundred dollars a night. The cartoonist Nast lectured for the season 1873-1874, engaging Parton to prepare his discourses and delivering them sometimes five

[1] J. R. Howard, *Remembrance of Things Past* (N. Y., 1925), 215-241.
[2] See J. B. Pond, *Eccentricities of Genius* (N. Y., 1900), for Redpath and his work; *Nation*, VIII, April 8, 1869. For the earlier history of the lyceum, see Fish, *The Rise of the Common Man*, 225.

The Lyceum Committeeman's Dream—Some Popular Lecturers in Character.

nights in a week.[1] He met with such dazzling success that Bennett's *Herald* started a mock subscription for the indigent artist who was laboring to save his family from want; for seven months' work he received forty thousand dollars—most of which evaporated with his other savings in the Grant-Ward failure. The formal instructive lecture everywhere gave way before the increasing demand of audiences for the humorous monologue, the dramatic recitation and the thinly disguised play.

In this popularized form the lyceum had a few years of radiant prosperity; but by 1874 it evinced decided signs of fading. Many of its best figures disappeared. Sumner died, Emerson's mind failed, Curtis was busied editing *Harper's Weekly,* and Colfax and Beecher were lost in clouds of scandal. It was necessary to turn to music to bulwark the failing institution, and in a single season the Redpath agency paid Max Strakosch ten thousand dollars for ten concerts. But the irretrievable decline of the lyceum was significantly revealed by the immortal Gilbert and Sullivan operas. These two masters began their collaboration in 1871 with "Thespis," and in the years 1878-1881 produced "Pinafore," "The Pirates of Penzance" and "Patience," which were shamelessly pirated and became enormously popular throughout America. People whose moral scruples prevented their attending plays went to hear the operas, and in New England especially they so appreciably took the place of the lectures that many lecture halls were remodeled to make their presentation possible.[2] Meanwhile, the Chautauqua movement had been founded in 1874 as an effort to promote the intensive training of Sunday school

[1] A. B. Paine, *Life of Th. Nast* (N. Y., 1904), 367. See Charles Francis Horner, *Life of James Redpath and the Development of the Modern Lyceum* (N. Y., 1926).

[2] Pond, *Eccentricities of Genius,* 533 ff.

teachers, and rapidly broadened into a partial substitute for the old-style lyceum of instructive aims.[1]

Nor did the newspaper, as an instrument of popular education, show just the progress after the war that was hoped of it. Progress there was, but it was chiefly in news gathering and commercial enterprise, with editorial tutelage less and less important. Fresh young men of ability, it is true, were called into the profession. In the decade from 1869 to 1879 Raymond, Greeley, the elder Bennett, Bowles and Bryant died; and as successors there appeared Charles A. Dana of the *Sun,* Manton Marble of the *World,* Whitelaw Reid of the *Tribune,* Henry Watterson of the *Louisville Courier-Journal,* Murat Halstead of the *Cincinnati Commercial,* and Joseph Pulitzer of the *St. Louis Westliche Post.*[2] Though these men had talents sufficient to support the tradition of "personal" journalism established before the war, two tendencies of the day were inimical to it. One was the fact that during the war newspaper readers had been taught to value the news columns far above the editorials. Now astute editors, profiting by the new methods taught by war-time necessities, paid their principal attention to the rapid, accurate and effective reporting of events. In assuming the editorship of the *Sun* (1868) Dana promised that "it will study condensation, clearness, point, and will endeavor to present its daily photograph of the whole world's doings in the most luminous and lively manner." [3] Indeed, the pungency, cynicism and sensationalism of Dana's news columns gave his journal

[1] J. L. Hurlbut, *The Story of Chautauqua* (N. Y., 1921), chaps. iv-vi.

[2] D. C. Seitz, *Life of Joseph Pulitzer* (N. Y., 1924) ; J. H. Wilson, *Life of Charles A. Dana* (N. Y., 1907) ; Royal Cortissoz, *Life of Whitelaw Reid* (N. Y., 1921) ; Henry Watterson, *"Marse Henry," an Autobiography* (N. Y., 1919).

[3] Wilson, *Life of C. A. Dana,* 381.

its success. The other tendency was the decentralization of the press. No journal after the war wielded as great an influence as the *Tribune* had done just before it. Throughout the West and South a multitude of new papers sprang into existence, and by means of the Associated Press supplied their readers with intelligence almost as full as that of the New York dailies. Among them were the *Chicago Evening Post* (1865), *Inter-Ocean* (1872) and *Daily News* (1875); the *Indianapolis News* (1869); the *San Francisco Examiner* (1865) and *Post* (1871); and the *Philadelphia Record* (1877).[1]

The Associated Press grew yearly in efficiency, and through its alliance with the Western Union Telegraph Company, the only telegraph system which had adequate national facilities, enjoyed almost a monopoly. Throughout this period it was not an incorporated body, but simply a loose organization of smaller regional associations, held together by a written compact for the exchange of news. The parent body, the New York association, acted as their clearing house, while it organized the exchange of intelligence with the European agencies and appointed correspondents in the ill-settled regions beyond the Mississippi.[2] Its dictation of policy was destined in the early eighties to produce a revolt of the Western press. Of great value, too, was the general introduction of stereotyping, which, begun during wartime, was now practised in all the greater newspaper establishments. Duplicate plates were made by means of paper matrices, and ten or twelve presses could strike

[1] It should be noted that several newspapers—the *N. Y. Evening Post, Springfield Republican* and others—showed striking political independence in 1872 and afterwards. See Allan Nevins, *The Evening Post: a Century of Journalism* (N. Y., 1922), chap. xvii; Richard Hooker, *The Story of an Independent Newspaper* (N. Y., 1924), chap. xvi.

[2] M. E. Stone, "The Associated Press," *Century Mag.,* LXX (1905), 299-310, 379-386; M. E. Stone and others, *"M. E. S." His Book* (N. Y., 1918), *passim.*

off a hundred thousand copies in two hours. Reporting took on still greater dignity, and the newspaper world could boast of figures like J. A. MacGahan, the noted correspondent who dealt with the Franco-Prussian War, the Russian expedition to Khiva and other stirring events.[1] Intellectually, there was no such advance, and Henry Adams tells us that he and young men like him turned away from newspaper life feeling that it offered them too few opportunities. They were repelled, too, by the venality of much of the press. Tweed kept dozens of New York journalists on his payroll, and by his menaces awed even Bryant's *Evening Post;* the news columns of the very best papers could be purchased or colored by big advertisers; and the *Independent* itself, for all its religious character, placed advertisements in its critical columns for a dollar a line and accepted a huge bribe from the firm of Jay Cooke for promoting the sale of Northern Pacific bonds by editorial puffs and special articles.[2]

As yet the bookstore was but a feeble institution, and throughout large areas of the country the public library was not merely unknown but unthought of. Parton in 1867 commented with surprise on the fact that Chicago boasted of three bookshops, which offered an assortment almost as large as any in the Atlantic cities and which had sold more than one thousand seven hundred sets of *Appletons' Cyclopaedia* and the *Britannica.* Visitors to San Francisco felt the same astonishment in seeing H. H. Bancroft's fine Market Street bookstore. But outside of the very largest cities there were usually no bookstores in the true sense of the word at all. Nor were there many libraries in the modern sense of the term;

[1] F. L. Bullard, *Famous War Correspondents* (Boston, 1914), 115 ff.
[2] *Nation,* XIX, Oct. 8, 1874; Gladden, *Recollections,* 234; Nevins, *Evening Post,* 385, 432.

no American collection of books in 1870 yet reached two hundred thousand volumes, though Europe counted more than twenty of that size. Indeed, there were only six libraries with as many as one hundred thousand volumes each—one the Library of Congress, with one hundred and eighty-three thousand; three in or near Boston —the Boston Public Library with one hundred and fifty-three thousand, the Harvard library with one hundred and eighteen thousand and the Athenæum library with a few more than one hundred thousand; and two in New York—the Astor Library with one hundred and thirty-eight thousand, and the Mercantile with one hundred and four thousand five hundred.[1] Of city and town libraries there were in 1875 about two thousand in the whole country with one thousand or more volumes each, and many of these were rubbish.[2] Even in the largest cities, moreover, the library privileges were restricted by unhappy rules. The Boston Athenæum collection was accessible for reference purposes, but only those who purchased shares at three hundred dollars each could borrow books. New York's largest library, the Astor, was not open for reference at night, and lent no volumes. Chicago had no provision for a free public library till in 1868 the merchant Walter Newberry died leaving a fortune estimated at four million dollars for one; and Philadelphia was similarly handicapped until the following year when Dr. James Rush left about one million dollars as an endowment.

The dearth of free public institutions gave a large field to private circulating libraries, but even they were not numerous, the entire number in 1870 being one thousand two hundred and forty-one, with an average

[1] A. R. Spofford, "Public Libraries of the United States," *Journ. of Social Sci.*, II, 92-114.
[2] U. S. Commissioner of Education, *Report 1899-1900*, I, xxxi.

of about two thousand volumes each. Massachusetts maintained an easy lead with one hundred and eighty-six, and states so populous and wealthy as Pennsylvania and Illinois had only eighty-six and seventy-nine respectively.[1] The American people in thousands of communities were, in fine, simply starved of well-selected books. They did not see good titles advertised; they found it difficult to buy if they did; and they had no opportunity to borrow. Only the subscription agent gave them a casual link with literature.

It was largely upon this cultural basis, and against these difficulties, that the new forms of intellectual betterment had to make their advance. The first clear manifestation of these forces came in the establishment of magazines which offered a medium for a broader, more realistic literature, and which created and guided a large new reading public. One weekly, the *Nation,* and four monthlies—*Scribner's, Lippincott's,* the *Galaxy* and the *Overland*—were founded at almost the same time, while *Putnam's Magazine* was reëstablished.[2] Each of the monthlies had its peculiar flavor and brought its own gifts. *Putnam's,* recommencing in 1868, kept a marked Knickerbocker character; *Lippincott's,* emerging the same year, presented an equally marked Philadelphia flavor in its contributions. The *Galaxy,* established in 1866, struggled bravely for a dozen years, and was a sheet anchor for many deserving authors. Bayard Taylor and E. C. Stedman were keenly interested in it and Taylor sold it many poems for his needy friend Sidney Lanier. But like *Putnam's,* it found the competitive pace too swift.[3] The cost of contributions was going up

[1] *U. S. Ninth Census* (1870), I, 475.
[2] Algernon Tassin, *The Magazine in America* (N. Y., 1916). For the *Overland Monthly* see W. F. Rae, *Westward by Rail* (London, 1870), 320 ff.
[3] G. H. Putnam, *George Putnam Palmer* (N. Y., 1912), 361.

rapidly; authors who a decade earlier had been content with from three dollars to five dollars a page now demanded at least from ten to twenty dollars, while much larger payments were required for special contributions. Magazine advertising as a source of revenue was virtually unknown. Not until the establishment of *Scribner's* in 1870 did any American monthly print other advertising than that of the books which its publisher issued. Even in the early seventies *Harper's* refused eighteen thousand dollars, with an air of Roman virtue, for a year's use of the last page by a sewing-machine company. *Putnam's*, after failing to attain a circulation of fifteen thousand, expired in 1871, while in 1878 the *Galaxy* was absorbed by the more vigorous *Atlantic*.[1]

It was by virtue of a new idea that *Scribner's Monthly* not only lived and prospered—its name was changed to the *Century* in 1881—but gained enduring distinction. *Harper's* and the *Atlantic* had aimed almost exclusively at literary achievement, though the *Atlantic* had done able political service during the war. But *Scribner's* had a definite ambition to lead public opinion in politics, religion, art and social ideals.[2] Under the guiding hand of Dr. J. G. Holland, a graduate of the efficient school of the *Springfield Republican,* and an able editor though a mediocre author, the monthly took a conspicuous stand in the advocacy not merely of civil-service reform and religious liberalism, but of international copyright, kindergarten instruction, tenement-house improvement and other causes. In its pages was struck faintly the note that was to be trumpeted by the muckraking monthlies at the turn of the century. But it was slow to grasp the best method for the elaborate discussion and exposi-

---

[1] See *U. S. Tenth Census* (1880), VIII, 115-116.
[2] Tassin, *The Magazine in America,* 287 ff.

tion of ideas, and its outstanding services to its first decade were in the fields of art and fiction.

Art and periodical literature had not hitherto been close handmaidens; and no illustrations or typography like those developed by *Scribner's* had been known in America. Alexander W. Drake, who was the art editor from the outset, hit upon many happy innovations. One was a new, freer, and more artistic form of wood engraving by a process in which the surface of the wooden block was prepared like a photographic negative, and the camera then used to reproduce upon it original drawings or paintings, which could be engraved more finely than ever before. Foremost among the engravers who were given fame by *Scribner's* was Timothy Cole, a young man of English birth who, having lost his business in the Chicago fire, had arrived penniless in New York, where the monthly employed him after 1875. Drake was responsible for an equally happy step when in 1876 he transferred the publication of the magazine to the care of Theodore L. De Vinne, a thoroughly trained printer of New York City who was soon to become the founder of the De Vinne press.[1] As Drake and Cole brought the art of wood engraving to the highest point it has ever reached in America, so De Vinne undertook to bring its typography and presswork to a new pitch of excellence. He was one of the few American printers conversant with the long and splendid history of his art and was eager to experiment with new types. He had finer and more powerful presses built, printing paper of better texture made, and special writing inks compounded. Under the driving ambition of these three craftsmen, *Scribner's* was soon acknowledged to be

[1] H. L. Bullen, "How Theodore Low De Vinne became America's Most Famous Printer," *Inland Printer*, LXIX (1922), 515-520; I. H. Brainerd, "T. L. De Vinne," *Printing Art*, XXXV (1920), 201-207.

the world's most beautiful magazine of general literature.[1]

With the same keen instinct for the future, *Scribner's* further emphasized its distinctive character by discarding long English serials, and giving warm encouragement to every token of originality among young American writers. The space given to moralistic literature steadily contracted, and *Scribner's* was shortly publishing the work of Joaquin Miller, Edward Eggleston, Bret Harte, George W. Cable and Thomas Nelson Page. It became the foremost patron of new authors, and especially of sectional voices; in a few years it was boasting that seven contributions by Southerners had appeared in a single issue.[2] Half a dozen years after the war it was evident that a new literature, displacing sentimentalism by realism and overthrowing a narrow Eastern regionalism by its democratic breadth, was coming in like an irresistible tide. Other magazines responded to it. The *Atlantic,* always alert for genuine talent, was publishing Bret Harte, John Hay, W. D. Howells, Clarence King, Henry James, Mark Twain, Maurice Thompson and Charles Egbert Craddock. A host of readers were buying the books of these authors.

Viewed as a social phenomenon, the rise of the fresh Western literature was a natural result of the overrunning of that section by highly literate men who found a tempting financial reward in its fictional exploitation.[3] The frontier had been settled by what Whitman called powerful uneducated persons and those who won an

---

[1] H. W. Ellsworth, *A Golden Age of Authors* (Boston, 1919), chaps. i, iii, v.

[2] L. F. Tooker, *Joys and Tribulations of an Editor* (N. Y., 1924), chaps. ii-iii.

[3] For the literary spirit in one Middle Western state, see Meredith Nicholson, *The Hoosiers* (N. Y., 1900), 134 ff., and Julia H. Levering, *Historic Indiana* (N. Y., 1909), 359 ff.

education turned naturally, like Lincoln, to the law and politics. Now it was full of figures like John Hay, a graduate of Brown; Bret Harte, the son of a professor of Greek in Albany Seminary; and Mark Twain, who had a fair common-school education and an excellent training in printing offices—not merely country offices but those of St. Louis and Philadelphia dailies.[1] Before the war these men would have found an inadequate market for their work; afterwards, thanks to the new magazines and the lecture system, they were amply rewarded. The instant and brilliant success of Bret Harte, indeed, showed how glittering the prizes might be. A typesetter and journalist in San Francisco, he became editor in 1868 of the *Overland Monthly,* which was planned to be the *Atlantic Monthly* of the Far West, and which, with its fresh reflection of life beyond the Rockies and high stylistic qualities, was pronounced by Englishmen to take rank with the best periodicals of the New or Old worlds. In the very second issue Harte captivated the reading public of America by "The Luck of Roaring Camp," and followed it immediately with "The Outcasts of Poker Flat" and other stories. A multitude of opportunities opened before him. In 1871 he made a triumphal progress to the East and accepted the munificent offer of the *Atlantic* to pay him ten thousand dollars for whatever he might write during the ensuing year, little or much.[2]

Harte had discovered the literary riches of the California slope, with the golden haze of the Spanish period mellowing its past and the picturesque days of the gold rush already receding into history. Without sacrifice of truth, he touched with a romance recalling Cooper's hand the gamblers, the Chinese, the reckless adventure

---

[1] A. B. Paine, *Mark Twain* (N. Y., 1912), I, chap. xix.
[2] M. A. De Wolfe Howe, *Memories of a Hostess* (Boston, 1922), 233.

and the varied scenery of the West.[1] It was the first
acquaintance of the East with the uncouth society of
ranch and mining camp; it was the first time that a literary artist had made use of Western barrooms, stagecoaches, quartz mills, gulches, sluice robbers and the
madroñas and *manzañitas* of the mountain sides. In
Joaquin Miller's work the more picturesque and grandly
scenic aspects of the West were combined with some of
the same social materials. His first volume was greeted
with praise in the *Overland Monthly;* his second found
him in England, where with his third (1871) it met a
cordial reception. The Eastern press of the United
States received him with supercilious reserve. "It is the
'sombreros' and 'serapes' and 'gulches,' we suppose, and
the other Californian and Arizonian properties, which
have caused our English friends to find in Mr. Miller a
truly American poet," observed the *Nation*. But little
by little the impression he made abroad found its reflection in his own land, particularly after he returned in
the mid-seventies to live in various Eastern cities. He
was one of the myth makers who sowed the wide new
West with legends and opened a whole new world of the
imagination to the reading public.[2]

The facts in Mark Twain's far more vigorous early
career which chiefly interest the social historian are his
rapid conquest of a half-reluctant national public and his
success in presenting the remote frontier as well as the
Mississippi Valley to the reading world. He emerged
in the East simply as another of the numerous tribe of
"funny men," the writer of a convulsing story about a
jumping frog, and a popular lecturer on the Sandwich

[1] F. L. Pattee, *A History of American Literature since 1870* (Boston,
1896), 63-82.
[2] Joaquin Miller, *Poetical Works* (S. P. Sherman, ed., N. Y., 1923),
38-39.

Islands.[1] Even his *Innocents Abroad,* for all its sale of one hundred and twenty-five thousand copies in three years, left him little more than a mere popular entertainer. But this was followed early in 1872 by *Roughing It,* a vivid picture of society on the Pacific Coast, which gave the East a fuller comprehension both of the wild frontier life of the region and of Mark Twain's powers. Charles Dudley Warner welcomed the opportunity to collaborate with him in *The Gilded Age;* the *Atlantic* not only accepted seven articles dealing with *Life on the Mississippi,* an unsurpassed picture of a river civilization that was already dying, but that august monthly had to pay the theretofore unapproached sum of two and a half cents a word for them. When *Tom Sawyer* appeared in December, 1876, it was appreciated in most quarters as at least a minor masterpiece. One evidence of Mark Twain's acceptance by austere circles was the fact that he was invited to make one of the principal addresses at the *Atlantic's* dinner in honor of Whittier's birthday (Dec. 17, 1877)—his speech unfortunately achieving an ever-memorable triumph of the malapropos.[2]

The Western writers not only conquered the East but Great Britain as well. When Mark Twain visited England in 1872 and again in 1873, he was lionized by English society, was shown high respect by Browning, Charles Reade, Turgenev and other eminent men and found his lecture halls jammed. After his return home Englishmen to whom Lowell or Holmes were mentioned were likely to say: "O, we can produce such cultured writers by the dozen; let us hear of Mark Twain, Bret Harte, and Artemus Ward." [3] Yet only Americans

---

[1] W. D. Howells, *My Mark Twain* (N. Y., 1910), expresses the early reluctance to accept the humorist.

[2] Paine, *Mark Twain,* II, chap. cxiv.

[3] Paine, *Mark Twain,* I, chaps. xc-xcii.

could appreciate the veracious social history embodied in Tom Sawyer's life in a river hamlet, in the account of Colonel Beriah Sellers and his dream of speculative millions, and in the description of mining-camp civilization in *Roughing It*. Only Americans, too, could fully appreciate the Western humor, a product of that stark battle with the frontier in which an ability to laugh offered the sole escape from realities which might otherwise have driven many settlers mad.

The literature of the West, including John Hay's *Pike County Ballads* and Eggleston's *Hoosier Schoolmaster*, had a quality of universality—for once the East had been West too—but in the South and New England also the seventies brought a burst of local-color writing of a distinctive sort. George W. Cable, a studious young accountant of New Orleans, published his first story, "'Sieur George," in *Scribner's* during the autumn of 1873, and rapidly followed it with others which appeared in book form under the title of *Old Creole Days* in 1879. In the Centennial year *Scribner's* began the publication of Irwin Russell's amusing poems in Negro dialect, continued till after the death four years later of the poverty-stricken, dissipated young author in New Orleans.[1] The Negro had stepped upon the stage beside the Creole, and the old Southern gentlefolk were about to assume a place with them. Thomas Nelson Page in the late seventies sent *Scribner's* his *Marse Chan*, a powerful story of Eastern Virginia, a family feud and two lovers united by death during the war, which threw a glow of autumnal romance over the old slaveholding aristocracy.[2]

Meantime Charles Egbert Craddock (Miss Murfree) discovered the Appalachians as a field for fiction and

---

[1] Irwin Russell, *Christmas Night in the Quarters and Other Poems* (N. Y., 1917)—see introduction by J. C. Harris.

[2] Roswell Page, *Thomas Nelson Page* (N. Y., 1923), 81.

brought them to general attention by *The Dancin' Party at Harrison's Cove* (1878) and later stories in' the *Atlantic*. She presented the quaint, shrewd mountain farmers of Tennessee; a gang of horse thieves and outlaws; moonshiners, hunters and feudists; the circuit rider and the grim officers of the law. Here was suddenly revealed an eighteenth-century society, with log cabins, spinning wheels, primitive ideas of justice and speech of Tudor flavor, hidden within a few hundred miles of Washington and Atlanta. And in these years Constance Fenimore Woolson was busy as a student of new social conditions in the lower South. Her tales of Florida, the Carolinas and Georgia just after the war, collected in 1880 in a volume called *Rodman the Keeper*, gave the North its first detailed picture of the changed conditions of life in this region. It was all new, strange and interesting.[1]

Nowhere did local color achieve a more artistic expression than in New England, where the ground had been broken long before the war. The *Atlantic* stories of Sarah Orne Jewett, collected in *Deephaven* and *Country Byways* (1877, 1881), showed the queer people of a decayed seaport and the inhabitants of scattered rural communities. It was high time that the old order was being photographed, Miss Jewett declared: "the old traditions have had time to die out even in the most conservative and least changed towns and a new element has come in. The true characteristics of American society, as I have said, are showing themselves more and more to the westward of New England. . . ."[2] Her *Deephaven* had a hundred counterparts on the New England map, with its indigent aristocracy, retired sea cap-

---

[1] M. G. Fulton, *Southern Life in Southern Literature* (Boston, 1917), 303 ff.

[2] Sarah Orne Jewett, *Deephaven* (Boston, 1877), 1-8.

tains, talkative widows, sedate spinsters and legends of heroism by land and sea. But already the more vigorous talent of William Dean Howells was tentatively turning to similar subjects. Nor should Aldrich, with his *Story of a Bad Boy* (1869) and his picture of rural New Hampshire in *Prudence Palfrey* (1874), be forgotten.[1]

The emergence of local-color fiction was a natural consequence of the growth of the republic, the development of sectional peculiarities and the destruction of political barriers to sympathy between its several parts. In earlier days the nation had a unity of character that was lost as the tide of population flowed beyond the Mississippi and as a new culture sprang into being in the Middle West, Northwest and Southwest. The one line of cleavage, that between North and South, was so great that literature found it difficult to overleap. But by 1870 there was a growing body of readers in the Middle West and the Far West eager for stories of New England life; an equal body in the East and the Far West who welcomed the songs and stories of the Mississippi Valley by J. J. Piatt, Will Carleton, Edward Eggleston and Mark Twain. The antipathy between South and North was slowly beginning to fade, and each side was willing to read of life in the other section with a relish seldom shown before 1865. Americans appreciated for the first time the breadth of social tradition sheltered by their land as they read of the Belles Demoiselles plantation and its gay Creole owners, of Huck Finn and the runaway slave, of Señor Altascar's curse on the Missourian as the latter took possession of his California ranch.

A sharp distinction between two types of the local

---

[1] W. D. Howells, *Literary Friends and Acquaintances* (N. Y., 1911), pts. i, iii and iv, offers an incomparable picture of literary New England in the seventies.

colorists' work is necessary. In two sections it had that vivid autumnal tinge produced by a social decay—in New England, drained of its best blood by emigration, and in the South, where the *ante bellum* system was in ruins. In other sections it was the crudely vigorous color of a bustling, fast-growing new country.[1] Before the Civil War neither the decline nor the development had reached a stage which gave the local colorists their full opportunity; now they made the most of it. Nor should we overlook the fact that Henry James's work, beginning with *Roderick Hudson* and *The American* (1875, 1876), was virtually the discovery of a new social frontier. Various observers commented in the seventies upon the growing number of American colonists to be found in every attractive town of the Continent; and it was noted that many who acquired culture abroad found it difficult to use it at home. They fell into "that melancholy process of vibration between two continents in which an increasingly large number of persons pass a great part of their lives; their hearts and affections being wholly in neither."[2] This group to which he belonged afforded James the material out of which he wrought his conscientious studies of a cosmopolitan society, his Americans thrown against an Old World setting of history, refinement and fixed social patterns. James was himself a social phenomenon, with his longing for "the denser, richer, warmer European spectacle" as a fund of suggestion for his art.[3]

One change of far-reaching significance, resulting largely from the establishment of the new magazines and the founding of energetic publishing houses like those

[1] See Horace Fiske, *Provincial Types in American Fiction* (N. Y., 1903).

[2] *Nation*, XIX, July 16, 1874.

[3] Henry James, *Nathaniel Hawthorne* (John Morley, ed., *English Men of Letters*, London, 1879), 12.

of Henry Holt, Charles Scribner and E. P. Dutton, was the creation of a really solid economic basis for authorship. Lowell in an address in New York near the end of his career remarked that in his boyhood only two Americans, Irving and Cooper, could have lived upon their literary incomes and they fortunately had other sources of revenue. "There are now scores," he said, "who find in letters a handsome estate." [1] The most important literary periodical in New York just after the war was the *Saturday Press;* to be accepted by it had been, as Howells said, nearly as signal a brevet of merit as to be accepted by the *Atlantic;* yet it paid contributors not a cent. It was quickly shouldered aside by *Scribner's,* which paid well.[2] No longer was it possible for a writer of Poe's originality and genius to starve for lack of a few dollars while he hawked his poems, tales and criticism from one miserly editor to another. Thoreau was a greater writer, if not a greater naturalist, than John Burroughs, yet Thoreau's income from his books and papers was zero while Burroughs was able to take advantage of a varied and eager market.[3]

The rise of the new literature was accompanied by the development of criticism in its modern form. Its origin was British in a double sense, for it owed the creation of its vehicle, the *Nation,* to a British newcomer and it was built upon the standards of the *Spectator* and *Saturday Review.* Our own so-called critics failed to divine the true necessity of the time. George Ripley, who headed the literary department of the *Tribune,* and the two Southerners, John R. Thompson and George Cary Eggleston, who successively managed that of the

---

[1] Horace Scudder, *James Russell Lowell* (Boston, 1901), II, 361.
[2] Howells, *Literary Friends and Acquaintances,* 70.
[3] Clara Barrus, *Life and Letters of John Burroughs* (Boston, 1925), I, 139 ff.

Evening Post, treated books with amiable superficiality, encouraging but not correcting or guiding authors.[1]   In the *North American Review* Lowell told his countrymen what to think of Carlyle's *Frederick the Great,* of Swinburne's poems and of many writers long dead; but after 1872 he devoted himself mainly to politics, poetry and scholarship.   The task of providing the United States with adequate literary criticism fell squarely upon the shoulders of E. L. Godkin, the brilliant Anglo-Irishman of thirty-three who on July 6, 1865, began publishing the weekly *Nation.*   It enlisted as contributors Longfellow, Lowell, Whittier, Howells, Frederick Law Olmsted, Bayard Taylor, Richard Grant White, Norton and a long list of academic worthies.   From the beginning it was doubly a power—a power in the critical domain, an even greater power, thanks to Godkin's acute, mordant and fearless pen, in the political world.[2]

Taken in its double character, it was such a weekly as no earlier period in American society could have supported.   For one reason, it was a product of the political and social problems entailed by the war.   The final and decisive impulse toward its establishment lay in the subscription of a large sum by James M. McKim, a philanthropic abolitionist of Philadelphia who had wished to establish a journal in behalf of the freedmen.   Of the seven main objects set forth by the prospectus, four directly concerned the problems offered by Southern Reconstruction and the emancipated Negroes.[3]   Moreover, before 1865 interest in public questions had not been of a character to give such a weekly any likelihood of a respectable circulation.   That interest had been intense, but in a

[1] Nevins, *Evening Post,* chap. xviii.

[2] Gustav Pollak, *Fifty Years of American Idealism* (Boston, 1915), 5 ff.; W. P. Garrison, *Letters and Memorials* (Boston, 1908), 142 ff.

[3] E. L. Godkin, *Life and Letters* (Rollo Ogden, ed., N. Y., 1907), I, 237.

partisan sense only, and without inclination toward an objective study of public questions. Finally, not until after the Civil War was there an audience sufficiently interested in the arts to care for the criticism which the *Nation* made available.[1] Godkin's British education gave him a novel point of view and an acquaintance with more mature institutions which were of the utmost value in his criticism of American life.[2] Editors, clergymen, lawyers and professors read his sound opinions on politics and transmitted them, in form dilute but recognizable, to a popular audience. Literary men read the *Nation's* comments on books and immediately profited.[3] It was shown incidentally that the weekly, not the monthly or the daily, was the best agency for criticism.

New manifestations of the country's increasing variety of interests were constantly appearing. Thus the comic weekly, after many abortive imitations of *Punch* and the continental journals, attained a vigorous life when in 1869 *Puck* was founded in St. Louis by Joseph Keppler, who had a remarkable *flair* for the humorous side of politics.[4] Later, in 1876, he entered the New York field, and the colored political cartoons became so popular that in 1877 an English-language edition was established. The first good financial weekly known in the New World, the *Commercial and Financial Chronicle,* was founded in the same year as the *Nation.* It had no such able editor as the *London Economist* boasted in Walter Bagehot, but in many features it was com-

[1] See Pollak, *Fifty Years of American Idealism,* 53.
[2] Brander Matthews, *These Many Years* (N. Y., 1917), 170 ff.
[3] See Ogden, *E. L. Godkin,* II, 66-67. "You always say what I would have said—if I had only thought of it." J. R. Lowell, *Letters* (C. E. Norton, ed., N. Y., 1893), II, 76. W. P. Garrison as literary editor was an invaluable aid to Godkin and a force of original power.
[4] Frank Weitenkampf, *American Graphic Art* (rev. edn., N. Y., 1924), chap. xiii; A. B. Faust, *German Element in the United States* (Boston, 1909), II, 361 ff.

parable with that standard journal, and it threw a strong influence upon the side of business honesty and conservatism. A marked feature of the day was the rise of the great commercial news companies, which had been negligible before the war, but not long after it were doing a business of ten millions dollars a year in New York City alone. The American News Company, which stood foremost, distributed throughout the country in 1866 no fewer than six hundred and fifty thousand copies of weekly newspapers, two hundred and ninety-six thousand copies of monthly magazines, and two hundred and twenty-five thousand of dime novels. It was largely due to these companies that the periodicals of the United States reached by 1878 a truly impressive circulation. It would be difficult to overestimate what these and other publications accomplished for the literary cultivation of the American people.

The same forces which gave vigor to a peculiarly American type of fiction were felt more feebly, but still realistically, in the drama. In 1874 Mark Twain made a play from *The Gilded Age* which he called "Colonel Sellers," and to which the capable actor John T. Raymond, playing the title rôle, gave a considerable success. It contained a broad satire upon American political and social corruption. The following year was produced B. E. Wolf's "The Almighty Dollar," which W. J. Florence made famous by his characterization of Judge Bardwell Slote, the congressman from Cohosh district —a typical American politician.[1] The foremost places among the writers for the stage were taken by Bronson Howard, who deserves the title of dean of American playwrights, and the enormously productive Dion Boucicault. Howard, a native of Detroit, would have graduated from Yale in the last year of the war, but his eyes

[1] M. J. Moses, *The American Dramatist* (Boston, 1911), 52.

failed him, and he turned to the theater. His first great success, a landmark in American drama, was "Saratoga," in 1870. Because of certain fresh and lively elements this mediocre comedy, produced by Daly in New York with Clara Morris sparkling in a leading rôle, enjoyed a tremendous run. On the hundredth night Daly gave the author a supper at which Mayor A. Oakey Hall presided. The best that we can say of American playwriting during these years, in which most literary men were frankly indifferent to the drama, is that "Saratoga" and the crude play, "Rip Van Winkle," which Joseph Jefferson transformed by his exquisite gift of character creation, contended for the highest crown of popularity.[1]

The stock companies were steadily waning, and the "star system" was slowly rising, as the years passed; but the best of the companies, like Wallack's in New York, Mrs. John Drew's Chestnut Street Theater in Philadelphia and the Boston Museum, were admirable even in decay. The difficulties of Augustin Daly in the metropolis exemplified the troubled career of the old-style manager. Daly was an affable, masterful man, with business capacity, the tact to handle a large company and the talent for writing a successful play himself. His "Horizon" was a picture of life on the frontier in the midst of Indian hostilities, while his "Divorce" was the first American play on the subject and was repeated more than two hundred times. Among his performers were Adelaide Neilson, Fanny Davenport, Charles Fisher, Mrs. S. H. Gilbert and young John Drew. In the early seventies one season after another gave him a notable success. But fortune seldom smiled long on Daly; on New Year's Day in 1873 the burning of his Fifth Avenue Theater cost him heavily and the Panic some months later almost ruined the theatrical business. In 1874-

[1] J. R. Towse, *Sixty Years of the Theater* (N. Y., 1916), 227.

1875 the manager failed to obtain three weeks' paying business in as many months, his new theater was maintained only by loans and the company for a time went to a half-salary basis. In the spring of 1876 the memorable revivals of Moody and Sankey at the Hippodrome affected all theaters unfavorably, while Daly's eighth season, 1876-1877, was a succession of failures; and in the fall he was forced to surrender his Fifth Avenue playhouse through inability to pay the rent. Under such circumstances it was no wonder that the "star" system, which enabled a speculative manager to dispense with costly troupes and give the public performances by one able actor "supported" by a company of nonentities, gained favor.[1]

In one artistic field, that of painting, the American advance rivaled that in the domain of *belles-lettres* and even began to promise a brilliant approach toward European achievement. When the war ended art occupied as sorry an estate as education or literature. New York had but a single mediocre statue of Washington in her streets and a mediocre bust of Schiller and several symbolic figures in Central Park. Washington had no statuary of value and the great Washington Monument, one third completed, had been halted for lack of funds. Boston had nothing but poor bronze statues of Webster, Emerson and Horace Mann. No American city had a public art gallery worthy of the name.[2] The nearest approach in New York, for example, was the gallery of the Historical Society, which had several hundred pictures, mostly portraits, and a few fine sculptures. Our two largest cities supported sturdy schools of art: Philadelphia's Academy of Fine Arts gave annual exhibitions and

[1] J. F. Daly, *Life of Augustin Daly* (N. Y., 1917), *passim*.
[2] See the *N. Y. Eve. Post*, Jan. 17, 1867, for a demand for a suitable gallery.

was proud of the marine painter James Hamilton, while
New York's National Academy of Design at its annual
showing in 1866 presented Weir's "The Gun Foundry,"
Homer's "Prisoners from the Front," Eastman Johnson's
"Sunday Morning," and portraits by William M. Hunt.
Yet their future seemed uncertain. It was one of the
few hopeful signs of the times that the demand for good
European paintings was keen. Many sales were made
in New York, and one of one hundred and sixty-eight
paintings brought more than one hundred thousand dollars. Several rich men had fine private collections of
modern canvases, notably August Belmont, A. T. Stewart—who paid seventy-five thousand dollars in gold for
Meissonier's "1807" [1]—and the public-spirited William
T. Blodgett, whose gallery at the time of his death was
worth fully two hundred thousand dollars.

But despite the lack of public galleries and the paucity
of schools, a small group of admirable artists were pushing their way to the front. Winslow Homer, a born
draughtsman of seafaring New England stock, had no
formal training save a month at the Academy of Design
and a few private lessons. After serving at the front
during the war as illustrator for *Harper's Weekly*, he
returned and began to exhibit paintings of war subjects,
which quickly established him as the foremost military
artist of the country.[2] His "Prisoners at the Front"
led to his election in 1865, at the age of twenty-nine, to
the National Academy. Elihu Vedder, of an old Dutch
family in New York, was chosen to the Academy in the
same year. The years immediately following the war
found James McNeill Whistler, John La Farge and John
S. Sargent studying abroad. Mary Cassatt, the daughter
of a Pennsylvania banker, began exhibiting in the Paris
salon in 1872, while Whistler simultaneously placed his

[1] *N. Y. World*, April 7, 1876.   [2] *The Arts*, VI, 185 ff.

portrait of his mother on view.   Edwin A. Abbey found
the stimulus for his career in the office of *Harper's
Weekly*, which also furnished a market for the work of
other brilliant young men—Joseph Pennell, Alfred Parsons, Howard Pyle and John W. Alexander.   Add to this
list of names George Inness, A. H. Wyant, Homer Martin and William Morris Hunt,[1] and it will be seen that
America had a distinguished school of artists and that a
new and vibrant spirit was in the air.   When La Farge
undertook the decoration of Trinity Church in Boston,
he was able to employ as his assistants Augustus St.
Gaudens, F. D. Millet and Edwin Champney.   One sign
of the times was the creation of a chair of art at Harvard
in 1875, which was occupied by the ideally fitted Charles
Eliot Norton, and another was the foundation of several
great art museums.

These museums were established not merely because of
a deepening public interest in art but because the accumulations of American capital were for the first time adequate.   One of them, the Corcoran Art Gallery at the
national capital, was the gift of a single rich banker of
Washington who in 1869 presented his own collections
with a generous endowment.   In Boston a number of
wealthy citizens, with the object of forming "a nucleus
of what may hereafter become, through the liberality of
enlightened friends of art, a representative" collection of
masterpieces, incorporated the Museum of Fine Arts in
1870, and opened it to the public on July 4, 1876.[2]   In
New York the sentiment in favor of a similar institution,
long stimulated by the press, bore fruit in a public meeting at the Academy of Music in November, 1869, when
a number of distinguished citizens were appointed a com-

[1] For art in Boston during the seventies, see Martha A. S. Shannon,
Boston Days of William Morris Hunt (Boston, 1923), 59 ff.
[2] *Art Journal*, I (1875), 212-213.

mittee to draft a plan of organization. A few such collectors as W. T. Blodgett gave liberally of money and artistic possessions to the Metropolitan Art Museum, as it was called, while the legislature authorized the parks department to raise a half-million dollars to erect a museum building in Central Park.[1] The original unit was completed in 1879, and its treasures opened to the public.

A postwar era which, amidst boodling, scandal and money grubbing, could produce *Scribner's* and the *Nation, Life on the Mississippi* and *Old Creole Days,* Edwin Booth in "Hamlet" and the Boston Museum of Fine Arts, was an epoch full of healthy and irrepressible growth in every cultural field. They represented achievements of enduring value, and indicated powerful and promising currents flowing beneath the surface of the life of the new nation.

[1] *Art Journal*, I (1875), 26-27.

CHAPTER X

THE DEEPENING OF AMERICAN CULTURE

NOTHING was more typical of the intellectual immaturity of the United States in 1865 than the state of its higher education. Harvard, as Bryce said later, was a struggling and poverty-stricken college, with vague relations to learning and research, loosely tied to a congeries of professional schools. Many of its courses were on the level of a present-day high school, and, except in science, it was impossible for any of its students to push beyond the weak training for the A.B. degree.[1] Yale's facilities were even more wretchedly insufficient. Its policies were shaped by a little group of Congregational ministers and a narrow church atmosphere stifled the teaching.[2] Its curriculum was antiquated, and the oldest professors were paid less than the youngest ministers in New Haven, while the scanty library fund was always exhausted before it was paid in. Princeton followed a course of study almost identical with that pursued by undergraduates when Madison was in the White House. The students recited in rooms that were "mostly ill-conditioned cellars and attics," and when in 1868 Dr. James McCosh became the head he pronounced the scientific apparatus and collections fit only to be burned. The University of Wisconsin had two or three very dilapidated buildings, a tiny uncatalogued library, five pro-

[1] C. F. Thwing, "President Eliot's Administration," *Harvard Grad. Mag.*, XVII (1909), 376.
[2] H. E. Starr, *William Graham Sumner* (N. Y., 1925), 80.

fessors and a few tutors; its critics declared that it was merely an academy for the village of Madison.[1]

There was everywhere an antediluvian flavor about the courses of study which explains Henry Cabot Lodge's remark that, in all his four years at Harvard, 1867-1871, "I never really studied anything, never had my mind roused to any exertion or to anything resembling active thought"—with the exception, he adds, of Henry Adams's course in medieval history.[2] Electives were virtually unknown outside the universities of Michigan and Virginia; and the hard-and-fast curriculum emphasized the ancient classics, ethics and rhetoric. In many institutions there were no modern languages taught, not even French and German. There was little science and laboratory practice was everywhere confined to a few experiments performed by the professor before his class. T. R. Lounsbury in all his college course at Yale never heard mention of any English author. Brander Matthews at Columbia had just one term in the history of English literature, but was not even here introduced to the writings of any authors or told to read them for himself. G. Stanley Hall at Williams was given no English literature save a driblet taught by the professor of rhetoric.[3] The colleges were used to the spectacle of professors filling several or even a half-dozen chairs at once. Thus Yale had one heroic savant expounding physics, astronomy, meteorology and mechanics, while at Columbia an intellectual Hercules dealt with moral and mental philosophy, English literature, history,

---

[1] J. F. A. Pyre, *Wisconsin* (N. Y., 1920), 159 ff. In comparison with the total population, the number of American college students was yet very small; in 1873 it was (exclusive of professional schools) only 23,000.

[2] H. C. Lodge, *Early Memories* (N. Y., 1913), 186-187.

[3] Brander Matthews, *These Many Years* (N. Y., 1917), 101 ff.; G. S. Hall, *Life and Confessions of a Psychologist* (N. Y., 1923), 158 ff.

political economy and logic.[1]   The method of teaching, for the most part, could not have been duller.   The students recited in much the same parrot fashion as in grade schools, for in general they were expected to acquire information rather than the ability to think. Brander Matthews tells us that he was never encouraged to go outside the textbooks, that no collateral reading was ever suggested, and that the professors lived in a splendid isolation from their students.   "All the exercises," testifies Dr. Hall regarding Williams, "consisted in hearing recitations."

It was no real justification of such pedagogic methods that the students were younger than now, the average age of Brander Matthews's class on entering Columbia in 1868 being sixteen.   Nor was there any justification for the refusal of most colleges to recognize the value of modern history, economics and the chief foreign tongues. Yale had no chair in either political economy or sociology till 1872 when William Graham Sumner was asked to fill both; [2] Columbia had no French, practically no history and but one hour weekly of economics.   Few of the three hundred and sixty institutions bearing the name of college or university were as well off as those named. As Andrew D. White said in 1874, most of them possessed no adequate faculties, no libraries offering any idea of the existing condition of knowledge, no illustrative collections or laboratories and next to no modern apparatus or instruments.   The ordinary sectarian institution would not consider for a moment going outside its own denomination for a teacher.   A visitor to most college towns, White added, would find the railway station and the county jail better built, heated and equipped

[1] This was Charles Murray Nairne.   See F. P. Keppel, *Columbia* (N. Y., 1914), 146.
[2] Starr, *Sumner*, 161.

than the halls of learning.[1]   In the Middle West especially—in Ohio, Indiana and Illinois—there was an excessive number of weak schools pretending to a collegiate rank which they never attained.   In their competitive greed for students they lowered their standards to such a degree as to injure the high schools in turn.

Equally striking in a survey of higher education was the fact that the very branches most important to the future growth of the nation were those most neglected. There was no scientific instruction in agriculture anywhere.   The first school of mines, that at Columbia, was only two years old when the war ended, and gave a slender three years' course.[2]   Instruction in technology was yet in its infancy, and the view still obtained that the proper function of the engineering college was to give students a superficial knowledge of technical methods and formulas, leaving them to be licked into shape by practical experience.   Shop practice in technical schools was almost unknown.   In medicine by 1870 there were more than fifty schools, but by present-day standards they were all wretched.   As yet there was little real distinction between surgeon and physician, as in England. Many of both the medical and law schools were wholly or in part proprietary—that is, money-making trade schools—and only nominally attached to the colleges whose names they borrowed.   In women's education, when the ambitious girl of 1865 looked about her she found only three or four institutions, Oberlin the most notable, of worthy standards.[3]

To produce the upheaval which changed and modernized the domain of higher education within two decades,

[1] A. D. White, "A National University," Nat. Educ. Assoc., *Addresses and Proceeds. for 1874*, 60.
[2] Keppel, *Columbia*, 118-120.
[3] See J. M. Taylor, *Before Vassar Opened* (Boston, 1914).

three primary causes interacted. The emergence of a half-dozen statesmen of education—Andrew D. White of Cornell (inaugurated 1867), James McCosh of Princeton (1868), Charles W. Eliot of Harvard (1869), Noah Porter of Yale (1871), James B. Angell of Michigan (1871), and Daniel Coit Gilman of Johns Hopkins (chosen in 1875)—provided the personal force that was needed. It was noteworthy that one of these men was a Scotchman, while the other five had studied or traveled extensively in Europe. Moreover, an outcry for a fresher, more practical and more advanced kind of instruction arose among the alumni and friends of nearly all the old colleges and grew into a movement that overrode all conservative opposition. The aggressive "Young Yale" movement appeared, demanding partial alumni control, a more liberal spirit and a broader course of study.[1] The sons of Harvard simultaneously rallied to relieve the university's poverty and demand new enterprise. Likewise, as an impulse toward greater social breadth and increased practical usefulness in university work, came the establishment of the land-grant institutions under the Morrill act. Education was pushing toward higher standards in the East, throwing off hidebound church leadership everywhere, and in the West finding a wider range of studies and a new sense of public duty.

The old-style classical education received its most crushing blow in the citadel of Harvard, where a young captain of thirty-five, the son of a former mayor of Boston and treasurer of Harvard, led the progressive forces. Five revolutionary advances were made during the first years of Dr. Eliot's administration.[2] They were the elevation and amplification of entrance require-

[1] Starr, *Sumner*, 161.
[2] J. H. Gardiner, *Harvard* (N. Y., 1914), 50.

ments, the enlargement of the curriculum and the development of the elective system, the recognition of graduate study in the liberal arts, the raising of professional training in law, medicine and engineering to a postgraduate level, and the fostering of greater maturity in student life. Most of these we may dismiss briefly. Standards of admission were sharply advanced in 1872-1873 and 1876-1877. By the appointment of a dean to take charge of student affairs, and a wise handling of discipline, the undergraduates were led to regard themselves more as young gentlemen and less as young animals. One new course of study after another was opened up—science, music, the history of the fine arts (with Charles Eliot Norton as lecturer),[1] advanced Spanish, political economy, physics, classical philology and international law.

In organizing postgraduate instruction upon a well-ordered basis Harvard was acting in response to a need which was clearly recognized at other institutions as well. True graduate training was unknown in America until after the war. Young men like Andrew D. White, G. Stanley Hall and Edmund J. James went naturally to Germany for their advanced study.[2] In 1871, however, Yale led the way for American institutions by concentrating all her nonprofessional graduate work into a distinct school. The next year Harvard went a step further by stiffening the requirements for the degree of A. M. and providing that the two new degrees of Ph. D. and Sc. D. might be conferred after three years of residential study. It was not, however, until the Johns Hopkins University was opened in Baltimore in 1876, as the result of the bequest of a wealthy merchant

---

[1] M. A. De W. Howe, *Letters of Charles Eliot Norton* (Boston, 1913), II, 3 ff.

[2] See G. S. Hall, *Life and Confessions of a Psychologist*, 183.

of that city, that an American university devoted itself primarily to research and the training of scholars.[1] Under the presidency of Daniel Coit Gilman a notable faculty was gathered there, and young college graduates soon began to feel that it was not necessary to go abroad for their intensive training, though the old tradition continued strong for another generation.

About the adoption of the elective system raged one of the most famous nation-wide battles in the history of American collegiate education. Harvard, like nearly all other colleges, still cleaved in 1864 to a deadening routine of subjects prescribed for all students. The following year the elective plan began to receive a trial, and when Dr. Eliot took office, it was so rapidly extended that by 1875 seniors had only one prescribed course and juniors only three. By 1883-1884 the system was carried even into the freshman year. All this struck other colleges as radically wrong. Dr. McCosh, who brought so much prestige with him from Scotland, took a stand midway between the old method and the new. He supervised the planning of a new curriculum whereby the first two years were devoted almost wholly to required subjects while in the last two an increasing freedom was permitted. With wonted Scotch vigor he declared that Harvard allowed immature and lazy youths to concoct a worthless program of easy studies and that every student should be made to master certain basic branches.[2] Presidents Eliot and McCosh met in a spectacular joint debate on the subject in New York. The question could be settled only by time, and time has ended it by a compromise. But at the moment Dr. Eliot's bold

[1] Fabian Franklin, *The Life of Daniel Coit Gilman* (N. Y., 1910), 182 ff.; D. C. Gilman, *The Launching of a University* (N. Y., 1906), *passim*. See the *Nation* (N. Y.), XX, Jan. 28, 1875, for penetrating comment on Gilman's plans.

[2] E. M. Norris, *The Story of Princeton* (Boston, 1917), 204.

course struck the shackles from the students in college after college.

It was a victory won upon a wide front. Cornell University was opened in 1868 on the elective principle; and freedom of study had much to do with its success, the undergraduates by its third year outnumbering those of any other three colleges in the state.[1] Michigan, which had pursued the same plan for a much longer period, met with an equally popular response. The inevitability of final triumph for the elective system was shown in dramatic fashion by Frederick A. P. Barnard's conversion to it at Columbia. As a teacher in the South, he had been familiar with the historic elective system of the University of Virginia and had strenuously opposed it. But in 1867 he was struck by the need for the teaching of French and German at Columbia, and when he learned that Harvard had introduced them into the regular course, demanding no Latin or Greek after the freshman year, he decided that the elective plan was identified with progress. Arguing with the trustees, he pointed out that times had changed; young men no longer preferred the polite learning of 1830, but wanted practical knowledge—the living tongues, the sciences, the arts—and the colleges should keep step with the world.[2] Unfortunately the trustees were adamant. Columbia and Yale remained, in fact, the two institutions which throughout this period clung stubbornly to their old curricula. The difference between them was that President Barnard labored earnestly to liberalize Columbia, while President Noah Porter, a highly conservative cleric, did his best to resist many new tendencies at Yale.

But if the increased breadth of higher education owed

---

[1] A. D. White, *Autobiography* (N. Y., 1905), I, 347, 353, 355.
[2] Margaret McM. Barnard, *Memoirs of Frederick A. P. Barnard* (John Fulton, ed., N. Y., 1896), chaps. xv-xvi.

much to a half-dozen Eastern leaders, it owed still more
to the Morrill act of 1862, which both re-created Western education and added a new wing to the Eastern edifice. Primarily, of course, its purpose was the provision
of education in agriculture and engineering, but actually
its effects touched all branches of instruction. It led to
the reorganization in 1866 of the University of Wisconsin, by which that university was given a strong president in place of a weak chancellor, while the curriculum
was broadened with the practical studies fairly in the
foreground. It caused the founding of the University
of Illinois (1867), which, in the words of its chief parent, the rugged Jonathan B. Turner, was intended to be
"a peculiar university," one which "our posterity can
erect into the strongest, broadest, and best university on
the face of the earth." [1] From it, also, sprang the universities of California (1868), of Minnesota (1868)
and of Kansas (1864), the Massachusetts and Texas
Agricultural colleges and other institutions. Most strikingly among its results, it brought to fruition the plans
for a new, broader and better university which Andrew
D. White, a wealthy young New Yorker had been forming during his years of teaching at Michigan and of study
and observation at Oxford and in Germany.

The rapid rise of Cornell University, under the double impetus of the Morrill land endowment of nine hundred and sixty thousand acres and an initial fund of five
hundred thousand dollars presented by Ezra Cornell,
was the most remarkable phenomenon in higher education during the postwar decade.[2] The institution
opened in 1868 with about four hundred students and
an adequate faculty. President White laid down four

[1] Allan Nevins, *Illinois* (N. Y., 1917), 30.
[2] For a study of the founder, see A. B. Cornell, *True and Firm: a Biography of Ezra Cornell* (N. Y., 1884).

"foundation ideas": a close union of practical and liberal instruction; nonsectarian control; a fruitful alliance between the university and the state school system; and the concentration of revenues for higher education. He called also for other innovations—for the steady development of scientific studies and for partial alumni control of the government. The university had to contend with much detraction, misrepresentation and poverty, but it was blessed by the vision of both White and Cornell. A characteristically happy invention of White's was the visiting lectureship undertaken by some eminent scholars: Lowell gave a course upon early English literature, Louis Agassiz upon biology, and Freeman and Froude upon English history. Goldwin Smith, newly arrived from England, consented to occupy the chairs of English and constitutional history from 1868 to 1871. Both White and Cornell were firm believers in coeducation, and soon obtained a handsome gift for the erection of a separate residential hall for women in the university. From another donor came the money to build and equip an engineering building, and the technical branches were developed so rapidly that an impressive exhibit was made at the Centennial. Meanwhile the president's ideas regarding architectural planning were carried into effect on the heights overlooking Lake Cayuga with superb results.[1]

Yet in the Middle West, with the aid of the new land-grant funds, some of the varied innovations which Cornell epitomized were given even greater emphasis. Coeducation received a trial under the friendliest auspices. The University of Iowa had admitted women in 1858; the University of Wisconsin had opened a special normal department for them in 1863; and Ohio State University

[1] A. D. White tells the story of Cornell's early years with great literary charm in his *Autobiography*, I, 330-427.

registered them from the outset in 1870. A heavy pressure of public opinion led the universities of Michigan and Illinois to fling their doors wide open to them in 1870. At the University of Illinois—at first called the Industrial University—there was a powerful movement to exclude liberal studies, specialize in practical branches, and diffuse knowledge among the farmers and mechanics by an elaborate system of correspondence.[1] It was with difficulty that the university head persuaded the indignant agricultural societies of Illinois that there was a legal provision against exclusion of the classical studies. But generally in the West there arose a feeling that the doors of higher education had at last swung wide for the producing masses, for women as well as for men, and for utilitarian as well as cultural pursuits. To many the new democratic movement in education was a fervent crusade.[2]

It was inevitable that the growth of agricultural instruction should be discouragingly slow, for the harsh fact was that before 1870 scientific agriculture had not made sufficient progress to constitute a subject for college teaching. That literary farmer, Donald G. Mitchell, attacked the land-grant colleges as delusive. Better, he growled, put a few thousands into the distribution of one or two sterling farm journals than a few millions into these pretentious institutions.[3] He demanded that the agricultural professors offer "some practical demonstration upon the land of the faith they hold and teach." For some time one college after another indeed presented a spectacle of almost utter failure. That of Massachusetts wasted many years and many thousands of dollars.

[1] Nevins, *Illinois*, 45 ff.
[2] See Illinois Agricultural Society, *Trans.*, 1867-1870, for an expression of this spirit.
[3] *Nation*, II, June 19, 1866.

The Illinois Industrial University had only forty-five students in agriculture in 1875-1876, and only twenty-three when the year 1879 opened. Wisconsin's record was still worse, for the agricultural department had just one graduate before the year 1880.[1]

In the long run, however, scientific agriculture was bound to take sturdy root. Cornell, after many vicissitudes, brought from the State College of Iowa an able professor, Isaac P. Roberts, who united practical experience and theoretical knowledge. His success at Cornell was immediate, and his long period of service from 1874 to 1903 covered the pioneer period in agricultural education.[2] The Michigan Agricultural College became a thriving center immediately after the war. Though there was little teaching of agriculture at Wisconsin, several experiments, notably the demonstration of the remarkable qualities of Manchurian barley, were important. Illinois in 1877 found an able professor of agriculture in George Morrow, one of the most prolific writers of the time on farm topics, while it possessed the leading horticultural scientist of the country in Jonathan Burrill, the first investigator to suggest and prove the bacterial theory of the origin of diseases in plants.[3] When Dr. McCosh assailed the agricultural colleges in the mid-seventies, President White was able to make a vigorous answer. He could assert that although the Sheffield Scientific School had not a single agricultural student, the experiments of two professors there upon fertilizers had already repaid the nation a hundredfold for its land grant to Connecticut.[4]

[1] Pyre, *Wisconsin*, 181, 271.
[2] E. O. Fippin, *Rural New York* (L. H. Bailey, ed., *Rural State and Province Series*, N. Y., 1921), 85 ff.; White, *Autobiography*, I, 367 ff.
[3] Nevins, *Illinois*, 69 ff.
[4] A. D. White, "Scientific and Industrial Education in the United States," *Pop. Sci. Mo.*, V (1870), 170-191.

Whereas in agriculture the edifice had to be built from the very foundations, in engineering the Morrill act did little more than create a score of technological colleges where a half dozen had existed before. The Massachusetts Institute of Technology had been established just before the war to supply a complete system of industrial education; [1] the Stevens Institute was already giving excellent instruction in mechanical engineering; and there were good technical schools at Troy and Worcester. Yet the land-grant universities lent immediate strength to the principle that engineering could be taught practically as well as theoretically. President White, who would have liked to set up a machine shop, knew that the trustees would regard the project as chimerical and therefore met the expense of a power lathe and other machinery from his own pocket until the building presented by Hiram Sibley was ready. Having collected the largest private architectural library in America, he made it the basis of an excellent architectural department. Following the example of Columbia, the land-grant University of Wisconsin opened courses in civil engineering, mining and metallurgy early in the seventies. At Illinois some of the first shop courses in America were being taught by Stillman W. Robinson, and before 1878 three departments—mechanical engineering, civil engineering and architecture—were vigorously on their feet. Year by year the business world was being converted to the fact that college graduates, with their thorough grounding, made eventually the best engineers.

If agricultural education was nonexistent in 1865 and engineering education very rudimentary, medical teaching was a social disgrace. [2] The proprietary colleges with

[1] See J. P. Munroe, *A Life of Francis A. Walker* (N. Y., 1923), for the development of the Massachusetts Institute of Technology.
[2] G. M. Towle, *American Society* (London, 1870), II, chap. xi.

Major Powell on the Colorado,
1868.

Andrew D. White,
Cornell.

Charles W. Eliot,
Harvard.

A Laboratory at the Massachusetts
Institute of Technology.

Science and Scholarship.

which the nation was sown, chiefly joint-stock corporations which furnished the least possible tuition for the
highest possible price, poured out a stream of quacks and
incompetents.   Even the best schools came nowhere near
the standards demanded in Europe.   Thus at Harvard
the students were required to attend only two courses of
lectures, not quite four months long; then, if they could
present certificates from some medical school or doctor
showing that they had studied three years in all, and
could pass a nominal examination, they were given their
degrees.[1]   The would-be doctor in all parts of America
seldom had more than a poor high-school education before he began his studies.   Turned loose upon society in
this way, he frequently began to kill his patients through
the grossest malpractice.[2]   The darkness that prevailed
among medical graduates is indicated by the opinion of
the head of the Harvard school in 1870 that written
examinations were impossible since "a majority of the
students cannot write well enough." [3]

Year in and year out the need for reform was proclaimed by leading physicians, medical associations and
educational experts, but with little effect.   The first substantial step toward a sound basis was that forced at
Harvard.   Against an incredible weight of conservative
opposition, President Eliot compelled the medical school
to place itself on the standard academic basis, giving
three full years of eight or nine months each.   He rallied the keen-witted Oliver Wendell Holmes of the medical faculty to his side.   When the overseers hesitated, he
brought forward proof that several shocking deaths in
the town of Quincy had been traced to the ignorance of a

[1] Gardiner, *Harvard*, 48; C. W. Eliot, *A Late Harvest* (Boston, 1924),
193 ff.
[2] U. S. Commissioner of Education, *Report for 1870*, 384 ff.
[3] Eliot, *A Late Harvest*, 33 ff.

recent graduate. In response to his efforts laboratory training was given its due place and the students were required to pass severe written examinations. Simultaneously with the other reforms, the Harvard corporation in the early seventies took full charge of the school's finances, removing it from its semiproprietary basis, and furnishing money enough for new professors and courses. By the Centennial year other schools were beginning to show the effect of Harvard's example.[1]

In the teaching of law, too, Harvard blazed a path. The university law school was utterly transformed following the appointment of a single man, C. C. Langdell, as Dane professor in 1869 and dean a year later. When he arrived it was still modeled, like all other schools in America, upon a lawyer's office.[2] The fee was the same as that charged by lawyers, the faculty had no formal meetings, the students were not divided into classes save for the moot court, and no examinations whatever were given. The most important part of the instruction was furnished by eminent lecturers from outside. Though nominally the course was of eighteen months, actually it might be finished with diligence in a year. At the Columbia law school, a semiproprietary institution, all of the instruction, save a course on medical jurisprudence by a physician, was given by the owner, Theodore W. Dwight.[3] His appeal was mainly to the memories of his students whom he fed predigested information. But Langdell, a member of the New York bar renowned for his prodigious learning and industry, believed that law was a science and that the way to study it was to go to

[1] T. F. Harrington, *The Harvard Medical School* (J. G. Mumford, ed., N. Y., 1905), III, chaps. xxxii-xxxvi.
[2] See *Nation*, XXII, Feb. 17, 1876, for the New York Bar Association's report indicting the wretched requirements for admission to the bar.
[3] Matthews, *These Many Years*, 133.

the original sources; and upon this principle he based a reconstruction of all law teaching.

His new method, the "case method," was hailed by Sir Frederick Pollock of Oxford as "the best way, if not the only way, to learn law." Instead of setting his students to learn legal principles by rote from textbooks, Langdell sent them to the reports in the library to dig out the actual cases from which the principles were derived. In reciting, they were expected to set forth the issues and appraise the justice of each decision, perhaps explaining how it would have been modified to accord with a postulated change of facts. The study took on new interest and vitality; for the first time a fierce eagerness was observed among the young men pursuing the courses. As Senator Lodge testified, the case system taught also the history of the common law and equity, and made the great judges and chancellors of England and America not mere footnote names "but living men whose influence upon the law, whose views and whose lives, were all of interest and moment." [1] At the same time Langdell and Eliot gave the school new standards, a longer period of study, better equipment and faculty members who were not lawyers of established repute but merely able teachers. The legal profession viewed these changes askance and many men scoffed at a dean who sent his students to the precedents of the Middle Ages. But as the graduates entered lawyers' offices, it was found that their grasp of legal concepts and ability to think for themselves made them priceless. [2]

Coeducation, we have noted, was given national breadth and irresistible impetus by the land-grant colleges. Nevertheless, the distrust of higher education for

[1] Lodge, *Early Memories*, 246.
[2] Gardiner, *Harvard*, 201; C. W. Eliot, "Langdell and the Law School," *Harvard Law Rev.*, XXXIII, 518-524.

women remained so keen, especially in the East, that T. W. Higginson felt it necessary to publish in the *Atlantic* a sarcastic essay, "Should Women Learn the Alphabet?" An eminent Boston physician, Dr. E. M. Clarke, issued a volume on *Sex in Education,* which presented "proof" that the physical impediments to sex equality in higher education were insuperable.[1] Influential leaders of opinion maintained that women would unsex themselves and lose every feminine grace if they undertook the same routine as men; they would soon be wearing bloomers and going in for rough outdoor sports!

The chief blow against these paleolithic beliefs was struck by the establishment, in the very heart of the conservative East, of three colleges exclusively for women: Vassar in 1865,[2] and Smith[3] and Wellesley[4] just a decade later. Various "female colleges" had been scattered throughout the country, but not even the best offered courses of true college grade. Vassar was established by a rich brewer of Poughkeepsie; Smith by Sophia Smith of Hatfield, Massachusetts, who left in 1870 about $365,000 for an institution to give young women advantages equaling those of men; and Wellesley by Henry Towle Durant, a wealthy Boston lawyer. A brewer, a spinster and a lawyer—the diversity of these figures illustrates the breadth of the new movement. Of the three colleges, Smith insisted from the outset upon standards precisely as high as those of the best men's universities, and maintained these standards despite the difficulty of obtaining adequately pre-

[1] See the answer to this volume: Anna C. Brackett and others, *The Education of American Girls* (N. Y., 1874).

[2] B. J. Lossing, *Vassar College and Its Founder* (N. Y., 1867), 20 ff.; J. M. Taylor and Elizabeth H. Haight, *Vassar* (N. Y., 1915), 61-84.

[3] L. C. Seelye, *Early History of Smith College* (Boston, 1923), chaps. i-ii.

[4] Florence Morse Kingsley, *The Life of Henry Durant* (N. Y., 1924), 235 ff.

pared students. The other two rapidly raised their requirements.

The general growth of colleges and universities in vigor and wealth was surprisingly consistent in view of the check which the Panic of 1873 gave all American activities. The work of McCosh at Princeton, a college which he gave its greatest administration until the arrival of Woodrow Wilson, was the outstanding achievement in conservative educational circles.[1] Even Yale, under the reactionary Noah Porter, and despite the fact that expansion was retarded by the existence of the Sheffield School, seeming to offer utilitarian studies to those who wanted them, felt an awakening. The first university art school in America began its instruction there in 1869, and numerous important gifts were received.[2] Meanwhile, besides Johns Hopkins, three other noteworthy endowed universities were founded in the seventies—Lehigh,[3] endowed by a rich Pennsylvania coal operator named Asa Packer; Vanderbilt University,[4] to which the "Commodore" gave generously; and Boston University,[5] founded by certain wealthy New England Methodists.

The genuineness of American interest in advanced knowledge in these years was especially evident in the scientific and historical fields. E. L. Youmans, the leading apostle of a new movement to give science a large place in education, issued a manifesto on the subject in 1867 under the title of *The Culture Demanded by Modern Life*. Containing papers by Huxley, Tyndall,

[1] V. L. Collins, *Princeton* (N. Y., 1914), 221 ff.
[2] Yale College, *Annual Catalogues for 1869-1870; 1872-1873; and 1875-1876.*
[3] *Appletons' Annual Cyclopedia* (N. Y., 1861-1903), XIX (1879), 713.
[4] *Am. Ann. Cyclop.,* XIII (1873), 486.
[5] J. M. Buckley, *A History of Methodists in the United States* (Philip Schaff and others, eds., *The American Church History Series,* V, N. Y., 1893-1896), 527.

Liebig and others and a belligerent introduction, it was as influential as Youmans's popular lectures. Four years later he visited Europe to arrange with men of science for the publication of a long list of scientific works to be called the *International Scientific Series*.[1] These books were to be brought out simultaneously in several nations and languages, and despite many difficulties, a library of more than fifty volumes resulted. Another of Youmans's useful achievements was the establishment in 1872 of the *Popular Science Monthly*, which aimed to expound every important new principle or theory of science along with a discussion of problems of real practical interest.[2]

Yet highly distinguished American men of science remained rare, and their contributions to world knowledge were inadequate. During the Centennial year a writer complained in the *Popular Science Monthly* that, for every research published in the United States, at least fifty appeared in Europe.[3] "Our meagre catalogue" of original investigators, he said, would be filled out by "fifteen or twenty chemists and physicists, as many mathematicians and astronomers, and a somewhat larger number of zoologists, entomologists, botanists, and geologists." The United States, he concluded, might possess, all told, twenty men of really notable scientific station, though none who compared with Tyndall or Helmholtz. Asa Gray was teaching a second generation of botanists at Harvard. Louis Agassiz, returning in 1868 from his trip to Brazil to make a second excursion to the warmer waters of North America three years later, was enabled by the liberality of John Anderson to found

[1] John Fiske, *A Century of Science and Other Essays* (*Miscellaneous Writings*, X, Boston, 1902), 64 ff.

[2] Grant Overton, *Portrait of a Publisher* (N. Y., 1925), 61.

[3] F. W. Clarke, "American Colleges *versus* American Science," *Pop. Sci. Mo.*, IX (1876), 467 ff.

his practical school of natural science at Buzzard's Bay in 1873, and died late that year. We have from Dr. Eliot a testimonial to the difficulty of finding any fit guides for the filling of professorships; and to the men just named he added only three others, M. F. Maury, the oceanographer, who died the same year as Agassiz, Jeffries Wyman, the anatomist, and D. H. Storer, the expert on fishes.[1] Benjamin Silliman the younger was continuing his work as chemist and mineralogist at Yale; James Dwight Dana was in the midst of his career as geologist there; and Joseph Henry, the physicist, at the national capital was placing the new science of meteorology upon a firm basis.

Certain special contributions to human knowledge had, thanks to the national preoccupation with the development of the West, a picturesquely memorable character. The dashing personality and high talents of Clarence King gave a special interest to his labors in mapping geologically the face of the Far West.[2] This young Rhode Islander, graduating from Yale in 1868, seemed marked for a more brilliant career than he actually achieved. He organized for the government the geological survey which ran like a ribbon with the Union Pacific along the fortieth parallel, and his main reports (1876-1877) constituted one of the most important scientific works of the time. During a visit East late in 1866 he won Congress to a plan for a government survey across the whole Cordilleran system at the widest point, and was placed in charge of the undertaking. The obstacles were enormous; but King organized his parties, imbued them with his own enthusiasm, and pushed the undertaking with such energy that in 1870 he was able to

[1] See Diana F. M. Corbin, *Life of Matthew Fontaine Maury* (London, 1888).

[2] Century Association, *Clarence King Memoirs* (N. Y., 1904), esp. 262 ff.; Henry Adams, *Education of Henry Adams* (N. Y., 1918), 311.

publish an admirable scientific study of the ore deposits of the region surveyed. Then came King's crowning service to science and the country. There had sprung up an intense rivalry in the Western field between the engineer corps of the army and the so-called Hayden Survey, and its bitterness threatened to cripple both.[1] King, laboring through his political friends and the National Academy of Sciences, was the chief instrument of settling the feud by obtaining the creation on March 3, 1879, of the United States geological survey as a bureau of the interior department. President Hayes promptly appointed him its first director, and though he remained in office only two years, he outlined the broad general principles upon which it has since been conducted.

Equally striking was the career of Major J. W. Powell. Coming out of the Civil War with the loss of his right arm, he possessed a fund of geological knowledge which led to his appointment to a professorship in the Illinois Wesleyan University. Two years later he began the exploration of the Rocky Mountains and of the Green and Colorado rivers, which was made ever memorable by his heroic boat trip of 1869 down the Grand Canyon.[2] When the geological survey was established, Powell was made director of the new bureau of ethnology, and upon Clarence King's resignation, succeeded him as head of the survey.[3] In exploration there was no more eminent name than Powell's, but in ethnology he had his superior. This was the period in which Lewis H. Morgan's contributions to that science reached their

[1] F. L. Hayden published *Sun Pictures of Rocky Mountain Scenery* (N. Y., 1870) ; *Geological and Geographical Atlas of Colorado* (1877).
[2] L. R. Freeman, *The Colorado River* (N. Y., 1920), chap. x; F. S. Dellenbaugh, *Romance of the Colorado River* (N. Y., 1909).
[3] J. W. Powell, *Exploration of the Colorado River of the West and Its Tributaries* (Wash., 1875).

greatest importance.[1] Already before the war, he had published his engrossing volume on the league of the Iroquois Confederacy, the first of all really scientific works on the Indian. Now he brought forth his *Consanguinity and Affinity* (1868) and his *Ancient Society* (1877), which long stood as the two most notable works upon anthropology theretofore written in America. Morgan founded his own school, and his original methods and high literary gift are illustrated in such papers as "Montezuma's Dinner" (1876), a critical examination of current notions regarding Aztec civilization. During 1877 the Peabody Museum of American Archæology and Ethnology at Harvard moved into its first building; and its annual reports introduced a young Swiss-American named A. F. Bandelier, who with unusual literary talent was devoting himself to these studies in the far Southwest and in old Mexico.

To this somewhat slender specification of advanced scientific activity we should, of course, add mention of creditable, if isolated, achievements in other fields. Professor O. C. Marsh of Yale made extensive paleontological expeditions into the dangerous regions held by the Indians. A fact which spoke well for the serious reading public was the sturdy existence for some years of the *Journal of Speculative Philosophy,* edited by W. T. Harris, of St. Louis. We should add that there was a time at the close of the seventies when the Royal Society of London had three Americans on its list of foreign members: Simon Newcomb the astronomer, Asa Gray, and Benjamin Peirce the mathematician.[2] Such facts as these were significant of a growing range and depth of scholarly inquiry. But they did not prove that the United

---

[1] F. W. Putnam, "Sketch of Hon. Lewis H. Morgan," Am. Acad. of Arts and Sciences, *Proceeds.,* XVII, 429-436.

[2] *Nation,* XXVI, Jan. 24, 1878.

States had attained the rank in such pursuits that its wealth and population warranted; nor did they give an adequate conception, on the other hand, of the broad intellectual advance which took place between 1865 and 1878.

The salient feature of this advance may be summarized in the statement that during these years the evolutionary theory, with all that it implied in science, philosophy and religion, dawned upon the United States. Few Americans understood it at the close of the war. Darwin's *Origin of Species* in 1859 had challenged alert students by the boldness of the theory, the range and coolness of the speculation and the skilled mastery of the argument; but such was the preoccupation with sectional strife that only after Appomattox did the nation slowly awaken to its significance. In characteristic American fashion, it was awakened less by studying Darwin himself than by reading Herbert Spencer's comprehensive application of Darwinian views, and Spencer's chief disciples, E. L. Youmans and John Fiske. The clash between scientific-minded young men and their theological-minded elders rapidly extended over a broad front. Youmans in 1865 collected seven thousand dollars to help Spencer publish his *Synthetic Philosophy;* Fiske, a brilliant young war-time graduate of Harvard, wrote many magazine articles on the subject.[1]

But, as was to be expected, the principal struggle centered largely in the colleges. Noah Porter conducted a class in Spencer's *First Principles* with the object of refuting the book, and found that his students had all become evolutionists. At Harvard President Eliot signalized his elevation to office by inviting Emerson to deliver a course of lectures on "The Natural History of the Intellect," and Fiske a course on "The Positive Philos-

[1] J. S. Clarke, *Life and Letters of John Fiske* (Boston, 1917), I, 327.

ophy." In other words, Fiske was asked to expound Comteism and differentiate it from Darwinism, thus explaining ideas which many people regarded as the very summation of infidelity and atheism. "The days of old fogyism here are numbered, and the young men are to have a chance," he exulted. Youmans promptly arranged for the publication of the lectures in full in the *New York World* (1869-1870), and the consequence was an immediate wave of alarm over what ministers called "Harvard's raid on religion." But President Eliot met the charges with composure and asked Fiske to repeat the lectures the next year with an additional course on English evolutionary thought.[1] As the sale of books by Fiske, Spencer and Huxley reached impressive proportions and every advanced seat of learning spread the new ideas, the more bigoted opponents of evolution loosed their shafts with reckless fury. They bitterly abused Cornell University and its president. White retaliated with a lecture in Cooper Union on "The Battlefields of Science," showing how blind religionists throughout the ages had combated various advances in knowledge. This lecture, frequently repeated, was eventually expanded from a little book into his large treatise on *The History of the Warfare of Science with Theology* (1896).[2] Meanwhile the growing influence of evolutionary thought was confirmed by visits from the most eminent British scientists. Tyndall lectured in America with great effect during 1872-1873, Huxley made a tour of the United States in 1876, giving many addresses, and Spencer himself arrived in 1882.

The period—essentially a transition period—closed with evolution still on trial, but with the verdict in its favor clearly inevitable in all really well-educated cir-

[1] Clarke, *John Fiske*, I, 380.
[2] White *Autobiography*, I, 425.

cles. Some scientists, like Asa Gray, accepted Darwin's principal views at once; some, like the geologist Dana, were converted to a half-hearted belief by the slow passage of years; and others, like the elder Agassiz, remained obstinate opponents to the end. But the topic was discussed everywhere, it insensibly but strongly modified the outlook of all thinking men upon life, and it widened the intellectual horizon of the nation. Men might angrily denounce naturalistic theories and cleave fanatically to their faith in a supernatural creation precisely six thousand years ago. They might attempt, as McCosh did in several books, to "reconcile" Genesis and geology. But the important fact is that they were set to thinking, and that even resentment of the new doctrines had its intellectual value.[1]

It was in these domains just outlined, if anywhere, that the texture of American life was proof against the charge of superficiality. That charge might be brought against the hectic rush of business to skim the cream from the natural resources of the continent; it might be brought against our literature, which was for the most part but skillful reporting. It might also be brought against our social thinking—we had no counterpart for the English group represented by Carlyle, Ruskin, Mill and Leslie Stephen. But it could hardly be brought against the undaunted and fairly sure-footed efforts of the colleges to keep pace with the rapid growth of human knowledge and to anticipate the needs of the nation for better trained men and women. Nor could it be alleged against the devoted efforts of a small but brilliant band of scientists to give American research a creditable position before the world, nor against the absorbed attention which the educated public granted to new scientific

[1] See S. H. Haywood, "Spiritual Pirates," *Pop. Sci. Mo.*, VI (1874-1875), 601.

doctrines. Of Herbert Spencer's works twenty thousand copies were sold in America while scarcely the first small edition had been distributed in England; large editions of Mill, Darwin, Comte and others were bought, and their ideas were traceable in all the leading magazines, reviews and books of a thoughtful nature.[1]

[1] The *N. Y. Tribune*, Sept. 22, 1876, printed in one extra number all of Huxley's addresses in America, giving them a circulation to fully a hundred thousand people.

CHAPTER XI

Two Memorable Years:
1873 and 1876

LIKE a black dividing line, the Panic of 1873 cuts across the history of the thirteen years following the Civil War. On the one side lies the sunshine of buoyant commercial prosperity; on the other the gloom of depression, economy and poverty. When the struggle ended at Appomattox, the economic strength of the North had sufficed to throw off immediately a slight reaction which manifested itself in 1865, and a somewhat greater trade depression in 1868. From 1869 to 1873, however, business showed an abounding prosperity;[1] and the crash of Jay Cocke's banking house in the summer of the latter year seemed to many almost unportended.

Factors which were felt throughout the world played a prominent part in causing the depression, and the United States did not stand isolated in facing this storm.[2] In nearly every part of the globe the same sharp dividing line marked off a period of expansion from one of stagnation and poverty. Germany had a panic at precisely the same time as the United States, which spread at once to France and Belgium and thence to England and all parts of the world. This profound check was evident in new communities based on agriculture like Australia and South Africa; it was felt in all the populous industrial

---

[1] Horace White, "The Financial Crisis in America," *Fortnightly Rev.*, XXV (1876), 820.
[2] D. A. Wells, *Recent Economic Changes* (N. Y., 1889), chap. 1.

regions like New York, Lancashire and Westphalia. It
even manifested itself in Japan and in South America.
Certain causes of a world-wide nature, as well as merely
national impulses, must therefore be sought. Among
them stands prominently a costly epidemic of wars. Our
Civil War, the disastrous French invasion of Mexico, the
Austro-Prussian conflict, England's quixotic assault upon
Abyssinia, the South American wars centering about the
dictator Lopez and the Franco-Prussian War piled up a
heavy economic debit. There was besides an excessive
construction of railways in Central Europe and Russia.
The heavy indemnity which France paid Germany,
eleven hundred million dollars, and the opening of the
Suez Canal also resulted in profound economic disloca-
tions. Everywhere currency inflation, with rising prices,
wages and speculation, made itself conspicuous, and pro-
voked a sharp reaction.

In America cautious observers had expressed a fear that
the currency was too much inflated, that railways were
being overbuilt, that there was overtrading, and that a
luxurious mode of life was demanding excessive impor-
tations from Europe. Federal extravagance, complained
the critics, had become outrageous, while state extravagance was equally bad. David A. Wells, as special commissioner of the revenue, pointed with alarm in 1869
to the rapid drift of energetic men from pursuits directly
productive of wealth to occupations connected with commerce, trade or speculation.[1] The consequences were
seen in a marked growth of population in the commercial
centers, a striking increase in the number and cost of
business buildings, and a spirit of trading and gaming
rife everywhere. The number of business firms in the
United States in 1870 was 431,000, and in 1871 it had

[1] Special Commissioner of Revenue, *Report for 1869; American Annual
Cyclopedia* (N. Y., 1861-1903), IX (1869), 260.

leaped to the astonishing total of 609,904.[1] All this, as
Wells said, indicated not a healthy growth but an unhealthy fever induced by inflated paper currency.

To protect this inflation, Congress in the spring of
1868 suspended, by a large majority, any further contraction of the currency, leaving the huge volume of war-
time greenbacks reduced by only about one fifth. The
federal notes in circulation stood at three hundred and
fifty-six million dollars, and Secretary Boutwell actually
increased this sum in 1871-1872. This bloated credit
system made speculation inevitable.[2] Moreover, the violent ebb and flow of this inflated currency in the financial
capital of the nation, New York, was responsible for
wide oscillations in the money market and consequent
disturbances of a grave nature. Since notes of the national banks were legal tender in payment of all debts,
they tended to accumulate each winter and each summer
at New York, while in the late spring and fall—especially in the fall, when crops were being moved—money
became scarce. Thus at one period speculation flourished and the price of stocks and bonds rose to excessive
heights; then the ensuing stringency compelled all holders
to sell, with the result that prices fell unduly low. Furthermore, the periods of stringency produced hardships
that were felt from the Atlantic to the Rockies. The
wheat and corn buyers of the West, the cotton factors
of the South, could hardly find currency enough to pay
for the crops; and they had to sell the crops again at once
because their banks were unable to get adequate credit
in New York. Receiving delayed payments and lower
prices than the world market really justified, the farmers
could not meet their debts with the storekeeper, nor the

[1] *Commercial and Financial Chronicle* (N. Y.), Jan. 24, 1873.
[2] D. R. Dewey, *Financial History of the United States* (A. B. Hart, ed.,
American Citizen Series, N. Y., 1907), 371.

storekeepers with the jobbers.   In all, the monetary and
credit system of the country was radically defective and
was certain to accentuate any passing crisis.[1]

To add to the dangers of the situation, a heavy drain
upon the nation's specie supply was caused by its debts
to foreign nations.   The United States had borrowed
abroad in great quantities during the years 1861-1868,
its obligations reaching one and a half billion dollars.
This meant an annual interest charge in 1868 of eighty
millions; and other payments, quite apart from those
made for ordinary imports, brought the total annual levy
up to about one hundred and thirty million dollars.   The
trade balance also was decidedly against the United States.
For a time after the war the foreign demands were met
by a transfer of government bonds to European account,
but this resource soon came to an end.   It then became
necessary to export specie, and this disturbed the American money market.[2]

The financial situation became more and more plainly
perilous as the seventies moved on.   By February of
1873 the best commercial organs were expressing their
apprehension of a crisis.   The inflation of credits had by
this time reached an unprecedented height; in the five
years from 1868 to Sept. 12, 1873, the national bank
deposits increased only forty-three million dollars, but
the bank loans for the same period rose by two hundred and eighty-three million dollars.   That is, the aggregate debt had risen fifty per cent, while the aggregate
circulating capital had increased only seven and one
half per cent.   Since all the debts of the country had
to be paid out of its circulating capital, the danger was

[1] Henry Clews, *Our Monetary Evils; Some Suggestions for Their
Remedies* (N. Y., 1872) ; *Com. and Fin. Chron.*, Dec. 14, 1872.
[2] *U. S. Statistical Abstract for 1921*, table 482.   Imports passed
the $600,000,000 mark in 1872, almost twice as much as before
the war.

clear.   Moreover, the fires in Portland, Boston and Chicago had caused a demand for floating capital to take the
place of that which had been annihilated.   It took credit
to finance the rebuilding; and during 1872 Chicago alone
was estimated to have borrowed fifty millions in the New
York market.   Finally, the burden of railway paper
grew constantly heavier; the wildcat methods and frequent exposures undermined the confidence of foreign
investors and the companies had to obtain their credit at
home.[1] The *Nation* might point out in 1872 that, of the
three hundred and sixty-four listed railroads, only one
hundred and four paid dividends at all, and sixty-nine of
these paid less than ten per cent; but the dazzled citizen
fixed his eyes on the thirty-five which paid ten per cent or
more.[2]

Harbingers of the oncoming storm slowly multiplied.
During 1871 there were only 2,915 failures in the United
States, but in 1872 the number suddenly leaped to 4069,
involving a loss of more than $121,000,000.[3]   There
had been danger of a general panic after the Chicago fire
in the fall of 1871.   Nearly a year later, when the
Grant-Greeley campaign was rising to its height in September, grave disturbances were avoided only by the in-
tervention of the government, Jay Cooke and other
strong financial interests.   In the spring of 1873 the
money market was again so badly shaken that some of
Jay Cooke's associates begged him not to carry forward
the Northern Pacific syndicate, then being formed.[4]
Throughout the first half of the year the Credit Mobilier
scandal was gathering force, throwing Congress into a
state of demoralization and accentuating the general dis-

[1] *Com. and Fin. Chron.*, Oct. 14, 1872; Jan. 4, 1873.
[2] *Com. and Fin. Chron.*, Sept. 7, 21, 1872. The *N. Y. Times*, Sept.
16, 1873, editorially denounced the wildcat railway investing.
[3] *Com. and Fin. Chron.*, July 15, 1876.
[4] E. P. Oberholtzer, *Jay Cooke* (Phila., 1907), II, 400.

trust of big business. Meanwhile New York had been deeply agitated by insurance and banking scandals,[1] causing a severe strain upon the money market, already inadequate to sustain the top-heavy structure of debt.

The crash came in September. An atmosphere of dread was created when on September 8 the New York Warehouse and Securities Company and five days later Kenyon Cox and Company, in which Daniel Drew was a special partner, failed. The gloom thickened as rumors spread that George Opdyke and Company were in grave danger.[2] On Wednesday the seventeenth stocks came down with a run on the New York market; and in all the offices which had burdened themselves with un-marketable collateral consternation reigned. Grave re-ports spread to Boston, to Washington and to Philadel-phia, where President Grant had just arrived to spend the night at Jay Cooke's home at "Ogontz." Still Jay Cooke's firm, the pillar of the nation during the Civil War, was generally considered unshakable. Yet, just before eleven the next morning, before business had fairly begun, the doors of his New York office were suddenly closed.[3] This step, taken by the partner in charge after consulting with a group of bank presidents, electrified the city. When the news was laid before Jay Cooke at the Philadelphia office, he ordered the doors of the house swung to, and then turned his face away from his asso-ciates, tears streaming from his eyes. A few minutes after noon his Washington branch and the First Na-tional Bank in Washington were shut, making the sus-pension complete.

The failure was a financial thunderbolt, stupefying the

[1] *Com. and Fin. Chron.*, April 11, 1873. See also *ante*, 193-194.
[2] *N. Y. Tribune*, Sept. 9, 10, 14, 15, 1873; *N. Y. Herald*, Sept. 14, 1873.
[3] Oberholtzer, *Jay Cooke*, 422 ff.

country. The New York Stock Exchange, after a moment of startled silence, was thrown into an uproar such as the oldest member could never remember hearing.[1] In Philadelphia the telegraph bulletin from New York caused the entire stock board to rush pell-mell into the street and down to Jay Cooke's doors to verify the report. A newsboy shouting an extra "all about the failure of Jay Cooke" was arrested by a horrified and incredulous policeman. In Washington word of the failure reached a criminal court during a murder trial, and it was hastily adjourned, the judges, lawyers, witnesses and spectators hurrying into the avenue to learn further news.[2]

In itself the failure was a blow certain to cause widespread but not universal demoralization. The real fright and dismay of the failure lay in its disclosure of the half-suspected fact that the aggregate indebtedness of the business world was far too great to be paid out of the circulating capital. The instant this disclosure came that bright September day, every business man clutched simultaneously at the means of payment. This frenzied rush for ready money, with the weaker trod ruthlessly underfoot, constituted the panic.[3] Nothing could be done, in essentials, but let the storm blow itself out. Several houses failed the same day as Jay Cooke, and thereafter came a steady succession of crashes. Fiske & Hatch went down in New York, carrying with them all hope of an immediate financial reorganization of the prostrate Chesapeake & Ohio; the Lake Shore Railroad failed; the Union and the National Trust companies were forced to suspend. At eleven o'clock on the third

---

[1] *N. Y. Tribune*, Sept. 19, 1873; *N. Y. Eve. Post*, Sept. 18-20, 1873.
[2] Oberholtzer, *Jay Cooke*, II, 424.
[3] Horace White, "The Financial Crisis in America," *Fortnightly Rev.*, XXV (1876), 810 ff.

day of the Panic, September 20, the governing committee closed the New York Stock Exchange, taking this
unprecedented step "to save the entire street from utter
ruin."[1] President Grant, Secretary Richardson and other
high government officers hurried on the fourth day to the
Fifth Avenue Hotel and summoned Commodore Vanderbilt and other financial leaders to their apartments to
offer advice.   Grant remarked that the first need of the
situation seemed to be for "a week of Sundays;" but
more heroic measures had to be taken.   For ten days, the
Stock Exchange was kept closed; the banks, pooling their
resources, for the first time issued the now familiar clear-
ing-house certificates; and the government, acting on the
counsel of men who believed the chief cause of the Panic
was a lack of money, released thirteen millions of greenbacks from the treasury for the purchase of government
bonds.[2]   But these steps proved the merest palliatives.
The country was like a debilitated patient, who rallies
from a sudden stroke of illness to face a slow convalescence.   Before it lay a long era of prostration, which
was simply "a period of painful and impossible effort
to pay a large amount of indebtedness with a relatively
small amount of capital"—a period in which business
had to readjust itself to a much smaller, narrower, but
more solid basis.

As the weeks passed, the evil effects of the Panic made
themselves felt in widening circles.   Five national banks
in Chicago suspended, and other Western business and
financial houses failed as disastrously as those in the East.
Jay Cooke and Company was found to have assets worth
$15,996,212 to balance against its liabilities of $7,939,-
409; but it was long before it could pay all its creditors

[1] N. Y. Tribune, Sept. 19, 20, 22, 1873.
[2] A. D. Noyes, Thirty Years of American Finance (N. Y., 1909),
18; Dewey, Financial History, 372.

—so great was the difficulty of realizing on its assets—
and Cooke never resumed business in his old capacity.[1]
The year ended with more than five thousand commercial
failures in the United States for the twelvemonth, the
liabilities aggregating $228,500,000, or nearly twice as
much as the preceding year. There were then eighty-
nine railways defaulting on their bonds, among them the
Boston, Hartford and Erie, the Kansas Pacific, the Northern Pacific, the Missouri, Kansas and Texas, and the
Rock Island. The total bond issues on which interest
payments were thus suspended aggregated very nearly
four hundred millions.[2] Deposits in the national banks
had fallen off more than a hundred millions during the
second half of 1873. Still the gloom over the country
thickened, and still firms continued to fall like lines of
dominoes, each toppling over some neighbor.[3]

The actual panic, naturally, was of brief duration,
and in a few months anybody with good collateral could
borrow money at four per cent.[4] But the crisis, the
Fury outraged by the violation of the laws of sound
finance, was pursuing innocent and guilty alike with her
vengeance and bringing her heaviest lash upon the backs
of the poor—the laboring factory hand, the sweated garment worker, the small savings-bank depositor. The
first disastrous effects were evident in a stoppage of work
on long lines of railway. The mileage built in 1874
was only 1,940, less than one third the average of the

---

[1] Oberholtzer, *Jay Cooke*, II, 437.

[2] *Com. and Fin. Chron.* Jan. 10, 1874. By October, 1874, there
were one hundred and eight defaulting lines, and by midsummer of 1876
some forty per cent of all American railway bonds were under default.
Com. and Fin. Chron., Oct. 10, 1874; July 1, 1876. By the opening
of 1876 the railway bonds in default reached $789,367,000.

[3] The failures in these years may be summarized as follows: 1871—
2915 concerns for $85,252,000; 1872—4069 for $121,056,000;
1873—5183 for $228,499,000. *Com. and Fin. Chron.*, Jan. 24, 1874.

[4] White, "Financial Crisis in America," *Fortnightly Rev.*, XXV, 810 ff.

preceding five years.[1] Nearly a half-million laborers were thrown out of work, partly or wholly, by this suspension. Rolling mills, machine shops, foundries and other industries connected with rail transportation followed. When the ironmasters of the country met in Philadelphia late in the spring after the Panic, they found that, of the six hundred and sixty-six furnaces in the United States, only four hundred were in operation. Subsidiary industries, one by one, shut down as demands and payments for their goods failed. Unemployment steadily mounted.

As the winter of 1874-1875 came on, long bread lines and demands for outdoor and indoor relief in New York. Boston and Chicago testified to a chilling drop in the social temperature. Despite the abundant harvest, wrote B. F. Nourse, "many thousand families will be nearer to hunger than for many years for lack of employment, and the circle of enforced idleness, disability, and poverty widens daily." [2] Radicalism was appearing among the unemployed of the great cities, and there was a grim significance in the demands which some socialistic bodies were making—demands for work on public enterprises, advances of money or food for one week to all who were in actual want, and the stopping of all eviction for non-payment of rent. Immigration ground sharply toward a stoppage, and workless aliens began departing by tens of thousands. From nearly four hundred and fifty thousand in 1872, the arrivals dropped to one hundred and thirty thousand in 1877, the lowest number since the tide of the Civil War was turned at Gettysburg.

For the first time since the war the virtue of economy returned in all sections and among all classes. A hundred tokens pointed to the refusal of the mechanic, the

[1] *Nation* (N. Y.), XXI, July 1, 1875.
[2] *Com. and Fin. Chron.*, Aug. 7, 1875.

clerk, the lawyer and the merchant to buy anything which they did not absolutely need.[1] The shipments from abroad of coal, textiles, metals, dressed and undressed hides and drugs fell off in 1874 and again in 1875. Most striking of all was the refusal of the American people to send to Europe for goods that could in any light be regarded as luxuries. Thus, the importation of silks dropped by more than one third between 1873 and 1878, that of tea by almost one half, and that of carpets almost disappeared, falling to one eleventh of the old total.[2] The leading financial journal estimated that in the first calendar year after the Panic, Americans retrenched their private expenditures by not less than four hundred million dollars. Part of the money saved by this stern economy went into the savings banks, which at once heavily increased their deposits. An inevitable phenomenon of the day was a prodigious amount of moralizing on the wickedness of luxury and the disciplinary value of adversity; every pulpit rang with it. At an early date it drew from Henry Ward Beecher a tart sermon rebuking the unctuous souls who expected the depression to clear away all the miasmatic "rottenness" of the time and bring back a golden age of simplicity, sobriety and industry. The moralizing drew from the *Nation,* also, some biting remarks concerning "the cheap, sick-bed morality of a panic." [3]

Work was not only hard to obtain, but what work could be got paid lower and lower wages.[4] In Massachusetts a particularly careful survey of wages for this

---

[1] *Com. and Fin. Chron.,* Aug. 22, 1874.

[2] *London Economist,* XXXII, Dec. 26, 1874; XXXVI, Sept. 21, 1878.

[3] *Nation,* XVII, Oct. 9, 23, 1873.

[4] Edith A. Abbott, *Wages of Unskilled Labor in the United States* (Chicago, 1905), 363. See also F. W. Smith, *The Hard Times* (Boston, 1877).

period shows that all the wage-earning groups in the year 1872 were receiving some thirty-six per cent more than in 1860, but that immediately a sharp decline began. By the end of 1875 wages had dropped nearly ten per cent, and by the close of 1878 they had fallen more than five per cent further, near which level they remained until 1880 brought a turn for the better.[1] Professional men—doctors, dentists, lawyers—reduced their charges by one half, and the churches were compelled to cut the salaries of their already ill-paid ministers. There was an alarming increase not merely in penury but in all that it entailed—illness, ignorance, discontent, crime. It was quickly reported that the city streets showed a distinctly larger number of young women driven to prostitution, and the jail records more men driven to theft.[2]

One consequence of the depression was the sudden emergence of the "tramp evil." The "bummer" of the Civil War had been succeeded by a small vagrant class after peace came, but it was never troublesome. Now the countrysides swarmed with hoboes. In some Eastern sections, like the Berkshires, they formed an organized brigandage, associating with professional criminals and beggars, camping in the woods, stealing, drinking and fighting. Their ranks were recruited by reckless young men wandering about in search of employment. From all over the East came reports of thefts, incendiary fires, rapes and even murders committed by vagrants. In some New England towns during 1877 people on the outskirts were forced to abandon their homes, and in Massachusetts alone there were said to be a thousand vagabonds roaming the rural communities. In parts of

---

[1] C. D. Wright, "Comparative Wages, Prices and Cost of Living," Massachusetts Bureau of Labor, *Sixteenth Ann. Rep. for 1885*.

[2] W. G. Moody, *Land and Labor* (N. Y., 1883), chap. xii. Statistics of pauperism may be found in the *U. S. Tenth Census* (1880), XXI, xix.

the Middle West the nuisance was almost as great, and every summer brought its stories of outrages by small cohorts.[1] Late in June, 1876, some two hundred tramps stopped a train on the Rock Island Railroad and ran it into Beardstown, Illinois, where the city marshal and his constables had a bloody encounter with the invaders. Another threatening gang temporarily occupied and terrorized Jacksonville, Illinois. Elsewhere in these states during 1876 revolver fights between trainmen and tramps became so frequent that trains on some railroads had to be especially guarded.

A natural consequence of the reduced consumption of goods and the accompanying "glut" was a marked and sometimes astonishing fall in the prices of commodities. It would not be too much to say that the cost of articles used by the average American family dropped about one fifth or one sixth in the five years after Jay Cooke's failure.[2] House rents fell slightly in most cities, and heavily in some, while in the East the charge for table board dropped by one fifth or even one fourth. Real estate suddenly found a stagnant market, and in innumerable instances became worth less than the mortgages it bore. Luxuries like silks and jewelry had almost no sale at the most astonishing reductions. The market for pianos and organs was kept active only by a combination of price-slashing and the introduction, for the first time in American history on a large scale, of the instalment system of buying; furniture and clothing grew steadily cheaper. But perhaps the most striking single item was pig iron, which sold for fifty-three dollars a ton in Philadelphia in the fall of 1872, and six years later was worth just sixteen dollars and fifty cents.[3]

[1] See *Nation*, XXVI, Jan. 24, 1878, on "the tramp evil."

[2] Aldrich Committee, *Senate Report*, 52 Cong., 2 sess., III, pt. i.

[3] See "Report on the Necessities of Life," *U. S. Tenth Census* (1880), XX. However, large swings in pig-iron prices are not rare.

Quite naturally, under the influence of the rigid economy practised in all sections and the distrust that the
plain investor felt for all new commercial enterprises,
money began to accumulate rapidly. "Such a plethora
and surplus of virgin capital was never before dreamed
of on this virgin continent, so-called," wrote Horace
White.[1] Savings banks, not in spite of but because of
the depression, were wonderfully prosperous. When
Hayes became president the eight states of New England,
New York and New Jersey had six hundred and thirty-
nine savings banks, with more than two million depositors and nearly eight hundred millions in deposits.

Yet the skies seemed for a time to grow steadily
blacker. During 1874 there were five thousand eight
hundred and thirty business failures in the United States,
during 1875 no fewer than seven thousand seven hundred and forty, and in the Centennial year the number
climbed to nine thousand and ninety-two.[2] The sections which enjoyed the largest measure of prosperity
were the farming districts of the Central West and the
mining regions of the Far West. Business was weighed
down by a millstone of bad debts and debilitated by the
rottenness inherited from previous years. There were
very nearly nine thousand failures for the year 1877.
In the closing months the rapid succession of frauds,
forgeries, disgraceful failures of several banks and trust
companies and embezzlements of securities cast an increased shadow over the financial community.[3] Not
only were the actual losses from these breaches of trust
heavy, making everybody suspicious of business, but they
produced an angry and exaggerated outcry against Wall

[1] Horace White, "The Tariff Question," *Journ. of Social Science,*
IX (1878), 117-131.
[2] *Com. and Fin. Chron.*, Jan. 15, 1876.
[3] *Com. and Fin. Chron.*, Jan. 5, 19, 1878.

Street as a den of robbers. Indeed, the year 1877 may rank as one of the blackest in the nation's annals. It had opened with the country in the throes of a disputed presidential election, threatening civil war; it had brought disastrous labor revolts and a hot discussion of the silver question, producing a fear of rash currency legislation. When the year ended a trained economist, Horace White, wrote that the industries of the nation were never, in the memory of living men, so smitten with paralysis. The farmers almost alone held up their heads. "All else is a weary and aching mass of unemployed or half employed capital, misdirected talent, and underpaid labor, to which commerce gives the generic name of glut." [1]

The year 1878 seemed to many people to leave the United States at the bottom of a deeper gulf than ever before. The number of failures reached an unprecedented total. There were no fewer than 10,478, and the liabilities totaled $234,383,000, or more even than in the black year 1873.[2] More than half the iron and steel furnaces were idle the whole year, while the price of their product was lower than at any time since colonial days. Unemployment seemed to be increasing rather than decreasing while the relations of capital and labor were more inflamed than ever before.[3] Yet actually the nation was at the turning of the tide and the skies were about to brighten rapidly. One great process essential to recovery, the process of deflation, had now been completed—a deflation both industrial and financial.

Financially, this deflation aroused a fierce sectional and group antagonism, which found both political and social expression. Few topics so agitated the American

---

[1] Horace White, "The Tariff Question," *Journ. of Social Science*, IX (1878), 117-131.

[2] Moody, *Land and Labor*, 191.

[3] Am. Iron and Steel Assoc., *Report for July, 1878*.

public during these years as the currency question. The advocates of cheap money argued that the continuance of the industrial depression was in great measure due to the steady contraction of the currency under the legislation of 1873 and 1875 for the demonetization of silver and the gradual retirement of greenbacks. They demanded the issue of large sums of unsupported government currency, the remonetization of silver, the payment of government bonds in less valuable media than gold, and repeal of the act by which the government was to resume specie payments on January 1, 1879. The hard-money party advocated resumption of specie payments, maintenance of the full gold standard, and payment of the national debt in that coin. Our interest in this contest lies in noting the fact that it was essentially a contest between the West, which needed and owed money, and the East, which had and lent it—between the debtor and the capitalist. Easterners spoke bitterly of repudiation, and of the demands of "loafers, gamblers and bankrupts;" Westerners spoke with equal anger of creditors who imposed a grinding slavery upon their debtors, and made them pay back a cheap dollar with a costly one. Eventually the hard-money party won, and on Jan. 1, 1879, the country passed quietly upon a specie-paying basis. The number of dollars in circulation per capita, which in 1865 had been $31.18, was $20.43 in 1872, and in 1878 was down to $16.95. The total number of dollars in circulation had shrunk from more than one billion at the close of the war to less than three fourths that amount in 1878. Here was the basis for a great future upheaval by the debt-paying West.

In the midst of this period of hard times, and three years after the Panic, there came a year when the people for a time sought deliberately to cast aside their cares, and gave themselves up to an impressive commemoration of their country's birth.   All could agree that a century's perspective yielded genuine cause for national pride whatever temporary difficulties America might be facing.   The celebration took the form of a great exposition, formally opened for its five months' career on May 10, 1876, in Fairmount Park in Philadelphia with imposing ceremonies.[1]   This sixth of the world's great fairs, and the first to be held in the United States, was in most respects an exhibition of which the United States might feel proud.   Though its architecture was mediocre, Americans were, as might be expected, pleased by its mere size. They boasted that the Main Exhibition Building was the largest structure in the world, and that with four other great halls and a half-hundred smaller buildings scattered through the two hundred and thirty-six acres of grounds overlooking the Schuylkill, the exposition surpassed the previous Paris and London fairs.[2]

Never had any attraction so focused national interest or brought such crowds from all parts of the nation. The railways reduced the round-trip rates from all points east of Omaha by one fourth, and since many foreigners wished to see the West, the same special rate was made on round-trip fares from the coast to the Missouri.   Chicagoans had to pay $34.50 for their round-trip tickets; residents of New Orleans $68.02; of Denver $106.50; and of San Francisco $204.[3]   On a single day, Pennsylvania Day, no fewer than 274,919 visitors entered, the greatest throng that any exhibition had ever attracted.   There were very nearly ten million visitors and more than eight million paid admissions.   Funds had been raised partly by private subscriptions, partly by

[1] N. Y. World, N. Y. Herald, N. Y. Tribune, May 11-12, 1876.
[2] Appletons' Ann. Cyclop., VI (1876), 262 ff., has a comprehensive description of the Exhibition.   See also Report of the Exhibition and numerous handbooks and guides.
[3] N. Y. Tribune, Jan. 21, 1876.

donations from Philadelphia, Pennsylvania and several neighboring states, and partly by a federal loan; and with receipts of about $3,800,000, the great fair was financially a success. At the outset a fierce debate raged round the question whether the Exhibition should be open on Sunday. Among church members, those who regarded the Exhibition as a place of amusement, took one side, those who thought of it as an educational institution the other.[1] In the end the management bowed to the guardians of the old Puritan Sabbath and followed British precedent in deciding for Sunday closing. Perhaps it was, as the *New York Tribune* said, all the more truly a national exposition in thus conforming to the national habit.[2] But in one respect the directors were thoroughly "liberal": they allowed the sale of liquor and turned a neat penny in auctioning the privilege to the highest bidder.

The best exhibits of the Centennial were unquestionably those of industrial and commercial interest, for European manufacturers were eager to enlarge their footing in the American market. American pride, indeed, was hurt by the indifference of the Continental nations to an effective display in the field of fine arts and craftsmanship. Not a single French painter of fame was represented, while the German and Austrian canvases were even more insignificant.[3] The British made better use of their opportunity. Their exhibit included examples of Gainsborough, Reynolds and other classic painters, and such moderns as Millais, Holman Hunt, Turner and Alma-Tadema. For the first time hundreds of thousands of Americans saw a foreign master. Decidedly

[1] *Nation*, XXII, May 11, 1876.
[2] *Nation*, XXII, May 1, 1876.
[3] W. D. Howells, "A Sennight of the Centennial," *Atlantic Monthly*, XXXVIII (1876), 93-107.

more influential upon the public taste, however, were the exhibits of furniture and household decorations, the British entries again arousing admiration by their completeness and beauty. Here was presented evidence of the astonishing renascence in household taste which England was experiencing, and the fine Lambeth faïence, Eastlake furniture and Minton tiles, together with the examples of exquisite cabinet work in Jacobean and Queen Anne's days, delighted American women. Germany sent an arresting display of fine porcelain, and France specimens of her best textiles. Excited attention was also given to the bronzes, porcelains, and lacquer wares of the Japanese, which had been an almost complete novelty but now found a growing favor in American homes.[1]

American art, however, proved surprisingly better than the critical public had anticipated. It is true that the statuary was bad, and that painting had its atrocity in a "Battle of Gettysburg" by Rothermel, depicting an appalling slaughter of Confederates. But in this section there was much to stir the national pride. Not only was the early school—Stuart, Copley, Allston, Rembrandt Peale and others—well represented, but the vigorous young artists of the time were there: Winslow Homer, Alden Weir, Thomas Moran, Eastman Johnson, La Farge with his really fine "St. Paul," and others. Though sculpture, with Hiram Powers and W. W. Story as the best-known workers represented, was less distinguished, the art collection as a whole was a revelation to multitudes of Americans.[2]

The essential symbols of American talent and progress were, however, not here but in Machinery Hall. There stood the majestic Corliss engine, a mighty athlete

---

[1] *Senate Exec. Docs.*, 48 Cong., 3 sess., no. 74.
[2] *Nation*, XXIII, Aug. 3, 1876.

of steel and brass, the enormous flywheel revolving with the power of sixteen hundred horses and making the whole building quiver. Another symbol lay in the sewing machines with which this hall seemed flooded, cramming every corner and overflowing from every alcove. Still another was the Woman's Pavilion,[1] with its acre of products of feminine industry, from textile designs by women trained in the Massachusetts Institute of Technology to a complete materia medica from the Women's Medical College of Philadelphia. Never before had a collective display of women's work been attempted, and its scope impressed many a scoffer at the feminist movement. Another symbol of America's essential interests lay in an exhibit of ores and mining processes by the Western states. Still another was the demonstration of the work of the Waltham watchmakers, busy with their fine machinery, and of the Trenton ceramic workers.

As an instrument for the education of the three million or more individuals who visited Philadelphia the Centennial could be pronounced an entire success. Outside the highly cultured Eastern circles, few Americans as yet traveled widely, and here they found all the world brought together for their inspection: the shawls and jewels of India, the bronzes of France, the lacquer ware of Japan, South African ivory and ostrich feathers, Brazilian woods, and Hawaiian corals and shells. They could admire the quaint peasant costumes of Sweden and Austria, and compare Swiss watches and Black Forest clocks. The educational exhibits were of especial value, for two of the Centennial buildings were devoted entirely to the kindergarten training of children, and the showing made by Belgium, Germany and Switzerland went far toward destroying the complacency and self-sufficiency then characteristic of

[1] *Appletons' Ann. Cyclop.*, VI (1876), 272.

American educators.[1]   Many a youngster received at the Centennial an enthusiasm for mechanical processes and possibilities which shaped his entire life.   The visitor could see manufactured before his eyes a thousand articles —newspapers (the *New York Herald* had a plant there), tacks, shoes, carpets, clothing, candies, bricks; he could see a variety of new inventions in operation, from the typewriter to the pneumatic tube for parcel carrying. The agricultural exhibit, which was of astonishing scope and interest, lent its aid to the new scientific movement in farming.[2]

It was an exposition, as it was an anniversary, which could not but stimulate a patriotic pride in American achievement; and yet reflecting people were painfully aware that in many respects the year 1876 was an infelicitous time for America to place herself on exhibition. Not only was economic distress still widespread, but the epidemic of political scandal and corruption which began in Grant's first administration had not yet run its course. Lowell expressed this thought by the speech he put into Brother Jonathan's mouth when Miss Columbia asked him what she should display at the Centennial:

> Show 'em your Civil Service, and explain
> How all men's loss is everybody's gain; . . .
> Show your new bleaching-process, cheap and brief,
> To wit: a jury chosen by the thief;
> Show your State Legislatures; show your Rings;
> And challenge Europe to produce such things
> As high officials sitting half in sight
> To share the plunder and to fix things right;

[1] U. S. Commissioner of Education, *Reports for 1876, 1877* and *1878*, *passim*.

[2] For a tribute to the efficiency of the Exhibition and the good manners of the American visitors, see *N. Y. Tribune*, Sept. 22, 1876. The foreign restaurants, particularly the Vienna bakery and the *Trois Frères Provenceaux*, had their influence.

> If that don't fetch her, why, you only need
> To show your latest style in martyrs—Tweed.[1]

Tweed was indeed exhibited to Europe in dramatic fashion. Escaping from jail in the closing days of 1875, he found his way to Cuba and Spain, and the next autumn was recognized in Vigo, through one of Thomas Nast's internationally circulated cartoons, and captured. The frigate *Franklin* brought him home to the Ludlow Street Jail,[2] and in this prison he shortly died (April, 1878).

Into the whole reeking series of exposures which crowded upon one another during the spring and summer of 1876 it is unnecessary to go in detail. The first event, the acquittal of Babcock upon the charge of sharing the Whisky Ring's profits, brought no comfort to the public, since few were assured of his innocence or of the propriety of the president in upholding him.[3] Then came the impeachment of Secretary Belknap of the war department on the charge of taking money for the grant of a post tradership in Indian Territory; the issuance of an official report upon General Schenck's misconduct while minister to England; the publication of the Mulligan letters, which indicated that Blaine had accepted improper favors from railway interests;[4] and the exposure, by committees which the Democratic House had appointed, of the rottenness which had honeycombed half of the executive departments. President Grant's own display of nepotism, his acceptance of lavish gifts

[1] J. R. Lowell, "The World's Fair, 1876," *Nation*, XXI, Aug. 5, 1875. See the *N. Y. Tribune's* editorial of May 8 on the ironic reminders of the Centennial, also the *Nation's* editorial, XXII, Jan. 27, 1876.

[2] *N. Y. Herald*, Oct. 22, Nov. 24, 1876.

[3] See *N. Y. World's* summary of press opinions, Feb. 26, 1876.

[4] *N. Y. Tribune*, June 6, 1876.

and his carelessness of appearances, were all open to censure.[1]

Month by month, too, corruption was still being stripped bare in the states and cities of the land. Governor Tilden in March reported upon his overthrow of the notorious "canal ring" in New York, which in the preceding five years had stolen or wasted not far from fifteen million dollars. Yet Albany was still far from clean, and that spring the lobbyists of the horse railways of the metropolis had no difficulty in defeating the Husted rapid-transit bill by purchasing votes at from two hundred and fifty dollars to fifteen hundred dollars each.[2] In Maryland a Democratic ring was proved to have stolen right and left; in Connecticut the Democrats who controlled the legislature sold a United States senatorship to William H. Barnum, an illiterate politician, for a gift of twenty thousand dollars to the state committee.[3] A legislative report upon crime in New York City showed that many officers of the police department and district attorney's office were working hand in glove with thieves, gamblers and keepers of brothels and sharing in their plunder. In Washington there was a hot debate upon the frauds of the District ring which "Boss" Shepherd was accused of heading. Shepherd, as the chief force in a new District government created in 1871, had done a wonderful work in renovating the ill-paved, ill-built, unsanitary capital, and had earned the title of the Baron Haussmann of Washington; but his and his associates' financial methods left much to be desired.[4] Worst of all was the corruption exposed in

---

[1] See the *N. Y. Tribune's* caustic arraignment, May 12, 1876, and also the *N. Y. Herald*, May 8, 1876.

[2] T. P. Cook, *Life and Public Services of Hon. S. J. Tilden* (N. Y., 1876), 189; *N. Y. Tribune*, May 8, 1876.

[3] *N. Y. Tribune*, May 16, 1876.

[4] For the condemnatory report of a congressional investigating com-

Philadelphia itself, where a "gas ring" had stolen nearly eight million dollars within a few years.[1]   Throughout the year the Beecher-Tilton scandal kept recurring and left the immense public influence of Beecher—who if not guilty of the adultery charged was certainly guilty of weakness in other regards—temporarily shattered.[2]

It was a year to make Americans ashamed rather than proud; and the most hopeful fact of the time was that this sense of shame, this appreciation of the contrast between the pretentious national Exhibition and the seamy, shabby aspect of American civic life, was earnestly expressed.   A change had come over the national temper, and the easy tolerance of the late sixties was being replaced by a new sternness.   The editorial columns of the press harped constantly upon the national humiliation, and great Republican organs like the *New York Tribune* and *Chicago Tribune* bitterly assailed the corruption in the administration.   The pulpit, the civic organizations, the professional leaders, the men of letters of the nation, all showed their mortification and resentment.   The country was awakening, and this fact was itself a sign of convalescence from the long moral sickness which had followed the war.   The evils were superficial rather than deep-seated, and they had at last aroused so deep a revulsion that a cure was seen to be indispensable.   An era of reform was about to open.[3]

mittee on Shepherd's grandiose eighteen-million-dollar scheme, see *Senate Rep.*, 49 Cong., 1 sess., no. 453.

[1] *N. Y. Tribune*, Jan. 4, 1876; S. P. Orth, *The Boss and the Machine* (Allen Johnson, ed., *Chronicles of America Series*, New Haven, 1918-1921, XLIII), chap. vi.

[2] For the fall of Beecher in public esteem, see the *Nation*, XVIII, June 3, 1874; XXI, July 8, 1875.

[3] This condemnation extended to the business corruption of the period; and the reckless financial methods of the Lackawanna, the Delaware and Hudson, the New Jersey Central, and the Lehigh railroads, which invested greedily in anthracite lands and attempted to establish a monopoly, were bitterly excoriated. See *N. Y. Tribune*, Sept. 8, 14, 1876.

One unmistakable evidence of this healthy new spirit was the campaign of 1876, which displayed more aspects of social interest than any other presidential contest since 1860.[1] It signalized the fact that the nation had returned to the two-party system, and that the old undisputed sway of the Republicans, itself a fertile cause of corruption, was at an end. It revealed an impatient and nation-wide demand for a cleansing of the Augean stables. The utter disgust of independent voters for the misrule under Grant, the softening of old war-time animosities and fears, the commercial depression which bred a demand for change—all these seemed to give the Democrats a prospect of victory. The result was that by midsummer the struggle had attained a heat and excitement not witnessed for many years. The Republicans were forced to nominate Hayes, a man of unquestioned integrity and zeal in reform, and the Democrats chose a nominee of greater ability and equally high character in Tilden. Not always does the hectic excitement of our presidential campaigns constitute a wholesome symptom, but in 1876 the electioneering fervor was as a bracing new wind blowing through the country. The one unfortunate fact was the character of the Republican contest. While the Democrats quite properly centered their fire upon Grant's unsavory record, the Republicans, in order to avoid the defensive, strenuously endeavored to revive the hatreds of the Civil War. Hayes himself, though by nature averse to Blaine's tactics of "waving the bloody shirt," ordered his followers, especially in the West, to lay emphasis upon the "dread of a Solid South, rebel rule, etc."[2]

[1] P. L. Haworth, *The Hayes-Tilden Disputed Presidential Election* (Cleveland, 1906), leans toward Hayes; H. T. Peck, *Twenty Years of the Republic* (N. Y., 1906), 115 ff., leans toward Tilden.

[2] Mary Abigail Dodge (*pseud.* Gail Hamilton), *Biography of James G. Blaine* (Norwich, Conn., 1895), 422.

Election day in the East proved gloomy and rainy. In New York City, where the streets were quiet and deserted as the hours wore on, the vote was heavy. As night fell men began to gather in spite of the continued downpour, and in front of the *Herald* bulletin board a crowd of ten thousand hailed the first scattering news with cheers. The rival party headquarters at the Fifth Avenue Hotel and the Everett House were jammed, and the pool rooms, heavy with smoke and the reek of liquor, were filled almost to suffocation.[1] By midnight the news indicated that Tilden had won a decisive victory; and the next morning his triumph was proclaimed by nearly all the American press, even the *New York Tribune* conceding it. But in the first hours after midnight an editorial council of the *Times* decided that the election was really doubtful, and declared in the first edition that Hayes might yet be president. At daybreak John Reid, the managing editor, left the *Times* office, woke Zachariah Chandler, the Republican national chairman, from a sleep of utter exhaustion, and told him that victory might yet be wrested from the jaws of defeat. The result was the hasty dispatch of telegrams reading, "Don't be defrauded" and "Can you hold your state?" to doubtful regions; and later in the day Chandler sent to his distant lieutenants the famous message, "Hayes has 185 electoral votes and is elected."[2]

The excitement of the ensuing days brought out the essential stuff of the American people as nothing had done since Johnson's impeachment. In New York crowds assembled before the bulletin boards in such numbers that traffic at certain points was virtually stopped; on the second afternoon following the election the mul-

[1] *N. Y. Herald*, Nov. 8, 1876.
[2] Haworth, *Disputed Election*, chap. v; E. H. Davis. *History of the New York Times* (N. Y., 1920), 133.

titude in front of the *Herald* office extended across the whole area below City Hall Park and blocked the vehicles on Broadway as far south as Bowling Green. Similar scenes were enacted in other large cities. The apprehension of the Democrats lest their candidate should be set aside—cheated of his victory when he had received a popular majority of more than a quarter million, and if the white vote alone was counted, of almost one and a quarter million—became intense. Yet only a few men indulged in threats of violence. The *New York Express* talked about "the use of the sword;" and the *World* said that if Tilden was counted out, "Many times 40,000 Americans will know the reason why." But the vast majority of Democrats condemned such utterances, and Tilden himself set an unforgettable example of calmness and moderation.[1] The *Nation*, intensely anxious that a solution be found, suggested that one Republican elector might switch his vote to Tilden; and the rumor thereupon started that Godkin's friend James Russell Lowell, who was a Massachusetts elector, meant to adopt this course—a rumor which Lowell quickly disposed of.[2] But as the weeks passed the people grew calmer, and at length, when the Electoral Commission reported in favor of the seating of Hayes, the whole controversy was ended without the slightest disturbance.

The presidential battle had had many deplorable aspects: the atrocities committed on helpless blacks at the South, the frauds of election officers in various states, the violent party animosity afterward, the efforts on both sides to purchase electors, the bargains between Southern leaders and friends of Hayes, the offer of governmental

[1] John Bigelow, *The Life of Samuel J. Tilden* (N. Y., 1895), II, 111-115.

[2] H. E. Scudder, *James Russell Lowell* (Boston, 1901), II, 216; anon., "A Disputed Election or A Failure to Elect," *Nation*, XXIII, Nov. 30, 1876.

rewards to disreputable Southern Republicans. Many people felt as if the worst sewage of American politics had been churned and emptied to give off a poisonous miasma; that neither Hayes nor Tilden really deserved the presidency. Yet when all was ended the careful student of affairs had reason to feel heartened rather than discouraged. The close approach of the Democratic party to victory demonstrated the disgust of the electorate for the boodling and mismanagement which had disfigured the Republican administration. It indicated that thereafter two parties, not one, would control the destinies of the republic and would furnish a vigilant check upon one another. Above all, the moderation and sobriety displayed by the average American under terrific strain, the serene emergence of the country from a bitter contest that in many another nation would have ended in civil war, were a striking testimonial to the essential steadfastness and orderliness of the American people.[1]

[1] See W. M. Evarts in C. R. Williams, *Life of Hayes* (Boston, 1914), I, 535; Haworth, *Disputed Election*, 342. An important and somewhat discreditable rôle was played in this campaign by the Grand Army of the Republic, which responded zealously to the waving of the bloody shirt by such men as Logan. This organization of veterans of the federal armies in the Civil War had been founded in 1866 in Decatur, Illinois, and had now become powerful. Its national encampment in Indianapolis in 1876 was virtually a grand Republican rally, with vociferous denunciation of "rebel brigadiers" and tumultuous cheering for Hayes. Already the G. A. R. was interested in pension legislation and was influential in the halls of Congress. On the other hand, its social and philanthropic activities were highly useful, and in ten thousand Northern localities it taught certain redeeming lessons of patriotism.

CHAPTER XII

HUMANITARIAN STRIVING

WHEN the Thirteenth Amendment was assured of victory, and William Lloyd Garrison locked the forms of the *Liberator* for the last time, the veteran abolitionist turned to the advocacy of temperance, "free trade" and woman suffrage.[1] This change of front was a symbolic act. It evinced the compelling reason why humanitarian zeal should manifest itself in a variety of new ways after 1865. The idealistic energy which had formerly been largely absorbed by the antislavery cause was now free to express itself in solicitude for the poor, the defective and the defenseless. The increasing urbanization of the nation, moreover, in connection with the hard times following the Panic, thrust certain problems more insistently into the foreground, such as poverty, public health, sweatshop abuses and child labor. The nation awoke after the war to find conditions existing in its largest cities which till then it had fondly thought confined to Manchester, Paris and Naples. As a result, the late sixties witnessed the first large and concerted movement against the city slums, the first scientific efforts in behalf of public health, the opening of a new chapter in penal reform, and the movement for the prevention of cruelty to animals. The seventies brought the organization of the Women's Christian Temperance Union and the first national ticket of the Prohibition party, the efforts of Clara Barton in behalf of the Red Cross, the

[1] Goldwin Smith, *The Moral Crusader: William Lloyd Garrison* (N. Y., 1892), 176.

318

rise of the National Association for Woman Suffrage, and the founding of the State Charities Aid Association in New York.

The slum, recently a mere name, had become a firmly rooted American institution. New York City had a hundred thousand slum dwellers, sheltered in nearly twenty thousand tenement houses, many of which were the vilest rookeries.[1] The cellar population alone—the troglodytes—approached nearly twenty thousand people. In some districts there was a congestion which had probably never been equaled in any other great city of Christendom. The tenements, erected by grasping speculative builders, were crowded together in solid blocks, with rear houses jammed in behind those facing the street. They were unheated, and most of the houses had no connection with the sewer. In such an immense and notorious rabbit warren as Gotham Court on Cherry Street each home consisted of two rooms and housed an average of from five to seven people.[2] In Boston, where the slum district was smaller than in New York but hardly less repellent, the construction of tenements after the war amazed all observers. By the time of the Panic more than one fifth the whole population, or about sixty thousand people, dwelt in the twenty-eight hundred registered tenement houses. What tenement life sometimes meant in human misery can best be suggested by a brief excerpt from an official report describing a tenement home not a half mile from the Boston City Hall.[3]

The room was unspeakably filthy; the furniture two or three old chairs and an old dirty table. No fire, and the room damp, dark, and cold. It was the only room the

[1] N. Y. Eve. Post, Aug. 31, 1865.
[2] See Jacob Riis, How the Other Half Lives (N. Y., 1890), chaps. i-iv; also New York Metropolitan Board of Health, First Ann. Rep. (1871).
[3] Boston Bd. of Health, Report for 1873.

family occupied except a little dark box in the corner with no window in it—a part of the room itself partitioned off for a bedroom. And such a bed! The two oldest children were dirty and ragged and leaning against the window on the side of the room. . . . The youngest was . . . about worn out and apparently half starved. . . . Its only clothing was an undershirt scarcely reaching to the waist, and the child's body, face, hands, and hair were reeking with the vilest filth; and the child was pinched with the cold.

Many mill towns of Massachusetts and other Eastern cities were just as shockingly overcrowded. Fall River, a conspicuous example, reported tenements where a dozen people dwelt in three rooms, or fifteen in four.[1]

Throughout the slums of the cities, so few were the sanitary precautions, death stalked almost unchecked. In the congested parts of New York typhoid, smallpox, scarlet fever and, above all, typhus fever were never idle. A wretched building in East Seventeenth Street, a stone's throw from the mayor's house, sent thirty-five typhus patients to the city fever hospital in a single year, while nearly a hundred more were treated at home.[2] Garbage was allowed to collect in many streets until they became almost impassable; in 1866 some fifteen hundred loads were removed from the Fourth Ward in a few days, and yet some streets were still ridged two feet high with the deposits. The city sewers, unconnected as yet with any main trunk lines to carry the contents far out into the tide-scoured bay, simply emptied under the piers of the Hudson and East rivers. The nation's second city, Philadelphia, presented a spectacle that was not a whit better. A large slum district existed on Bedford and St. Mary streets, crowded by people exhibiting a revolt-

[1] F. W. Draper, "The Homes of the Poor in Our Cities," Mass. State Bd. of Health, *Fourth Ann. Rep. for 1872* (*Mass. Pub. Docs.*, IV, no. 31), 396-441.
[2] N. Y. Metropolitan Bd. of Health, *Report for 1869*.

ing squalor and vice. The town was so exceedingly dirty that in 1870 the street authorities removed a thousand loads of filth a day over a period of two and a half months.[1] Hogs still roamed a large area of the city. A considerable part of the population was supplied with drinking water from the Delaware River, into which the sewers threw thirteen million gallons of waste daily, which was carried by the tides to the induction pipes.[2]

The result was writ large in mortality figures that seem, by the standards of a half century later, barbarous. During the winter of 1864-1865 New York had more than two thousand cases of smallpox and more than six hundred deaths. Philadelphia in the first year of peace lost seven hundred and seventy-three victims to typhoid fever and three hundred and thirty-four to typhus. A year later, in 1866, cholera appeared and claimed nine hundred and ten lives. During 1869 and 1870 the Philadelphians suffered from a scourge of scarlet fever, which was responsible for one thousand seven hundred and fifty-five deaths in the two years and which left hundreds of deaf, crippled or mentally enfeebled persons behind it. Then in 1871 ensued a terrible smallpox epidemic which threw both New York and Philadelphia into mourning. It killed over eight hundred people in the former city, more than ever before in its history, while in the latter the deaths nearly reached two thousand.[3] Boston, Baltimore and Washington were all ravaged by the same powerful epidemics. The most casual investigation showed that a great part of the deaths were preventable by better housing and a few elementary measures of sanitation. Thus in the reeking slums of the

[1] Philadelphia Bd. of Health, *Reports for 1868* and *1869*.
[2] The Philadelphia Bd. of Health complained of malodorous half-open sewers. See *Report for 1870*.
[3] N. Y. Metropolitan and Philadelphia Bds. of Health, *Reports for 1866-1872*.

Fourth Ward of New York it was found in 1863 that one resident in twenty-five perished, while in the open, well-built Fifteenth Ward, only one resident in sixty.[1]

The necessity for reform was one to which no intelligent body of citizens could long remain blind, and public-spirited men arose in the largest Eastern cities to demand action. New York City, leading the way, obtained in 1866 a state enactment creating an efficient municipal health board, which was headed by the public-spirited merchant Jackson S. Schultz. Within four years it had closed virtually all the cellars and basements used for foul lodgings.[2] It had completed a survey of the tenements and ordered the owners to effect alterations making them decently habitable. Vaccination had been applied to most of the population without resorting to compulsion and the causes of cholera had been vigorously dealt with. The board in 1868 forced the removal of all downtown slaughterhouses, of which there had been twenty-three in a single half-ward, to points above Fortieth Street. At the same time the first collecting sewer to free the pier slips from the accumulation of waste was built, and others rapidly followed.[3] Meanwhile Massachusetts was being persuaded to create her state board of health (1869)—a far-reaching step which stimulated all the cities of the Bay State to improve their sanitation and to attack disease.[4] Two years later the legislature gave

[1] One half of New York City's population furnished three fourths of the total sickness and mortality. See N. Y. Metropolitan Bd. of Health, *Report for 1871*; also *N. Y. Eve. Post*, Aug. 31, 1865.

[2] Elisha Harris, "Health Laws and their Administration," *Journ. of Social Science*, II (1870), 176-187.

[3] *U. S. Tenth Census* (1880), XVIII, 571.

[4] G. C. Whipple, *State Sanitation* (Cambridge, Mass., 1917), I, 39 ff. The other state health boards established were those of Louisiana (1867); California (1870); Virginia (1872); Minnesota (1872); Michigan (1874); Maryland (1874); Alabama (1875); Georgia (1875); Colorado (1876); Wisconsin (1876); Mississippi (1877); New Jersey (1877); Tennessee (1877); Illinois (1877). N. S.

Boston a tenement-house law far in advance of the old
code. It was also necessary for Boston to attack the
problem of sewage disposal, and in 1875 the city established a commission to prepare a plan for main sewers
stretching far out into the harbor.[1] The Philadelphians
already had their board of health, which labored as vigorously as a corrupt administration would let it.

If these conditions existed in the three largest and
wealthiest cities of the East, the state of affairs in backward Southern centers and the raw, fast-growing Western municipalities may be easily imagined. Memphis in
1870, a city of forty thousand, had practically no sewage arrangements or health administration at all, though
built in part on swampy soil. New Orleans, then easily
one of the most insalubrious cities in the world, was—
despite the establishment of the Louisiana board of health
soon after the war—in even worse case. "The soil is
saturated almost to its surface," ran an official report in
1880, "and saturated very largely with the oozings of
foul privy vaults, and the infiltrations of accumulations
on the surface of the streets and in the rear of houses."
The drainage was totally ineffective.[2] Charleston and
Mobile presented the same spectacle. All the Southern
cities were habituated to frightful epidemics. Memphis
in 1873 was attacked from three quarters at once—by
yellow fever, smallpox and cholera. The people fled in
a panic, leaving half the houses vacant. Some seven
thousand cases of yellow fever were reported and about
two thousand deaths; cholera attacked one thousand and
slew two hundred and seventy-six; and smallpox reaped
a heavy harvest among the Negroes.

Shaler, ed., *The United States of America* (N. Y., 1894), III, 1227-
1228.
   [1] Boston Bd. of Health, *Report for 1878*.
   [2] *U. S. Tenth Census* (1880), XXIX, 276.

Among the people who filled the slums of the large cities there was one large group which is deserving of special notice. A product partly of the war, partly of the trend toward city life, the sweated woman worker suddenly appeared in large numbers. In the North the invasion of the industrial field by women did not halt in 1865, for the shortage of labor remained acute; the competition with discharged soldiers simply pushed these women lower in the economic scale.[1] Both East and West their lot was frequently pitiable, for they were protected neither by the laws nor by trade unions. In New York City alone there were seventy-five thousand women workers who lived on the ragged edge of misery. In the first year of peace, with prices rising to an unprecedented height, fifteen thousand or more of them, employed in shops and factories, earned only from two dollars and fifty cents to four dollars a week. Yet they were far more fortunate than the wretched stratum of women employed as pieceworkers on cheap garments.[2] In the Middle West women were glad to earn from three dollars to five dollars weekly, and those in the Chicago and Cleveland sweatshops labored for even less. A union movement was inevitable. Susan B. Anthony became head of the Workingwomen's Protective Association;[3] women's labor organizations were born in the cigar-making, printing and shoe-making trades. Yet these protective efforts, taken in the aggregate, could accomplish little.[4]

Despite the poverty which stared every city dweller in the face, remedial or relief institutions were few and painfully weak. The settlement house was unknown; the

[1] N. Y. Eve. Post, July 13, 1865.
[2] Nation (N. Y.), IV, Feb. 21, 1867.
[3] J. R. Commons and Associates, History of Labour in the United States (N. Y., 1918), II, 133.
[4] R. T. Ely, Labor Movement in America (rev. ed., N. Y., 1905), 82.

slum mission was just taking root; the institutional church and the Salvation Army were unborn. Efforts at the erection of cheap model houses, though familiar in England, were unheard of in America. In Boston Dr. H. P. Bowditch, of the state board of health, was spurred by the misery of the tenements to incorporate a coöperative building company, which opened the first of five groups of "cottage-flats" in 1872. In Brooklyn Alfred T. White, a philanthropic gentleman who had studied housing in England, built two admirable sets of model tenements in 1877-1878.[1] But this was all. A. T. Stewart's model hotel for working girls, with its excessively rigid rules, proved a failure. As yet refuges, shelters and asylums were few and the free clinic and "milk station" were unknown. Not until about 1870 was there even so obvious a form of philanthropy for children as the fresh-air work in Boston and New York, undertaken in the former city by the North End Mission, and in the latter by the newspapers coöperating with religious workers.[2]

On the other hand, agencies of vice and impoverishment carried on their work with only the slightest impediment. New York officials in the late sixties confessed to six hundred and ninety-seven disorderly houses in the city and two thousand five hundred and seventy-four prostitutes; but these figures were notoriously too low, and one authority placed the entire number of such resorts at about seven hundred and seventy-five and that of the fallen women at fully twelve thousand. Outside of a few states, the saloon flourished in nearly every town of any size. The census of 1880 showed that the four hundred and ninety-two cities of the country with a

[1] *Appletons' Ann. Cyclop.*, XVI (1876), 735.
[2] G. B. Bartlett, "The Recreation of the People," *Journ. of Social Science*, XII (1880), 141.

population of more than five thousand each supported about eighty thousand liquor establishments; and the census authorities estimated the whole number of drinking places in the country at perhaps one hundred thousand, or one for about every fifty inhabitants. This was a showing distinctly discreditable to the habits of the nation. No fewer than one hundred and eighty-five towns admitted having houses of ill-fame, while ninety-four boasted that they were quite free from them, and two hundred and fifteen furnished no information whatever.[1] The public attitude toward them was utterly unenlightened, for as yet it was believed that they should be "regulated" instead of stamped out. A sanitary committee in New York reported in 1867 in favor of controlling the social evil as in continental Europe, with official inspection and regulation; and this recommendation, written by three able physicians, was emphatically indorsed by the *Nation*.[2]

As yet little attention was being given to a really scientific study of social distress, its causes and remedies. Good-hearted people were shocked by the desperate need of the Negroes who came thronging north to the border cities, by the squalor of the Eastern slums and by the misery that followed the Panic of 1873. Only here and there was an earnest soul attempting an expert appraisal of social maladjustment. Charles Loring Brace, the benefactor of the New York working boy, published his illuminating study of the "dangerous classes" in the metropolis and showed how education could prevent the

[1] Philadelphia reported the largest number, 517; New Orleans reported 365. Baltimore roughly estimated hers at 300; Chicago hers at 200, and New York mendaciously declared there were only 183 within her precincts. *U. S. Tenth Census* (1880), XXI, liv ff.

[2] *Nation*, IV, Feb. 21, 1867. Professional abortionists flourished in many cities; their advertisements were common in the press; one, Mme. Restelle, was notorious in New York City. She was actively prosecuted by Anthony Comstock, then starting his career.

juvenile from becoming a criminal. On the other hand a few years later appeared R. L. Dugdale's epochal work on *The Jukes: A Study in Crime, Pauperism, Heredity, and Disease* (1877).[1] The author undertook to demonstrate the powerful influence of heredity in producing poverty and vice; and tracing one notorious family tree, he showed that the descendants of a certain woman whom he called Ada Jukes had cost the state of New York more than a million dollars since 1800. Dugdale placed great faith in industrial training, but his book plainly pointed to the need for some check upon the multiplication of the diseased and vicious. Such men as he and Brace were the vedettes of the new scientific sociology that was soon to emerge.

Official provision for the poor, both in city and country, was rude, unsystematic and wretchedly administered. One great city after another furnished outdoor relief on the most lavish and careless scale.[2] In Brooklyn, which became the classic illustration for a generation afterward of the perils attaching to such loose charity, the number of people who asked and received help doubled between 1872 and 1877; and in the latter year one person in every sixteen in the city was receiving public aid. The whole system there was an inherent part of the municipal corruption of the time. When it was found in 1878 that the entire system was illegal, it was suddenly discontinued; yet to the surprise of observers no increased demand fell upon private or public relief agencies, and no unusual suffering appeared.

In the smaller cities and in the country, unsupervised county relief was the rule. When a family fell into

[1] See *Nation*, XIV, Oct. 19, 1872, for a review of Brace's volume; XXIV, July 26, 1877, for Dugdale's book. Brace pointed out that one third the adult criminals of New York state were illiterate, and two thirds of those in New York City jails were foreign-born.

[2] A. G. Warner, *American Charities* (3d edn., N. Y., 1919), 211.

hopeless pauperism, it was packed off to what most states called the poorhouse. We have altogether too clear a picture of the degradation and suffering which these institutions represented. In New York, where the county poor farms and city almshouses together cared for 13,698 paupers in 1867, and many more later, the typical building was in constant disrepair, badly ventilated, and the food coarse and poorly cooked. "Here the innocent are mingled with the vicious," reported the state authorities just after the war; "young and simple-hearted children with their callous and corrupt elders; the sexes mingled indiscriminately by day and often by night." [1] In Ohio there were six thousand five hundred paupers in equally wretched circumstances. [2] Of course there were advanced counties where the provision was fairly good, but the state inspector after the war found that, on the whole, the condition of the infirmaries was "not only deplorable but a disgrace to the State and a sin against humanity." Most other states were in the same situation, or even worse. Edward Eggleston in *The Hoosier Schoolmaster* draws a repellent sketch of an Indiana poorhouse and indicates the shame and degradation felt by all respectable folk who became its inmates.

There were two groups, the pauper insane and the pauper children, whose lot was especially painful. Despite the pioneer efforts of Dorothea Dix before the war, [3] the system of caring for the insane was discouragingly bad. The New York poorhouses sheltered one thousand eight hundred and forty-two such unfortunates in 1867, who were confined sometimes in heavily grated cells, sometimes in gloomy cellars, and sometimes in bare dun-

[1] N. Y. Bd. of State Charities, *Report for 1867*.
[2] Ohio Bd. of State Charities, *Report for 1868*, 186.
[3] C. R. Fish, *The Rise of the Common Man (A History of American Life*, VI), 258-260.

geons as dark as midnight; while more than two hundred of the helpless creatures were in chains or otherwise tightly secured.[1]   Ohio officers reported finding some insane patients in nudity and filth and others with feet frozen off.   As for the children, New York two years after the war had more than twelve hundred, many of whom had been born in the poorhouses, and all of whom suffered physically and spiritually from debasing contacts.   The official reports speak of small children confined in rooms near the cells assigned to maniacs and crying with horror and fright at their situation.   A similar account comes from Ohio.[2]   Those children could count themselves fortunate who were bound out, like Riley's "Little Orphant Annie," to families which needed their labor and which made at least a perfunctory promise of giving them kind treatment.   Some states were even more indifferent to their helpless wards than New York and Ohio.

Reform was bound to come, even though slowly. The most powerful impulse was furnished by the rapid creation of state boards of charities to supervise all institutions of relief, public and private, and to suggest means of improving them.[3]   The Massachusetts board, established in 1863, was followed during the five years after the war by the formation of similar bodies in New York, Rhode Island, Pennsylvania, Ohio and Illinois. The Bay State body quickly distinguished itself in the establishment of two schools for teaching deaf mutes by articulation, one in Boston, the other the Clarke Institution at Northampton.   In New York the board in 1868 brought out a report on poorhouses and almshouses

[1] N. Y. Bd. of State Charities, *Report for 1867.*

[2] "Simply brutal," was the phrase used by the Ohio board.   Ohio Bd. of State Charities, *Report for 1867,* 12.

[3] F. B. Sanborn, "Poverty and Public Charity," *North Am. Rev.,* CX (1870), 347 ff.

which the press used in a campaign for reform. This report demanded the building of a state institution adequate to care for the insane, a demand met by the completion of the Willard Asylum, which had been authorized in the last year of the war. In 1873 the board also made an effort to arouse public sentiment for the better care of destitute children. Meanwhile in Illinois the officers were exposing county abuses of a terrible nature: the inhuman practice of farming out the patients to the lowest bidder, who systematically starved them; the insufficient medical care of the sick; the neglect of children, "almost without exception uninstructed and untrained;" and the failure to separate the two sexes, so that the numbers of illegitimate children within the poorhouse walls were shocking.[1] The Ohio board called not only for better treatment of juveniles and the insane, but for the establishment of district workhouses for vagrants and petty criminals and of reform schools for wayward girls. This last was one of the crying needs of the time everywhere. For example, in Connecticut a special commission had just estimated that delinquent girls below the age of sixteen numbered about five hundred. Massachusetts, here as elsewhere in advance of most states, had established an industrial school for girls at Lancaster.[2]

States which neglected their poor in this fashion, it is not surprising to find, paid little attention to their prisoners. During the latter years of the war the jails had been but half-filled, the commitments of male convicts falling off enormously.[3] But when the war closed, the amount of crime increased alarmingly, from one half to three fourths of the new convicts in many penitentiaries

---

[1] Ill. Bd. of State Charities, *Report for 1870;* Warner, *American Charities,* 435 ff., for state work.

[2] *Appletons' Ann. Cyclop.,* XIX (1879), 874.

[3] *Nation,* V, Aug. 22, 1867.

being former soldiers or sailors.[1]   At this moment an inquiry was made into the condition of American prisons and reformatories by E. C. Wines and Theodore W. Dwight and presented to the New York legislature as a 500-page report (1867).   They found that the United States was far behind Europe in the convict systems used. The American prison industries, once so boasted, were poorly managed.   In some states, including New York, the politicians had laid hands on all prison appointments. In the Southern states the convicts were leased to contractors in gangs, and nobody could travel through the section without hearing, as Sir George Campbell did, terrible stories of outrage and abuse.[2]   Nowhere was there a proper inspection of the lower prisons; the county jails were, as a Michigan report said, "moral pest-houses, foster-places of idleness, and schools of crime;" and in every state the lack of classification was glaring.   Even Massachusetts had no satisfactory system until 1870.[3]

What a thoroughly bad penitentiary might be was revealed in 1878 by a report in Tennessee upon the state prison in the heart of Nashville.   Two men and sometimes three were locked in a cell seven feet long and three and a half feet wide, compelled to breathe air tainted by the open buckets used for wastes; and the sick were "thrown into a hospital lacking in the decency and comfort of a pig-sty."   The mortality rate was fearful, for scurvy and typhus fever were almost constant, and epidemics spread with fearful rapidity, until the prison became a menace to all Nashville.[4]

[1] E. C. Wines and T. W. Dwight, *Report on the Prisons and Reformatories of the United States and Canada*—made to the New York legislature, Jan., 1867.
[2] George Campbell, *White and Black* (N. Y., 1879), 384.
[3] *Appletons' Ann. Cyclop.*, XIX (1879), 600.
[4] Tenn. State Bd. of Health, *Report for 1878.* See *Appletons' Ann. Cyclop.*, XIX (1879), 539, for equally shocking data upon Kentucky prisons.

The two great principles of prison reform about which the discussion of the postwar years centered were the indeterminate sentence and the adaptation of penal discipline to the regeneration, rather than the punishment, of the offender. Here the influence of British example, and especially of the so-called Irish prison system instituted by Sir Walter Crofton, was potent.[1] Two important events in the field of penal reform occurred almost simultaneously: the establishment of a prison where the new reformative principles could be applied, and the formation of a national body to enunciate and expound them. The New York legislature authorized the Elmira Reformatory in 1869, and the state commission which drew up plans for it reported that the new name would be given genuine meaning. "We propose to make the sentences substantially reformation sentences," they said. "We propose that, when the sentence of a criminal is regularly less than five years, the sentence to the Reformatory shall be until reformation, not exceeding five years." In 1870 Dr. Wines was instrumental in forming the National Prison Association.[2] Its declaration of principles called for a progressive classification of prisoners, a system of rewards for good conduct, a constant insistence upon reformation, and the indeterminate sentence. Already the walls of Elmira were rising, and under Z. R. Brockway of Detroit as its able manager, the new plan was given partial scope when the institution opened in 1877.

Despite the carelessness and easy optimism of the American public before 1873, despite the depression and discouragement afterward, reform pushed steadily into new fields. One of the most creditable humanitarian

[1] F. H. Wines, *Punishment and Reformation* (rev. edn., N. Y., 1919), chap. x.

[2] The *Proceedings* of this body are a valuable source of information.

movements was that of Henry Bergh for the protection
of dumb beasts.   The son of a wealthy New York ship-
builder, he returned in 1864 from a consular position in
St. Petersburg so moved by the daily scenes of brutality
to animals which he had witnessed that he resolved to
devote himself to their protection.[1]   Well aware of the
work which the British Royal Society for the Prevention
of Cruelty to Animals had been doing for forty years,
Bergh was responsible for chartering an American Society for the same purpose in New York in the spring of
1866, and the legislature at Albany was induced to pass
an adequate law for the protection of dumb animals.   He
then turned his attention to enforcement.   A picturesque
figure, with his tall, lanky figure, long face and intense
eyes framed by heavy black hair—the very image of a
Puritan reformer—he was to be seen on the streets at all
hours watching for infractions.

One of his first tasks was to stop the cruel overloading
of horses on the city omnibus lines; and he won wide
publicity for the new society when he began halting the
cars at leading junction points, making passengers alight
to reduce the weight, and even knocking troublesome men
into the gutters.[2]   Soon he undertook to expose the dan-
gerously unsanitary conditions under which a great part
of the city's milk was produced, coming from cattle in
the last stages of tuberculosis, fed on garbage, and milked
in filthy underground stables.   Bennett, Frank Leslie
and other publishers joined in the clamor which compelled an abatement of the evil.[3]   Nor did public opinion fail to respond to Bergh's insistence upon humane
methods of transporting and killing cattle.   It also gave

[1] S. H. Coleman, *Humane Society Leaders in America* (Albany, 1924),
33 ff.
[2] *Nation*, II, June 11, 1866.
[3] See H. C. Brown, ed., *The Last Fifty Years in New York* (N. Y.,
1926), 219.

due support to his vigorous campaign against dog fights, cock fights and rat or badger baiting, sports which still had a devoted following in the New York slum districts.[1]

That the American people saw the need of this humane movement is shown by its growth; for it spread at once to other states. Societies were incorporated in city after city, and by the year of the Panic, when Bergh made a speech-making tour as far west as Chicago and St. Louis, the Society for the Prevention of Cruelty to Animals was a thoroughly national institution. Lieutenants of ability came forward to support the founder. In New England, where general indignation was aroused in the spring of 1868 by a horse race in which both horses were driven to death, George T. Angell, a prominent Boston lawyer, became the energetic head of the Massachusetts Society for the Prevention of Cruelty to Animals. His society had the shooting of live pigeons abolished by law while it was still legal elsewhere; and it was he who saw the merit of the Englishwoman Anna Sewell's story *Black Beauty* (1877), to which American humane workers gave a circulation of literally millions as a pamphlet. In Illinois Edwin L. Brown, who labored to reform the outrageous conditions at the Chicago stockyards, and in New York Elbridge T. Gerry, a brilliant young attorney who distinguished himself as a prosecutor, proved invaluable leaders.[2]

It is a singular fact that the organized protection of children was, in large degree, an outgrowth of the protection of dumb animals. In 1874 a little girl of nine, beaten, gashed and starved by her foster mother in a New York tenement, was brought into court as an animal—

[1] Coleman, *Humane Society Leaders,* 49.
[2] Coleman, *Humane Society Leaders,* chaps. ii, iv, x; A. B. Faust, *German Element in the United States of America* (Boston, 1909), II, 446.

Clearing out a rookery in New York City.

Henry Bergh begins the work of the S.P.C.A.

for the law sanctioned no interference between parent
and child—on the complaint of the Society for the Prevention of Cruelty to Animals   Jacob Riis has described
the scene on that bitter winter day, when the unclothed
mite was brought into the court room, "carried in a
horse blanket, at the sight of which men wept aloud. I
saw it laid at the feet of the judge, who turned his face
away, and in the stillness of that court room I heard a
voice raised claiming for that child the protection men
had denied it, in the name of the homeless cur on the
streets." In the dingy court room was born the New
York Society for the Prevention of Cruelty to Children,
organized by Bergh, Gerry and other humanitarians.[1]
Other cities adopted the idea. Children had been
trained to beg and steal; they had been whipped
into hazardous occupations; they had been exposed
to surroundings of vice and obscenity. All these
abuses, together with physical cruelty to minors, were
attacked. Like its predecessor, the new society was
criticized for officiousness, but it quickly made itself
respected.

But such undertakings, commendable as they were,
were of less importance than the temperance movement
and the woman's rights movement, two mighty causes
destined to enlist millions and within a half century to
write their results into the federal Constitution. Both
were revivals of prewar movements which, thrust into
the background by the slavery struggle, now emerged
with greater strength than ever. Both entered upon new
phases, including a far more aggressive part in politics
than had been previously attempted.

The liquor evil just after the war seemed to be attaining formidable proportions. The reliance of the federal
government upon liquor taxes for revenue gave drinking

[1] Coleman, *Humane Society Leaders*, chap. iii.

a new respectability.[1] Immigration assisted its growth, for the Germans of the Middle West checked the prohibition legislation which had been attempted there, and the Irish and Italians of the East supported the saloon. The capital investment in liquor grew from twenty-nine million dollars in 1860 to sixty-seven million dollars in 1870 and one hundred and ninety-three million dollars in 1880. With this prosperity to embolden them, the liquor manufacturers and retailers entered politics to protect themselves against heavier taxation or antisaloon enactments. In cities like New York they allied themselves with the dominant gangsters, and the Whisky Ring frauds showed that they were able to corrupt high federal officers and reach their polluting hands into the very precincts of the White House. The old-fashioned warfare against the dramshop was seen to be quite ineffective. It was well represented at this time by the activities of John B. Gough,[2] then at the height of his career as a temperance lecturer—a voluble and eloquent agitator of English birth who had himself been rescued from youthful drunkenness and regarded intemperance as equally a sin and a disease.[3] But new forces were about to come into play and make the older methods seem antiquated and inadequate.

The prewar movement for state prohibitory laws, so successful in the North during the fifties, had suffered serious reverses during the conflict. When the war ended, only Massachusetts and Maine were "dry," and a vehement popular revolt in the former commonwealth led to the restoration of the license system in 1868.[4] In

---

[1] On the heavy postwar drinking in the South, see Robert Somers, *The Southern States since the War* (London, 1871), 245.

[2] J. B. Gough, *Platform Echoes* (Hartford, 1885), *passim*. See the *Nation*, VIII, April 1, 1869.

[3] Fish, *The Rise of the Common Man*, 265.

[4] See *Appletons' Ann. Cyclop.*, XIX (1879), 579, for a long historical

Maine prohibition continued in force, and the question whether it was a success or not was one upon which national opinion sharply divided. Several Central states, notably Michigan, Ohio and Illinois, stood vacillating at the end of this period between license and prohibition. However, the antisaloon forces labored strenuously for local-option legislation, and before 1878 a considerable list of cities, including Cincinnati and Dayton in Ohio, and Gloucester and Portsmouth in New England, allowed no dramshops. In some other places saloons were forced to operate under costly licenses.

Meanwhile a militant prohibition party had come into existence throughout the East and Middle West. This party, state and national, grew out of the order called the Good Templars, which, founded about ten years before the war, was by now the country's largest and most powerful temperance organization.[1] The first state political organization was formed in Ohio during the summer of 1869; and that fall five hundred delegates met in Chicago at the call of the Templars to perfect a national party. The platform demanded statutory abolition of the liquor traffic, and supported woman suffrage as the most effective means of reaching that goal. It was a bold step, for during a half century temperance leaders had insisted that the movement would be wrecked if it ventured on the tempestuous sea of party politics. Nationally the early results seemed disappointing. John Black, Green C. Smith and Neal Dow, the three presidential candidates in 1872, 1876 and 1880, failed to receive twenty-six thousand votes among them. But in certain states the party showed an impressive and increas-

article on prohibition in Maine. For Massachusetts, see *Am. Ann. Cyclop.*, VII (1867), 480; *Nation*, VIII, April 1, 1869. See *Nation*, XIII, April 4, 1872, for comment on the situation in the Middle West.
[1] E. H. Cherrington, *Evolution of Prohibition in the United States* (Westerville, Ohio, 1920), chap. vi.

ing vigor, and a long list of towns went "dry" under local option.

Much more spontaneous was the emergence of a powerful woman's temperance movement. The seed of the Women's Christian Temperance Union was dropped as if by accident. Late in 1873 a well-known health reformer of Boston, Dr. Dio Lewis, delivering a series of temperance addresses, urged the women of Jamestown and Fredonia, New York, and Hillsboro, Ohio, to begin a praying crusade to close the saloons. This effort, though a failure in New York, succeeded at Hillsboro, and spread through southern Ohio with astonishing effects. The country was startled to hear that in city after city squads of women were singing hymns before the saloon doors and even entering to hold prayer at the bar.[1] In Dayton and Chicago the women were insulted by street loafers; in Cincinnati they were received with respect; in Zanesville they persuaded the city council to stop the sale of drink. A hundred women marched in Chicago to the city hall to ask the council to keep the saloons closed on Sunday. Along the Eastern Seaboard and as far west as San Francisco, the strange outburst manifested itself. Its direct effects were evanescent, but indirectly it accomplished a great object. The church women of Chautauqua, New York, called a national convention of temperance women in Cleveland, which in the late summer of 1874 organized the Women's Christian Temperance Union. It grew swiftly, and when five years later Frances E. Willard was elected its head, it could already claim to be one of the real powers of the land.

This formidable participation of women in the temperance struggle was, from one standpoint, merely a part

---

[1] *Nation*, XVIII, March 19, 1874; A. M. Schlesinger, *New Viewpoints in American History* (N. Y., 1922), 151-152.

of the growing emancipation of the sex. In view of the war services of the women, the feminist leaders, when the war ended, believed they had as good a title to the ballot as the liberated Negroes. Bombarding Congress with petitions they tried to obtain for their sex the right to vote as a part of the proposed Fourteenth Amendment. They were totally unsuccessful, for though such leaders as Gerrit Smith, G. W. Curtis, Garrison and Greeley believed theoretically in equal suffrage, even they objected to imperiling the amendment by making it too broad.[1] But despite their failure in getting the word "male" omitted from the second section of the Fourteenth Amendment, the women steadily pushed their campaign for the vote. Susan B. Anthony and Elizabeth Cady Stanton were in the forefront of the effort. The year 1867 found them fighting in New York for the admission of women to the state constitutional convention; it found them conducting a hot struggle in Kansas for an equal-suffrage clause in the new constitution. "We speak in schoolhouses, barns, sawmills, log cabins with boards for seats and lanterns hung around for lights, but people come twenty miles to hear us," wrote Miss Anthony. On election day the suffrage amendment got nine thousand and thirty votes out of a total of about thirty thousand—the first votes ever cast in the United States for the enfranchisement of women.[2] Then the devoted pair established a suffrage weekly called the *Revolution*. Despite some help from the eccentric George Francis Train, it soon died leaving Miss Anthony ten thousand dollars in debt—a sum which she gallantly paid to the last cent by lecturing and writing.[3]

[1] Ida M. Harper, *Life and Work of Susan B. Anthony* (Indianapolis, 1898-1908), I, chap. xv; Schlesinger, *New Viewpoints*, 146-148.
[2] Harper, *Susan B. Anthony*, I, chap. xvii.
[3] Harper, *Susan B. Anthony*, I, chap. xviii.

One difficulty with the movement was that at first many people refused to take it seriously. Most intellectual circles would have regarded it as freakish had it not possessed the advocacy of John Stuart Mill, who lent it the dignity of a great philosophical reform.[1] In May, 1869, the National Association for Woman Suffrage was born, with Mrs. Stanton as president, and its annual conventions in Washington aroused great interest. Senator Hoar and Vice-President Wheeler were among the early converts. Almost simultaneously the Woman Suffrage Association was established, with Henry Ward Beecher as head, to demand equal suffrage through a federal amendment.[2] The opponents of the movement objected that under equal suffrage women would no longer be regarded with reverence, that family life would be unsettled by sex equality, and that the feminine intellect was incapable of dealing with civic issues. The suffragists, said the *Nation*, shirk one point discreditably: "the existence and enormous influence in life and manners, and above all on the social position of women, of the sexual relation." [3] The only substantial gains came when Wyoming and Utah territories gave women complete political equality, while a few states granted them the vote in school elections.

Women were pushing into the professions in ever-increasing numbers. Anna Howard Shaw presented a striking instance. Born in England and brought to the Michigan backwoods, she became so intent upon an education that she supported herself by teaching and needle-

---

[1] "His support was of course invaluable," said the *Nation*, XVII, May 17, 1874.

[2] Elizabeth Cady Stanton, Susan B. Anthony and others, *History of Woman Suffrage* (N. Y., 1882-1922), II, chap. xxvi. There was a sharp difference in the temper of the two associations, the National being decidedly the more radical. See M. A. De Wolfe Howe, *Causes and Their Champions* (Boston, 1926), 194 ff.

[3] *Nation*, VII, Nov. 26, 1868.

work while she studied. Just after the war, while working in Big Rapids, she was fired with the ambition to become a minister.[1] That year, though her family offered her an education at Ann Arbor if she would desist, the young woman of twenty-three filled a pulpit thirty-six times, and the following spring a Methodist conference voted to admit her to the ministry. By an heroic struggle she finished her education at Albion College and the theological school of Boston University, at one time during the latter course living in an attic room on bread and milk. Finally obtaining her diploma in 1878, she took up a pastorate—along with suffrage work—that fall on Cape Cod. Of women journalists there was now a brilliant group in New York: the Cary sisters, Kate Field, "Fanny Fern," Mary Mapes Dodge, Mrs. Croly and "Gail Hamilton" (Mary Abigail Dodge). One of the best-known physicians in the city was Mary Putnam Jacobi, the daughter of the publisher G. P. Putnam and the first woman to graduate from the École de Medicine in Paris. We need not list the American sculptresses like Harriet Hosmer and Anne Whitney, the actresses like Charlotte Cushman, the singers like Clara Kellogg. When the British feminist Emily Faithfull visited the United States in the late seventies, she attended a reception at which literally hundreds of women workers of repute, in dozens of fields, were present.[2]

In reality, there were two sides of this woman's economic movement. One was represented by the irresistible forward thrust of countless daughters of farmers and wage-earners, eager for a life of light, clean and sedentary labor that would leave their evenings free for

---

[1] Anna Howard Shaw, *The Story of a Pioneer* (N. Y., 1915), chap. iii ff.

[2] Emily Faithfull, *Three Visits to the United States* (Edinburgh, 1884), chap. ii.

recreation or rest. They had no journals or lecturers, made no noise, and holding old-fashioned ideas about marriage, cared nothing about "independence" from men. Yet they raised the number of women over sixteen working in factories, offices and stores to 364,819 in 1870, and 644,208 in 1880. The more vocal side of the movement was represented by the women's-rights advocates who insisted that their sisters should become brokers, lawyers, ministers and editors, thus asserting their equality with men in ambition and capacity.[1]

The rise of women's clubs represented another phase of woman's aspiration to partake more richly of the life about her. Two women shortly after the war gave this movement its first impetus—Julia Ward Howe and Mrs. J. C. Croly. The former was the leading spirit in the New England Women's Club, organized in Boston on February 16, 1868. Many a reform took its beginning in the club's quiet Park Street rooms. "When I want anything in Boston remedied," said Edward Everett Hale, "I go down to the New England Women's Club!"[2] The Sorosis of New York City was born of the indignation of Mrs. Croly when she was excluded from the press dinner to Dickens on the ground of her sex. It grew rapidly in numbers and influence; and it was talked of, envied and imitated all over the nation.[3] To thousands of women the club movement of the seventies opened new vistas of activity and usefulness. These women, busy during the war with innumerable new tasks, could not go back to the sheltered idleness of the fifties. At first the clubs were conservative in aim,

[1] *U. S. Twelfth Census* (1900), volume on *Occupations*, xlix ff.
[2] Laura E. Richards and Maud Howe Elliott, *Julia Ward Howe* (Boston, 1916), I, 283 ff.
[3] H. A. Bruce, *Woman in the Making of America* (Boston, 1912), 228; Mrs. J. C. Croly, *Jennie Juneiana: Talks on Women's Topics* (Boston, 1864); Schlesinger, *New Viewpoints*, 150-151.

emphasizing study and cultural pursuits, but with the example of the New England Club before them, they soon annexed large provinces of civic and philanthropic activity. "They make women strong-minded," an irritated male remarked. "At any rate," rejoined Lucy Stone, "that is better than being weak-minded!" Meanwhile, of course, some outstanding women were pursuing reform activities quite independently. One was Clara Barton, a native of Massachusetts, who began in these years her patient crusade for American membership in the Red Cross.[1] Another was Elizabeth C. Hobson, the foremost figure in the great movement—inspired partly by Florence Nightingale's work in England—which led to the opening in 1873 of schools of nursing at Bellevue in New York City and in Boston, New Haven and Philadelphia hospitals.[2]

The greatest single force supporting the principal humanitarian movements of the time was, of course, the church, though its organized participation seemed singularly slender. The American people were a thoroughly religious people, and the denominations exercised an immense power in behalf of such causes as temperance. The country had 72,459 church congregations in 1870 with more than sixty-three thousand buildings in use. The Methodists, with 25,278 congregations, stood first, attesting the evangelical energy of Wesley's followers; then came the Baptists with 15,829 congregations, and the Presbyterians with 7,824; while the Catholics made a fast-growing fourth, with 4,127 churches.[3]

These sects were by no means as harmonious as they should have been. When the war closed, the Meth-

[1] W. E. Barton, *Life of Clara Barton* (Boston, 1922), II, chaps. viii-x.
[2] On hospital training schools, see *N. Y. Eve. Post*, July 16, 1876.
[3] *Compendium, U. S. Ninth Census* (1870), 514-527.

odists, Baptists and Presbyterians were divided into hostile sectional organizations, North and South, and in all three denominations this schism persisted. The Catholics and Episcopalians fortunately escaped any such division. Necessarily the cleavage was damaging to church morale and vigor, and the exasperations which accompanied it were unchristian. Yet its consequences were not wholly evil, as the Southern Presbyterian Church showed by its brave and independent labors among the freedmen, challenging the emulation of the Northern branch. Moreover, in matters of doctrine there was a growing tendency in most churches to overlook former differences, and the Old and New School Presbyterians of the North, long separated, were joyously reunited in 1869.[1]

In the country as a whole the devotion of the greater part of the population to religious ideals rendered the prestige of the clergy, especially in educated communities, very high. They were, to a notable extent, the intellectual as well as moral leaders of society, and were encouraged in the large cities to take a prominent part in public affairs.[2]

Two ministers, in fact, stood out as great national leaders: Henry Ward Beecher and Phillips Brooks. The strength of Beecher lay, as earlier, in his oratorical power, his strong faith in righteousness, his unconventionality of discourse, and, not least, his adherence to a theology adapted to the needs of the day. He accepted evolution and preached its essential principles with boldness. Phil-

---

[1] L. W. Bacon, *History of American Christianity* (Philip Schaff and others, eds., *American Church History Series*, XIII, N. Y., 1895), 351-355; Mark Mohler, "The Episcopal Church and National Reconciliation," *Pol. Sci. Quar.*, XLI, 567-595.

[2] T. D. Woolsey and others, *The First Century of the Republic* (N. Y., 1876), 485; R. E. Thompson, *History of the Presbyterian Church* (*American Church History Series*, VI), chap. xiv.

lips Brooks, a finer scholar and a man of higher literary gifts, was distinguished chiefly as an intensely earnest preacher, whose eloquence enforced spiritual truths with a rare power. There were other ministers whose influence, though more local, was powerful—Henry W. Bellows and O. B. Frothingham in New York, James Freeman Clarke in Boston, and William H. Furness in Philadelphia.[1] Though the clergy as a whole was then, as later, shockingly ill-paid—in the whole state of Connecticut just after the war only seven ministers received twenty-five hundred dollars a year and none more than three thousand—its power was very great. The half-starved pastor of a small town would almost invariably be found serving on school committees, managing the lyceum, taking charge of charitable enterprises, delivering addresses and, in short, acting as a community leader.

Yet the church of this mid-Victorian period was thoroughly conventional in its methods and organization.[2] Though social life was changing rapidly, it failed to respond. The cities were expanding, immigrants were arriving by millions, and the nation was fast being industrialized, but the church clung in the main to the aims of a rural age. The most spectacular religious enterprise of the seventies was the series of revivals held by Dwight L. Moody, an eloquent but narrowly dogmatic exhorter, and his aid, Ira D. Sankey, who possessed a fine tenor voice and a gift for the direction of massed choirs. These revivals were conducted in many parts of the country and excited wide attention even in the great cities.

[1] Of the many lives of Beecher, the most valuable are W. C. Beecher, Samuel Scoville and Mrs. H. W. Beecher, *A Biography of Henry Ward Beecher* (N. Y., 1888), and Lyman Abbott, *Henry Ward Beecher*, (Boston, 1903). See A. V. G. Allen, *Life and Letters of Phillips Brooks* (N. Y., 1900), and D. D. Addison, *The Clergy in American Life and Letters* (London, 1900), chaps. ix and x.

[2] H. K. Rowe, *History of Religion in the United States* (N. Y., 1924), 141 ff.

Much needless worry was caused among the religious by the "Continental Sabbath," one of the results of the immigrant invasion.   Still more alarm was felt among Protestants over a supposed intent of the Catholic Church to gain control of education, or to obtain a share of the public-school funds for its parochial schools.   Certain moves in the latter direction in the early seventies in New York evoked a stern popular resentment, which was voiced aggressively in *Harper's Weekly*, inspired some of the best cartoons of Nast, and drew emphatic statements from President Grant and other national leaders.

The chief social force of a religious nature was not a denominational agency at all, but the Young Men's Christian Association which had been introduced from England into the United States in the fifties.   By 1874 its branches were thickly sown in this country and Canada, numbering very nearly a thousand and counting fully a hundred thousand members.   Of these branches more than a hundred either owned buildings or had funds for the purpose of erecting them.   The Young Women's Christian Association, which had come into existence before 1865 for the benefit of girls in stores and offices, also found a soil in which it flourished.   Both organizations exhibited a healthy movement away from mere religious activities toward study classes, lectures, concerts and athletics.[1]   But of efforts to go into the city districts where newly arrived immigrants lived and combine charitable and evangelical activities in the slums, there were few.

If the humanitarian activities of these years, seen as a whole, betray many glaring gaps and strange oversights, we must remember that the labors and agencies of our own time will seem, to the view of posterity, very nearly

[1] See *Nation*, IV, May 16, 1867, on the decline of church-going; XIII, Dec. 7, 1871, on the Young Men's Christian Association.

as ragged and inadequate. Social needs always outrun social provision to meet them. The seventies were strangely indifferent to many evils other than those we have mentioned. They paid no attention to the fraudulent and health-wrecking nature of the patent-medicine business, with its enormous sale of kidney pills, tonics, bitters and blood purifiers. Though nearly all groceries were commonly adulterated, sometimes in the most unhealthful way, there was no movement on foot for purer foods.[1] Cream was mixed with gums and white glue; oleomargarine was frequently adulterated with horse fat; baking powders were largely made of alum; and it was said that at least half the vinegar sold in the large cities contained poisonous preparations of lead, copper or sulphuric acid. There was no systematic effort to reduce the high infant mortality of the time, and dark ignorance was manifest everywhere in the care of young children.

The wealthy philanthropist, too, was singularly rare when we consider how rapidly fortunes were being piled up. Above all other givers of the day loomed the benignant figure of George Peabody, born in America but of London residence, whose occasional visits evoked a fervent welcome. Gladstone said of him that "he taught us how a man may be master of his fortune, not its slave." Indeed, his benevolences amounted in the aggregate to eight and a half million dollars. The greatest single object to which he devoted his wealth was the promotion of education in the South, to which he gave, as endowment of the Peabody Fund, in 1867, three and a half million dollars; but he was also a liberal benefactor of cultural institutions at the North. It was unfortunate for the country that there were not more men like him or Peter Cooper, or even like A. T. Stewart, whose philanthropies were smaller but highly credi-

[1] *Appletons' Ann. Cyclop.*, XIX (1879), 2 ff.

table.[1]   The gifts of James Lenox and Samuel J. Tilden toward what is now the great public library in New York, of Vanderbilt and Cornell to found new universities, were evidence of an increasing sense of the heavy public obligation imposed by the possession of wealth. But this obligation was not so fully recognized as it was in the next generation.   Yet, despite all reservations, the thirteen years after the war may be pronounced years of creditable progress in liberal and humanitarian fields.

[1] For contemporary sketches of Peabody and Stewart, see *Am. Ann. Cyclop.*, IX (1869), 557, and XV (1875), 735.

CHAPTER XIII

RECOVERY IN SOUTH AND WEST
(1873-1878)

WHILE the spirit of humanitarianism was showing a steady growth throughout the nation, conditions in the South revealed a marked improvement over the dark years immediately following the war. Politically, it is true, the white Southerners found their cup brimming over with bitterness during Grant's first administration; but economically and socially, even in these confused years, there was a certain amount of progress. The use of federal authority to support the enfranchised Negroes insured the temporary domination of nine states (Virginia and Texas escaped) by the grotesque tyranny of Carpetbaggers and freedmen,[1] and the sufferers of this tyranny had to content themselves with covert and irregular obstruction. For several years the South was racked by an upheaval of violence and disorder unparalleled in our history. Then in one state after another, as Grant's first term ended and his second advanced, the craft and tenacity of the whites triumphed. To outward view the turmoil seemed to deaden most of the constructive energies of the Lower South and to add new losses to those resulting from the war; but a short period of peace proved that its effects had not been so disastrous as the Southerners had supposed.[2]

The history of all governments upheld by the bayonet

[1] See *U. S. Statutes at Large*, XIV, 428, for the famous Reconstruction act of 1867.

[2] W. A. Dunning, *Reconstruction, Political and Economic* (A. B. Hart, ed., *The American Nation*, N. Y., 1904-1913, XII), chaps. xi, xiii.

shows that some secret organization for resistance, like the Carbonari of Italy or the Tugendbund of Germany, is almost certain to spring into violent activity. None of these bodies is more picturesque than the Ku Klux Klan. First organized, in 1866, in Pulaski, Tennessee, it spread rapidly to other states. In 1867 a grand convention in Nashville gave the Klan the name of "the Invisible Empire," chose General Nathan B. Forrest its Grand Wizard, and appointed a hierarchy of subordinate officers— Genii, Grand Dragons, Grand Titans and Grand Cyclops.[1] The activities of the night-riding members, disguised with robes and masks, at once attracted national attention. Primarily an agency for terrifying unruly blacks and disciplining troublesome Carpetbaggers, the Klan accomplished, especially at the outset, certain healthy objects. It was really needed in those communities where the Negroes were heavily predominant and had fallen under the sway of malevolent white men.[2]

There was, however, another and worse side of its activities. While thousands of reputable Southerners joined the Klan and a similar body called the Knights of the White Camelia with the intention of using only orderly means of maintaining the ascendancy of their race, thousands of irresponsible and reckless men also joined. Outrages were soon being perpetrated on a wide scale, in some of which the Klan had no part but for others of which it was blamable.[3] Just in proportion as the Radicals in Congress aroused anger by their measures, the Klan and the Camelia showed aggressive-

[1] For constitution and ritual, see W. L. Fleming, ed., *Documentary History of Reconstruction* (Cleveland, 1906-1907), II. chap. xii.

[2] See A. W. Tourgee, *A Fool's Errand* (N. Y., 1879), for a picture of a Carpetbagger's experiences.

[3] The activities of the Klan are thoroughly treated in the congressional *Ku Klux Report*, occupying thirteen volumes of *House Rep.*, 42 Cong., 2 sess., no. 22.

ness and turbulence. They recruited their members, in many districts, from ready-made bands of vigilantes which had already sprung up on the model of the pre-war slave patrol. They were encouraged, moreover, by a sectional tradition of violence which for generations had marked life in the South and which had grown appallingly stronger as the war closed.[1]

The fall campaigns of 1868 sent a portentous wave of disorder across the states in which Congress seemed to be assuring a Negro domination. In South Carolina there was a series of political assassinations designed to keep the Negroes from the polls.[2] In Mississippi the Klan resorted to numerous murders and assaults for the same purpose. In Alabama, where ten thousand men were enrolled in the Klan, the lawlessness was even more pronounced.[3] But it was in Louisiana that conditions became most alarming. General Rousseau compared the population of New Orleans to a volcano ready for an explosion. Cutthroat gangs giving themselves such names as the "Seymour Tigers" or "Swamp Fox Rangers" roamed the town assaulting harmless Negroes, and in some of the outlying parishes murder was committed on a wholesale scale, the Negroes being killed like vermin.[4] Frightened by the degeneration of the Klan, General Forrest and his aids formally dissolved it in March, 1869, and after that date, though it maintained vitality for some time, it steadily lost cohesion and strength.[5] As the state and national organizations dis-

[1] C. W. Ramsdell, *Reconstruction in Texas* (Columbia Univ., *Studies*, XXXVI), 219; *House Exec. Doc.*, 42 Cong., 2 sess., no. 268.

[2] A. A. Taylor, *The Negro in South Carolina* (Wash., 1924), 189.

[3] J. W. Garner, *Reconstruction in Mississippi* (N. Y., 1901), 287; Secretary of War, *Report for 1870*.

[4] *Ku Klux Report*, I, 20 ff.

[5] J. C. Lester and D. L. Wilson, *The Ku Klux Klan, Its Origin, Growth and Disbandment* (N. Y., 1905), 128. But see S. L. Davis, *Authentic History of the Ku Klux Klan* (N. Y., 1924), 125.

appeared, most of the outrages became simply the work of local mobs. The dissolution of the Freedmen's Bureau in 1869, with the departure of its officials from every district and county, removed in some states a restraint of great value. In one capital after another legislation was passed in an effort to cope with the terrorism. Thus "Parson" Brownlow, the Radical governor of Tennessee, called his legislature in special session during 1868, and night riders who disturbed the peace were made liable to a penitentiary term of not less than five years. Moreover, the communities which connived at or failed to prevent Klan outrages were subjected to pecuniary damages.[1] Other states followed with drastic legislation, and in several it was made legal to hunt down and shoot any disguised man. When such enactments proved totally useless, the federal government took a hand. In the spring of 1871, simultaneously with an inquiry by a congressional committee, the so-called Ku Klux law came into effect, declaring that groups of rebels might be regarded as "unlawful combinations" against the national government and that, in any terrorized community, the president might suspend the writ of *habeas corpus* and declare martial law.[2]

In June, 1871, the first important trials under the Ku Klux act took place in Oxford, Mississippi, where after stormy scenes—for the town rapidly filled with excited men who threatened a clash with the soldiery— indictments were found against twenty or thirty night riders.[3] In South Carolina nine intractable counties were quickly brought to a more sober temper, and when it became evident that the United States was in grim earnest, dozens of mob ringleaders fled to Mexico or the

[1] *Acts of Tennessee, for 1868* (Extra Session), 18 ff.
[2] *U. S. Statutes at Large*, XVII, 13.
[3] *Ku Klux Report* (Mississippi volume), 936 ff.

Caribbean islands. Many others were arrested and taken to Columbia for trial, where there were a number of convictions and sentences of imprisonment.[1] Wherever disorder raised its head in other parts of the South, federal troops were quickly dispatched. Their use evoked a storm of Southern wrath, but it was effective in hastening the return of peace. Thus by the time of the presidential campaign of 1872, the South was in a virtual state of subjection to armed force.[2]

To Southern whites the one rift in the gloom was the fact that in some of the states their party, the "Conservatives," by dint of superior numbers, or adroitness, was triumphing over the "Radical" elements. The Republicans lost control of Tennessee as early as 1869, and Georgia and North Carolina were "redeemed" by the Democrats in the following year. But this left the six states of Florida, South Carolina, Alabama, Mississippi, Louisiana and Arkansas, all with a heavy majority of Negro voters, struggling still to escape from the slough. The disparity between the numbers of the races was such that the Conservatives were but little assisted by the congressional restoration of suffrage and the right to hold office, in 1871-1872, to almost all the Southern whites.[3] It is not the story of corruption, incompetence and extravagance at the six state capitals which most concerns us here; it is the social effects of this misgovernment. Such a carnival of misrule as took place throughout the Lower South, such bickering between the Radical factions as convulsed Louisiana, could not fail to depress all business and all society.[4]

[1] J. S. Reynolds, *Reconstruction in South Carolina* (Columbia, 1905), chap. v.
[2] Dunning, *Reconstruction, Political and Economic*, 205.
[3] *U. S. Statutes at Large*, XVII, 142.
[4] A prejudiced but interesting treatment is H. A. Herbert, ed., *Why the Solid South?* (N. Y., 1890). The *Ku Klux Report* puts the increase

The grafting and extravagance were most spectacular in South Carolina, where the Carpetbaggers and their Negro followers stole with barefaced impudence under Governors Scott and Moses, and stopped only when the third Radical governor, Chamberlain, took steps in 1874 to end the scandal.[1] Here in the state house at Columbia the marble countenances of Robert Y. Hayne and George McDuffie looked down upon the strangest legislative body that has ever sat in the United States, three fourths of its members colored men of every hue from the octoroon's swarthy pallor to the deepest black and of every type from the polished house servant to the rough field hand. The rascalities perpetrated under the cloak of a purchase of "supplies" or "sundries" were almost ludicrous. These entries covered such items as Westphalia hams, imported mushrooms, plush velvet *tête-à-têtes*, garters, chemises, gold watches, perfumes and a metal coffin. The agency of government which was kept in the most efficient operation was the fine barroom of the state house, which was open from eight in the morning till two or four o'clock at night, though large quantities of wine and spirits were also sent to the members' rooms. During four years more than two hundred thousand dollars was spent for state-house furniture, leaving at the end just $17,715 worth in the building. In refurnishing the capitol the grafters bought $650 French mirrors, $60 chairs, $600 timepieces and $60 imported china spittoons.[2] But it was not in such crude and obvious ways that the greatest thefts were perpetrated. School funds were stolen; money in huge quantities was wasted in railways and other internal "improvements;" and the

in the debt of the eleven states between the beginning of Reconstruction and 1872 at nearly one hundred and thirty-two million dollars.

[1] Vividly described in J. S. Pike, *The Prostrate State* (N. Y., 1874).

[2] South Carolina Assembly, Committee on Frauds, *Report for 1877*; *Nation* (N. Y.), XXIII, Feb. 28, 1877.

Treasury was looted by every possible means. In other states the peculations were hardly less glaring.[1]

The social and economic evils flowing from this mismanagement of Reconstruction were enormous. The embitterment of racial relations, the destruction of white morale, the interference with labor readjustments, the strengthening of the old Southern curse of violence, were in all a calamity which defies measurement. But some faint indication of the force of the evil may be found in one aspect of it which can be gauged with fair precision —the increase in tax burdens and the depression of property values. The people of Arkansas, when Reconstruction began in 1868, owed about $3,500,000 in state debt, had almost no county debt, and possessed $319,000 in the treasury. Seven years later the state owed at least $15,700,000, and most of the counties were practically bankrupt. For this huge burden of debt of $115 for every voter, the Arkansans had practically nothing to show.[2] The situation in Louisiana was even worse. The state tax rose from forty-five cents on the hundred dollars in 1861 to $2.15 in 1872; yet in spite of these cruel levies, the debt increased from about $11,000,000 just after the war to $50,597,000 at the beginning of 1875.[3]

No other part of the Union was half so poor as the South; yet the South groaned under levies which were unapproached elsewhere. The first census after the war showed that, despite a much lower per-capita wealth, the state charges in Louisiana were $21.85 for every thousand dollars' worth of property, against $7.47 in New York; in Mississippi they were $17.86 as against $6.44

[1] See Garner, *Reconstruction in Mississippi*, 190, 203-204; C. W. Ramsdell, *Reconstruction in Texas*, 205.
[2] Charles Nordhoff, *The Cotton States in the Spring and Summer of 1875* (N. Y., 1876), 29 ff.
[3] Nordhoff, *The Cotton States in 1875*, 45-51.

in Pennsylvania. With every year until the Reconstruction governments were overthrown, the burden tended to grow heavier.[1] When computed according to wealth, it was a more oppressive taxation, in all probability, than has ever been borne before or since in the United States. The consequence was a general inability of property values in the Lower South to rally as they should have done. Edward King wrote in *Scribner's* in 1874 that there were hundreds of investment opportunities in South Carolina that would never be utilized so long as the tyrannical and corrupt government remained in power. He found valuable plantations in Louisiana abandoned and a strong conviction prevalent that to invest in New Orleans was utter folly.[2] Visitors to Montgomery in 1874 found the market place filled with auctioneers presiding over sheriffs' sales, while the town and surrounding country complained of poverty and even destitution.

Yet the depression could not continue, for politically the disease brought its own remedy in a determined movement by the white voters to throw off forever the burden that had been saddled upon them. In the elections of 1874 Alabama and Arkansas were carried by the Conservatives, who also came close to victory in Louisiana and Florida, while in South Carolina a Radical governor pledged to reform was chosen. Early in 1875 the Conservatives made good their claim to control of the lower house in Louisiana.[3] Not even a state like Mississippi, where the Negro majority was overwhelming, could long resist the tide. Armed clubs, organized by white leaders, showed themselves ready to plunge the

[1] See tables in the *Nation*, XIV (1872), 198 ff.

[2] Edward King, "The Great South," *Scribner's Monthly*, VI (1873), 257-288.

[3] For the struggle in Arkansas preceding the Democratic victory, see J. M. Harrell, *The Brooks and Baxter War* (St. Louis, 1893); Powell Clayton, *The Aftermath of the Civil War in Arkansas* (N. Y., 1915).

state into racial warfare to redeem its government, and the Radical governor was reluctantly forced to compromise with them.   In the fall of 1875 the Conservatives carried the state elections by a majority of thirty thousand, and their legislature immediately forced the resignation of the governor and superintendent of education.[1] Thus by the summer of 1876 the political revolution which gave the white Southerners full control of their states was seen to be approaching completion.   Only Florida, Louisiana and South Carolina remained in Radical hands.   That fall the Conservatives waged a desperate struggle with such success that the election left in each of the three states two sets of claimants for office.   In Florida the Democratic candidates were promptly seated; but in Louisiana and South Carolina they were not permitted to take control until the newly seated President Hayes made it clear that he would refuse to allow the use of federal bayonets to compel acceptance of the Republican nominees.[2]

The news of race riots and brutal clashes abruptly ceased.   The Negroes, where well-behaved, were, except in rare instances, left unmolested, and their rights were far more fully recognized than ever before.   Everywhere the Southern population felt a new impulse of hope, a sense that now their land, with the last hated Northern garrison withdrawn, belonged to themselves.   They had time to breathe freely and to look about them.   Within a year or two it was borne in upon them that, after all, progress had not been halted in even the darkest Reconstruction days.   A great part of the producing area had been little affected by the Reconstruction maladies; while for the obvious reason that Southern wealth rested upon

[1] Garner, *Reconstruction in Mississippi*, 196-200.
[2] P. L. Haworth, *The Hayes-Tilden Disputed Presidential Election* (Cleveland, 1906), 92 ff., treats both state contests in detail.

agriculture, it felt the effects of the industrial depression after 1873 much more slightly than the North. The cotton yields rose almost steadily and prices remained good.[1] Farmers who had never made money since the war made it during these years, and every season the South emerged with less debt than before. In 1875 the *Financial Chronicle* pointed to the wonderful change in a half-dozen commonwealths, and predicted that the North would some day be surprised at the wealth quietly developed in the section. Here and there, as in North Carolina, poverty remained the rule. Moreover, the unprecedented yield of cotton was not a wholly favorable sign, for it meant that there was too little mixed farming, too much of the old one-crop system, with its vicious credit basis. Yet despite the handicap of this system, which often permitted the local dealer to appropriate one fifth or one fourth the whole crop in return for advancing money and supplies, the section as a whole was prospering.[2]

In the South in general the number of small farmers continued to increase, partly through the break-up of old plantations, partly through the occupation of neglected lands. It was a section in which the poor man, white or black, found it remarkably easy to establish his independence. Not merely Arkansas and Texas but Louisiana, Georgia and Florida each had millions of acres lying uncultivated at prices so low that the farmer could pay for his holdings from the profits of two first-rate cotton crops.[3] In North Carolina, a half-empty commonwealth, fair cotton land even in 1878 could be had for five dollars an acre and up. The small farmers of Geor-

[1] See *Commercial and Financial Chronicle* (N. Y.), Sept. 13, 1879, for summary.

[2] For the one-crop system and its evils, see E. A. Smith, "Report on Cotton Production in Alabama," *U. S. Tenth Census* (1880).

[3] U. S. Commissioner of Agriculture, *Report for 1874*, 215 ff.

gia were observed by the Centennial year to be a remarkably prosperous class. They had little or no debt, money circulated rapidly, and steady improvements were seen in their buildings, implements and methods. Across the Mississippi River a pioneer agriculture was fast pushing west and south. The movement of settlers virtually doubled the population of Texas in the seventies and almost trebled the number of farms, while it sent the population of Arkansas past the million mark early in the eighties.[1] The whole social texture of the South was changing. Year by year it was becoming a more democratic region, one decidedly more modern and alert in its outlook and much more like the Middle West in its manners and psychology.

This transformation was materially assisted in the late seventies by the development of a considerable list of resources besides agriculture. Railways had pushed into regions which possessed mineral or lumber wealth. Thus the yellow-pine region of Arkansas was penetrated by the Missouri Pacific and the Iron Mountain lines, and countless sawmills sprang up; while in Alabama and Tennessee rich new coal and iron districts were tapped by rail. In 1870 the site of Birmingham was a cotton field. The following year a land company, with railway support, founded the city, and by 1878 it was a thriving iron center with more than three thousand people. The production of coal in Alabama exceeded two hundred thousand tons that year, and the census just afterward credited her with fourteen steel and iron plants.[2] Cotton, despite a paucity of capital after the Panic, furnished the basis for a vigorous manufacturing industry in the South. The production of cotton-seed oil and oil cake became

[1] *Compendium, U. S. Tenth Census* (1880), 333.
[2] *Appletons' Annual Cyclopedia* (N. Y., 1876-1902), XVI (1876), 8; Fleming, *Reconstruction in Alabama,* 767 ff.

important in Louisiana and Texas, while the census of 1880 showed North Carolina to have thirty-three textile factories,[1] Georgia forty-four, Alabama eighteen, South Carolina fourteen, and Mississippi nine. In Tennessee and Georgia the value of the annual lumber output had reached nearly five million dollars. North Carolina boasted of no fewer than one hundred and eighteen tobacco establishments, with a product valued at two million two hundred and fifteen thousand dollars, while the making of sugar and molasses employed much capital in Louisiana. New Orleans, still the great Southern metropolis, possessed five large refineries by the end of the seventies.[2] Industrial and railway centers, such as Chattanooga and El Paso, which had hardly been heard of before the war, sprang into prominence.

The sturdy growth of manufacturing gave the South an entirely new social and economic class, composed of the mill operative, the miner and the foundryman. Particularly did the textile industry confer invaluable advantages upon the poor whites who furnished most of its hands. It gave employment to girls and women who would otherwise have remained household drudges; it increased the family income and raised the standard of living; and it was the means of offering a rather abject and miserable rural population a taste of a wider, livelier town life. The child-labor evil which accompanied it was not yet regarded with much reprobation. All over the South the income yielded by the new industries had a stimulating effect, and by 1878 the worst phases of poverty were vanishing. "Within the last year or two," one Southerner wrote, "broadcloth is often seen and

---

[1] See Nordhoff, The Cotton States, 108; Appletons' Ann. Cyclop., XVI (1876), 609.

[2] For Southern industry, see Compendium, U. S. Tenth Census (1880), 944 ff.

ladies wear costly outfits." Carriages were still little used, as being too costly, but well-kept buggies were numerous. A strong taste for travel had revived, and mountain resorts, watering places and mineral springs were finding a large custom, while the practice of going to Northern centers was being resumed. Indeed, the love of travel was now more widely spread than before the war, having been stimulated by the campaigning of the conflict and the breaking-up of old homes and associations. In cities like New Orleans, Richmond and Charleston the *ante-bellum* festivities were fast reviving.[1]

Not merely the worst of the poverty but the worst of the old provincialism, aristocratic arrogance and quarrelsomeness was disappearing. It was now possible to engage in trade or the baser professions without loss of caste. In the *ante-bellum* South a gentleman could be a planter, a lawyer or an officeholder, but little else; now young men crowded into business with alacrity, and felt pride in attaining distinction as physicians, journalists, teachers or engineers. The section was no longer dominated by a semifeudal set of rural ideals. The spirit of lawless individualism which had long been one of the curses of the section could not be stamped out in a few years, and manifested itself in countless personal affrays, duels and murders based upon a mistaken idea of "honor." But little by little the social, the ethical and the intellectual codes of the South were being modernized.

No element in this revolution was more remarkable than the change in the status of women, a change produced primarily by the rough buffets which sent Southern girls to work outside the home. In the old days they had moved in an atmosphere compounded of Cavalier

[1] A South Carolinian (*pseud.*), "South Carolina Society," *Atlantic Monthly*, XXXIX (1877), 682.

tradition, the *Waverley* romances and pure moonshine. But the outcome of the war compelled them to become equals instead of weak dependents.[1] It forced tens of thousands of sheltered women to do all the washing, cooking and sewing; it sent innumerable widows and orphaned daughters to support themselves by opening boarding houses, acting as dressmakers, or managing shops. In rural districts the oversight of many a plantation and farm fell upon feminine shoulders. A multitude of Southern girls married the crippled wrecks who came back from the battlefields, and helped establish new homes by labor in the schoolroom, over the counter and in garden and field. Thanks to the rebirth of Southern education, within a generation it was asserted that the public schools had made it possible for every maiden, however humbly born, to become independent. This new outlook of womanhood seemed to many old-fashioned people profoundly disturbing, and they asserted that the young men no longer paid women a proper deference; but shrewd observers perceived that the change in standards was wholesome.[2]

The rise of a new Southern culture, of a society that knew and cared about books, newspapers and schools far more than before, was also evident by 1878. After all the educational turmoil and errors of Reconstruction days, an uneven but distinctly valuable school heritage had been left by the Carpetbaggers. For the first time, mandatory provisions for free public education were generally found written into Southern constitutions. For the first time, too, provision was made for a uniform system of school taxation and for the education of

[1] A. W. Calhoun, *A Social History of the American Family* (Cleveland, 1917), III, 11 ff.

[2] J. L. Underwood, *Women of the Confederacy* (N. Y., 1906), 65; see also W. F. Tillett, "Southern Womanhood as Affected by the War," *Century Mag.*, XLIII (1891-1892), 9-16.

Negro children. Such a state as South Carolina, which had kept its public schools on the pauper level before the war, was now forced to give them respectability, place them under adequate state supervision, and raise their enrollment year by year. By the Centennial year more than fifty thousand white and seventy thousand colored children were in the South Carolina schools.[1] All over the section there was a rapid strengthening of public education.

Southern colleges and universities shared in the educational revival. Indeed, there is no more heartening chapter in Southern history than that which relates their grim persistence against a flood of calamities—the poverty of their old supporters, the refusal of the Carpetbag legislatures to appropriate state funds to any but coracial institutions, the enforced admission of Negroes to the administration and classes. The Louisiana State University was kept alive by the devotion of Colonel David French Boyd, its president, and a few heroic professors, who remained at their posts without pay to prevent the seizure and sale of the property.[2] Too poor to buy clothes, to eat butter or sugar, to afford the slightest material or intellectual luxury, the faculty struggled on, though the university often seemed at its last gasp; one session had an average attendance of only four professors and six students. The University of Mississippi fared somewhat better, for though several Carpetbaggers and Scalawags were placed on the board of trustees, the resources were not quite cut off. In South Carolina the whites actually lost control of the state university for a time. Several Negro trustees were appointed and the

[1] E. W. Knight, *The Influence of Reconstruction on Education in the South* (Teachers College, Columbia Univ., *Contribs. to Education*, no. 60), 88 ff.
[2] Fleming, *Documentary History of Reconstruction*, II, 199.

doors opened to Negro students, whereupon the faculty members resigned and the young aristocrats of the state angrily erased their names from the books; but all this was quickly ended when the whites regained political ascendancy, and the institution slowly recovered after 1876. The universities of North Carolina and Alabama were made "Radical" and declined to utter insignificance; but they also began a steady revival as strictly white institutions after the Centennial year.

Thus, all together, when the nation took stock of its resources at the end of the seventies, the "New South" was already a reality. Many of its people were better educated, better clothed, better governed, and more thoughtful and alert than when the incubus of slavery, with all the fictitious wealth it represented, rested upon their shoulders. Yet they still faced a multitude of problems dismaying in their complexity and gravity. Great numbers of the whites remained, as they had been during Reconstruction, poor, ill-educated, overburdened, and filled with resentment against the North. The old kindliness and pleasantness of Southern life seemed to have disappeared. Under pressure of the war and its aftermath, and of the fiercer competition of the new era, the former hospitality, geniality, and individualistic flavor of existence had been lost. But the section as a whole was upon an improved basis, adjusting itself to a sounder economic system, and responding to higher social and intellectual ideals.

However amazing the recovery of the war-stricken South, it was surpassed by the construction of a wholly new America in the West. This process, so far as may be judged from outward appearances, suffered little check from the Panic and the ensuing depression. Indeed, the Northern and Western farmer whose lot had been so harsh in the late sixties and early seventies found himself at least in many localities, in a comparatively happy position as the seventies wore on.   The hard times touched him but indirectly and lightly.   Hamlin Garland has related for us the history of a typical Western family tilling three hundred acres of Iowa prairie during these years.[1]   Month by month settlement thickened and the comforts of civilization increased.   The wild meadows were fenced; lanes of barbed wire replaced the winding wagon trails; groves of Lombard poplar and larch took the place of aspen, hazel and cottonwood.   Baseball nines sprang up, and the Eastern newcomers brought fairs, conventions and Fourth-of-July picnics.   Here and there a farmer added an ell to his house, and painted his barn.   The daughter of the Garland household wanted an organ, the mother ingrain carpets, and the boys a spring wagon.   A steadily improving collection of farm machinery lightened the burdens of the husbandmen. There occurred a year or two, thanks to the appointment of the elder Garland as superintendent of a Grangers' elevator, of town life, lasting until the farmers proved so much readier to take a speculator's price from the commercial elevators than a fair market price from their own that the enterprise failed.   The crops were enormous and the prices good; only when the weather turned against the farmer, or the chinch-bug, debouching from northern Illinois and southern Wisconsin, threatened the prairie wheat, did the pinch of poverty return.

These were years of increasing crop yields, of fair if not steady prices and of dropping transportation costs, during which it became evident, both abroad and at home, that America was immeasurably the world's greatest single source of food.[2]   The fertile prairies, netted by

[1] Hamlin Garland, *A Son of the Middle Border* (N. Y., 1917), 173 ff.
[2] Finlay Dun, *American Farming and Foods* (London, 1881), 421 ff.; *Appletons' Ann. Cyclop.*, XIX (1879), 165.

a railway system which brought them next door to the European capitals, were forcing the yeoman farmer of Yorkshire and the *junker* of Prussia to the wall. American bread was baked for the table of the Berlin workman, American cheese was eaten by the French artisan, and American bacon used for the breakfast of the British clerk. The farmer still endured a multitude of hardships and many injustices, but he had an interlude of five years of lighter burdens and increased compensations. Wheat growing was stimulated between 1875 and 1880 by a series of crop failures in Western Europe which, causing a demand that had never existed before, could be satisfied only by heavy American imports.[1] Argentina as yet was wholly unknown as a factor in the world's wheat trade, shipments from India were almost negligible, and even Russia sent but a small quantity westward compared with her later exports. In short, the prairie farmer occupied a favored position in an eager market. Nor was it by wheat exports alone that he turned a handsome penny. The provision merchants of London and other European cities sold our pork and corned beef in large quantities, while in 1875 there sprang up a brisk trade in refrigerated meats.[2]

In Oregon and Washington the number of farms more than doubled in the seventies and the value of livestock more than trebled. This region plainly needed only clear railways to California and the Great Lakes to leap forward in startling fashion; and the railways were coming. But it was in Utah that the changes of the decade were most important. These changes preceded the death of Brigham Young, and were traceable to the steady seeping in of an immigration which gave Utah 144,000

[1] D. A. Wells, *Recent Economic Changes* (N. Y., 1889), 172 ff.
[2] J. T. Critchell and Joseph Raymond, *A History of the Frozen Meat Trade* (London, 1912), 190 ff.

people by 1880.   Brigham Young's end on Aug. 29, 1878, removing the last of a great group of state builders—for Heber Kimball had died in 1868 and George Smith in 1875—merely attested the durability of the Mormon institutions.   His funeral occasioned such an outburst of popular grief as the West has seldom witnessed.[1]   But those who had supposed that his death would result in church schisms and disintegration found themselves mistaken.[2]   After a brief interregnum John Taylor, an Englishman by birth and the president of the Twelve Apostles, became head of the church.   The real weakening of the Mormon theocracy was caused by the steady increase of the Gentile community in strength. Utah would have grown still faster than it did but for the difficulty of marketing agricultural products.[3]

On the great plains the cowboy was now in his heyday and the cattle kings were reaching the height of their prosperity.   Texas alone by the late seventies had five and a half million cattle, while all the range lands of the far Northwest were being occupied.   Indeed, even from Oregon and British Columbia increasing numbers of shapely, compact beeves, of a better stamp than the Texas longhorns, were herded over the Rockies and grazed for a year in Wyoming, upper Colorado or Nebraska before being sold.   In the wide expanse of the Great West by 1878 there were probably eleven million or more cattle.[4]   Stock raising in Montana had resulted as early as 1874 in the driving of large herds to the Union Pacific stations and was now a thriving industry, its round-ups and other features carefully regulated by

[1] Deseret News Steam Printing Establishment, *Death of President Young* (Salt Lake City, 1877).

[2] L. E. Young, *The Founding of Utah* (N. Y., 1923), chap xl.

[3] H. H. Bancroft, *History of the Pacific States of North America* (San Fran., 1882-1890), XXI, 750 ff.

[4] Secretary of War, *Report for 1878*, 38 ff.

the legislature. The price of meat rose rapidly, and whereas ordinary stock cattle for range herds had sold for four or five dollars in 1874, by 1878 they were worth eight dollars a head. The packing industry expanded, the size of the herds increased, and moneyed newcomers from Britain and the Eastern states poured in to give the cattle business a higher, more systematic organization.[1] Great ranching corporations were organized, and began to crowd upon the private cattlemen. They and others introduced blooded bulls, and the stock was rapidly improved. Live cattle were now also being shipped abroad in astonishing numbers, visibly affecting the English market, while in the late seventies America grew to be the largest exporter of cheese in the world, sending nearly sixty thousand tons in 1878 to England alone.

The fertile West responded to the world's need with a series of record-breaking crops. The total yield of all cereals increased from a little more than 1,500,000,000 bushels in 1873 to more than 2,400,000,000 in 1879.[2] It was enabled to do this partly by the abundance of labor and partly by the continuous improvement in farm machinery. The heavy gang plow, the spring-toothed harrow, the McCormick self-rake harvester, with five hands binding grain behind it, and the hay loader were now seen almost everywhere. The corn planter of modern type, which drops the corn in even crossrows permitting of two-way cultivation, also came into widespread use late in the seventies.[3] On the great

[1] R. A. Clemen, *The American Livestock and Meat Industry* (N. Y., 1923), 185 ff.

[2] See Dun, *American Farming*, 435; Edward Atkinson, *The Distribution of Products* (N. Y., 1885), 231 ff.

[3] Waldemar Kaempffert, ed., *Popular History of American Invention* (N. Y., 1924), II, chap. vii; A. H. Sanford, *Story of Agriculture in the United States* (Boston, 1916), chaps. xii-xiii. For farm wages, see U. S. Commissioner of Agriculture, *Report for 1879*, 145.

farms of the Pacific slope the combined harvester and thresher, drawn by a steam engine and pouring out twelve bushels of grain a minute, was already familiar. Science was lending a greater and greater aid to the farmer—a fact attested by the circulation of such books as Emerson and Flint's excellent *Manual of Agriculture* and by the establishment of the nation's first agricultural experiment station in Connecticut in 1875.

When the farmer faced the problem of transporting his wheat and corn to market, he found himself, thanks partly to the Granger legislation but most largely to the intense rivalry among many railway lines, fairly free from the piratical gouging he had suffered before the Panic. Whereas before that event the ordinary Chicago-New York rate had been about twenty cents a bushel, by the spring of 1876 it was down to twelve cents, and it was reported that some contracts had been made for nine cents.[1] The result was an unprecedented increase in rail traffic and sore distress among the lake and canal companies. The lines west of Chicago maintained somewhat exorbitant rates, but even these were measurably reduced. In consequence, and despite much overcharging by elevator men and commission dealers, the farmer's price for wheat came ever closer to the New York price. Hardly once between the Panic and the close of 1878, a period when all other products were sagging, did the price of no. 2 spring wheat fall below $1.10 in the Eastern markets, while it repeatedly exceeded $1.50 and averaged between $1.30 and $1.40—figures which, in view of the increased purchasing power of the dollar, spelt a very satisfactory return.[2]   Other

---

[1] Atkinson, *Distribution of Products*, 231 ff.; same author, *Industrial Progress of the Nation* (N. Y., 1890), 33 ff.

[2] See Atkinson, *Distribution of Products*, 246 ff., for New York prices in gold of staple farm products.

prices also remained high—so very high that in 1876 and later the cost of meats elicited widespread complaint from British and American consumers.[1] The farmer was not growing rich, indeed, much poverty remained; but in some Western districts he was being partly compensated for his sufferings of a few years earlier.

The worst years for agriculture, as measured by wheat prices, were 1874–1875; but in compensation these were years of comparatively high returns for the corn farmer, particularly in the eastern half of the great North Central region. Indeed, the first year after the Panic was one of almost unprecedented profits for the corn grower of this belt. In the Centennial year the farmer did not do so well; but in 1877 the crops of the North and West were good and the prices were high. Wheat reached 85 cents a bushel in December at the Iowa markets, and the wheat farmers of the whole North Central region, according to government statistics, had an average gross return of no less than $15.11 an acre. It is no wonder that Eastern financial journals, reviewing the year, spoke of the farmers' position as exceptionally good. In 1878 there was a slump—though the same journals continued to speak of agriculture as doing well—but 1879 was once more a year of exceptional prosperity. The wheat growers of the eastern North Central states, according to the same government figures, made the astonishing sum of $20.72 gross an acre. Farther west they fared much worse. But it is impossible to measure the farmers' profits and losses by crop prices alone. He was now benefiting greatly in the Middle West by increased crop diversification. He could buy his manufactured commodities at reduced prices, while labor costs were falling. He knew better how to meet blizzard, drought and chinch bug. As population increased and land values

[1] N. Y. World, Feb. 22, 1876.

doubled and trebled, he reaped a rich "unearned increment." [1]

With industry paying so badly while farming paid slightly better than before, and with many a man raising twenty dollars' worth of wheat on land that had cost him only ten dollars, population did continue to increase rapidly. In 1874 the final entries under the homestead act exceeded one and a half million acres; in 1874, two million acres; and in 1878, more than two and a half million. Many workmen from the cities and towns took permanently to the land. The population of Minnesota rose in this decade from 440,000 to 780,000, and that of Nebraska from 123,000 to 452,000. The westward drift of men of small capital was reflected in the first formidable appearance of farm tenancy as a feature of American agriculture. The census of 1880 showed that about a fourth of the farmers of the country did not own their land, and that tenancy was greatest in the Negro districts and the new regions of the West. But most Western tenants were simply young men who were rapidly saving money to buy land, and who within a few years would own the farms which they were working.

Largely because of their new economic welfare, the Western farmers in the late seventies showed less and less legislative activity. They were also chilled by the defective operation of the ill-drawn Granger laws. Thus, Minnesota in 1875 repealed her rate-regulatory law and provided for a single railway commissioner with general powers of inspection and little more; Wisconsin the following year abandoned her stringent Granger law;

---

[1] Crop prices are carefully tabulated in *Bulletins* no. 514 and 515 of the United States Department of Agriculture (1917), entitled "Wheat, Yields Per Acre and Prices, by States, 1866-1915," and "Corn, Yields Per Acre and Prices, by States, 1866-1915." See the *Commercial and Financial Chronicle's* January reviews of the preceding year, 1878 and 1879.

and Iowa did likewise in 1878. The half-formed farmers' parties were melting away and disappearing into the Greenback movement, which was far from being a purely agrarian party. The Greenback-Labor alliance polled a million votes in 1878, but its platform dealt with currency and labor questions rather than with direct farm grievances. Its chief appeal in the West was to the debtor class, to resentment against the contraction of greenbacks and the demonetization of silver, and to dissatisfaction with the presidential settlement of 1876. This Western debtor sentiment forced the passage of the Bland-Allison silver-coinage act of 1878. Naturally, also, the Grange lost strength. Its rather disastrous coöperative ventures discredited it; and its social and educational objects did not suffice to hold the attention of members who had little economic interest in it. An atmosphere of comparative quiescence spread over parts of the Middle West.

Yet events were to prove it only temporary. The elements of future revolt were still there needing only to be reawakened by another wave of hard times. The mortgaged farmer still groaned under outrageous interest charges by Eastern capitalists.[1] In Minnesota the exactions of elevator companies and the alleged manipulations of a millers' "ring" gave Ignatius Donnelly,[2] campaigning against them, a strong following. Indeed, the Western branch of the Greenback-Labor party, recruiting its strength chiefly among the farmers, though malcontents and soft-money enthusiasts of every calling joined, cast more than a half-million votes in 1878. The West could not hope for an indefinite continuance of high European prices, and the amazing grain yields of

[1] *Com. and Fin. Chron.*, Jan. 20, 1877.
[2] J. D. Hicks, "Political Career of Ignatius Donnelly," *Miss. Valley Hist. Rev.*, VIII, 80 ff.

1878 and 1879, a biennium in which nearly five billion bushels were poured upon the world, broke the markets sharply and revealed the fact that the problem of a glut would soon be formidable.

On every hand occurred kaleidoscopic changes in population and development. Not merely the larger cities—Chicago with 500,000 people, St. Louis with 350,000, San Francisco with 235,000, Kansas City with 56,000, Minneapolis and St. Paul with 88,000—showed unceasing growth, but new cities emerged all over the West. By 1878 settlement in Kansas and Nebraska had overspread all the well-watered area, and along the streams—the Republican, the South Platte, the Kansas and the Arkansas—had reached the western boundaries. In Minnesota in 1870 the frontier line of population still clung to Lake Michigan on the north, but now it thrust west along the Canadian border till it met the ninety-seventh meridian. The tide of farmers overlapped into eastern Dakota, green each spring with wheat, and was steadily pressing west and north. Colorado, the Centennial state, made an amazing growth, the belt of settlement widening from a narrow strip along the immediate base of the Rockies to cover the greater part of the mountains and plains—nearly two hundred thousand people.[1]

While in the West as a whole mining was irresistibly being thrust into second place by agriculture, two great stampedes in rapid succession—the Black Hills gold rush of 1875-1876 and the Leadville silver rush of 1877-1878—attracted national attention. Both had all the picturesqueness of the Nevada and Montana rushes a decade earlier, and the former involved the nation in another outbreak of Indian hostilities, while it helped lay the foundation for a new state. Rumors of the exist-

[1] *U. S. Tenth Census* (1880), volume on *Population*, xix-xx.

ence of gold in the Black Hills, then part of the Sioux reservation in Dakota, aroused a feverish eagerness, as the year 1875 opened, to invade the reservation.[1] During the summer troops under Sheridan, Terry and Crook succeeded in damming back most of the eager throng of miners, but it was clear that next year the tide would overpower them. The stage was set for an Indian war. With the beginning of 1876 gold hunters poured into the Black Hills so rapidly that there were four thousand there by March 4; the angry Sioux took the warpath under Red Cloud and Spotted Tail; and the fighting which followed had a tragic climax when Custer, pursuing the enemy, was drawn into ambush and his force annihilated on June 25, 1876.[2] But the Indians were quickly worsted. The opening of mines, which in the next quarter century were destined to furnish a hundred million dollars' worth of precious metals, and the expulsion of the Sioux were factors of first importance in preparing the way for statehood.

Greater romance, if far less difficulty and danger, attached to the discovery, or rather rediscovery, of mineral wealth at Leadville.[3] Here gold had been found early in the sixties, and Oro City had risen, roared with life and died to a shell. Placer mining had feebly continued, and for sixteen years "heavy sands" and huge boulders which interfered with the work had been moved to one side. But in 1876 an investigative miner took

[1] R. I. Dodge, *The Black Hills* (N. Y., 1876), 16 ff.; *Senate Exec. Docs.*, 44 Cong., 1 sess., no. 51; Secretary of the Interior, *Report for 1875;* 686 ff.; *1876,* 390 ff.

[2] Secretary of War, *Report for 1876;* F. S. Dellenbaugh, *George A. Custer (True Stories of Great Americans*, N. Y., 1917), chap. xix; J. K. Dixon, *The Vanishing Race* (Garden City, N. Y., 1913), 168 ff.; P. E. Byrne, *Soldiers of the Plains* (N. Y., 1926), 104.

[3] Frank Fossett, *Colorado: A Historical, Descriptive, and Statistical Work* (Denver, 1876), 404 ff.; H. H. Bancroft, *Pacific States*, XX, chap. ix.

samples of ore which yielded between twenty and forty ounces of silver to the ton, and further exploration revealed enormous lead carbonate deposits rich in silver. Leadville in the late summer of 1877 consisted of some twenty shanties; by the end of 1879 the population was estimated at thirty-five thousand.[1] In Leadville, in Deadwood, in several other swarming new mining towns of the West, there were repeated the scenes of turbulence and dissipation which had made Virginia City and Bannack notorious a decade earlier.[2]

California, a nation in itself, stood apart from the remainder of the West in the complexity of its social scene. The growth of population, the depression consequent upon the Panic and the decreased flow of gold from the mines, the liberation of an army of Chinese from the work of railway building, all combined to produce a critical social situation which came to a climax in 1877-1878 at a period of unprecedented distress among the laboring people. The crash of mine stocks and the Eastern depression had thrown on the streets thousands of ignorant workmen responsive to any incendiary agitator. They had genuine grievances. There was some truth in the charge that the Chinese, nearly one hundred and fifty thousand of whom were now under the control of six great Chinese companies, had forced down wages and narrowed the scope of employment; in the shoe factories, for example, the Chinese outnumbered the whites four to one, and the pay had declined from twenty dollars a week in 1870 to nine dollars in 1878.[3] These and other themes of discontent were seized upon by labor agitators, foremost among

---

[1] *Appletons' Ann. Cyclop.*, XIX (1879), 156 ff.
[2] Bancroft, *Pacific States*, XX, chap. ix.
[3] Charles Nordhoff, *California for Health, Pleasure, and Residence* (N. Y., 1883), chap. xiv.

whom was Dennis Kearney, a young Irish ex-sailor who owned a draying business, and whose earnest, flashy eloquence made him the idol of the more violent workingmen. He began addressing great mass meetings on the sand lots, his mouth "full of oaths, gallowses, and conflagrations," and inciting his hearers to violence against the wealthy residents of the city, on the one hand, the poor persecuted Chinese on the other. The radical laboring men of San Francisco were quickly organized into a political party, which set forth a series of vigorous demands: that the government should be wrested from the hands of overweening millionaires; that the country should be rid of cheap Chinese labor; and that land monopoly be destroyed by effective legislation.[1]

It was evidence of the sound sense of Californians that, while the movement failed utterly in its appeal to violence, it scored a complete victory in its demand for social and political reform. The labor party elected a constitutional convention, which in 1878-1879 gave the state a greatly improved instrument of government. Heavy restrictions were laid on the legislature, which had come to be regarded as a tool of rich corporate and private interests; lobbying was made a felony; provisions were inserted for the taxation and control of railways, steamship lines and other carriers and corporations; and storage and wharfage charges were placed under state regulation.[2] It was high time. In this great and wealthy state the amount of poverty was shocking, and a few thousand citizens were rich while hundreds of thousands eked out a bare existence, their chances to rise in life unnaturally restricted by corporate and individual selfishness.

[1] J. F. Rhodes, A History of the United States (N. Y., 1893-1919), VIII, 186.
[2] Bancroft, Pacific States, XIX, 351 ff., 373 ff.

California laborers had no welcome for the Chinese.

The Ku Klux Klan operating in North Carolina.

White Supremacy in the Seventies.

Though of the eight hundred and fifty thousand people of the state hardly one quarter lived upon farms, California dated the definite ascendancy of the farming interest over all others from the early seventies. Not only did the small farmers and fruit growers steadily encroach upon the "cow country" but also upon the vast farming estates, which the passing years were steadily proving to be unprofitable.[1] These estates were an unquestionable evil, stunting the growth of the commonwealth, and limiting opportunity and equality to an extent which inspired in Henry George—a California editor throughout these years—the zeal for land and tax reform which found expression in *Progress and Poverty* (1879). Some of the largest farms, like that of Dr. Glenn at Jacinto, were famous. Lying on the west bank of the Sacramento, twenty-three thousand acres of this enormous holding were under cultivation and a much larger area lying fallow. Glenn kept hundreds of men, fifteen hundred horses and mules, and a line of fifty gang plows busy at one time.

One social trait of the fast-growing West, its deference toward women, was of increasing national importance. The freedom of the West offered women new careers and broadened activities, and because women were so badly needed, they attained a new dignity in the social scale. California just after the war had three men for every woman, Washington had four, Nevada eight, and Colorado twenty. So great was the demand for a feminine element in the Pacific Northwest that a whole shipload of women was sent out from New York, by special arrangement, to be teachers, clerks and housekeepers. Women were "objects of a sort of crude, fierce worship" and were treated not merely as man's equals but "as a

[1] J. S. Hittell, *Resources of California* (San Fran., 7th edn., 1879), chap. viii.

strange and costly creation," whose whim ought to be
law. If unmarried the attractive woman had suitors
without end, and if married, she could warn her husband to be deferential—"if he don't, there's plenty
will." Women workers in a town like Denver commanded pay four times as high as in Chicago, with board
and room thrown in. The pioneer woman of the West,
moreover, in facing frontier conditions necessarily developed an individualism, resourcefulness and courage
which made men regard her with respect. She fought
Indians, she managed ranches, she preached, doctored
and taught. It was with good reason that the West
exalted woman to sovereignty, granting her social privileges unknown in the East, and that the Western school
of fiction paid her the same honor. When Wyoming
in 1869 gave universal suffrage to women, they at once
set to work and purged Cheyenne of its brothels and
gambling saloons and forced the nomination of better
territorial officers.[1]

In a hundred diverse ways it was evident by the close
of the seventies that the West was gaining maturity.
To attest the variety of its resources it had innumerable
new industries—salmon packing, wine making, fruit
growing, a great Northwestern lumber business, coal
mining in Colorado,[2] borax shipments from the Mojave
Desert. It had come into the closest contact with the
East in the decade since the completion of the transcontinental railway, and tourists were familiar with its
scenic wonders from Estes Park to the Yosemite. James
Gordon Bennett demonstrated in the Centennial year
just how close the two oceans had drawn by paying half
the cost of a special train which made the New York-

[1] W. M. Raine, *Wyoming, A Story of the Outdoor West* (N. Y.,
1908), 163 ff.
[2] For Colorado's varied development, see Secretary of the Interior,
Report for 1875, 122 ff.

San Francisco trip in eighty-three hours and thirty-four minutes. If the South showed where the reconstructive energies of the nation were working most vigorously, the Far West showed where its capacities for new construction were being most effectively expressed.

CHAPTER XIV

EMBATTLED INDUSTRY

(1873-1878)

THE Panic of 1873, like every other panic since 1837, was accompanied by convulsions in the field of labor. Indeed, the constant growth of unemployment, the cruel drop in wages and the general hopelessness of the industrial outlook produced in 1877 one of the most violent revolts of labor in American history. Somewhere between two and a quarter and three million people were idle who would gladly have worked,[1] and as all times of labor surplusage necessarily are, it was a black period for labor unions. Strikes were easily defeated, and the threat of a lockout was usually sufficient to enforce the acceptance of a wage cut. The employers, seeking to free themselves from the restrictions which labor had imposed in the boom years after the war, resorted to blacklists and legal prosecutions, so that it became difficult for unions to find men of ability and energy to serve as their leaders.[2] During the depression the number of really effective national trade unions fell from about thirty to eight or nine, most of which were nearly penniless.[3] In New York City, where the roster of union men had once reached forty-four thousand, it

[1] For the unemployment figures in Massachusetts from 1875 to 1878, see W. G. Moody, *Land and Labor in the United States* (N. Y., 1883), 160.

[2] G. E. McNeill, ed., *Labor Movement* (Boston, 1887), 398.

[3] Mary R. Beard, *A Short History of the American Labor Movement* (N. Y., 1920), 81.

dropped to about five thousand, and in Cincinnati to about one thousand.

As the manufacturers who engaged in blacklisting should have foreseen, an inevitable consequence was the formation of secret labor societies. The repression which drove Southerners into the Ku Klux Klan drove Northern workingmen into unions veiled by ritual, grip and password. One of the largest and mildest of the underground organizations was the Sovereigns of Industry, an indirect offshoot of the Grange, which by 1876 enrolled forty thousand members, most of them in New England. It gave prominence to coöperative purchasing activities, and never embarked on industrial warfare. Another was the Industrial Brotherhood, which gained sufficient strength to dominate the National Labor Congress in 1874.[1]

Most important of all was the Knights of Labor, which had been founded in Philadelphia as early as 1869,[2] and to the development of which we shall later refer. But the one which attracted the most attention in the mid-seventies was a sinister body among the Pennsylvania coal workers called the Molly Maguires.[3] It was a product, on the one side, of the harsh conditions under which the miners worked, and, on the other, of the naturally lawless temper of the Irish miners. At first the criminal activity had been unorganized, but the Molly Maguires arose as a secret ring which controlled

[1] J. R. Commons and Associates, *History of Labour in the United States* (N. Y., 1918), II, 17 ff., 196.
[2] T. V. Powderly, *Thirty Years of Labor* (Columbus, Ohio, 1890), 134.
[3] J. D. McCabe (*pseud.* E. W. Martin), *History of the Great Riots, together with a Full History of the Molly Maguires* (Phila., 1877); F. W. Dewees, *The Molly Maguires* (Phila., 1877), 160 ff.; J. F. Rhodes, *A History of the United States* (N. Y., 1893-1919), VIII, 52-87; Allan Pinkerton, *The Molly Maguires and the Detectives* (N. Y., 1878), 522.

the several lodges of the Ancient Order of Hibernians in the anthracite counties and directed and concealed the crimes. Its operations centered in Schuylkill and Carbon counties, though it was known throughout the anthracite area. It began resorting to secret acts of violence as early as 1862; and until it was crushed in 1876 through the efforts of one James McParlan, a Pinkerton detective who was employed by the enterprising head of the Reading Railroad, it made increasing use of assassination, mutilation, and destruction of property.

While such violence was happily an isolated phenomenon, the revolutionary tinge which the philosophy of the labor movement began to assume was noticeable all over the North. It was impossible for American socialism in its modern character to emerge till after the Civil War; it was inevitable that it should then emerge with considerable vigor. The Lassallean agitation in Germany, beginning in 1863, and the propagandist activities of the International Workingmen's Association, which Karl Marx founded in London in 1864, were two European sources from which it drew strength.[1] The large German immigration to the United States furnished a ready soil for its growth. In 1868 there appeared the Social party of New York, a short-lived organization of Lassallean views, and by the close of 1870 several sections—French, Bohemian and German —of the International Workingmen's Association had been formed. These foreign-born socialists found sympathy and assistance among some native American intellectuals who had imbibed the ideas of Fourier and Owen in the forties and fifties.[2]

Under the leadership of F. A. Sorge, a Saxon immi-

[1] Commons and Associates, *History of Labour*, II, 204.
[2] C. R. Fish, *Rise of the Common Man* (*A History of American Life*, VI), 189-190.

grant who deserves to be called the father of American socialism, the Marxian organization rapidly developed vigor and promise.[1] During the years just after the Panic, when the discontent and agitation among the workers offered them numerous recruits, it proved able, despite a vast deal of internal bickering, to extend its structure over a great part of the North and the Middle West, especially where the German-Americans were strong, and to call a considerable body of native Americans under its banner. The persistent quarrel between the Marxian and Lassallean wings, the former intent primarily upon building up strong trade unions and the latter eager rather for political action, was one of the chief factors in crippling it. Of course it was too weak to win any political victories, and it was repulsed in its efforts to gain control of the labor movement. The socialist delegates to the National Labor Convention convoked in Pittsburgh in 1876, who hoped to swing that body to the advocacy of state management of industry, were easily overpowered by the Greenback element. But the socialist leaders and journalists did lay a foundation for the more powerful movement of the early twentieth century.[2]

Meanwhile the hard-pressed workingmen of the United States were being irresistibly thrust into political activity of a more practical nature. In the wake of the Panic, workers' parties rapidly appeared not only in New York and Illinois but in Pennsylvania, Ohio and Connecticut. Everywhere that labor suffered from depression a ground swell of radicalism manifested itself. The campaign of 1872 had already been marked by a

---

[1] Morris Hillquit, *History of Socialism in the United States* (N. Y., 1910), 178-181, 187-191.

[2] Commons and Associates, *History of Labour*, II, 230 ff. R. T. Ely, *Labor Movement in America* (N. Y., 1886), analyzes the social forces at work.

convention of Labor Reformers in Ohio, attended by delegates from a dozen states, which first nominated David Davis and later Charles O'Conor for president. The party stood for a shorter workday (ten hours as the first step in factories), the grant of federal aid to co-operative undertakings, the extinction of monopolies, Chinese exclusion and universal education. Other labor conventions met, notably one in Massachusetts in 1875, which nominated Wendell Phillips for governor.[1] By the close of the Centennial year there were indications that this Labor Reform movement was headed toward an early fusion with the Greenback movement, which at the same time was rising like some tremendous tide among the farmers of the West and Northwest. The two had many differences, but also much in common; they might be regarded as really branches of a single party which was pressing certain industrial and economic issues that the two old parties refused to touch. United they might grow into a strong independent party, holding the balance of power between the Republicans and Democrats. On both sides, as 1878 opened, the demand for fusion was being voiced.[2]

That year, the fourth since the Panic, found many laboring men in what they felt an almost intolerable position, and yet one that was growing worse. In all the great cities, from Boston to Omaha, crowds of work-less and hungry men tramped the streets, hung disconsolately about the public squares, and joined in parades and mass meetings of protest.[3] To add to the discon-

[1] Workingmen in the election of 1876 cast but few of the Green-back-party votes for Peter Cooper. Commons and Associates, *Labour in the United States*, II, 240.

[2] Beard, *American Labor Movement*, 83; F. E. Haynes, *Third Parties in the United States* (Iowa City, 1919), chap. viii.

[3] For the earlier Tompkins Square riot in New York City, see *N. Y. Times*, Jan. 14, 1874. There were outbursts of violence by unemployed and hungry men in Cincinnati, Chicago and other cities in 1875-1876.

tent, one strike after another since the Panic had been ruthlessly crushed. Of a long series of labor defeats, one strike involving the anthracite workers of Pennsylvania [1] and another the toilers in the textile mills of New England,[2] attracted wide attention. Each occurred in 1875 and was the result of successive reductions of wages to starvation levels. Each resulted in the grimmest misery, the anthracite strike in especial involving women and children in a protracted ordeal of hunger and destitution. Workers the country over, watching them, were wrought up to a high pitch of uneasiness and indignation.

Such industrial battles as these were the prelude to the first great nation-wide conflict in American history: the railway strike of 1877. For some years events had been pointing to a desperate labor struggle on the transportation lines of the nation. Scores of railways were bankrupt, while others were hard pressed financially. The railway corporations saw themselves caught between the upper millstone of public regulation and the nether millstone of union demands. The employees, on the other hand, were exasperated by the repeated wage reductions in the years following 1873. On the New Jersey Central in 1875, for example, every engineer had stopped his train at midnight on a given day and left his engine where it stood—in field, roundhouse or on the street crossing. On the Grand Trunk between Detroit and Montreal a similar walkout had occurred. Since both strikes had been successful, the organizing agency—the

[1] Pennsylvania Secretary of Internal Affairs, *Annual Report for 1876-1877*, pt. iii; R. P. Porter, "The Truth about the Strike," *Galaxy*, XXIV (1877), 725; Andrew Roy, *History of the Coal Miners of the United States* (Columbus, Ohio, 1907), 99; Arthur Suffern, *Conciliation and Arbitration in the Coal Industry* (Boston, 1915), 213.

[2] *N. Y. Herald*, Jan. 19, 1876; McNeill, *Labor Movement*, 221 ff. French-Canadian immigrants began coming in to take the place of the strikers.

Brotherhood of Locomotive Engineers—gained an immense prestige from them, and its membership rose to fifty thousand or more.[1] Conductors, trainmen and trackmen as well as engineers belonged. Well financed, and ably led by its indefatigable head, P. M. Arthur, the union proved able to dictate terms in matters ranging from the reinstatement of a workman to the raising of wages.

The attitude of the seventies toward labor being what it was, it was natural for the railway managers to determine to break the strength of this powerful union. The corporations felt that they could count on public action to keep the roads clear for mails and necessary traffic. On the other hand, the railway men felt sure that a strike would be the signal for a sympathetic walkout in many other industries. Railway workers everywhere were chafing under unsteady work and lessened pay and eager for a demonstration of their bitterness. There should have been coöperation and mutual sympathy in meeting the burden of the industrial depression; instead, as the summer of 1877 opened, the atmosphere was electric with distrust and resentment.

The signal for the battle was a cut of ten per cent in railway wages, ordered in June and July, 1877, with peremptory suddenness for most lines east of the Mississippi. The first conflict came on the Baltimore & Ohio. On July 18, the day after the reduction became effective, strikers took possession of the B. & O. lines at many points and refused to let any freight trains leave. The governor of Maryland called out the whole militia force, and President Hayes [2] at once sent two hundred and fifty regulars to Martinsburg, West Virginia. At

[1] Commons and Associates, *History of Labour*, II, 67-68, 309.
[2] For his proclamation, see J. D. Richardson, ed., *Messages and Papers of the Presidents* (Wash., 1896-1899), VII, 447.

once the rail system of the nation north of the Potomac
and east of the Mississippi was half paralyzed. The
three other trunk lines to the west, the Erie, the New
York Central and the Pennsylvania, with their subsi-
diaries, were tied up; so were the coal roads, such as the
Lackawanna and the Reading. The strike spread across
the frontier to the Canada Southern, and beyond the
Mississippi to the Missouri Pacific and the St. Louis,
Kansas City and Northern. Its growth was essentially
spontaneous and the Brotherhood of Locomotive Engineers took no part in directing it.[1]

As the strike spread, it was accompanied by such de-
structive and bloody riots as the country had never before experienced in connection with labor troubles. The
desperation of the strikers, the presence of a large body
of tramps, and the increase in the "dangerous classes"
from the industrial malady, all furnished fuel for the
blaze. The first alarming outbreak occurred in Baltimore. Here on July 20 two regiments of the Maryland
militia were ordered under arms, one to proceed to Cumberland, Maryland, and restore the passage of trains, the
other to remain at the Baltimore armory. The former,
reaching Cumberland, was hemmed in there amid scenes
of disorder, and asked for reënforcements from the Baltimore troops.[2] When the latter marched out from the
Baltimore armory, they were greeted with brickbats,
stones and clubs. Revolver shots followed and the soldiers returned the fire. Many of the troops, pursued by
the infuriated crowd, had to take refuge in private homes
and escape by the back door or in civilian dress. When
the remainder entered the railway station in headlong
disorder, the structure was promptly set in flames. Only

---

[1] *Appletons' Annual Cyclopedia* (N. Y., 1861-1903), XVII (1877),
423 ff.
[2] Adjutant-General of Maryland, *Report for 1877.*

the arrival of the entire police force of the city, which stayed all night and repeatedly charged the mob, rescued the militia. When, the next day, federal troops arrived to restore order, nine persons had been killed, and more than a score lay wounded in Baltimore homes and hospitals.[1]

While the country was reading with alarm of this riot, a far graver disturbance had commenced in Pittsburgh.[2] With local feeling already highly inflamed, six hundred and fifty soldiers arrived on the scene from Philadelphia on Saturday afternoon, July 21. At five o'clock they came into collision with a large mob at the Twenty-eighth Street crossing, where the missiles of the rioters were met by several volleys of musketry and about twenty-five persons were slain and many wounded. As night fell, the troops were ordered into the round-house and machine shops to seek shelter. A fierce assault at once began on the roundhouse, and continued for hours by the light of blazing buildings and freight trains. The mob had broken into the gun shops, and volley after volley was poured into the windows. At dawn the roundhouse was set on fire by cars of flaming coke which had been pushed against it, and the military were in imminent danger of their lives. "Tired, hungry, worn out, surrounded by a mob of infuriated men yelling like demons, fire on nearly all sides of them, suffocated and blinded by smoke, with no chance to rest and little knowledge of what efforts were being made for their relief . . . the wonder is that they were not totally demoralized."[3] Yet they marched out and,

[1] Secretary of War, *Report for 1877;* J. A. Dacus, "The Great Strike," *Harper's Weekly,* Aug. 11, 1877.

[2] Rhodes, *History of the United States,* VIII, 23.

[3] Pennsylvania Legislative Committee on the Pittsburgh Riots, *Report for 1878,* I, 79, 176 ff., 485; *N. Y. Tribune* and *N. Y. Herald,* July 23-25, 1877.

*Union men taunting the "Blacklegs," Mahanoy City, Pa.,
1871.*

The great railroad strike of 1877—The Baltimore riot.

under a hail of bullets, retreated across the Allegheny River like veterans.

There had already begun a scene of shameful pillage, and with the mob now completely master of the situation, it steadily increased. Long lines of freight and passenger cars were broken open, looted and set on fire. The streets near the yards were filled with rioters carrying off furniture, clothing and provisions. Barrels of liquor were tapped and drunk on the spot; women appeared and seized laces, silks, parasols and small gas stoves. The incendiarism extended until two thousand freight cars, the machine shops, two roundhouses with one hundred and twenty-five locomotives, a grain elevator and other property had been destroyed. At three o'clock on Sunday afternoon the Union Depot, a large four-story building, was set in flames. The direct loss to the railways was variously estimated later at between three and ten million dollars, and the county actually paid damages of $2,765,891. As evening closed in and the mob began to enter private buildings and sack saloons, vigorous steps were for the first time taken to check the disorder. The next day armed companies of citizens appeared on the streets to reënforce the police, the entire militia of the state were out, and President Hayes ordered General Hancock to Philadelphia, where he immediately called for all the available troops of the Atlantic department.

As the rioting died down in Pittsburgh, however, it spread to other railway points east and west. In Reading on Monday, following the burning of a railway bridge, there occurred a skirmish between the militia and strikers, in which eleven men were killed and many wounded. Rioting at Buffalo on July 23, with danger at other points, led Governor Robinson to place the entire military force of the state under arms. As the strike reached the Mississippi Valley, the large rail centers, including Chicago, St. Louis and Indianapolis, were wholly cut off from the East, while sympathetic walkouts occurred in a wide range of industries. At Columbus and Zanesville, Ohio, crowds of miners, tramps and ruffians closed the mills, machine shops and factories, and were not quelled until the citizens themselves had enrolled in armed companies. In Chicago, four days after the Pittsburgh rioting, there was an angry collision between the police and the mob in which ten rioters were killed and scores were injured. United States regulars appeared immediately on the scene, and General Sheridan reached Chicago to take command on the twenty-ninth. In St. Louis a wild crowd surrounded the quarters of the police and firemen, taunting them and daring them to fight. San Francisco, Toledo, Louisville and other cities reported bloodshed and terrorism, and even in small towns a spark seemed enough to cause an explosion, while, to add to the dismay, news came that the coal miners were all striking.[1]

Despite the disorders, the railway strike aroused public sympathy, for the workers' objects seemed to have much justice behind them. The railway men asserted that they wanted only a living wage, declaring on the Baltimore and Ohio and some other lines that they were actually desperate from poverty. Here, they said, they could average only four days' work a week; they had to spend a good part of their wages in board at distant stations; and the pittance of from $1.35 to $1.75 a day paid to firemen and brakemen was insufficient for a decent existence. It appeared that on the New York Cen-

[1] Goldwin Smith, "The Labour War in the United States," Contemporary Rev., XII (1877), 529-541; R. P. Porter, "The Truth about the Strike," Galaxy, XXIV (1877), 725-732; Suffern, Conciliation and Arbitration, 234; Powderly, Thirty Years of Labor, 209-221.

tral the daily wage of firemen was but $1.58, and the average monthly pay $41.08. On other lines the situation was not always so bad, but it was grievous enough. The railways insisted that their wages were generally a third or more above those paid in 1860, and that the cost of living on January 1, 1877, was only 106 per cent of that on May 1, 1860; but the men replied that these figures were deceptive. We may well ask why such a line as the New York Central had cut its wages below what Vanderbilt admitted was a fair standard without requesting a single sacrifice of the shareholders. This great system had a nominal capital of about ninety million dollars, or twice its real capital, yet it stiffly maintained a dividend of eight per cent. Why should not Vanderbilt have reduced his rate to six per cent, an absolute easing of $1,780,000 annually, or far more than he was obtaining by the wage cut, with all the suffering and convulsion it entailed? [1]

The fact that within a surprisingly brief period the whole movement utterly collapsed throws light on the reasons for its disorders. The ill-paid men knew they did not have the means for a sustained effort, and the psychological effect of this knowledge had made many eager to strike a hard, violent blow. On July 26, the day of the rioting in Chicago, St. Louis and San Francisco, the workers showed signs of weakening in the East. Under the protection of the troops the trains quickly began running. The New York Central resumed full traffic on the twenty-sixth, and the Erie and the Pennsylvania on the twenty-seventh. By August 3 the revolt was ended on the most severely interrupted lines. "The property losses have to be made good by the taxpayers," said a Western newspaper. "The strikers have finally gone to work at the wages they

[1] *Springfield Republican*, Aug. 2, 1877.

refused. The dead are the only lucky ones in the entire affair." [1]

Indirectly, however, the great labor upheaval bore many of the fruits of success. Public attention was called to the fact that unemployment was greater than ever before in our history, that the suffering and despair of hundreds of thousands of workmen demanded sympathy, and that peremptory, czarlike edicts reducing wages by one tenth or more were really inexcusable. The railway managers learned what a terrible store of dynamite lay beneath their feet. With a general sense of shock the country, hitherto complacently sure that American society was too peaceful and prosperous to fear any such convulsions as France had just witnessed in the Commune, drew back as from an abyss.[2] Its first frightened impulse was to demand protection; many states passed conspiracy laws, while the old doctrine of malicious conspiracy was revived by some judges to strike at the labor unions.[3] Armories were hastily built. But while asking for protection against the lawless workmen, the public also demanded a more responsible and cautious attitude on the part of capital.

In spite of defeat, the labor movement reaped an important benefit in the emergence of a new spirit of solidarity among workingmen. The remarkable Greenback-Labor movement of 1878, in which the workers participated, was, in part, an aftermath of the strike.[4] As the name indicates, the party represented a union of the Greenback farmers of the West and the labor radicals

[1] *Iowa City Daily Press*, July 30, 1877.
[2] *Nation* (N. Y.), XXII, Aug. 2, 1877.
[3] *Nation*, XXII, Aug. 9, 1877; J. A. Dacus, "The Great Strike," *Harper's Weekly*, Aug. 18, 1877.
[4] Haynes, *Third Party Movements in the United States*, chap. x; for Greenback vote, see Edward Stanwood, *History of the Presidency* (Boston, 1898), 367, 409, 423.

of the East. The junction was effected at Toledo in February, where delegates from twenty-eight states united in declaring for "financial reform and industrial emancipation." Their demands covered a wide range of popular issues: currency inflation, free silver, encouragement of labor, discouragement of monopolies, exclusion of the Chinese, and the establishment of labor bureaus by the states and nation. A surprising popular support was elicited. More than a million ballots were cast for Greenback-Labor candidates, the greatest number of any third-party movement since the early days of the Republican party and fourteen Representatives were triumphantly seated in Congress.[1]

Meanwhile the first labor organization destined to a national scope and influence, the Knights of Labor, was beginning the reorganization which was to make possible its astonishing growth in the early eighties.[2] It had been founded four years after the war by Uriah S. Stephens, a Philadelphia garment cutter, and was a secret society with ritual, grip and password. Men usually called it "the five stars," with reference to the five asterisks that represented its title in all public notices. There were few restrictions upon membership, though it made an especial appeal to unskilled workers. At the beginning of the year 1878 a convention met at Reading, effected a central national organization and adopted a constitution.[3] As we should expect of an organization shaped during a period of harsh industrial depression, the Knights of Labor swung toward radical views. They followed the socialists in declaring that the state should

[1] E. E. Sparks, *National Development* (A. B. Hart, ed., *The American Nation*, N. Y., 1904-1918, XXIII), 144.
[2] F. T. Carlton, *History and Problems of Organized Labor* (Boston, 1911), 70 ff.
[3] Powderly, *Thirty Years of Labor*, 153 ff.; McNeill, *Labor Movement*, 251; Commons and Associates, *History of Labour*, II, 197 ff.

own and manage all public utilities, including railways. Socialistic, too, was their demand for a steady extension of coöperation, until private coöperative enterprises and government ownership between them should dominate a new and better society.

The year 1878 closed with the laboring classes still fumbling uncertainly for the type of association that would most effectively win them a betterment of conditions. Most of the surviving local trade unions held aloof from the Knights of Labor because it was of the "One Big Union" type and not a federated organization like the National Labor Union. Furthermore, they believed in wage bargaining, were hostile to political action and revolutionary theories, and had little taste for fraternizing with unskilled workmen. The highly trained craftsman felt he weakened the development of his union if he permitted any amalgamation with the weaker elements in industry. Such was the view of the cigar makers' union, and in particular of the president of local no. 144 in New York, an able young man named Samuel Gompers who had come to America from England during the war.[1] Gompers was aggressive, uncompromising, eager always to assert the power of the trade union, but firmly convinced that collective bargaining was the means to advance. During 1877 he had helped lead a desperate strike of the cigar makers against the tenement-house system of manufacturing, and had learned from its failure that a better method of organization was necessary—a method which would increase the membership dues for the purpose of building up a reserve fund, would offer benefit features in order to give the union stability, and would vest complete power over the local unions in the head of the national or international body. The railway unions, the typographical

[1] Commons and Associates, *History of Labour*, II, 306 ff., 321 ff.

union, the bricklayers' union and other bodies also held coldly apart from the Knights.

But labor had come a long road in the thirteen years since the Civil War. Its leaders during the sixties had regarded trade unions as the first step in a vast coöperative movement which should ultimately offer self-employment. The bodies which they organized, however, proved unable to survive the stress of unemployment and falling wages after 1873. In these black years had emerged a revolutionary movement, which in its extremer phase of German socialism had never become important, and which gave way to the milder but as yet quite impotent Knights of Labor, with its socialist and Greenback wings. However, in the background there was steadily and irresistibly emerging a new and formidable kind of trade unionism. Both types of organization had behind them the spirit of resentment left by the great revolt of 1877; in front of them they had the prosperity and strength of the new industrial period just dawning.

While labor was suffering a succession of misfortunes and defeats, capital found the hard times a blessing in disguise. From the standpoint of the business world, the dark years following 1873 were, in their enduring results, highly constructive. They took the whole excessive commercial structure built up during and after the war, knocked away the false and superfluous elements, strengthened those which were left, and began a drastic reorganization. Business was put on an athletic regimen; it became spare and fit and learned to use its wits to keep alive. As we shall see, the results were not long in showing themselves.

American manufacturers are at all times too ready to depend upon the "home market;" and one healthy effect of the Panic was to force them to supplement their reduced domestic demand by foreign conquests.[1] This took courage, for the depression was world-wide. But the circumstances were more favorable than a surface view indicated. It was an era in which new lands were being fast developed—Australia, Canada and other British colonies, Siberia and South America. American manufactures had a special adaptability to such lands. Our locomotives and railway cars were the only ones really suited to many freshly opened regions. American agricultural machinery went naturally to all countries where large-scale farming was practised, and the New Zealand farmer guided a South Bend plow while the Russian peasant drove a Chicago reaper. Indeed, the American iron and steel products broke into the European field in a way that alarmed Britons. The North British Railroad Company bought a fifteen-thousand-dollar steam shovel in America for its excavating, the first of the kind that England had seen, and even an American locomotive was sold to one of the English railways. Fruit syrups used in tropical America had once come from France, but the United States captured the entire trade by producing a richer, better flavored and cheap commodity.[2] A great many American factories, of course, sought and took orders at prices that meant no profit whatever, simply to keep their half-busy wheels turning. This activity, conjoined with the increasing shipments of farm products and the slump in imports, resulted in a decisive change in the balance of trade. The Centennial year saw the United States take a permanent place as a nation whose exports exceeded its imports. In only three years before that date (1857,

[1] See *Commercial and Financial Chronicle* (N. Y.), May 18, 1878, for a review of foreign trade expansion; Joseph Nimmo, jr., "American Manufacturing Interests," *N. Am. Rev.*, CXXXVI (1883), 507-525.

[2] *Appletons' Ann. Cyclop.*, XIX (1879), 189.

1862 and 1874), had the country shipped more goods abroad than it bought; in only three years during the rest of the century (1888, 1889 and 1894) did the imports exceed the sales.[1] It was a far-reaching change, which may be taken to mark the definite emergence of the United States as an industrial world power.

A natural process of concentration and consolidation in industry had been interrupted by the flush times after the war, and now it was suddenly accelerated and strengthened. Year by year thousands of weak, ill-managed businesses were thrown into bankruptcy—an average of no fewer than ninety-five hundred annually for the three years 1876-1878. Those survived which had the most capital, the greatest efficiency and the best marketing facilities. At the same time such leaders as Rockefeller perceived that cutthroat competition menaced the vitality of even the largest, best-managed plants. The result was the first slow and hazy shaping of those tendencies which in the eighties and nineties were to bring the trust problem before the nation as a giant menace. As yet there were no trusts anywhere, but there were pools and marketing or rate agreements, and they pointed out a broad highway toward monopoly.

The movement was led most spectacularly and effectively by the business genius who declared that "the American Beauty rose can be produced in its splendor and fragrance only by sacrificing the early buds which grow up around it." By 1870, it will be remembered, most of the smaller oil refineries had been obliged to

---

[1] See Katharine Coman, *Industrial History of the United States* (N. Y., 1910), 290 ff. This increase in exports coincided with a striking decay of the mercantile marine and shipbuilding, upon which British steel competition and the American tariff pressed disastrously. Already in 1865 the percentage of imports and exports carried in American bottoms was only 27.7; by 1879 it declined to 22.6. See D. A. Wells, *Our Merchant Marine* (N. Y., 1883).

capitulate to more efficient firms.[1] But John D. Rockefeller determined that a complete centralization should be
effected.   In 1872 he and other refiners, including William Rockefeller, O. H. Payne and H. M. Flagler, created
a great corporation—the South Improvement Company
—to obtain a monopolistic grip upon the Pennsylvania
oil by arranging for rebates from the railways serving
the oil regions.   The Pennsylvania, the New York Central and the Erie railways proved willing to grant heavy
rebates in view of the business which the new syndicate
felt able to guarantee—rebates heavy enough, indeed, to
crush all other refining agencies.   The Rockefeller interests further insisted that the railroads actually pay to
them a large part of the receipts from rival shippers!
But the moment the new arrangement went into effect
the independent producers rose in their wrath.   They
called meetings, drew up agreements, and laid so nearly
complete an embargo upon shipments to the South Improvement Company that it had to be disbanded.[2]

But Rockefeller kept up his fight.   The heavy overproduction of raw oil in the years 1873-1875 inclusive,
forcing petroleum rates down to ruinous levels, compelled one small refiner after another to go into bankruptcy or to sell out to larger corporations.   By the
year of the Panic the Standard Oil Company, which
Rockefeller had organized in Cleveland in June, 1870,
controlled one fifth of the oil capacity of the country,
and its profits that year were far in excess of a million
dollars.   This money was invested in extending the
business—a Rockefeller principle—in barrel factories, in
tank cars, in plant improvements and in gaining control

[1] G. H. Montague, *Rise and Progress of the Standard Oil Company*
(N. Y., 1903), 14-15.
[2] Montague, *Standard Oil*, 23-48; Ida M. Tarbell, *History of the
Standard Oil Company* (N. Y., 1904), I, chaps. ii-v.

of terminal facilities in New York.[1] All the while
Rockefeller continued to demand and to obtain special
favors in freight rates, and to make these rebates a
weapon in forcing competitive refiners to sell out to
him or accept his leadership. It is unnecessary to rehearse in detail the engrossing story of the steady rise
of the Standard Oil to dominance of the whole oil business. Its progress was irresistible. It formed a close
alliance with the Erie and the New York Central; it
carried on a bitter war with the Pennsylvania, which
had its own oil protégés, and utterly routed that line;
and it defeated all the interstate-commerce bills offered
in Congress—bills that would have quickly broken its
octopus grip.[2] As a result of these efforts, by the end
of 1878 the Standard Oil had perfected an "alliance"
which controlled virtually all the transportation of oil in
America, whether by railway or pipe line, and ninety-
five per cent of the refining. Its supremacy was unquestioned. In the path which Rockefeller had left were
strewn ruined men and abandoned plants; before him
lay an unquestioned control over tremendous sources of
wealth.

However harsh and at times unethical the practices of
the Standard Oil might be, the emergence of such a great
controlling organization was inevitable. One of the
conditions which made monopoly certain lay in the
railway practices of the period. The grant of special
rates to those shippers who, by superiority of capital or
enterprise, promised to supply the most freight was general, and the great lumbermen, the meat packers and
others profited only less than Rockefeller. A measure
of justification existed for such favors since the large
companies served as "eveners" of traffic. In the oil in-

[1] Tarbell, *Standard Oil Company*, I, 104-128.
[2] Montague, *Standard Oil*, 62-63.

dustry the fluctuation of production and prices, the uncertainty of the outlook three months in advance and the wastefulness of small companies, all militated in favor of a large-scale business. Monopoly was economical and efficient. It permitted the Standard Oil Company to exploit the export market to the utmost, to regulate home production in accordance with consumption, to place the refineries near the several markets, and to utilize by-products efficiently.

While one group of railroads coöperated with the refiners in establishing the petroleum monopoly, another group themselves established what closely approached a monopoly of anthracite. Here too all the conditions were favorable: a limited source of supply, which could be cornered, limited facilities for transportation, and a rapid disappearance of weak companies under the pressure of rising competitive costs. By 1870 the hard-coal business was practically controlled by six great corporations; the Reading Railroad, New Jersey Central Railroad, the Lehigh Valley Railroad, the Lackawanna Railroad, the Lehigh Coal and Navigation Company and the Pennsylvania Coal Company.[1]

What the railways did for coal and oil they naturally wished to do for themselves; and to the general public the most alarming movement toward monopoly was that of the trunk lines all over the country during the seventies. To railway heads, however, it seemed the only refuge from the ruin threatened by the rate wars of the period. These wars actually brought passenger fares between Cleveland and Boston in the summer of 1876 down to $6.50, while cattle were transported from Chicago to New York for a dollar a carload.[2] It was

[1] *Com. and Fin. Chron.*, Aug. 28, 1869; *N. Y. Tribune*, Sept. 8, 14, 1876.
[2] E. R. Johnson, *American Railway Transportation* (N. Y., 1903), 218; editorial, *N. Y. Tribune*, Sept. 12, 1876.

necessary to check the resulting losses by drastic measures. The first railway pool of real consequence was effected in the Middle West at the height of the Granger revolt, when the three great trunk lines between Omaha and Chicago, the Northwestern, the Rock Island and the Burlington, formed an association in 1870, agreeing that, since they had approximately the same facilities, they should divide the business equally. This agreement was successfully maintained throughout the seventies and was responsible for high freight rates. Other pools in the West and South, operating with more or less success, shortly sprang into existence.[1] Of especial importance was the Southern Railway and Steamship Association, developed under the masterful administration of Vice-President Albert Fink of the Louisville & Nashville. Originating in 1873, it grew rapidly to include most of the important lines of the old Confederacy, and it necessarily took on an elaborate organization. Rates on competitive traffic were determined by an executive committee which also apportioned the freight among the competing roads. At the end of the year each line paid a large part of its gross earnings into the pool, to be distributed by prearranged percentages.[2]

Much more difficult was the problem of arranging such agreements between the fiercely competing lines running from the Middle West to the Atlantic Seaboard; yet this also was accomplished. An understanding between the anthracite-coal roads in 1872 was quickly followed by efforts to control the relations between the trunk lines from Chicago to the coast. The first device was to arrange with certain large shippers to make them

[1] For early railway abuses, see N. Y. Assembly, *Document* no. 38 (1880); C. F. Adams, jr., *Railroads: their Origin and Problems* (N. Y., 1887).

[2] Slason Thompson, *Short History of American Railways* (N. Y., 1925), 196.

"eveners" of traffic; that is, they agreed to allot their freight among the several roads in such a way as to give each a stipulated share. The first eveners were the livestock shippers of Chicago and the Standard Oil of Cleveland, which were rewarded by rates that were utterly ruinous to their rivals.[1] There was a bitter outcry in the press and on political platforms, and in 1879 they were terminated; but already a better scheme to restrain competition was in hand. During 1877 two organizations were effected, one composed of the four great trunk lines, the Erie, the New York Central, the Pennsylvania and the Baltimore and Ohio; the other of the railways connecting Pittsburgh, Erie and Buffalo on the east with Chicago and St. Louis on the west. It was determined that of the westbound traffic from New York, the Erie and New York Central should each have thirty-three per cent, the Pennsylvania twenty-five per cent, and the Baltimore and Ohio nine per cent.

Not only the trend toward consolidation but also technical advances and inventions were stimulated by the Panic. Industry had to save money and utilize neglected materials as never before. Little by little, business was making use of the newest applications of chemistry, physics and engineering; little by little the sway of the rule-of-thumb superintendent was passing away and that of the expert technician arising. It now seems incredible that in the late sixties chemistry was virtually unknown as an agent in the manufacture of pig iron and steel; the blast-furnace manager of those days was a rough fellow who relied upon instinct to show him the condition of his furnace, as the dowser relied upon a hazel twig to locate oil. Nor was chemistry better known in the manufacture of soap, oil or paints. It is

[1] "Transportation and Sale of Meat Products," *Senate Report*, 51 Cong., 1 sess., III, no. 829.

an attested fact that a leading oil refiner spent thousands
of dollars just after the war in mixing perfumes with
the petroleum in an effort to deprive it of its offensive
odor.[1] Half the value of crude oil was still thrown
away, not merely because the gasoline engine was as yet
unknown but because industrial chemists had not
brought their test tubes to the discovery of its secrets.
Even in the field of mechanics slapdash methods reigned
almost absolute. In the seventies John Fritz, who
played so large a part in developing the steel industry,
used to make most of his drawings for new machinery
with a piece of chalk upon the floor of the pattern room,
and whenever a bit of mechanism was built, would announce: "'Now, boys, let's start her up and see why she
don't work."[2] The science of metallurgy was hardly
out of its swaddling clothes. Such an expert industry
as the making of optical glass, which had its feeble beginnings when Bausch and Lomb opened their Rochester
plant in the seventies, depended upon German assistance.

Much of Carnegie's success was attributable to his use
of scientific knowledge for the improvement of iron and
steel manufacture. At the Lucy Furnace, which he
erected in 1870, he employed a German chemist who
multiplied the effectiveness of the plant. Iron ore
which had enjoyed a high reputation was found in some
instances to be very poor, while mines which had been
neglected were discovered to be yielding a superior ore.
Nine tenths of all the gloomy uncertainties of pig-iron
manufacture melted away under the brilliant sun of
chemical science. The cheap ores of the celebrated Pilot
Knob Mine in Missouri had been despised, but the Ger-

---

[1] A. R. Leeds, "State Geological Surveys," *Pop. Sci. Mo.*, XIV (1873),
226-229; C. F. Chandler, "Report on the Quality of the Kerosene Oil
Sold in the Metropolitan District," N. Y. City Bd. of Health, *Annual
Report for 1870*, 3 ff.

[2] F. B. Copley, *Frederick W. Taylor* (N. Y., 1923), I, 101.

man aid found they were actually very rich and needed only special pains in the fluxing.[1]   Again, Carnegie began using certain profitable by-products which his competitors were ignorantly throwing away as wastes; for a time he bought the roll scale of a Cleveland rival, practically pure oxide of iron, at fifty cents a ton. With equal shrewdness he obtained control of the Dodds patents in England for carbonizing the faces of iron rails, and placed the first hard-headed rails in America on the sharp curves of the Pennsylvania Railroad, where the metals had worn out every six or eight weeks.

Where one corporation led others quickly followed. The Midvale Company in Philadelphia, for example, produced a group of daring innovators.   One was the president, William Sellers, who as a manufacturer of machine tools achieved a position comparable with that of Sir Joseph Whitworth in England.   An international jury which examined his display at the Centennial Exhibition paid it a glowing tribute and Whitworth himself called Sellers "the greatest mechanical engineer in the world."   One of his early draftsmen was Henry R. Towne, who in 1868 associated himself with Linus Yale in making the Yale and Towne locks and other ingenious and elaborate forms of hardware.   At Midvale, too, appeared Frederick W. Taylor, the future father of scientific management, a striking example of the new leader which only a highly organized and concentrated industry could produce. Cool and bold, he was animated by an intense faith in system, standardization and the application of scientific principles. Though not a college man, his was essentially the same outlook as that of the engineering graduates who were beginning to trickle into business.   The true science of engineer-

[1] Andrew Carnegie, *Autobiography of Andrew Carnegie* (Boston, 1920), 130 ff.

ing, said Taylor, started "when a few experts (who were invariably despised and sneered at by the engineers of their day) made the assertion that engineering practise should be founded upon exact knowledge of the facts rather than upon general experience and observation." He made himself one of these experts.[1] Industry was henceforth to need the help of science at every step, and the appearance of such men as Taylor showed that the fact was penetrating the industrial consciousness.

As the year 1878 came to a close there were indications here and there that the tide of depression had definitely turned and that a period of prosperity was near at hand. Railway building had revived. This was the year in which James J. Hill, with Canadian capital behind him, began the actual work of constructing what he called the St. Paul, Minneapolis, and Manitoba Railroad, destined to grow into the Great Northern. Another railway builder of eminence was stepping upon the stage in the person of Henry Villard, who in the years 1876-1879 was taking the steps in Oregon and Washington which were to enable him to complete the Northern Pacific. Foreign trade was mounting steadily. Immigration had begun sharply to increase, a sure evidence that employment was easier to find. The nation, in short, was emerging from one of the darkest half decades in its industrial history.[2]

If we were to select the one outstanding characteristic in which the America of 1878 differed from that of 1865, it might be summed up in the word "unity." When the war closed, the North was divided by a seem-

[1] Copley, *Taylor*, I, chap. x; see also *Frederick Winslow Taylor, a Memorial Volume* (N. Y., 1920), *passim*.

[2] J. G. Pyle, *Life of James J. Hill* (Garden City, N. Y., 1917), I, 63 ff.; Henry Villard, *Memoirs* (Boston, 1904), II, 131 ff.; *Commercial and Financial Chronicle*, Jan. 10, 1880.

ingly impassable line of hostility from the South; the Eastern states were farther removed from the Pacific slope than from Europe. The social conditions in Massachusetts and Alabama, in Pennsylvania and Colorado, were utterly dissimilar. Within these thirteen years important strides were made toward knitting the nation into closer unity politically, economically and culturally. The continental railways made it more compact; the newspaper, the magazine and the public school tended to make it more like-minded; the growth of wealth and the progress of industry gave it a greater identity of outlook. Sectional characteristics persisted, but even in the South, where the humiliations of Reconstruction still rankled, there was an increasing tendency for people to pride themselves on being participants in the common life of a great country. This growth of common traits and interests was to be greatly strengthened in the period of material and intellectual expansion just opening.

The chief element which supported this increased homogeneity was the economic revolution now evident throughout a great part of the nation. The North had emerged from the Civil War a full-panoplied industrial giant. Its people awoke to the realization of innumerable smoking factory towns, great slums, a strangely variegated tide of aliens pouring into the seaboard cities. This industrial conquest strode over the wide West, and even threw outposts into the new textile towns of the South. The Panic of 1873, which seemed to check the exuberant new commercial era, simply confirmed its sway, for the ensuing depression sheared away what was weak and false in the business structure and compelled a reorganization on stronger, more careful lines.

Yet the new industrialism was only the greatest among a hundred facts and tendencies which were remolding American life.   Despite its losses, the South could count an inestimable gain in the fact that, for the first time in history, it was adjusted to the healthful competitive forces, economic and social, of American life. The West of the Indian and buffalo had given way to a new West that was steadily losing every trace of wildness. The farmers had not merely shown a strength and cohesion undreamed of before; they had taken the lead in declaring that, if the industrial era had arrived, the excesses of industry must be checked by firm political control. The vicious tendencies of postwar readjustment were yielding to the idealism and progressivism typified by the civil-service-reform movement of Curtis and Schurz and by those reformers who, like Tilden, purified states and cities.   The universities had been transformed; the women's movement and the labor movement were rising to a new aggressiveness.   Between the Negro field hand and the Negroes who organized the Fisk University Jubilee Singers, what a gulf!   New forces in literature and art caught their color from the quicker, more vital tendencies of the time.   The Civil War had marked the end of one great era in American life; the dozen years of reorganization and readjustment which followed it marked the emergence of the new and modern republic.

CHAPTER XV

CRITICAL ESSAY ON AUTHORITIES

PHYSICAL SURVIVALS

MATERIAL illustrating industry and invention in the sixties and seventies is widely scattered. The original Sholes typewriter is in the museum of the Buffalo Historical Society. Specimens of Cyrus W. Field's Atlantic cables, 1865-1866, are in the National Museum in Washington, D. C. The same institution has an exhibit illustrating the development of photography, including stereoscopic portraits of postwar days and ambrotypes. At the Thomas A. Edison Laboratories in West Orange, New Jersey, are the original Edison phonograph and models illustrating Edison's work upon the telephone and electric light. The original of Lyman R. Blake's machine to sew shoe soles and uppers together is in the factory of the United Shoe Machinery Corporation at Beverly, Massachusetts, where are also models and photographs of machines later developed in shoe manufacturing. In Chicago both Swift and Company and Armour and Company have large collections of photographs, plans, sketches and similar material illustrating the development of the livestock-and-packing industry. The original Kelly steel converter is preserved by the Bethlehem Steel Company at its Cambria plant at Johnstown, Pennsylvania. A model of a petroleum refinery, together with other material upon the development of the petroleum industry, is to be found in the National Museum in Washington. The best commercial museum in the country is that in Philadelphia, with not merely a large library but also physical and pictorial material upon transportation and trade in this period. The Pullman Company in Chicago has models and illustrations of early Pullman cars.

A good agricultural museum is still a desideratum, but

the Department of Agriculture in Washington possesses the rudiments of one with pictures and a few models illustrating the improvement of farm machinery, the development of new crops and farm methods, and the rise of scientific agriculture. The offices of the International Harvester Company of America in Chicago possess many drawings, lithographs, photographs and models illustrating the development of the reaper. A museum maintained by the American Steel and Wire Company in Worcester, Massachusetts, contains full material on the early history of barbed wire. In the American Indian exhibits of the National Museum in Washington, and the exhibits of the Museum of the American Indian, Heye Foundation, in New York, is ample material for a study of Western Indian life in this period. The "Southwest Pavilion" of the Museum of Natural History in New York also contains varied collections upon the buffalo-hunting tribes and the village tribes of the Great Plains. Two Southern states, North Carolina in her Hall of History at Raleigh and Arkansas in her State Museum of History at Little Rock, have assembled a good many objects, pictures and records bearing upon Reconstruction. The Confederate Museum at Thirteenth and Clay Streets, Richmond, Virginia, while devoted in the main to war objects, also has exhibits upon Reconstruction.

The architectural remains of the period are many, and may be viewed in most towns and cities of the land. Trinity Church in Boston, completed in 1877, shows the perfection of the style evolved by Henry Hobson Richardson's study of the Romanesque churches of southern France. An admirable example of a fashionable home is to be found in the Theodore Roosevelt Memorial Museum at 26-28 East Twentieth Street, New York City. The furniture, hangings, pictures, bric-a-brac and books are in large part actual family possessions dating from Roosevelt's boyhood; the dwelling itself is an exact restoration. The current taste in sculpture is revealed by the numerous monuments erected to commemorate the exploits of the soldiers and sailors in the Civil War and in the popular "Rogers groups," a good collection of which can be found in the Essex Institute at Salem, Massachusetts. The best paintings of the period have been preserved in such galleries as the Metropolitan Museum of Art in New York City, the Boston Museum of Fine Arts and the Art Institute of Chicago. Feminine fashions are illustrated in the Essex Institute by carefully selected models, and in the National Museum by dresses worn by the wives of Presidents Grant, Hayes and Garfield. In general, pictorial representations of the significant industrial, agricultural, intellectual and artistic productions of these years can be found in R. H. Gabriel, ed., *The Pageant of America* (15 vols., New Haven, 1926-   ), of which seven volumes have appeared.

GENERAL BIBLIOGRAPHY

The bibliographical chapters appended to W. A. Dunning, *Reconstruction: Political and Economic, 1865-1877,* and E. E. Sparks, *National Development, 1877-1885,* in A. B. Hart, ed., *The American Nation: a History* (28 vols., N. Y., 1904-1918, XXII and XXIII), are sketchy but indicate some of the main sources for this period. Briefer but more recent bibliographies are appended to the following volumes of Allen Johnson, ed., *The Chronicles of America Series* (50 vols., New Haven, 1918-1921): Emerson Hough, *The Passing of the Frontier* (XXVI); S. P. Orth, *Our Foreigners* (XXXV); John Moody, *The Railroad Builders* (XXXVIII); same author, *Masters of Capital* (XLI); and Holland Thompson, *The New South* (XLII). These do not cover the ground, but they are suggestive. For Southern conditions there is a useful bibliography in W. L. Fleming, comp., *The Reconstruction of the Seceded States* (New York State Education Department, *Syllabus,* no. 98, Albany, 1905). A very comprehensive bibliography upon labor fills forty-six pages of the second volume of J. R. Commons and Associates, *History of Labour in the United States* (2 vols., N. Y., 1918), and the most important sources are carefully appraised. Reference need hardly be made to the standard but now somewhat antiquated book of Edward

Channing, A. B. Hart and F. J. Turner, eds., *Guide to the Study and Reading of American History* (Boston, 1912). It is supplemented on Western history by F. J. Turner and Frederick Merk, comps., *List of References on the History of the West* (Cambridge, 1922), and on agricultural history by L. B. Schmidt, comp., *Topical Studies and References on the Economic History of American Agriculture* (rev. ed., Phila., 1923). J. N. Larned, ed., *Literature of American History* (N. Y., 1902), is incomplete and now out of date, but has useful annotations upon important books. For American religious development, P. G. Mode, ed., *Source Book and Bibliographical Guide for American Church History* (Menasha, 1921), is helpful.

DOCUMENTARY SOURCES

The *Congressional Globe* (called the *Congressional Record* from 1873) and the Senate and House documents are indispensable for an understanding of the social problems of the period. Many of the latter publications are cited in the footnotes of this volume, and others may be found by a use of B. P. Poore, *Descriptive Catalogue of Government Publications to 1881* (Wash., 1885). Reference should be had to L. P. Lane, *Aids to the Use of Government Publications,* (American Statistical Association, *Quart. Publs.,* VII, no. 49). An indispensable work on Reconstruction in its social as well as political aspects is the comprehensive and admirably edited compilation by W. L. Fleming, *Documentary History of Reconstruction* (2 vols., Cleveland, 1906-1907). Equally valuable in the field of industry and labor is J. R. Commons and others, eds., *A Documentary History of American Industrial Society* (10 vols., Cleveland, 1910-1911), though, unfortunately, it treats chiefly of the period before the Civil War. It may be supplemented by P. H. Douglas, C. N. Hitchcock and W. E. Atkins, eds., *The Worker in Modern Economic Society* (Chicago, 1923), and L. C. Marshall, ed., *Readings in Industrial Society* (Chicago, 1918). Interesting material, some of it suggestive of further reading, is to be found in the fourth volume of A. B. Hart, ed., *American History Told by Contemporaries* (4 vols., N. Y., 1899-1901). Special mention should be made of the *American* (called from 1876 *Appletons'*) *Annual Cyclopædia*, a comprehensive, thorough and fairly accurate record of the chief events and developments of each year. Though based mainly on newspaper material, it represents a good deal of original research. For official presidential papers see J. D. Richardson, comp., *A Compilation of the Messages and Papers of the Presidents, 1789-1897* (10 vols., Washington, 1896-1899). The publications of the Bureau of the Census (Washington) are indispensable for population figures and other statistical data.

PERIODICAL LITERATURE

Special value attaches to the *Nation* (N. Y., 1865–   ), for its editor E. L. Godkin made constant efforts to deal with social topics in a lively, penetrating fashion. His point of view with regard to labor, the farmer and social reform was highly conservative and at times reactionary, but he always kept a critical attitude and he had marked capacity for stimulating generalization. *Harper's Weekly* (N. Y., 1857-1916), edited by G. W. Curtis, has little of value besides its editorials, pictures and cartoons, but the pictures are invaluable to the social historian. Those in *Frank Leslie's Illustrated Weekly* (N. Y., 1855-1922) are less numerous and illuminating. Among the religious weeklies a preëminent place was taken by the *Independent* (N. Y., 1848-   ), which under the editorship of Theodore Tilton (1866-1870) adopted a highly controversial tone. *The Christian Union* (N. Y., 1870-1893), edited 1870-1881 by Henry Ward Beecher, attained a wide influence till the Beecher-Tilton scandal weakened Beecher's hold on the public. A large number of religious journals had vastly more importance then than today. The *Round Table* (N. Y., 1865-1869) was a creditable literary weekly.

The *North American Review* (Boston, 1815-   ) specialized in ponderous articles upon economic, social and political topics of the day, but was usually more discursive than substantial. The *Atlantic Monthly* (Boston, 1857-   ) confined itself mainly to Eastern subjects, but *Scribner's Monthly* (N. Y., 1870-1881), printed many articles upon conditions in the Far West and South, while the *Galaxy* (N. Y., 1866-1877) dealt vigorously with Reconstruction and with labor questions. The *Overland Monthly* (San Francisco, 1868-1875; 1883-   ) is almost indispensable to an understanding of Western life. Among the popular publications, the *New York Ledger* (N. Y., 1844-1898) of Robert Bonner should be given attention as showing what the masses appreciated. The specialized magazines best worthy of attention are the *Scientific American* (N. Y., 1859-   ), for discovery, invention and technical progress; the *Popular Science Monthly* (N. Y., 1872–   ), for scientific culture; and the *Journal of Social Science* (N. Y., 1869-1909), which contains scholarly and acute essays upon social topics.

Among newspapers the *New York Tribune* (1841-1924) and the *New York Times* (1851-   ) were preëminent for correspondence from the West and South as well as for news articles. The *New York Herald* (1835; since 1924 *Herald-Tribune*) was not so valuable, especially after the elder Bennett's death, but more independent. For editorial comment the *Springfield Republican* (1824-   ) and the *New York Evening Post* (1801-   ) are most useful. The *Chicago Tribune* (1847-   ) was a liberal and aggressive journal until, in the middle seventies, Horace White was replaced as editor by Joseph Medill. C. A. Dana made the *New York Sun* (1833-   ) interesting by its bitter hostility to the Grant administration. All newspapers printed more elaborate correspondence from outlying points than is now the practice.

PERSONAL MATERIAL

Of autobiographies and memoirs an almost overwhelming number have been published in recent years. They supplement the older political biographies, which contain but a few sidelights of value to the social historian—John Sherman, *Recollections of Forty Years in the House, Senate and Cabinet* (2 vols., Chicago, 1895); G. S. Boutwell, *Reminiscences of Sixty Years* (2 vols., N. Y., 1902); A. K. McClure, *Recollections of Half a Century* (N. Y., 1902); and Hugh McCulloch, *Men and Measures of Half a Century* (Salem, Mass., 1888). On the reform movements there is matter of value in G. W. Curtis, *Orations and Addresses* (John Bigelow, ed., 2 vols., N. Y., 1885). More valuable than John Sherman's autobiography is John Sherman and W. T. Sherman, *Letters* (Rachel S. Thorndike, ed., N. Y., 1894)—an intimate correspondence. G. F. Hoar, *Autobiography of Seventy Years* (2 vols., N. Y., 1903), has interesting chapters on political corruption and on the Saturday Club of Boston. C. M. Depew, *My Memories of Eighty Years* (2 vols., N. Y., 1924), throws considerable light upon the relations of railroads and politics. Theodore Roosevelt, *An Autobiography* (N. Y., 1913), gives an account of an aristocratic New York household and of New York politics. Reference may also be made to Charles Sumner, *Works* (15 vols., Boston, 1870-1883), and to James A. Garfield, *Works* (B. A. Hinsdale, ed., 2 vols., N. Y., 1883).

Reminiscences by Southerners afford much detailed information upon the ruin and dejection of the South just after the war. Special value attaches to Joseph Le Conte, *Autobiography* (W. D. Armes, ed., N. Y., 1903); Mrs. Roger Pryor, *Reminiscences of Peace and War* (N. Y., 1904); and Susan D. Smedes, *Memorials of a Southern Planter* (Balt., 1887). See also Frances B. Leigh, *Ten Years on a Georgia Plantation since the War* (London, 1883).

The autobiographies, chiefly literary in interest, include two by veteran publishers: Henry Holt, *Garrulities of an Octogenarian Editor* (Boston, 1923), and G. H. Putnam, *Memories of a Publisher* (N. Y., 1915). Magazine editors are represented by R. U. Johnson, *Remembered Yesterdays* (Boston, 1923), with excellent chapters upon New York and Chicago in the seventies and the editorial office of *Scrib-*

ner's; W. W. Ellsworth, *A Golden Age of Authors* (Boston, 1919) ; and G. C. Eggleston, *Recollections of a Varied Life* (N. Y., 1910). Among the books by newspaper men are Henry Watterson, *"Marse Henry," An Autobiography* (2 vols., N. Y., 1919) ; E. P. Mitchell, *Memoirs of an Editor* (N. Y., 1923) ; S. B. Griffin, *People and Politics* (Boston, 1923). There is much of value in Hamlin Garland, *A Son of the Middle Border* (N. Y., 1917), with its autobiographical picture of Western farm life and literary Boston, in W. D. Howells, *Literary Friends and Acquaintances* (N. Y., 1900), in Mark Twain's *Autobiography* (A. B. Paine, ed., 2 vols., N. Y., 1924), and in Rebecca H. Davis, *Bits of Gossip* (Boston, 1905). Among books by clergymen special mention may be given Washington Gladden, *Recollections* (Boston, 1909), dealing with editorial work in New York and a ministry at Springfield, Mass. Much material upon music is offered in Walter Damrosch, *My Musical Life* (N. Y., 1923).

A good picture of social and political life in Washington is afforded by Mrs. John A. Logan, *Reminiscences of a Soldier's Wife* (N. Y., 1916). Brander Matthews, in *These Many Years* (N. Y., 1917), deals chiefly with education, letters and the drama in New York City. Another educator, G. Stanley Hall, *Life and Confessions of a Psychologist* (N. Y., 1923), treats of college life in New England and New York. Henry Cabot Lodge, in *Early Memories* (N. Y., 1913), describes his Boston youth and Harvard education. Michael Pupin, *From Immigrant to Inventor* (N. Y., 1923), and Jacob Riis, *The Making of an American* (N. Y., 1901), are valuable pictures of the struggles of immigrant youths to profit by American opportunities.

GENERAL SECONDARY WORKS

The best treatise on the political history of this period is James Ford Rhodes, *History of the United States from the Compromise of 1850* (8 vols., N. Y., 1899-1919), VI-VIII; it also contains chapters dealing with social history. Fuller attention is given to social development in E. P. Oberholtzer, *History of the United States since the Civil War* (3 vols., N. Y., 1917-1926, in progress). These three volumes cover the years 1865-1878, and present a mass of details interestingly and accurately, though without much effort at interpretation. C. A. and Mary Beard, *The Rise of American Civilization* (2 vols., N. Y., 1927), offers a briefer synthesis of the life of the period.

Considerable material upon economic topics is to be found in J. J. Lalor, ed., *Cyclopedia of Political Science* (3 vols., 1881-1884). Of the various economic histories of the United States there are unfortunately none upon a comprehensive scale. Perhaps the most usable and satisfactory is H. U. Faulkner, *American Economic History* (N. Y., 1924), which is soundly critical in tone and devotes special chapters to Western development and the agrarian revolution.

THE SOUTH: RECONSTRUCTION AND RECOVERY

For every Southern state there is a special monograph on Reconstruction, nearly all of them giving attention to social as well as political history. Among those of especial merit and thoroughness are W. L. Fleming, *Civil War and Reconstruction in Alabama* (N. Y., 1905); J. W. Garner, *Reconstruction in Mississippi* (N. Y., 1901)—more largely confined to politics; and J. S. Reynolds, *Reconstruction in South Carolina* (Columbia, 1905). All these volumes betray a certain Southern bias, and A. A. Taylor attempts a correction of the third one, in behalf of the Negro, in his *The Negro in South Carolina during the Reconstruction* (Wash., 1924). Two other monographs on South Carolina are Walter Allen, *Governor Chamberlain's Administration in South Carolina* (N. Y., 1888)—apologetic in tone, and J. P. Hollis, *Early Reconstruction Period in South Carolina* (Balt., 1905). Briefer studies than those by Fleming and Garner, and more largely political than either, are E. C. Woolley, *Reconstruction in Georgia* (N. Y., 1901); J. W. Fertig, *The Secession and Reconstruction of Tennessee* (Chicago, 1898); and H. J. Eckenrode, *Virginia during the Reconstruction* (Johns Hopkins Univ., *Studies,* XXII, 1904). Among the fruits of Professor Dunning's seminar are five excellent monographs in the Columbia University *Studies:* C. W. Ramsdell, *Reconstruction in Texas* (XXXVI, 1910); W. W. Davis, *The Civil War and Reconstruction in Florida* (LIII, 1913); J. G. deR. Hamilton, *Reconstruction in North Carolina* (LVIII, 1914); C. Mildred Thompson, *Reconstruction in Georgia, Economic, Social, Political, 1866-1872* (LXIV, 1915); and T. S. Staples, *Reconstruction in Arkansas, 1862-1874* (CIX, 1923). J. R. Ficklen has written the *History of Reconstruction in Louisiana* (Johns Hopkins Univ., *Studies,* XXVIII, 1910), through 1868, and Ella Lonn has dealt with *Reconstruction in Louisiana after 1868* (N. Y., 1918).

Books by travelers are highly important. A half dozen by Englishmen should not be neglected: Sir George Campbell, *White and Black* (London, 1879); W. H. Dixon, *The White Conquest* (London, 1876); David Macrae, *The Americans at Home* (Edinburgh, 1870); George Rose, *The Great Country* (London, 1868); William Saunders, *Through the Light Continent* (London, 1879); and Robert Somers, *The Southern States since the War, 1870-1871* (London, 1871). With these may be bracketed several by excellent Northern observers. Immediately after the war came Sidney Andrews, *The South since the War* (Boston, 1866); Whitelaw Reid, *After the War: a Southern Tour* (Cincinnati, 1866); and J. T. Trowbridge, *The South* (Boston, 1866). These represent the best type of journalism. Later came Edward King, *The Southern States of North America* (London, 1875)—a good sketch of Southern recovery. Two books which picture the South under Carpetbag misrule are Charles Nordhoff, *The Cotton States in 1875* (N. Y., 1876), and J. S. Pike, *The Prostrate State* (N. Y., 1874)—both based on a combination of first-hand observation and official evidence. These travelers' accounts may be supplemented by two novels of a North Carolina Carpetbagger, A. W. Tourgee: *A Fool's Errand* (N. Y., 1879), and *Bricks without Straw* (N. Y., 1880). Tourgee's biography by R. F. Dibble (Richmond, 1921) gives added value to his literary picture.

Secondary works of a general nature are numerous. W. L. Fleming has written a very readable account of *The Sequel to Appomattox* (*Chronicles of America Series,* XXXII), which is supplemented by Holland Thompson, *The New South* (same series, XLII). Also from the Southern point of view are two volumes in G. C. Lee and F. N. Thorpe, eds., *The History of North America* (20 vols., Phila., 1903-1907) : P. J. Hamilton, *The Reconstruction Period* (XVI), and P. A. Bruce, *The Rise of the New South* (XVII). Agriculture in the South is treated by R. P. Brooks, *The Agrarian Revolution in Georgia, 1865-1912* (Univ. of Wis., *Hist. Series,* III, no. 3, 1914), and manufacturing in Broadus Mitchell, *The Rise of Cotton Mills in the South* (Johns Hopkins Univ., *Studies,* XXXIX, 1921). H. A. Herbert, *Why the Solid South?* (N. Y., 1890), presents a series of essays explaining the race antagonism of Southern whites for the Negroes. They are of uneven value and biased.

For the Ku Klux Klan there are two principal treatises, neither wholly satisfactory: J. C. Lester and D. L. Wilson, *The Ku Klux Klan, its Origin, Growth, and Disbandment* (N. Y., 1905), and S. L. Davis, *Authentic History of the Ku Klux Klan* (N. Y., 1924). A penetrating treatment by W. G. Brown is included in his volume on *The Lower South in American History* (N. Y., 1902). For Southern education nothing approaches E. W. Knight, *The Influence of Reconstruction on Education in the South* (Teachers' College, Columbia Univ., *Contribs. to Educ.,* no. 60, 1913). Official relief work among the Negroes is described by P. S. Peirce, *The Freedmen's Bureau* (Univ. of Iowa, *Studies,* III, 1904). B. T. Washington, *Up from Slavery: an Autobiography* (N. Y., 1901), a book of unusual literary merit, and his *The Story of the Negro* (London, 1909) throw much light on the problem of race adjustment. A brief study, which illustrates the possibilities of research in the field, is J. L. Sellers, "The Economic Incidence of the Civil War in the South," *Miss. Valley Hist. Rev.,* XIV, 179-191.

THE MIDDLE WEST AND THE FARMER

The best general works upon farm discontent are S. J. Buck, *The Granger Movement* (*Harvard Hist. Studies*, XIX, 1913), and his briefer treatment, *The Agrarian Crusade* (*Chronicles of America Series*, XLV). A. E. Paine has written an account of *The Granger Movement in Illinois* (Univ. of Ill., *Studies*, I, 1904). In part this is supplemented by E. B. Usher, *The Greenback Movement of 1875-1884 and Wisconsin's Part in it* (Madison, 1911). The leading histories of the Grange itself are J. D. McCabe, jr. (*pseud.* E. W. Martin), *History of the Grange Movement* (Chicago, 1874) ; Jonathan Periam, *The Groundswell* (Cincinnati, 1874) ; and E. S. Carr, *The Patrons of Husbandry on the Pacific Coast* (San Francisco, 1875). The early pages of F. L. McVey, *The Populist Movement* (Am. Econ. Assoc., *Studies*, I, 1896), will be found of value. D. C. Cloud, *Monopolies and the People* (Davenport, Ia., 1873), is of assistance in interpreting the farmers' views. Valuable chapters in the political history of Minnesota and Kansas are to be found in E. W. Fish, *Biography of Ignatius Donnelly* (Chicago, 1892), and in T. A. McNeal, *When Kansas Was Young* (N. Y., 1922). Special attention is paid to Iowa in F. E. Haynes, *Third Party Movements since the Civil War* (Iowa City, 1916), and same author, *Life of James Baird Weaver* (Iowa City, 1919). A vast amount of manuscript and other material bearing upon American agricultural development has been brought together in the McCormick Agricultural Library in Chicago, which is the best collection for this type of research in the country.

THE FAR WEST

Two interesting accounts of the wilder West, devoted in part to this period, are Emerson Hough, *The Passing of the Frontier* (*Chronicles of America Series*, XXVI), and F. L. Paxson, *The Last American Frontier* (N. Y., 1910). The best comprehensive history is F. L. Paxson, *History of the American Frontier, 1763-1893* (Boston, 1924). For interpretative comment reference should be had to F. J. Turner, *The Frontier in American History* (N. Y., 1920). The public lands and the operation of the homestead act are discussed in Thomas Donaldson, *The Public Domain* (N. Y., 1881), in the *Public Land Report* (Wash., 1880), and in articles in A. C. McLaughlin and A. B. Hart, eds., *Cyclopedia of American Government* (3 vols., N. Y., 1914). The best volume, however, is B. H. Hibbard, *A History of the Public Land Policies* (N. Y., 1924).

The history of the Indian wars has been treated in considerable detail. Among the numerous works it is sufficient to name G. B. Grinnell, *The Story of the Indian* (N. Y., 1895); G. A. Forsyth, *The Story of the Soldier* (N. Y., 1900); J. P. Dunn, *Massacres of the Mountains: A History of the Indian Wars of the Far West* (N. Y., 1886); L. E. Texter, *Official Relations between the United States and the Sioux Indians* (Wash., 1896); and P. E. Byrne, *Soldiers of the Plains* (N. Y., 1926). The last-named is highly sympathetic with the Indians. So is G. B. Grinnell, *The Cheyenne Indians: Their History and Ways of Life* (2 vols., New Haven, 1923). Helen H. Jackson, *A Century of Dishonor* (Boston, 1885), deals rather emotionally with the Indians' wrongs. G. W. Manypenny, *Our Indian Wards* (Cincinnati, 1880), treats of efforts to civilize the savages. N. A. Miles, *Serving the Republic* (N. Y., 1911); Philip Sheridan, *Personal Memoirs* (N. Y., 1888); and G. A. Custer, *My Life on the Plains* (N. Y., 1874), are the best soldiers' autobiographies.

Emerson Hough has written a volume, at once expert and absorbing, *The Story of the Cowboy* (N. Y., 1897), which is supplemented rather than supplanted by P. A. Rollins's admirable, *The Cowboy* (N. Y., 1922). F. L. Paxson has written upon "The Cow Country" in the *Am. Hist. Rev.*, XXII, 65-86, and E. E. Dale upon "The Ranchman's Last Frontier" in the *Miss. Valley Hist. Rev.*, X, 34-46. Footnote references afford a guide to the more specialized works upon ranching.

The most interesting single volume upon mining in the West is C. H. Shinn, *The Story of the Mine* (N. Y., 1901), which unfortunately is restricted in the main to the Comstock Lode. Cy Warman has a companion volume on the opening of the Far West by the railways: *The Story of the Railroad* (N. Y., 1898). The rougher sides of the West are set forth in N. P. Langford, *Vigilante Days and Ways* (N. Y., 1893), and by Emerson Hough, *The Story of the Outlaw* (N. Y., 1907). Among travel books a preëminent place may be given to Samuel Bowles, *Our New West* (Boston, 1869), and W. F. Rae, *Westward by Rail* (London, 1874). An authoritative contemporary description, with detailed references to economic conditions, is L. P. Brockett, *Our Western Empire: or the New West beyond the Mississippi* (Phila., 1880). For a vivid account of a famous gunman see W. N. Burns, *The Saga of Billy the Kid* (Garden City, 1926).

BUSINESS, FINANCE AND INVENTION

The general financial background of the period is treated in a number of comparatively brief works. The most prominent are D. R. Dewey, *Financial History of the United States* (A. B. Hart, ed., *American Citizen Series*, N. Y., 1903); A. B. Hepburn, *A History of Currency in the United States* (N. Y., 1915); A. S. Bolles, *Financial History of the United States* (3 vols., N. Y., 1896); J. J. Knox, *History of Banking in the United States* (N. Y., 1900); W. O. Scroggs, *A Century of Banking Progress* (N. Y., 1924). Special attention should be given to A. D. Noyes, *Forty Years of American Finance* (N. Y., 1909), though the author deals in the main with the years following 1877. H. W. Lanier, *A Century of Banking in New York* (N. Y., 1922), is suggestive. The Greenback movement is thoroughly treated from the financial aspect by W. C. Mitchell, *A History of the Greenbacks* (Chicago, 1903). The beginnings of the silver movement may be studied in J. L. Laughlin, *History of Bimetallism in the United States* (N. Y., 1892), and in

"History of the Coinage Act of 1873," *Senate Miscel. Docs.*, no. 132, 41 Cong., 2 sess. The *Annual Reports* of the American Bankers Association may be studied (1875-1878).

Among volumes of value on the general economic background of the period may be mentioned D. A. Wells, *Recent Economic Changes* (N. Y., 1889), and same author, *Practical Economics* (N. Y., 1885), the former paying special attention to the concentration of industry, the latter to the effects of the tariff. G. F. Redmond, *Financial Giants of America* (2 vols., Boston, 1922), and Gustavus Myers, *History of the Great American Fortunes* (3 vols., Chicago, 1910), approach the subject of wealth respectively in a friendly and hostile spirit. Andrew Carnegie, *Triumphant Democracy* (N. Y., 1887), is devoted to an exhibition of America's industrial progress. The old volume by C. D. Wright, *Industrial Evolution of the United States* (Meadville, Pa., 1897), still has material of interest. The files of the *Commercial and Financial Chronicle* (N. Y., 1865-   ), are indispensable.

A large number of volumes, some of them excellent, have been devoted to the history of special industries. Two which deal interestingly with particular inventions are H. N. Casson, *The History of the Telephone* (Chicago, 1910), and Joseph Husband, *The Story of the Pullman Car* (Chicago, 1917). Brief but reliable is the Herkimer County (N. Y.) Historical Society, *The Story of the Typewriter* (Herkimer, 1923). Of importance also is A. B. Paine, *In One Man's Life, Being Chapters from the Personal and Business Career of Theodore N. Vail* (N. Y., 1921). Upon metals we have J. M. Swank, *History of the Manufacture of Iron in All Ages* (Phila., 1892); H. N. Casson, *The Romance of Steel* (N. Y., 1907); and J. R. Smith, *The Story of Iron and Steel* (N. Y., 1908). These are supplemented in part by Andrew Carnegie, *Autobiography* (Boston, 1920). J. V. Woodworth has written the history of *American Tool Making and Interchangeable Manufacturing* (N. Y., 1911). Flour milling is dealt with in the semicentennial issue of the

Northwestern Miller (St. Paul, 1923). For textiles see T. M. Young, *The American Cotton Industry* (N. Y., 1902); M. T. Copeland, *The Cotton Manufacturing Industry in the United States* (Cambridge, 1912); A. H. Cole, *The American Wool Manufacture* (2 vols., Cambridge, 1926); and W. C. Wycoff, *American Silk Manufacture* (Boston, 1887). F. J. Allen has written the history of *The Shoe Industry* (N. Y., 1916).

For the development of the oil fields in this period the two standard works are Ida M. Tarbell, *History of the Standard Oil Company,* (2 vols., N. Y., 1904), which is accurate, full and impartial, and G. H. Montague's slender volume on the *Rise and Progress of the Standard Oil Company* (N. Y., 1903). For coal, see Arthur Suffern, *Conciliation and Arbitration in the Anthracite Coal Industry* (Boston, 1915); Scott Nearing, *Anthracite: An Instance of Natural Resource Monopoly* (Phila., 1915); and Eliot Jones, *The Anthracite Coal Combination* (*Harvard Econ. Studies,* XI, 1914). See also H. R. Mussey, *Combination in the Mining Industry* (N. Y., 1905). There is material upon steel in A. Borglund, *The United States Steel Corporation* (Columbia Univ., *Studies,* XVIII, 1907); in H. L. Wilgus, *A Study of the United States Steel Corporation* (Chicago, 1901), and in the early chapters of Ida M. Tarbell, *Elbert H. Gary* (N. Y., 1926).

Volumes which have some bearing upon the Panic of 1873 and its results, though their value is small, are T. E. Burton, *Financial Crises* (N. Y., 1902), and G. H. Hull, *Industrial Depressions* (N. Y., 1911). Invention and its bearings upon industry are treated in E. W. Byrn, *Progress of Invention in the Nineteenth Century* (N. Y., 1900); George Iles, *Leading American Inventors* (N. Y., 1910), and Holland Thompson, *The Age of Invention* (*Chronicles of America Series,* XXXVII). Waldemar Kaempffert has edited *A Popular History of American Invention* (2 vols., N. Y., 1924), with many illustrations. Much work remains to be done on the industrial and financial history of the years following the Civil War. The best collection of source materials for this purpose has been brought together by the Business Historical Society in the Harvard Business Library.

TRANSPORTATION

It is impossible here to mention more than the outstanding titles in the vast mass of literature upon American railways during this period. The best histories of individual railroads are C. F. Adams and Henry Adams, *Chapters of Erie* (N. Y., 1886)—a caustic volume; H. S. Mott, *Story of the Erie* (N. Y., 1902)—more tolerant in tone; J. P. Davis, *The Union Pacific* (N. Y., 1894); E. L. Sabin, *Building the Pacific Railway* (Phila., 1919); G. D. Bradley, *The Story of the Santa Fé* (Boston, 1920); Stuart Daggett, *Chapters in the History of the Southern Pacific* (N. Y., 1922); E. V. Smalley, *History of the Northern Pacific* (N. Y., 1883); and W. H. Stennett, *History of the Chicago and North Western Railway System* (Chicago, 1910). Among the lives of railway builders are J. G. Pyle, *Life of James J. Hill* (2 vols., N. Y., 1917); *Memoirs* of Henry Villard (2 vols., N. Y., 1904); and E. P. Oberholtzer, *Jay Cooke, Financier of the Civil War* (2 vols., Phila., 1907). A monograph worth consulting is W. F. Gephart, *Transportation and Industrial Development in the Middle West* (Columbia Univ., *Studies*, XXXIV, no. 1, 1909). On the reconstruction of the Southern railways, see C. R. Fish, *The Restoration of the Southern Railroads* (Univ. of Wis., *Studies*, no. 2, 1919).

Good general accounts of railway building in this period may be found in John Moody, *The Railroad Builders* (*Chronicles of America Series*, XXXVIII), and Slason Thompson, *A Short History of American Railways* (Chicago, 1925). Other works which may be consulted are E. R. Johnson, *American Railway Transportation* (*Appletons' Business Series*, rev. edn., N. Y., 1912); C. F. Adams, jr., *Railroads: Their Origin and Problems* (rev. edn., N. Y., 1893); and A. T. Hadley, *Railroad Transportation* (N. Y., 1886). A work of special value is L. H. Haney, *A Congressional History of Railroads in the United States, 1850-*

1887, (Univ. of Wis., *Econ. and Pol. Sci. Series,* III, no. 2; VI, no. 1, 1908-1910). Important collections of source materials bearing upon the railroad history of the period can be found in the Harvard Business Library, the Bureau of Railway Economics in Washington, the library of the Wharton School of Business at the University of Pennsylvania, and the Scudder Financial Library at Columbia University.

LABOR AND IMMIGRATION

The most thorough treatment of the labor movement during the period is the discussion contributed by J. B. Andrews to the second volume of the monumental *History of Labour in the United States* (2 vols., N. Y., 1918), by J. R. Commons and Associates. There are a number of good brief histories, including G. G. Groat, *An Introduction to the Study of Organized Labor in America* (rev. edn., N. Y., 1926); F. T. Carlton, *History and Problems of Organized Labor* (N. Y., 1920); Mary R. Beard, *A Short History of the American Labor Movement* (N. Y., 1920); Selig Perlman, *A History of Trade Unionism in the United States* (N. Y., 1922); and S. P. Orth, *The Armies of Labor (The Chronicles of America Series,* XL). On special labor organizations there are several monographs. The more important are D. D. Lescohier, *The Knights of St. Crispin* (Univ. of Wis., *Econ. and Pol. Sci. Series,* VII, no. 1, 1910); E. C. Robbins, *Railway Conductors* (Columbia Univ., *Studies,* LXI, 1914); and C. D. Wright, "An Historical Sketch of the Knights of Labor," *Quart. Journ. of Econ.,* I, 137-168.

By far the most important volume by a labor leader for this period is T. V. Powderly, *Thirty Years of Labor, 1859-1889* (N. Y., 1890). In connection with it may be read the early chapters of G. E. McNeill, ed., *The Labor Movement, the Problem of Today* (N. Y., 1887). The part of women in industry is treated in Edith Abbott, *Women in Industry* (N. Y., 1910), and in Alice Henry, *The Trade Union Woman* (N. Y., 1915). For the eight-hour-day movement see G. E. McNeill, *Eight Hour Primer, the Fact, Theory and the Argument* (N. Y., n. d.). Much light is thrown on the radical side of the labor movement by F. Engels, *The Labor Movement in America* (N. Y., 1887), and by Morris Hillquit, *History of Socialism in the United States* (N. Y., 1910). Some interesting facts and ideas are presented in Robert Hunter, *Violence and the Labor Movement* (N. Y., 1914). R. T. Ely, *The Labor Movement in the United States* (N. Y., 1886), is a book of special insight.

The two best single volumes upon immigration are probably J. R. Commons, *Races and Immigrants in America* (N. Y., 1920), and P. F. Hall, *Immigration and its Effects upon the United States* (N. Y., 1906). S. P. Orth, *Our Foreigners* (*Chronicles of America Series*, XXXV), is sketchy but stimulating. G. M. Stephenson, *A History of American Immigration* (N. Y., 1926), emphasizes political aspects. Mary R. Coolidge, *Chinese Immigration* (N. Y., 1909), discusses that subject with detail and accuracy. For the cultural influences of various immigrant stocks, consult the excellent bibliography in Stephenson, *A History of American Immigration*, 283-302.

HUMANITARIAN REFORM

A series of volumes in this field may be called standard treatises. They include F. D. Watson, *The Charity Organization Movement in the United States* (N. Y., 1922); A. G. Warner, *American Charities* (rev. edn., N. Y., 1919); F. H. Wines, *Punishment and Reformation* (rev. edn., N. Y., 1919); and Edith E. Wood, *The Housing of the Unskilled Wage Earner* (N. Y., 1919). A good general treatment is Maurice Parmelee, *Poverty and Social Progress* (N. Y., 1916). Much light is thrown upon public health by G. C. Whipple, *State Sanitation* (Cambridge, 1917). The effort to prevent cruelty to animals is fully described by S. H. Coleman, *Humane Society Leaders in America* (Albany, 1924), and R. C. McCrea, *The Humane Movement* (N. Y.,

1910). Much information upon housing and slum conditions in New York city is presented by Jacob Riis, *How the Other Half Lives* (N. Y., 1890). The student should consult Henry George, *Progress and Poverty* (N. Y., 1890), for its incidental material upon American poverty.

Popular but sketchy accounts of the feminist movement are offered in H. A. Bruce, *Woman in the Making of America* (Boston, 1912), and in Belle Squire, *The Woman Movement in America* (Chicago, 1911). The third volume of A. W. Calhoun, *Social History of the American Family* (3 vols., Cleveland, 1917-1919), is highly valuable and contains a full bibliography. For the suffrage struggle the fullest record is to be found in Elizabeth Cady Stanton, Susan B. Anthony and others, *History of Woman Suffrage* (4 vols., N. Y., 1881-1902), completed in two additional volumes under the editorship of Ida H. Harper (1918-1922). Anna H. Shaw, *The Story of a Pioneer* (N. Y., 1915), is an engrossing volume. Jennie L. Wilson has written upon *The Legal and Political Status of Women in the United States* (Cedar Rapids, 1912), and Bertha Rembaugh upon *The Political Status of Women in the United States* (N. Y., 1911). The most valuable biography is Ida H. Harper, *The Life and Work of Susan B. Anthony* (3 vols., Indianapolis, 1898-1908). General aspects of feminism are dealt with in Kaethe Schirmacher, *The Modern Woman's Rights Movement* (N. Y., 1912), and Mrs. C. P. Gilman, *Women and Economics* (N. Y., 1909). For women's clubs the two best volumes are Mrs. J. C. Croly, *The History of the Woman's Club Movement in the United States* (N. Y., 1898), and Mary L. Wood, *History of the General Federation of Women's Clubs* (N. Y., 1912).

For prohibition the student should consult the early files of *Our Union*, published in New York by the Women's Christian Temperance Union. Frances E. Willard, *Glimpses of Fifty Years* (N. Y., 1889), is supplemented by A. A. Gordon, *The Beautiful Life of Frances E. Willard* (Chicago, 1898). Four general treatises on the prohibition movement are: E. H. Cherrington, *The Evolution of Prohibition in the United States* (Westerville, O., 1920); Daniel Dorchester, *The Liquor Problem in All Ages* (N. Y., 1888); J. G. Wooley and W. E. Johnson, *Temperance Progress of the Century* (Phila., 1903); and D. L. Colvin, *Prohibition in the United States* (N. Y., 1926).

EDUCATION

For the significant trends in elementary and secondary school education, such manuals as E. P. Cubberley, *Public Education in the United States* (Boston, 1919), and E. G. Dexter, *History of Education in the United States* (N. Y., 1904), give convenient summaries for this period. The careful student, however, will want to consult the voluminous annual *Reports* of the United States Commissioner of Education (Washington), beginning with 1867 and including digests of the reports of state superintendents of education. An index to the publications of the Bureau of Education from 1867 to 1890 may be found in Commissioner of Education, *Report for 1888-1889*, II, 1453-1551.

A really good history of university and college education is much needed. The best general guide, C. F. Thwing, *A History of Higher Education in America* (N. Y., 1906), has to be supplemented by histories of separate institutions and biographies or autobiographies of educators. *The American College and University Series* (G. P. Krapp, ed.) has special value. Its volumes include F. P. Keppel, *Columbia* (N. Y., 1914); J. H. Gardiner, *Harvard* (N. Y., 1915); J. M. Taylor and Elizabeth H. Haight, *Vassar* (N. Y., 1915); Allan Nevins, *Illinois* (N. Y., 1917); V. L. Collins, *Princeton* (N. Y., 1914); and J. F. A. Pyre, *Wisconsin* (N. Y., 1920). The history of Johns Hopkins University for these years is fully treated in Fabian Franklin, *The Life of Daniel Coit Gilman* (N. Y., 1910), and in D. C. Gilman, *The Launching of a University* (Balt., 1906). For Harvard see *The Harvard Book* (2 vols., Cambridge, 1874), and Charles W. Eliot, *A Late Harvest* (Boston, 1924). W. R. Thayer, *History and Customs of Harvard University*

(Boston, 1898), may also be consulted. L. W. Spring has published an excellent *History of Williams College* (Boston, 1917). For Cornell the important source is Andrew D. White, *Autobiography* (2 vols., N. Y., 1905). College and university catalogues and yearbooks should also be consulted.

LITERATURE, THOUGHT AND RELIGION

Upon literature the fullest general guide is furnished by W. P. Trent, S. P. Sherman, John Erskine and Carl Van Doren, eds., *The Cambridge History of American Literature* (4 vols., N. Y., 1917-1921). The bibliographies appended make further citations of titles unnecessary here. For a briefer treatment see F. L. Pattee, *A History of American Literature since 1870* (N. Y., 1915). American speculative movements are treated by Woodbridge Riley, *American Thought from Puritanism to Pragmatism* (N. Y., 1915), and in the field of politics by C. E. Merriam, *American Political Ideas, 1865-1917* (N. Y., 1920). The Southern literary awakening is described in W. M. Baskervil, *Southern Writers* (2 vols., Nashville, 1898-1903); in Carl Holliday, *A History of Southern Literature* (N. Y., 1906); and in M. J. Moses, *The Literature of the South* (N. Y., 1910).

For the production of books and for information about the book trade, the files of *The Publishers' Weekly* (title varies somewhat) are indispensable. The history of a number of magazines and newspapers has been worked out more or less adequately. Algernon Tassin has sketched the main outlines of a huge subject in *The Magazine in America* (N. Y., 1916). M. A. DeW. Howe, *The Atlantic Monthly and its Makers* (Boston, 1919), is brief but interesting. Journalism is treated in J. M. Lee, *History of American Journalism* (Boston, 1923); G. H. Payne, *History of Journalism in the United States* (N. Y., 1920); and W. G. Bleyer, *Main Currents in the History of American Journalism* (Boston, 1927). Gustav Pollak, *Fifty Years of American Idealism* (Boston, 1915), and W. P. Garrison, *Letters* and Memorials (J. H. McDaniels, ed., 2 vols., Cambridge, 1908), supplement Rollo Ogden, Life and Letters of Edwin Lawrence Godkin (2 vols., N. Y., 1907), in giving a history of the Nation and its editors. For particular newspapers the student should examine F. M. O'Brien, The Story of the Sun (N. Y., 1918); Elmer Davis, History of the New York Times (N. Y., 1921); and Allan Nevins, The Evening Post: A Century of Journalism (N. Y., 1922).

The volumes of Philip Schaff and others, eds., The American Church History Series (13 vols., N. Y., 1893-1897), all tend to slight the period immediately following the Civil War. Material of value may be found, however, in H. H. Carroll, The Religious Forces of the United States (American Church History Series, I), and Daniel Dorchester, Christianity in the United States (N. Y., 1895).

SCIENCE

Along with other phases of American culture, the history of science in the United States received attention from those who, in 1876, were celebrating the centenary of American independence. Among the more notable summaries were: Simon Newcomb, "Abstract Science in America, 1776-1876," N. Am. Rev., CCL (1876), 88-123; A. S. Packard, jr., "A Century's Progress in American Zoology," Am. Naturalist, X (1876), 591-598; and F. A. P. Barnard, "The Exact Sciences," and Theodore Gill, "Natural Science," both in The First Century of the Republic (N. Y., 1876). The present-day student, however, can find fuller accounts of these and other branches of science for this period in such works as R. T. Young, Biology in America (Boston, 1922), G. P. Merrill, The First One Hundred Years of American Geology (New Haven, 1924); E. F. Smith, Chemistry in America (N. Y., 1914), and C. N. Lauer, Engineering in American Industry (Boston, 1924). The activities of the leading scientific institution of the period are described in G. B. Goode, The Smithsonian Institution, 1846-1896 (Washington, 1897).

The impact of evolutionary thought upon the American mind is best studied from the sources. Among the volumes of importance are Asa Gray, *Darwiniana* (Boston, 1878); James McCosh, *The Development Hypothesis: Is it Sufficient?* (N. Y., 1876), and John Fiske, *Darwinism and Other Essays* (Boston, 1885). There is much material in three biographies; D. C. Gilman, *Life of James Dwight Dana* (N. Y., 1899); Elizabeth C. Agassiz, *Louis Agassiz, His Life and Correspondence* (Boston, 1885); and J. S. Clark, *The Life and Letters of John Fiske* (2 vols., Boston, 1917). In John Fiske, *A Century of Science and Other Essays* (Boston, 1899), there are essays upon evolution and upon E. L. Youmans.

THE FINE ARTS

The standard histories of American painting all have a distinct value for the period: Sadakichi Hartman, *A History of American Art* (2 vols., Boston, 1901); Samuel Isham, *History of American Painting* (N. Y., 1905); and C. H. Caffin, *Story of American Painting* (N. Y., 1907). The tendencies in sculpture may be discovered in Lorado Taft, *The History of American Sculpture* (rev. edn., N. Y., 1924), and in music in L. C. Elson, *The History of American Music* (rev. edn., N. Y., 1925). The taste of the period in domestic architecture can be understood by consulting Samuel Sloan, *Sloan's Homestead Architecture* (Phila., 1866), a fully illustrated handbook already in its second edition in 1867. A brief historical treatment will be found in Henry Van Brunt, "Development and Prospects of Architecture in the United States," in N. S. Shaler, ed., *The United States of America* (3 vols., N. Y., 1894), and in J. W. Dow, *The American Renascence: A Review of Domestic Architecture* (N. Y., 1904). In some respects still more can be gained from Fiske Kimball and G. H. Edgell, *A History of Architecture* (N. Y., 1918).

For the drama one of the most stimulating volumes is J. R. Towse, *Sixty Years of the Theatre* (N. Y., 1916). Montrose J. Moses, *The American Dramatist* (rev. edn., Boston, 1926), Mary C. Crawford, *The Romance of the American Theatre* (rev. edn., Boston, 1926), and T. A. Brown, *History of the New York Stage* (N. Y., 1903), should also be consulted. For the Boston stage, Eugene Tompkins and Quincy Kilby, *The History of the Boston Theatre, 1854-1901* (Boston, 1908), is of first importance.

INDEX

ABBEY, E. A., early career of, 262.

Abilene, Kansas, as cattle market, 36, 125.

Adams, Charles Francis, on Mill. 231.

Adams, Henry, on Boston life 95; on Washington, 96; on corruption, 200; as teacher, 265.

Advertising, outdoor, 227; influence of, on press, 242; in magazines, 245.

Agassiz, Louis, founds Wood's Hole school, 282-283.

Agricultural journals, circulation of, 156-157.

Agriculture, in the South, 8-11; and share system, 18-20; and break-up of plantations, 20-21; and Southern crops, 25; Southern improvements in, 29-30; machinery of, 46; Western expansion of, 118-120; and "bonanza farms," 120-121; in California, 148-149; and Western population, 154-155; inventions for, 157-159; hardships of, 159-162; education for, 267, 272-276; experiment station for, 369; and tenancy, 371. *See also* Agricultural journals, Farmers.

Air brake, invention of, 99.

Alabama, railways destroyed in, 4; guerrillas in, 6; destitution of, 11; Negro labor in, 17; constitution of, 27; Carpetbag rule in, 349-355; redeemed, 356; results of misrule in, 356; textile mills in, 360.

Alabama, University of, postbellum history of, 7, 364.

Aldrich, T. B., writings of, 253.

Alexis, Grand Duke, tour of, 113.

Allen, Henry W., emigrates, 17.

Allison, W. B., in Senate, 164; and Credit Mobilier, 190.

American News Company, work of, 258.

Ames, Oakes, and Credit Mobilier, 188-190.

Amusements, and city life, 89-90; rural, 156; in South, 208; theater, 93, 218; circus, 224-225; lyceum, 239. *See also* Sport.

Anderson, Mary, and star system, 89.

Anson, A. C., and baseball, 219.

Anthony, Susan B., and woman's rights, 324, 339-340.

Apartment houses, in New York, 208.

Appleby, John F., perfects binder, 157.

Arapahoe Indians, relations with, 101-109; treaty with, 110; as farmers, 115.

Architecture, and urban changes, 89-90; domestic taste in, 203-205. *See also* Housing.

Aristocracy, in the South, 21-22; in New York, 90-91; in Boston, 94-95; in Washington, 96.

Arizona, postwar growth of, 152, 153.

Arkansas, destruction in, 2-4; desperadoes in, 6; migration to, 23; constitution, 27; Carpetbag rule in, 349-355; redeemed, 356; debt increase of, 355-356; growth of, 359.

Armour, Philip D., career of, 36-37.

Armstrong, S. C., and Hampton Institute, 16.

433

Art, development of, 260-263; bibliography, 431-432. *See also* fine arts by name.

Art galleries, founding of, 262-263.

Arthur, P. M., and rail strike, 385.

Arthur, T. S., writings of, 233.

Asbestos, introduction of, 85.

Associated Press, growth of, 241-242.

Astor, William B., career of, 91.

Athletics, increased activity in, 219-224.

Atlanta, ruin of, 3; rebuilt, 8, 30.

Atlantic cable, laying of, 86.

Atlantic Monthly, character of, 245, 247-248.

BALTIMORE, riots at, 385-388.

Baltimore & Ohio, reaches West, 64.

Bandelier, A. F., work of, 285.

Banking, expansion of, 47-48; defects of, 198, 199; prosperity of, 303. *See also* Finance.

Barbed-wire, introduced, 35 *n.*

Barnard, F. A. P., as educator, 271.

Barnard, Judge G. C., corruption of, 180, 196, 200.

Barnum, P. T., and circus, 224-225.

Barton, Clara, and American Red Cross, 343.

Baseball, reorganization of, 219-221.

Bathrooms, increase of, 205-206.

Bausch & Lomb, optical work of, 403.

Beadle, Erastus, and dime novels, 235-236.

Beards, universality of, 210.

Beecher, H. W., trial of, 227; as novelist, 234; as editor, 236; on the Panic, 300; influence of, 313, 344-345; as suffrage leader, 340.

Beer, increased use of, 46, 211-212.

Bell, A. G., invents telephone, 87-89.

Bennett, J. G., jr., and polo, 219; engages transcontinental train, 378.

Berea College, founded, 15.

Bergh, Henry, and humane movement, 333-335.

Bessemer process, use of, 33-35.

Bibliography of period 1865-1878, 408-432.

Bicycling, craze for, 223-224.

Billy the Kid, career of, 131.

"Black Crook," production of, 93.

Black Friday, history of, 200-201.

Blaine, J. G., and Credit Mobilier, 189; and railway schemes, 191; public attitude toward, 227; and Mulligan letters, 311.

Bland-Allison act, passage of, 372.

Blodgett, W. T., as art patron, 261, 263.

Boarding houses, rôle of, 214, 215.

Bonner, Robert, as editor, 236.

Book distribution, methods of, 236-237. *See also* Literature.

Boston, paving, 83; fire, 85; social life, 94-95; literary taste of, 234; libraries, 243; art museum, 262; slums, 319-320; public health, 321-323.

Boston University, founded, 281.

Bowles, Samuel, on Pacific railroad, 51; and Western food, 52-53.

Boyd, D. F., as educator, 363.

Brace, C. L., as sociologist, 326.

Bridges, built after war, 80-81.

Brooks, Phillips, influence of, 344-345.

Brownlow, W. G., as governor of Tennessee, 352.

Bryant, W. C., literary activities of, 229, 237-238.

Buffalo Bill. *See* Cody, W. F.

Buffaloes, numbers and destruction of, 112-114.

Burroughs, John, champions Whitman, 213.

Business, expansion of, 25, 291-292; failures in, 294-298, 303, 397; bibliography, 421-423. *See also* Commerce, Finance,

Manufacturing, Mining, Panic of 1873.

Butler, B. F., in Washington, 95-96.

CABLE, G. W., literary career of, 251.

California, development of, 146-148, 376-377; farming in, 148-149; factories in, 149; culture of, 150; and Chinese problem, 150-152, 375; radicalism in, 174-175; depression in, 375-376.

California, University of, early years of, 150.

Cameron, Simon, as politician, 180-181.

Canned foods, introduced, 76.

Carnegie, Andrew, adopts Bessemer process, 34-35; as industrial organizer, 403-404.

Carpetbaggers, rule of, 349-357. See also Southern states by name.

Case method of teaching law, 278-279.

Centennial Exhibition, history of, 306-10.

Central Pacific Railroad, construction of, 53-54.

Chandler, Zachariah, and campaign of 1876, 315.

Chaperons, use of, 212-213.

Charities, provision for, 327-328; state boards of, 329-330. See also Freedmen's Bureau, Philanthropy.

Charleston, devastation of, 3; public health in, 13; rebuilding of, 30.

Chattanooga, development of, 360.

Chautauqua, founded, 239-240.

Cheyenne Indians, life of, 101-105; fighting with, 105-109; treaties with, 110; restiveness of, 115.

Chicago, steel making in, 34; meat packing in, 36-38; factories in, 46; growth of, after war, 79-80; fire, 84-85; newspapers, 241; bookshops, 242; libraries in, 243; population of, 373; railway riots in, 390.

Chicago & Northwestern Railroad, built westward, 57; consolidation of, 65.

Chicago, Burlington & Quincy Railroad, built westward, 57; consolidation of, 65.

Children, books for, 234 n.; labor of, 360.

Chinese, as railway laborers, 54-55; as a California problem, 150-152, 375.

Christian, G. M., and milling, 38-39.

"Chromo Civilization," Godkin's phrase, 226-227.

Churches. See Religion.

Circus, development of, 224-225.

Cities. See Urban changes, and cities by name.

Claflin, Tennessee and Victoria, 214.

Clark, W. A., career of, 139-140.

Clemens, S. L. See Mark Twain.

Clothing, manufacture of, 44-45.

Coal, efforts to monopolize anthracite, 400.

Cody, W. F., as scout, 112; as author, 235.

Coeducation, growth of, 273-274, 279-280.

Cole, Timothy, as wood engraver, 246.

Colfax, Schuyler, on Utah conditions, 144; and Credit Mobilier, 189-190.

Colleges and universities, development of, 264-281. See also colleges by name.

Colorado, and Indian wars, 106-109; and mining, 134-140; and Leadville rush, 374-375; coal mining in, 378.

Colorado Springs, founded, 217.

Columbia University, growth of, 265-267, 271.

Commerce, with the South, 7-8; of Middle West and East, 37, 38; on the Great Lakes, 65-67; on

Mississippi, 67-69; with Utah, 145; with California, 149; with the Middle West and Europe, 163; and the Fisk-Gould raid, 199; and import trade, 299-300; and export trade, 395-397.

Commercial and Financial Chronicle, founded, 257.

Comstock Lode, development of, 136-138.

Coney Island, attractions of, 93.

Congress, and Reconstruction, 26-30; coarseness of tone of, 96; and Indian problem, 107-108; on Indian treaties, 115.

Constitutions, new Southern, 26-30.

Cooke, Jay, mansion of, 204; failure of, 290, 295-296; assets of, 297-298.

Cooper, Peter, career of, 92, 347.

Coöperation, by labor, 71-72; by farmers, 171-173.

Corliss engine, at Centennial, 308.

Corn, increased acreage of, 154-155; prices of, 163, 165.

Cornell, Ezra, benefactions of, 272-273.

Cornell University, rise of, 271-275.

Corruption, in politics, 163-165, 178-190; in business, 190-202; in Centennial year, 310-313.

Cotton, prices of, 7; tax on, 10; crops, 23-24; changed methods of selling, 25-26; enlarged acreage of, 29-30; manufactures, 359-360.

Cowboys, life of, 124-128, 129-130, 133, 367-368; bibliography, 420.

Craddock (*pseud.*), Charles Egbert, writings of, 251-252.

Credit Mobilier, history of, 188-190; effects of, 294-295.

Crime, on frontier, 131-132, 140-141, 201; in Northern states, 201, 202, 301-302; and heredity, 327; as affected by Civil War, 330-331; and punishment, 331-332. *See also* Ku Klux Klan.

Croly, Mrs. J. C., as editor, 341; club leader, 342.

Croquet, craze for, 223.

Currency, inflation of, 289-293, *See also* Finance.

Custer, George A., and Indian warfare, 110-112.

DAKOTA, Indians wars in, 104-107, 374; settlement of, 117, 120; population of, 154; and Black Hills rush, 373.

Daly, Augustin, as manager, 259-260.

Damrosch, Leopold, as symphony conductor, 90.

Dana, C. A., and Tweed Ring, 187; as editor, 240-241.

Darwinian theory, battle over, 286-289.

Davis, Rebecca H., on New England writers, 229; as novelist, 234.

Deering, William, manufactures binders, 157.

Densmore, James, and typewriter, 88.

Denver, as mining center, 134-135.

Department stores, growth of, 91-92.

De Vinne, T. L., career of, 246-247.

Diamond swindle, in Southwest, 192.

Dickens, Charles, second American visit of, 230-231.

Diet, changes in, 76, 77, 210-211.

Dime novels, vogue of, 235-236.

Divorce, growth of, 215, 216.

Dodge City, Kansas, and Western development, 113, 125, 131.

Dodge, G. M., as railway engineer, 55.

Dodge, Richard I., on buffalo slaughter, 112-114.

Donnelly, Ignatius, in politics, 174-175, 372-373.

Drake, A. W., and *Scribner's*, 246-247.

Drama, writers of, 258-259.
Dress, women's, 209; men's, 210.
Drew, Daniel, career of, 194-199, 295.
D r e w Theological Seminary, founded, 195.
Drinking, rarity in homes, 211-212; at Centennial Exhibition, 307. *See also* Temperance.
Dugdale, R. L., on the "Jukes," 327.
Duke, James and Washington, careers of, 5.
Dwight, T. W., and prison reform, 331.

EADS, J. B., and bridge, 81.
Eastlake furniture, use of, 206, 308.
Economic conditions, bibliography, 421-423. *See also* Agriculture, Business, Commerce, Finance, Labor, Manufacturing, Mining, Panic of 1873, Railroads.
Eden Musée, in New York, 93.
Edison, T. A., early inventions of, 87.
Education, among freedmen, 15-16; in Utah, 143; college and university, 264-281; at Centennial, 309-310; under Reconstruction, 362-364; bibliography, 428-429.
Eggleston, Edward, literary career of, 236, 251.
Eggleston, G. C., as editor, 236, 255.
Eight-hour day, movement for, 71-72.
Elective system in universities, battle over, 270-271.
Elevated railroad, in New York, 82.
Elevator, for passengers, 77-78.
Eliot, Charles W., as educational leader, 268-271, 277-279.
Elmira Reformatory, founded, 332.
El Paso, development of, 360.
Emerson, R. W., influence of, 229; mind of, fails, 239.

Engineering education, growth of, 276.
Epidemics, in the cities, 320-322; in the South, 323.
Erie Railroad, consolidation of, 64; and "Erie War," 195-197.
Evolution, battle over, 286-289.
Export trade, growth of, 395-397.

FAMILY LIFE, in Utah, 144-145; general character of, 212-216; in slums, 319-320; in West, 377-378.
Farmers, revolt of, 162-168; in Grange, 169-173; in politics, 173-177; improved condition of, 364-372; tenancy of, 371; bibliography, 419. *See also* Agriculture.
Far West. *See* Frontier, and states by name.
Field, Cyrus W., and Atlantic cable, 86.
Finance, buoyancy of, 31-32; railway, 60-63; and the farmer, 165-166; excesses of, 190-201; and the Panic, 290-298, 303-304; bibliography, 421-423.
Fisk, James, career of, 195-199; murder of, 201.
Fisk University, founded, 15; Jubilee Singers of, 15, 407.
Fiske, John, writings of, 286-288.
Flagler, H. M., and oil industry, 42, 398.
Florida, Reconstruction in, 26-29; under Carpetbag rule, 349-356; redeemed, 357.
Flour milling, development of, 38-40.
Football, development of, 221-222.
Freedmen's Bureau, relief work of, 10-18.
Fritz, John, and steel industry, 35, 405.
Frontier, and Indian warfare, 101-112, 115, 373-374; buffalo destruction on, 112-114; colonization of, 116-123; and ranching, 124-133; and min-

ing, 133-153; conditions on, after 1873, 364-379; bibliography, 419-421.
Furniture, styles of, 206-208.

GALAXY, career of, 244-245.
Gambling, prevalence of, 140, 202.
Garland, Hamlin, on rural hardships, 166; on New England writers, 230; on Western development, 365.
Garrison, W. L., and reform, 318.
Georgia, destruction in, 2-4, 8; destitution in, 11; and Negro labor, 18; and new economic leadership, 22; and Reconstruction, 26-28; Carpetbag rule in, 349-352; redeemed, 353; textile mills in, 360.
Germans, as immigrants, 48, 120, 121; and Brooklyn Bridge, 80; influence musical taste, 90; in New York City, 93; train American scholars, 269.
Gerry, E. T., and humane movement, 334-335.
Gilbert and Sullivan, early operas of, 239.
Glidden, Carlos, and typewriter, 88.
Godey's Lady's Book, vogue of, 236.
Godkin, E. L., on American wealth, 202 n.; on boarding houses, 214; on the Beecher-Tilton trial, 227; founds Nation, 256-257.
Gompers, Samuel, labor organizer, 394.
Gough, J. B., and temperance, 336.
Gould, Jay, as head of Erie, 64, 100; and Governor Fenton, 180; financial career of, 194-199.
Grand Army of the Republic, activities of, 317 n.
Granger movement, history of, 169-173; achievements of, 176-177; decay of, 371-372.
Grant, U. S., ethical defects of, 179; at Long Branch, 217; and

Grant-Ward failure, 239; and Panic of 1873, 295-297; and nepotism, 311.
Gray, Asa, at Harvard, 282.
Great Lakes commerce, decline of, 65-66; as check on rail rates, 67.
Greenback-Labor party, rise of, 372, 393-394. See also Greenback question.
Greenback question, 166-167, 292-294, 305.

HALL, A. Oakey, and Tweed Ring, 183-184.
Hampton Institute, founded, 16.
Harte, Bret, and California life, 140, 150; literary career of, 229, 247-249.
Harvard University, development of, 243, 264, 268-271, 277-279; athletics at, 221-222; library of, 243.
Hatch, C. P., invents tank car, 41.
Hay, John, in South, 22; as poet, 251.
Hayes, R. B., and Washington society, 96; in campaign of 1876, 314-317; and South, 357; and rail strike, 385-386.
Health, public, in South, 12-14; in American cities, 319-323; state boards of, 322; bibliography, 426.
Hearth and Home, revived, 236.
Higginson, H. L., in South, 22-23.
Higginson, T. W., and Negro songs, 15.
Hoffman House, built, 78; manager of, 201.
Holladay, Benjamin, and stage lines, 51-53; and Indians, 106.
Holland, J. G., writings of, 232-233; as editor, 245, 247.
Holley, A. M., steel manufacturer, 34.
Holliday, C. L., as railway builder, 59.
Holmes, Mary J., vogue of, 234.
Homer, Winslow, early career of, 261.

Home furnishing, heating, 76; lighting, 76-77; furniture, 206-208, 308.

Homesteading, growth of, 118-119; drives out ranches, 132-133.

Hotels, character of, 78-79; in New York, 92-93.

Housing, model, 324-325. *See also* Architecture.

Howard, Bronson, as dramatist, 258-259.

Howard, O. O., and Freedmen's Bureau, 15.

Howard University, founded, 15.

Howells, W. D., upon divorce, 216; literary work of, 228, 230, 247, 253.

Humanitarianism, bibliography, 426-427. *See also* reform movements by name.

Humane movement, 332-335.

Hunt, R. M., as architect, 89, 208.

Hunt, W. M., as artist, 261-262.

Huntington, C. P., as railway organizer, 54-56.

Huxley, Thomas, lectures of, 287-289.

IDAHO, early development of, 138.

Idealism, expressions of, 263, 318-348.

Illinois, and railway regulation, 168-169; farm radicalism in, 173-176; Granger laws victorious in, 176.

Illinois Central Railroad, extends to Gulf, 65; land sales of, 119.

Illinois, University of, early history of, 271-275.

Immigration, increases after war, 48-49; decreases after Panic, 299; bibliography, 426. *See also* nationalities by name.

Import trade, declines after 1873, 299-300.

Independent, influence of, 236; advertisements in, 242.

Indianapolis News, founded, 241.

Indians, numbers and life of, 101-106; wars with, 106-109, 115, 373-374; treaties with, 110; bibliography, 420. *See also* tribes by name.

Ingalls, J. J., early career of, 182.

Insurance, in South, 4; expansion of, in North, 47; scandals in, 193-194.

Intellectual interests, growth of, 228-263; bibliography, 429-430.

International influences, on home furnishing, 206, 308; on literature, 230-232, 234; on education, 268-270; on science, 281-282, 285, 286-287; and Panic of 1873, 290-291; at Centennial, 307-310; on American industry, 395-397. *See also* Immigration.

Inventions, for railways, 36-37, 41, 97-100; in milling, 39; typewriter and telephone, 87-89; bibliography, 423. *See also* inventions and inventors by name.

Iowa, and rail regulation, 169; Grange in, 170; farm radicalism in, 173-175.

Irrigation, in the West, 132; in California, 149.

Italian immigration, increase of, 49.

JAMES, Henry, and European travel, 226; novels of, 254.

James, Jesse, career of, 201-202.

Jefferson, Joseph, as actor, 89, 259.

Johns Hopkins University, early history of, 269-270, 281.

KANSAS, growth of, 116-117, 154; immigrant hardships in, 120; locusts in, 160; radicalism in, 174; political corruption in, 182.

Kansas City, growth of, 117, 373; and Jesse James, 202.

Kearney, Dennis, career of, 375-376.

Kelly, William, steel process of, 33.

Kerosene lamps, become universal, 76-77.

King, Clarence, in the Sierras, 153;
and diamond swindle, 193;
writings of, 247, 283-284.
Knights of Labor, history of, 381,
393-395.
Knights of St. Crispin, rise and
fall of, 72-73.
Ku Klux Klan, history of, 349-
353; federal legislation against,
352-353.

LABOR, hours and wages of, 69-
71; and eight-hour day, 71-72;
and trade unions, 72-74, 380-
383; and Greenback-Labor movement, 372; after 1873, 380-
384; strikes, 384-392; bibliography, 425-426.
Labor Reformers, convention of,
384.
La Farge, John, early career of,
262; at Centennial, 308.
Land grants, to railways, 63; to
state universities, 118; sales of,
119-120. See also Homesteading.
Langdell, C. C., in Harvard Law
School, 278-279.
Leadville, silver rush at, 373-375.
LeConte, Joseph, as teacher, 150.
Lee, Robert E., as educator, 5 n.
Legal education, improvements in,
267, 278-279.
Lehigh University, founded, 281.
Libraries, public, 242-243; private,
243-244.
Lighting, changes in, 76-77.
Lincoln, Nebraska, railway to, 58;
history of, 121-122; university
at, 123.
Literature, changes and develop-
ment of, 228-238, 247-258;
bibliography, 429-430. See also
Magazines, and authors by name.
Lodge, H. C., on Harvard educa-
tion, 265; on legal education,
279.
Longfellow, H. W., literary posi-
tion of, 229, 236.
Lord & Taylor department store,
erection of, 77.

Louisiana, war losses of, 8; land
values in, 21; farms in, 24; Reconstruction in, 26-28; and Carpetbag rule, 349-356; redeemed,
357; manufacturing in, 359-
360.
Louisiana State University, postbellum history of, 363.
Lowell, J. R., quoted, 257n., 310-
311.
Lyceum, reorganization of, 238-
240.

MACY, R. H., and department
stores, 91.
Magazines, agricultural, 156-157;
growth of, 236, 244-251;
bibliography, 412-413.
Manufacturing, expansion of, 32-
36; tendency of, toward consolidation, 45; westward thrust
of, 45-46; effect of, on daily
life, 76-79; in the South, 259-
260; improved basis of, after
panic, 395; and technological
advances, 396-405.
Maretzek, Max, as impresario, 90.
Mark Twain (pseud.), on steamboating, 68; in California, 150;
on typical Southern home, 207;
and subscription publishing, 237-
238; literary career of, 247-
251; as dramatist, 258, 263.
Marriage, early age of, 215.
Massachusetts Institute of Technology, early history of, 276.
Matthews, Brander, on education,
265-266.
Maury, M. F., scientific work of,
283.
McClellan, G. B., and diamond
swindle, 192.
McCosh, James, as university head,
264, 270, 275; on evolution,
286.
McGuffey, W. H., school readers
of, 155.
Meat packing, development of, 35-
37; and export trade, 366; expansion of, 367-368.

Medicine, professional training for, 267, 276-278, 343. *See also* Health.

Michigan, University of, innovations at, 271, 274.

Middle West. *See* Frontier, and states by name.

Miles, N. A., on Indian warfare, 110-111; and Buffalo Bill, 112.

Miller, Joaquin, literary work of, 247-249.

Mining, rapid development of, 133-141.

Minneapolis, as milling center, 38-40; growth of, 117, 373.

Minnesota, growth of, 116-118, 154, 371; seeks immigrants, 121; political radicalism in, 174-175, 372.

Minnesota, University of, enrollment at, 123.

Mississippi, destruction in, 4, 11; Negro labor in, 18; Northern farmers in, 22; increased number of farms in, 24; and Carpetbag rule, 349-356; redeemed, 357.

Mississippi, University of, postwar history of, 363.

Modjeska, Helena, and star system, 89.

Molly Maguires, rise and fall of, 381-382.

Montana, early development of, 138-140.

Montgomery Ward & Company, founding of, 172.

Moody and Sankey, revivals of, 260, 345.

Morals, decline in political, 178-190; decline in business, 190-202; sexual, 213-215.

Morgan, L. H., pioneer anthropologist, 284-285.

Mormons, as builders of Utah, 141-146.

Morris, Nelson, and meat packing, 36-37.

Muhlbach, Louisa, vogue of, 234.

Muir, John, in California, 150; education of, 155.

Munn *v.* Illinois, decision in rate case, 175-176.

Music, and urban life, 89-90, 218; light opera, 239.

NAST, Thomas, and Tweed Ring, 184, 311; and lyceum, 238-239.

Nation, founding of, 244; influence of, 256-257.

Nationalism, growth of, 253, 405-406. *See also* Sectionalism.

Nebraska, population of, 156; and locust plague, 160; later growth of, 371.

Negroes, postwar migrations of, 9; epidemics among, 12-13; religious life of, 13-14; economic progress of, 15; education of, 16, 362-364; melodies, 15; handicrafts, 16; acquire farms, 19-21; in political control, 26-29; and Carpetbag rule, 349-356; after Reconstruction, 357-358.

Nevada, and mining development, 135-138.

Newcomb, Simon, scientific work of, 285.

New England Women's Club, influence of, 342-343.

New Mexico, development of, 152-153.

New Orleans, ruin and recovery of, 3, 7; opera in, 218; and public health, 323; manufacturing in, 360; gayety in, 361.

Newspapers, in California, 150; general changes in, 240-242; bibliography, 413. *See also* newspapers and editors by name.

New York (state), corruption in, 179-180.

New York Central Railroad, consolidation of, 63-64; and strike of 1877, 387; wage policy of, 391.

New York City, rapid transit in, 82; paving in, 83; fire dangers in, 83-84; social life in, 90-94; and Tweed Ring, 182-187;

apartment houses in, 208-209; theater in, 218; newspapers in, 240-241; libraries in, 243; stock companies in, 259; statuary in, 260; Metropolitan Museum in, 263; slums of, 319-320; public health in, 320-323; labor troubles in, 380-381, 384 n.

New York Evening Post, character of, 241-242.

New York Ledger, vogue of, 236.

New York Sun, and Tweed Ring, 187; postwar character of, 240.

New York Times, in campaign of 1876, 315.

New York Tribune, character and influence of, 240-241.

New York World, and Tweed Ring, 187; character of, 240.

North Carolina, destruction in, 2; Negroes in, 17; increased farms of, 24; Reconstruction in, 26-28; and Carpetbag rule, 249-252; redeemed, 353; textile miils in, 360.

North Carolina, University of, postwar history of, 364.

Northern Pacific, commenced, 58-59; financial methods of, 60-61; and buffalo, 114; completed, 405.

Nursing, schools of, 343.

OHIO, regulates rail rates, 169.

Oil industry. See Petroleum.

Oleomargarine, introduction of, 211.

Omaha, bridge at, 57; immigrant center, 116; growth of, 117.

Opera, grand, in New York, 90-91, 218; in New Orleans, 218; light, 239.

Oregon, postwar growth of, 152.

Ouida, vogue of, 234.

Overland Monthly, founding of, 150.

PAGE, T. N., literary career of, 251.

Painting, progress in, 260-262; at the Centennial, 308; bibliography, 431.

Panic of 1873, history of, 290-299.

Park Avenue Hotel, built, 78.

Parkman, Francis, writings of, 233.

Parton, James, on Tammany misrule, 179-180; as author, 233.

Pauperism, after Panic, 301. See also Poorhouses.

Paving, of American cities, 82-83.

Payne, O. H., and oil industry, 398.

Peabody, George, benefactions of, 347.

Pennsylvania Railroad, and oil business, 42; and consolidation, 64; and air brake, 99.

Petroleum, growth of industry, 39-41, 397-400; refining of, 41-42.

Philadelphia, paving in, 83; social life in, 93-94; newspapers in, 241; libraries in, 243; theaters in, 259; corruption in, 312-313; slums in, 320-321; public health in, 321, 323.

Philanthropy, progress of, 243, 271-273, 324-329, 347-348. See also Charities, Freedmen's Bureau.

Pillsbury, C. A., as miller, 38-40.

Pittsburgh, rioting at, 388, 389.

Plankington, Jacob, 36-37.

Plummer, Henry, as road agent, 140-141.

Polygamy, in Utah, 144-145.

Poorhouses, wretched condition of, 328-330. See also Pauperism.

Population, of South, 1; of cities, 75, 93, 373; growth in West, 116-118, 154, 371. See also Immigration.

Porter, Noah, as author, 233; as educator, 271.

Portland, Maine, fire in, 84.

Postal service, improvement of, 86-87.

Powell, J. W., scientific work of, 153, 284.

Prices, of crops, 7, 163-165; 370-371; of land, 21; after Panic, 302-303.

Princeton College, development of, 264, 268, 270.

Prisons, condition and reform of, 331-332.

Professions, training for, 267, 269, 276-279. *See also* professions by name.

Prohibition. *See* Temperance.

Prostitution, extent of, 325-326.

Public domain. *See* Homesteading, Land grants.

Public health. *See* Health.

Publishing, organization of, 236-237; by subscription, 237-238; new firms for, 254-255.

Pulitzer, Joseph, as editor, 240.

Pullman car, development of, 46, 97-98.

Putnam's Magazine, career of, 244-245.

RAILROADS, in South, 3-4, 8; Western development of, 50-51; transcontinental, 51-56; other trunk, 56-59; overexpansion of, 59-63, 294-295; consolidation of, 63-65; improved in comfort and safety, 96-100; sell land, 119-120; and agriculture, 162-164; and stock watering, 164; state regulation of, 168-169, 371-372; failures of, 298-299; rate wars of, 400-401; pools of, 401-402; bibliography, 424-425. *See also* railroads by name.

Ranching, development, 124-127; typical ranches, 127-129.

Reade, Charles, novels of, condemned, 213; prices paid for books by, 231.

Reconstruction, history of, to 1870, 26-30; history of, from 1870, 349-360; of education, 362-364; bibliography, 416-418.

Redpath, James, and lyceum, 238-239.

Reform, bibliography, 426-428. *See also* reform movements by name.

Refrigerator cars, invention of, 36-37.

Reid, Whitelaw, in South, 22; as editor, 240.

Religion, evangelistic, 260, 345; census of, 343; and sectionalism, 343-344; and clergy, 344-346; bibliography, 430, 431. *See also* Evolution.

Richardson, H. H., as architect, 89-90, 409.

Richmond, ravaged by war, 3; rebuilt, 7, 30.

Rockefeller, J. D., early career of, 42-44; as head of oil industry, 397-400.

Roe, E. P., novels of, 232-233.

Roebling, J. A., plans Brooklyn Bridge, 80.

Rogers groups, popularity of, 206.

Roosevelt (elder), Theodore, death of, 92.

Roosevelt, Theodore, on cowboy life, 128, 133.

Rural life, in South, 8-24; in California, 148-149; in Middle West, 154-176, 364-366; under Reconstruction, 355-356; in Far West, 366-368, 377.

SABBATH. *See* Sunday.

Salt Lake City, growth of, 141-142.

San Francisco, growth of, 146-147, 373; Chinese in, 152; newspapers of, 241; bookstores of, 242; political agitation in, 375-376; labor troubles in, 390.

Savings banks, growth of, 147; failures in New York, 194.

Scandinavian immigration, growth of, 49.

Scholarship, achievements in, 281-289.

Schurz, Carl, on South, 5; as reformer, 407.

Science, advances in, 281-289; used in industry, 402-405;

bibliography, 430-431. *See also* sciences and scientists by name.

Scribner's Monthly, character of, 244-247; rate of pay of, 255.

Sculpture, popular, 206; progress in, 260, 308.

Sectionalism, and New York hotels, 92; in literature, 247-254; in churches, 343-344; decline of, 405-406.

Shaw, Anna Howard, career of, 340-341.

Shaw University, founding of, 15.

Sherman, J., on industrial growth, 32.

Sherman, W. T., march of, to sea, 2; and Indian fighting, 104-107.

Shepherd, A. R., work of, in Washington, 90, 312.

Sholes, C. L., invents typewriter, 87-89.

Simms, William Gilmore, poverty of, 11.

Sioux, life of, 101-105; fighting with, 106-109, 115, 373-374; treaties with, 110.

Slums, and housing reform, 319-321.

Smith College, early history of, 280-281.

Socialism, in America, 382-383.

Society for the Prevention of Cruelty to Animals, founded, 333-334.

Society for the Prevention of Cruelty to Children, founded, 335.

Somers, Robert, quoted, 12, 29.

Sorge, F. A., and Socialism, 382-383.

Sorosis, founding of, 342.

South, bibliography, 416-418. *See also* Reconstruction, and states by name.

South Carolina, desperadoes in, 6; destitution of, 11; Negro labor in, 18; increase in farms of, 24; and Reconstruction, 26-30; and Carpetbag rule, 349-356; redeemed, 357; textile mills in, 360; education in, 362-363.

South Carolina, University of, postwar career of, 363-364.

Southworth, Mrs. E. D. E. N., vogue of, 234.

Sovereigns of Industry, history of, 381.

Spalding, A. G., and baseball, 219.

Speculation. *See* Finance.

Spencer, Herbert, *American influence of, 231-232, 285-289.

Sport, growth of, 219-224.

St. Louis, and river traffic, 69; and Eads bridge, 81; population of, 117.

Stagecoach lines, after the Civil War, 51-53; in New York City, 81-82.

Standard Oil Company, history of, 43, 397-400.

Stanford, Leland, and Central Pacific, 54-57.

Stanton, Elizabeth Cady, and suffrage movement, 339-340.

Steamships, increased use of, 48-49.

Steel, manufacture of, 33-36.

Stewart, A. T., Southern sales of, 7; builds Park Avenue Hotel, 78; career of, 91-92; and model housing, 325.

Stokes, E. S., murders Fisk, 201; later career of, 201 *n.*

Straight University, founding of, 15.

Strikes, before 1873, 73; after 1873, 384-392.

Suffrage, Negro, 26-29, 351-357; and women, 338-340, 378.

Summer resorts, growth of, 217.

Sumner, W. G., and Yale, 266.

Sunday, rigidly kept, 212; at Centennial, 307; affected by immigration, 346.

Sutro, Adolph, builds tunnel, 136-137.

Swift, Gustavus, career of, 37-39.

TAMMANY, misrule of, 179-180; and Tweed Ring, 182-186; revolt against, 186-187.

Tariff, fosters new industries, 33; injures farmers, 167.

Taxation, inequality of, 167-168; under Carpetbag rule, 355-356.

Taylor, Bayard, home of, 204.

Taylor, F. W., as industrial manager, 404.

Telegraph, expansion of, 86.

Telephone, invented, 87-88.

Temperance, progress of, 211-212, 335-338; bibliography, 427-428.

Tennessee, race relations in, 18; increase in farms of, 24; and Reconstruction, 27; and Carpetbag rule, 349-352; redeemed, 353; lumbering in, 360.

Texas, violence in, 6; land prices in, 21; migration to, 23; ranching in, 124-126; population increased, 359; manufacturing in, 360.

Theater, popularity of, 89, 93, 218; stock companies in, 258-260.

Thomas, Theodore, as symphony conductor, 90; New York career of, 91.

Tilden, S. J., and Tweed Ring, 187; and Canal Ring, 312; as philanthropist, 348; and campaign of 1876, 314-317.

Timrod, Henry, poverty of, 11.

Tournaments, a Southern amusement, 208.

Trade unions, before 1873, 72-74; after 1873, 380-383. See also Labor.

Tramps, increase of, 301-302.

Transit, in New York and other cities, 81-82.

Transportation. See Railroads, Stagecoach lines, Steamships, Transit.

Travel, in summer, 216-217; European, 226; Southern, 361.

Trust companies, established, 48.

Turner, J. B., educational leader, 272.

Tweed, W. M., corrupts legislature, 180; and Tweed Ring, 182-186; exposure and defeat of, 187, 311.

Typewriter, invented, 87-89.

Union Pacific Railroad, building of, 53-57; financial troubles of, 62-63; and buffalo, 113; and land sales, 119; effect of, on Utah, 145-146; effect of, on California, 174.

Universities. See Colleges and universities.

Urban changes, multiplicity of, 75-86. See also cities by name.

Utah, postwar development, of 144-146; later growth of, 366-367.

Vanderbilt, Cornelius, as railway organizer, 66-67; personality of, 91; financial battles of, 194-199; as philanthropist, 281; labor policy of, 391.

Vanderbilt University, founded, 281.

Vassar College, founded, 280-281.

Vedder, Elihu, early career of, 261.

Villard, Henry, as railroad builder, 405.

Virginia, destruction in, 2-4; Negroes in, 17-18; social changes in, 381.

Virginia City, Montana, population of, 139.

Virginia City, Nevada, mining boom at, 136-138; life in, 140.

Wages, postwar level of, 69-71; fall after Panic, 300-301; difficulties over, 380, 385, 391-392.

Wanamaker, John, and department store, 91.

Ward, E. S., steel magnate, 33.

Washburn, C. C., as miller, 38-40.

Washing machines, wide distribution of, 76-78.

Washington (city), Negroes in, 9; street paving in, 83; social life in, 95-96; growth of, 152; municipal corruption in, 312.

Washington (state), development of, 377-378.

Washington, Booker T., quoted, 9 n.; at Hampton Institute, 16.

Watterson, Henry, as editor, 240.

Wellesley College, founding of, 280-281.

Wells, D. A., on economic conditions, 31, 69-70, 291.

Westinghouse, G. M., as inventor, 98-99.

Wheat, milling of, 38-39; increased acreage of, 154-155, 365-366; prices of, 161, 165, 369-370.

Whistler, J. M., early career of, 261.

White, A. D., as educational leader, 266, 272-273; on science and theology, 287.

Whitman, Walt, literary career of, 213.

Wichita, Kansas, history of, 121-122.

Williams College, instruction at, 265-266.

Wines, E. C., and prison reform, 331.

Wire nails, introduction of, 35.

Wisconsin, University of, development of, 264, 272-273, 275.

Women, in the Grange, 170-171; education of, 267, 273-274, 279-281; at Centennial, 309; as sweated workers, 324; and temperance, 338; and suffrage, 338-340; and professions, 341-342; and clubs, 342-343; improved Southern position of, 361-362; Western position of, 377-378; bibliography, 427.

Women's Christian Temperance Union, early history of, 338-339.

Woolson, Constance F., literary work of, 252.

Wyman, Jeffries, scientific work of, 283.

Wyoming, women suffrage in, 378.

YACHTING, international, 223.

Yale & Towne, makers of locks, 404.

Yale University, athletics at, 221-222; development of, 264, 268-269, 271.

Yellow fever, epidemics of, 323.

Youmans, E. L., scientific labors of, 281-282, 286-287.

Young, Brigham, career and personality of, 141-145; death of, 367.

Younger, Cole and James, desperadoes, 201.

Young Men's Christian Association, and athletics, 222; general work of, 346.

Young Women's Christian Association, work of, 346.